Talking About Leaving

Why Undergraduates Leave the Sciences

Elaine Seymour and
Nancy M. Hewitt

Westview Press
A Member of the Perseus Books Group

Copyright © 1997 by Westview Press, A Member of the Perseus Books Group

Published in 1997 in the United States of America by Westview Press, 5500 Central Avenue, Boulder, Colorado 80301–2877, and in the United Kingdom by Westview Press, 12 Hid's Copse Road, Cumnor Hill, Oxford OX2 9JJ

Find us on the World Wide Web at www.westviewpress.com

A CIP catalog record for this book is available from the Library of Congress.
ISBN 0-8133-8926-7 (hc.)—ISBN 0-8133-6642-9 (pbk.)

The paper used in this publication meets the requirements of the American National Standard for Permanence of Paper for Printed Library Materials Z39.48–1984.

10   9   8   7   6   5   4   3   2   1

Contents

Tables

Figures

Acknowledgments

The authors wish to acknowledge the generous financial support for this project by the Alfred P. Sloan Foundation. We also thank the Sloan Foundation staff, and particularly Dr. Hirsh Cohen for his encouragement, suggestions, and critique of the work in progress.

We thank the seven institutions who took part in the study, particularly the deans, faculty, and administrative staff of the science and mathematics departments and colleges of engineering who hosted our research activities, and the institutional records staff who provided the student samples. We also thank those faculty who invited us to discuss the study and gave us the opportunity to validate our findings with students in a wider array of institutions.

We thank the many colleagues with whom we have discussed our work for their suggestions and critical review. Among these, we especially thank Dr. Anne Lanier of the National Science Foundation who first suggested we undertake this study and who has followed its progress throughout; and Drs. Angela B. Ginorio (Director, North West Center for Research on Women, the University of Washington), and J. Rolf Kjolseth (Department of Sociology, the University of Colorado) for their careful review of the manuscript and good editorial suggestions.

We thank our transcribers, Linda Thornton and Emily Miller, for their accurate reproduction of the interviews, and the members of our research team, especially Anne-Barrie Hunter and Lois Dahnke, for their fidelity in processing and managing the data, and for their critical contributions throughout the project. Turning our original (1994) report of some 550 pages into a more compact volume, without losing the complex and subtle nature of our participants' observations, has been a considerable challenge. If we have succeeded, it is largely due to Anne-Barrie Hunter's fine editorial and publication skills and her respect for the integrity of the text data. We also thank our other research team members, especially Jill Schwaninger and Liane Pedersen-Gallegos, who ensured that other projects continued uninterrupted at times when preparation of the book claimed our attention. We thank our indexer, Maureen Connors for her humor and patience as well as for her good work.

To the 460 students who took part in the study, we offer our warmest thanks for their generosity and candor in discussing their experiences. We offered them nothing in return except the promise to tell their stories as faithfully as we knew how. We hope they will be pleased with the outcome.

Elaine Seymour
Nancy M. Hewitt

1

Overview

Background to the Study

Whenever traditional practices are called into question and new practices are proposed, it is always worth asking, Why at this time? Who seeks these changes? Who resists them? and, By what rhetoric do they support their positions? When our study began in the spring of 1990, concern that there might be something fundamentally wrong with science and mathematics education was just beginning to be expressed. In 1995, at the time this book was in preparation, a national movement was already underway to improve the quality of, and increase participation in, science and mathematics education from kindergarten to graduate school. As we shall illustrate, the debate which prompted this movement had a number of sources and dimensions, not all of which were academic, and the nature of the argument changed over time. Three issues were dominant at the outset: science and mathematics education was failing to foster science literacy in the population; too few undergraduates and graduates were recruited and retained to meet the nation's future needs; and the sciences recruited too exclusively among white males—thereby depriving the nation of the talents of women of all races and ethnicities, and of men of color.

From the mid-1980s, the Higher Education Research Institute (H.E.R.I.) at U.C.L.A. drew attention to a decline in the percentage of freshmen choosing to enter and remain in mathematics and science-based majors (Astin, 1985; Astin et al., 1985, 1987; Dey, Astin & Korn, 1991; Astin & Astin, 1993). Their findings were based on longitudinal surveys of large national samples of freshmen at two- and four-year institutions. In a series of articles based on Cooperative Institutional Research Program (C.I.R.P.) data,[1] Green (1989a, 1989b) described a twenty-year decline in freshman interest in undergraduate science majors (from 11.5% in 1966 to 5.8% in 1988), with an abrupt drop from 1983. The largest portion of this decline was evident in mathematics (from 4.6% to 0.6%) and the physical sciences (3.3% to 1.5%). Between 1966 and

1989, freshman interest in mathematics fell by four-fifths. The sharpest, most recent decline in enrollment occurred in engineering and computer science (from 12.0% in 1982 to 8.6% in 1988).

The future for all of these disciplines appeared to be further undermined by: a decline in the proportion of students choosing careers in science and mathematics teaching (from approximately 22% of freshman in 1966 to approximately 9% in 1988); a shift toward the preparation of science and mathematics teachers through education, rather than via disciplinary, majors; and a growing disinclination among young women to choose a career in high school mathematics teaching. Green refers to this as the loss of a "captive population" of women who, historically, had been "a key resource in the pool of potential science instructors, as well as key role models for women" (1989b, p. 37).

The American Freshman surveys, and (by 1991), U.S. Census data, clarified that potential graduates in science, mathematics and engineering (S.M.E.) were lost in the transition from high school to college by undergraduate switching into non-S.M.E. majors, and by declining enrollment in advanced S.M.E. degrees. Collectively, these losses began to be referred to as "leakage" from the S.M.E. "pipeline." In their 1993 C.I.R.P. report, Astin and Astin indicated that between freshman and senior years, S.M.E. majors suffered a relative student loss rate of 40 percent. Losses ranged from 50 percent in the biological sciences and 40 percent in engineering to 20 percent in the physical sciences and mathematics (when the transfer of former engineering majors into these disciplines is taken into account). Taken as careers, both engineering and the health professions lost over half of their entrants (53% and 51% respectively). The National Science Foundation (N.S.F.), the National Academy of Sciences, and the Office of Technology Assessment (O.T.A.) were among the first public bodies to debate the extent and causes of problems in science education and to promote discussion of ameliorative action. A 1987 National Academy of Sciences discussion paper concludes:

> There is still movement into the mathematics, science and engineering (M.S.E.) pipeline during the college years. However, at each stage, the net effect of the movement in and out of the pool is loss. The cumulative impact of these losses is substantial. Over 50 percent of the high school seniors surveyed dropped out of the M.S.E. pipeline by the end of their first year in college. Some returned later on. However, by college graduation, only 35 percent of the high school seniors who planned on M.S.E. majors had stayed with their plans. This suggests that, during the college years, more attention should be paid to preventing migration out of science (p. 29).

The Report of the Task Force on the Engineering Student Pipeline (Engineering Deans' Council, 1988) also estimated the rates of loss to other majors, and from school altogether, as varying between 30 percent and 70 percent in four-year engineering schools (where deans and faculty gathered the data). They discovered that few engineering schools maintained longitudinal retention data in which the persistence of freshmen cohorts was tracked.

This pattern of loss was also documented in a series of collaborative studies by the N.S.F. and U.S. Department of Education (cf., N.S.F., 1990a), and in the work of Hilton and Lee (1988). The greatest losses (estimated at between 34% and 40%) were found among high school graduates who abandoned their intentions of entering an S.M.E. major at or before college enrollment. During college, the highest risk of S.M.E. switching (a further 35%) occurred in the transition from freshman to sophomore year, and included those who moved into other majors and those who left college altogether. Hilton and Lee reported the loss between freshman and junior years as two percentage points (from 7.5% to 5.4%). From the start of junior year to graduation, the attrition rate dwindled to 0.8 percent. Very few students transferred into S.M.E. majors after college enrollment, and there was always a net loss. These estimates were thought likely to be conservative as many institutions do not require formal declaration of major until the end of sophomore year when the primary period of risk is already past.

As to gender differences in losses from the sciences, Strenta and his colleagues (1993) reported the persistence rates of men in S.M.E. majors varied between 61 percent for highly selective institutions to 39 percent for national samples, while the comparative rates for women ranged between 46 percent and 30 percent. Astin & Astin (1993) observed that absolute losses were greater among men, but, because the proportionate loss of women was greater, their under-representation increased during undergraduate S.M.E. education. In the same report, they documented high loss rates among that smaller proportion of S.M.E. entrants who are Hispanic, black, or native American. Only one-third of Hispanics, one-half of blacks, and one-half of native Americans who enrolled in S.M.E. majors graduated in them.

Some academic commentators also expressed concern that S.M.E. losses came from a pool of disproportionately able undergraduates (Green, 1989a, 1989b; White, 1992). Green observes that in 1988, 45.3 percent of college entrants intending to enroll in S.M.E. majors had final high school G.P.A.s of A or A- compared with 26.3 percent for students planning non-S.M.E. majors.[2] This finding is underscored by the N.S.F.'s (1990a) report that, of high school graduates entering four-year institutions with A or A-/B+ grades and at least 10 semesters of math and science, a consistently higher proportion entered S.M.E. majors than entered non-S.M.E. majors. Approximately 20 percent of the same well-prepared, high-ability group entered lower-level colleges, and another 20 percent did not enroll in any type of college. Able students were lost both immediately before S.M.E. enrollment and at some point over freshman and sophomore years. Green (1989b) summarizes his concerns thus:

Not only do the sciences have the highest defection rates of any undergraduate major, they also have the lowest rates of recruitment from any other major. In short, science departments lose a huge proportion of their potential clients—the academically-able and intellectually-motivated students who enter college with a genuine interest in studying science (p. 478).

Declining enrollment in advanced S.M.E. degrees by American-born students also attracted alarm (cf., Atkinson, 1990; Hilton & Lee, 1988; Massey, 1989; O.T.A., 1989; Pool, 1990; N.S.F., 1990a). Hilton and Lee (1988) described the failure of able S.M.E. undergraduates to continue into graduate school as the second greatest source of loss from the pipeline.[3] The 1989 O.T.A. report blamed stagnation in the academic job market and observed, "Graduate enrollments have been sustained largely by foreign students who have helped to compensate for the decline in enrollments by U.S. citizens" (p. 9). The 1992 edition of National Science Indicators (N.S.F., 1993a) also reported that between 1971 and 1991 the number of science and mathematics doctorates awarded to non-U.S. citizens rose 135 percent (170 percent in engineering), while those awarded to U.S. citizens fell by 10 percent (19 percent in engineering). A National Academy of Sciences analysis of the bi-annual Survey of Doctoral Recipients (cf., N.S.F., 1990a) estimated that in 1988, foreign students accounted for more than 28 percent of Ph.D.s in science, mathematics and engineering.

While the academic community was discussing the implications of these studies, public debate about the state of science and mathematics education focused on information of a different but related kind; namely, international studies comparing school children's achievements. The 1988 report of the International Association for the Evaluation of Educational Achievement received particular media attention. In comparing the achievements of U.S. children and those of 17 other countries, it found only average levels of competence in mathematics and science for U.S. 10 year-olds, which, by age 14, dropped to 14th place, and to the lowest ranks by the end of high school. This concern has recently been moderated, but not assuaged, by re-evaluation of national and international data.

One important consequence of the public debate generated by this body of work has been an effort, spearheaded by the National Research Council, to establish teaching and assessment standards for K-12 mathematics and science education (cf., N.R.C., 1993). However, these standards are not (unlike those of many other countries) mandatory.

Evidence of declining scientific literacy in the population, and of reduced numbers of S.M.E. graduates available for research, development, or teaching, has also generated expressions of concern that America's international competitiveness in the science and technology-dependent sectors of the U.S. economy would be undermined as a consequence of these trends:

From a broader perspective, there is a growing concern over our country's future ability to compete in the global market (Mullis & Jenkins, 1988, p. 5).

The U.S., two decades ago, led its economic competitors in the number of scientists and engineers it produced relative to its population. But, today, Japan—with half the U.S. population—produces more engineers than the U.S. (N.A.S.U.L.G.C., 1989, p. 36).

Arguments of this nature gave strong impetus to initial efforts to revitalize science education, although they have more recently been called into question. As Gomory and Cohen have argued (1993), some important growth industries, and the countries that have profited most from them, depend more on good design, production techniques, and marketing than on international leadership in academic science. Nevertheless, expressions of economic nationalism, and anxieties about the nation's prosperity in the fast-approaching second millennium seem likely to fuel science education reform efforts for some time to come.

The response of the academic and professional community has been differently expressed. A series of commissions, task forces, conferences, and working groups—sponsored by the N.S.F., the National Academy of Sciences, Sigma Xi, the National Association of State Universities and Land Grant Colleges (N.A.S.U.L.G.C.), and the American Association for the Advancement of Science (A.A.A.S), and others—began to collectively brainstorm the causes and consequences of low interest in, and high attrition from, mathematics and science at all educational levels. The most influential of these include the 'Neal Report' (N.S.F., 1986), the Report of the Disciplinary Workshops on Undergraduate Education (N.S.F., 1988), and the Sigma Xi "Wingspread Conference" of the National Advisory Group (1989). Each represents the collective wisdom and experience of higher education administrators and educators, officers of learned bodies, and representatives of the scientific community, industry and government. The Neal Report pointed to flaws in the undergraduate experience: lab instruction, at worst, was said to be "uninspired, tedious and dull"; lab facilities and instruments were described as limited and "obsolete"; teaching was inadequate and poorly organized and reflected little knowledge of modern teaching methods; teaching materials were out of date, and curricular content failed to meet students' varied and emergent career needs. The report segmented its account by types of institution, disciplines, and to some degree, by the special difficulties of under-represented groups. It also noted a decline in the number of S.M.E. graduate students choosing academic careers, and thus a growing shortage of engineering faculty since 1976 and of mathematics faculty since 1981. Surveying the condition of undergraduate S.M.E. education overall, it warned that, "all sectors of undergraduate education in mathematics, engineering, and the sciences are inadequately responsive to either its worsening condition, or to the national need for revitalization and improvement" (N.S.F., 1986, p. 3).

The N.S.F. workshops on undergraduate education (1988) were divided by disciplines, and faculty identified problems common across S.M.E. undergraduate education, and specific to their own disciplines. They highlighted the second-class status of teaching compared to research: "The most important thing N.S.F. can do for science education is to increase the prestige and respectability of teaching" (Physics Workshop, p. 75). They also pointed to, "inadequate pre-college instruction,...deteriorating instructional facilities, and lack of funding for research efforts involving students" (Geo-science Workshop, p. 3). The Chemistry Workshop specifically identified "widespread, fundamental and long-standing problems in lab instruction in chemistry [as having] the greatest effect on retention of students...in the first two years of the undergraduate curriculum" (Chemistry Workshop, p. 5).

The National Advisory Group of Sigma Xi (1989) focused on problems with the physical and pedagogical context of undergraduate learning, insufficient accountability and flexibility in curricula, and the unmet needs of traditionally under-represented groups. Losses from S.M.E. majors were thought to reflect a poor balance between faculty research and teaching, large classes, inadequate academic and emotional support for students. They were also a consequence of using entry-level courses as a gate-keeping mechanism, "to protect more advanced courses from all except the most able, and the most committed" (p. iv). An important new note was, we feel, struck: "In addressing these topics and some of their concomitant issues, it became evident that attitudes and perceptions are, in themselves, significant topics" (p. vi).

The forum approach highlighted many elements likely to have bearing on the causes of S.M.E. attrition. However, without systematic investigation we could not know whether all of the pertinent issues had been raised, or which elements mattered more than others. Furthermore, even at the Sigma Xi meetings—where it was recognized that, "students' perceptions of the undergraduate curriculum in science, mathematics and engineering, and the faculty perceptions of the same curriculum, are by no means congruent" (p. iv)—the perceptions of students were not solicited.

The O.T.A. reports (1988, 1989) addressed attrition by comparing studies of S.M.E. baccalaureate productivity in higher education institutions of different types. They documented the better record of liberal arts and historically black colleges and of technical institutions, compared with state and research universities. They cited the self-study programs of the 50 private liberal arts colleges in the 'Oberlin Group' which identify the features of undergraduate education found to work in favor of higher S.M.E. completion rates: higher selectivity in enrollment, lower faculty-student ratios, and higher faculty-student interaction (monitoring, advising, counseling, and student involvement in faculty research). Replication of these conditions was argued to reduce the risk of attrition. Porter (1990) also found higher completion rates in those colleges with smaller classes, enhanced contact with faculty, and greater enrollment

 # students who want to drop/ change majors
- doing poorly

selectivity. Knowing 'what works' in smaller, privileged, and highly selective settings does not necessarily constitute a test of what causes or cures attrition in other contexts, nor does it tell us what else might work. Nevertheless, the greater success of small liberal arts colleges in recruiting, and retaining, science and mathematics majors (including women and students of color) has prompted some larger institutions to consider their methods. It has also encouraged groups of smaller institutions to build on their success by promoting what they perceive as the best ways to present science and mathematics to undergraduates. The longest-established, and most wide-ranging of these endeavors is that of the Independent Colleges Office "Project Kaleidoscope" (1991, 1992, 1995).

An overarching concern reflected in many reports, studies and commentaries in the late 1980s was that, by the end of the century, the nation would face a shortfall in the supply of qualified scientific and technical personnel at all levels (cf., N.S.F., 1990a, 1990e; Atkinson, 1990; Pool, 1990; N.A.S.U.L.-G.C., 1989). Although this fear subsequently proved unjustified, and is increasingly being replaced by the concern that graduates from particular disciplines, especially physics, are actually facing underemployment and unemployment, it nevertheless played an important early role in promoting the reform of science education.

Tobias (1990, 1992a), Heylin (1987), and others have pointed to the significance of another widespread belief in shaping the way that recruitment and retention issues have been addressed—that the ability to understand mathematics and science is limited to a relatively small proportion of the population:

> Chemistry, and much of the rest of science in this country, has been working for far too long under an implicit assumption that scientific competence is disproportionately concentrated in that roughly 40 percent of the population represented by white males (Heylin, 1987, p. 3).

This assumption bolsters a related belief—that some, even most, switching from S.M.E. majors is 'appropriate' or 'normal' (cf., N.S.F., 1990a). S.M.E. faculty expect some fallout (even at a fairly substantial rate) because those presumed to lack sufficient natural ability to continue are thought to discover their limitations, and/or their true vocation for some other discipline, and leave. By this perspective, the function of the traditional 'weed-out' system is to assist this process. Where S.M.E. attrition is regarded as largely inevitable or appropriate, recruitment rather than retention is seen as the appropriate way to address pipeline concerns. The perceived shortfall crisis, therefore, prompted a search for mathematics and science talent in populations which had, hitherto, received less attention, namely, women, students of color and students with disabilities. Interest in non-traditional groups as a source of S.M.E. enrollment also coincided with growing concern (expressed by researchers, educators, and the professional and academic associations of women and minority groups) that women, students of color and students with disabilities were under-represented among S.M.E. undergraduates and graduate students, faculty and administrators for reasons other than ability. (The debate about why this has occurred, and the research which informs it, are discussed briefly below, and in more detail in Chapters 5 and 6.) The movement to increase the participation and retention rates of under-represented groups has yielded disappointing results despite considerable outlays of money and effort.[4] This can be explained, we suggest, by unresolved contradictions in its focus and strategy. If programs addressing under-representation are primarily shaped by a search for undiscovered talent, while the structural and cultural barriers to enrollment and persistence among under-represented groups remain obscure or unaddressed, such programs cannot succeed.

Reasons for Attrition among S.M.E. Majors

Prior to 1990, there was no body of work that had explored the range of factors contributing to attrition among both male and female undergraduates, different racial or ethnic groups, and different S.M.E. majors. Theories of attrition based on research tended to be limited in scope. Studies focused on particular groups (often women), were offered as by-products of research into other issues, addressed one possible cause of attrition (e.g., inadequate high school preparation), or used one kind of theoretical approach (e.g., institutional data analysis, or psychological theories of motivation). Some of the commonest observations on S.M.E. attrition had no basis in research at all. For example, several national reports speculated that increases in the numbers of foreign teaching assistants and faculty were a likely source of impediments to the progress of women in S.M.E. majors. Among these, Vetter writes:

> A growing problem for American students is the language barrier between them and many of their foreign teaching assistants and faculty. While this is a problem for both sexes, foreign teachers are said to provide an additional handicap for women...The retention rate for women in engineering, from freshman year to bachelor's degree, has dropped drastically...It may reflect some of the student-faculty problems for women who must work with foreign men in what the latter may perceive as a submissive role (1988, p. 737).

Although the validity of this supposition had never been tested, its repetition allowed attention to be diverted from the experience of female S.M.E. students with American-born faculty and peers. Concentration on what were, perhaps, peripheral difficulties, in effect, circumvented inquiry into the significance for attrition of mainstream cultural practices.

The only national data on the causes of S.M.E. attrition are those derived from the National Longitudinal Survey and the 'High School and Beyond' surveys conducted by the Department of Education.[5] Students were found to switch out of S.M.E. majors into other majors for two main reasons: 43 percent said that they found non-S.M.E. majors more attractive (a finding similar to that of the University of Michigan study [Manis et al., 1989] discussed later in this section), and 31 percent stated that they found the work 'too difficult'. Unfortunately, these findings raise more questions than they answer, including what students mean by the 'hardness' of science, mathematics and engineering. Nor do we learn what elements of students' experiences in S.M.E. courses were so unsatisfactory that other disciplines seemed more appealing.

Faculty opinion surveys were also a source of attrition theories. A Carnegie Foundation (1989) survey of 5,500 faculty in all disciplines reported that nearly three-quarters of faculty thought undergraduates were seriously under-prepared in academic and study skills. The accuracy of this perception, and the role played by under-preparation in S.M.E. attrition, were unknown. However, work by Strenta and his colleagues (1993) on the causes of attrition among women at highly prestigious institutions called into question the significance of pre-admission measures of 'developed abilities', compared with women's adverse reactions to negative pedagogical and peer group experiences in their first two years.

The only studies of attrition grounded in actual student experience were those which explored the problems of women in science and engineering majors. Studies of female S.M.E. graduate students reported psychological alienation, and lowered self-esteem as common responses to their graduate school experiences and as significant factors in their decisions to leave. The Illinois Valedictorian Project (cf., Widnall, 1988) which followed the college progress of 80 high school seniors of high ability (both male and female) also reported a significant loss by sophomore year of previously high self-esteem among women, and a lowering of career ambitions despite high performance levels. Over the same period, the self-esteem and career aspirations of their male peers rose. Some clues to understanding this phenomenon arose from the findings of a series of studies sponsored by the American Association of Colleges (Hall & Sandler, 1982, 1984, 1986). Hall and Sandler described the experiences of women students, faculty, and administrators in the sciences as "chilling." They documented the rudeness of male peers experienced on a daily basis, and the role of undergraduate instructors in maintaining classroom inequalities, both by disattention and by overt discrimination. Where faculty conveyed messages of lower expectations for women, women of high ability were prompted to lower their academic and career ambitions and to under-achieve.

Studies of persistence among students of color in all majors alerted researchers to another factor in attrition—the negative consequences for academic progress of insufficient financial support. Mohrman (1987), Rotberg (1990), Wilson (1990), and Porter (1990), discussed the disproportionately negative consequences for students of color of reductions in the level of public support available to all students. Mohrman predicted that almost one-third of low-income students of all racial and ethnic groups would drop out of school completely if public grants were to be eliminated. Wilson found students took longer to complete their baccalaureates, or dropped out, partly because they could not meet their college tuition and everyday living expenses. While students of color had the lowest college completion rates for reasons which had not been explored or explained, the very highest drop-out rates occurred among students of all races and ethnicities who did not receive grants. Rotberg reported debt burdens to have greatest impact on the college attendance rates of students of color because both their family resources and their expected future earnings tended to be lower. Other aspects of student financial problems with bearing for attrition were: the increasing cost of higher education at a time of inflation; a decline in the real value of student aid as a percentage of tuition costs; and the creation of a debt burden for half of all graduates by a shift in emphasis from grants to loans. Porter found that four-year degree programs were no longer a viable option for most undergraduates. Most undergraduates who left college did so in freshman year: those with federal grants showed significantly more persistence beyond the first year than those without them. He also found financial problems were especially acute for students of color, and the main cause for high college drop-out rates among Hispanics and blacks at four-year institutions was breakdown of their attempts to carry full course loads while working to meet tuition and living expenses.

Several different approaches are discernable in those few studies which have directly sought reasons for S.M.E. attrition. The development of predictive models by which to identify those students who are most likely to persist is exemplified by the work of Levin and Wyckoff (1988) among engineering students. Ability in mathematics was found to be the best single predictor of engineering success (better than S.A.T., college or high school G.P.A. scores), followed by choice of an S.M.E. major on the basis of interest in the subject. Though models predicting individual success in S.M.E. classes are useful for development of better screening procedures, they are limited as ways to explain attrition rates which are disproportionately high among particular groups.

Silberman (1981) and Carter and Brickhouse (1989) explored the learning problems of S.M.E. students by comparing the beliefs of faculty and students about the nature of science. They reframed the attrition issue as: What makes a subject so 'difficult' that some students drop out or fail? In a study of 1,200 students taking Chemistry 116 at Purdue University, they found that the 'difficulty' of the class was very differently perceived by the students who took it, and by the faculty who taught it. Faculty took a more determinist view of students' chances of mastering the material: they believed the subject material was inherently hard, and expected a certain proportion of the students in each cohort to be unable to 'get it'. They conceded, however, that hard material might be mastered with sufficient background knowledge, interest and effort. Students did not accept the 'inherently difficult' view of the material. They maintained a 'democratic' theory of education, believing it should be possible to teach so as to clarify the complexities of chemistry for students who were adequately prepared: such students should be able to 'score' good grades with sufficient personal effort and faculty help. They also stressed remedies within the control of the individual student or teacher more often than did faculty. This is a particularly useful line of inquiry because it begins to clarify what frustrates students about 'hard' classes, and identifies some sources of faculty resistance to pedagogical reform initiatives. The academic difficulties experienced by many S.M.E. students, and the apparent difficulty of many faculty in responding to them, may be visualized as a structural conflict between the élitism and predestinarianism of science (cf., Merton, 1942, 1970, 1973) and the demo-cratic, consumerist approach which students bring to college from high school and the wider society.

Five bodies of research which illustrate the value of seeking to understand how students process their experiences in S.M.E. classes, and the conditions under which they function well are: the work of Manis, Sloat, Thomas and Davis at the University of Michigan on factors affecting choices of S.M.E. majors (1989); Tobias' (1990) exploration of the introductory science and mathematics class experiences of high ability students from other disciplines; Lipson's (1992) secondary analysis of interview data from the Harvard-Radcliffe study of women in science (cf., Tobias, 1990); Treisman's series of calculus teaching experiments at Berkeley (cf., Treisman, 1992); and those of Hudson (1986) in physics at the University of Houston. Manis and her colleagues interviewed: high-ability women who had decided not to enter science majors; women who entered them, but left; women who remained through to senior year; and matched samples of men. At the end of freshman year, 71 percent of all women reported a variety of negative experiences in S.M.E. classes, and 61 percent described specific class experiences (most commonly in mathematics and chemistry) which had dampened their interest in science and undermined their motivation to continue. The characteristics of such classes were (in order of importance): poor teaching or organization of material; hard or confusing material, combined with loss of confidence in their ability to do science; cut-throat competition in assessment systems geared more to weeding out than to encouraging interested students; dull subject matter; and grading systems that did not reflect what students felt they had accomplished. Many of those who stayed in science also complained about poor teaching and an unpleasant atmosphere. Male students who had gone through the same experiences were much less troubled by the competitive atmosphere, the grading system, and the dullness of the subject matter. Both male and female switchers reported that negative experiences in freshman science were more important than positive experiences in other fields in reaching their decision to leave. Sophomore switchers confirmed the salience of the issues raised by freshmen, and cited the quality and availability of faculty advice and support as critical in their decision to persist or leave.

Tobias (1990) approached the issue of the leaking pipeline by asserting the existence of a 'second tier' of untapped scientific ability among able people who choose to work in other disciplines, but possess sufficient interest and preparation to pursue S.M.E. fields. Such people might, she proposes, be persuaded to enter, or return to, science were a more flexible approach to curriculum and teaching methods adopted, and different modes of thought accommodated. Tobias found seven high achievers in other fields (five women and two men, including one faculty member) who had considered, but rejected, a career in science, but who were sufficiently well-prepared to take freshman or sophomore science and mathematics classes, and asked them to undertake one semester in a science or math class of their choice. Her findings from this experiment are derived from each participant's diary of their learning experiences, and from open-ended interviews. Her participants described the 'apprenticeship model' of scientific pedagogy, and the 'maleness' of its culture. They offered detailed commentaries on the thinking processes required by science and mathematics, and how these differed from those to which they were accustomed in other disciplines. They commented on the counter-productive effects of curve-grading, and aggressive competition among peers, and faulted the narrowness of syllabus content and lack of application in the teaching of concepts. Two of the seven volunteers reported they had struggled with a desire to abandon the experiment before the end of the semester.

Tobias's monograph includes an account of Lipson's (1990) secondary analysis of qualitative interview materials from a longitudinal data set of Harvard-Radcliffe women in science (Lipson, 1992; Ware et al., 1985, 1986, 1988). Lipson draws on interview data with first-year S.M.E. switchers and persisters in order to clarify the issues contributing to their decisions to stay, or to move into non-science concentrations. She found a pattern in which persisters evoked external explanations for their difficulties in science courses, while switchers cited their own inadequacies as the cause. Switchers rejected the culture of competition, and felt that commitment to science meant losing the chance of a well-rounded, liberal education. These findings square with those from several other studies of college women, as reviewed by Widnall (1988) and Baum (1989).

Treisman's work is important because, along with Tobias's earlier work on math anxiety (1978), it questions the assumption that the pool of people 'able' to tackle mathematics or science is limited. It calls into question theories of attrition based on extrinsic variables rather than learning experiences. It also offers empirical support for a student-centered approach to mathematics teaching which, though not uncommon in other disciplines, has not been widely employed in the traditional pedagogy of mathematics, science, or engineering. In a now-famous series of experiments, Treisman identified, and successfully replicated, the interaction and study patterns of Asian-American students who did well in his calculus classes with black students who performed poorly. He discovered that key elements in student success were: group study and support; students' awareness of their teacher's high expectations; the shared experience of success in solving problems of a progressively challenging nature; and the building of self-confidence. Jaime Escalante's success in preparing minority students from poor East Los Angeles families for the Advanced Placement test in calculus, and Bonsangue and Drew's (1992) evaluation of a calculus workshop program for Latino students built on the Treisman model, suggests that Treisman's success cannot be dismissed as a function of the high intellectual calibre of his Berkeley students or of his own high ability as a teacher. As the classic Hawthorne experiments of the 1930s remind us, the strong effects in a desired direction created in a group that feels its performance is a matter of special importance to the experimenter (in this case, the teacher) should not be underestimated (cf., Mayo, 1966). Hudson's earlier (1986) experiment with students in introductory physics classes also underscores Treisman's results. Hudson found that weaker performances could be improved by making assessment practices serve as a learning tool: where the results of tests were given to students in a diagnostic manner with feedback on specific areas of weakness and with time to remedy learning difficulties in a program of self-study, students with lower scores for mathematical and reasoning ability were able to perform to the required class standard.

The implications of this body of research and experimentation are clear: S.M.E. attrition cannot be viewed as a natural consequence of differential levels of ability; classroom climate and activities play critical roles in determining the students who do, and do not, persist within S.M.E. majors. However, when we began our own study in the spring of 1990, the work of teasing out the whole range of factors contributing to high S.M.E. attrition rates had not been attempted, despite some promising leads in particular directions. Nor had a framework been developed to express the relative contribution of different factors to each other. It was this combination of tasks which we set out to accomplish.

Study Objectives

In the spring of 1990, we began a three-year study whose aim was to discover, and to establish the relative importance of, the factors with greatest bearing upon the decisions of undergraduates at four-year colleges and universities to switch from science, mathematics and engineering majors into disciplines which are not science-based. On the presumption that the institutional context in which science, mathematics and engineering education takes place is likely to have some effect on retention and attrition, we chose seven institutions to represent the types of four-year colleges and universities which contribute most to the national supply of baccalaureate scientists, mathematicians and engineers. Because information about the causes of S.M.E. attrition was limited, we made no presumptions about the kinds of factors which might be involved, nor about their relative importance. We adopted an ethnographic approach which was grounded in the assumption that undergraduates are expert informants who are well-placed to describe the strengths and limitations of their educational experiences: where students abandoned their intention to major in an S.M.E. discipline, only they can explain how they weighed particular elements in the network of events leading to their decision. We assumed that particular pieces of information (especially high school preparation, class grades, S.A.T. math scores, G.P.A., etc.), were likely to have important bearing on their educational fortunes. However, without some understanding of how students interpret and respond to these biographical facts, their actions cannot be predicted or explained.

Within our overall aim for the project, we included a number of specific objectives:

*   to identify sources of qualitative difference in the educational experience of science, mathematics and engineering under-classmen at institutions of different types

*   to identify aspects of the structure, culture, pedagogy, or other features of science, mathematics and engineering departments, schools and colleges which encourage attrition or impede retention for the whole undergraduate population, and for important sub-sets of it

*   to compare and contrast the causes of attrition from science, mathematics and engineering majors found among male students of color, and among women of all races/ethnicities, with those of white males

*   to estimate the relative importance of the factors found to contribute to S.M.E. attrition

As most departments and colleges do not keep enrollment, persistence, and attrition records, our first task was to establish field 'switching' and field persistence patterns by groups of disciplines. We defined 'switching' so as to include both leaving a declared S.M.E. major for a non-S.M.E. major, and declaring a non-S.M.E. major, despite an original intention to enter an S.M.E. major. Undergraduates who had moved from one S.M.E. major to another were not counted as switchers.[6] 'Persistence' was taken to mean intending to graduate, either in the S.M.E. major originally chosen, or in another S.M.E. major. We wanted to know: what proportions of undergraduates stayed in the major they originally chose or intended to enter; what proportion moved into another major in the same broad group of disciplines; what proportion moved into majors outside their original group; and how the switching and persistence patterns of S.M.E. majors compared with those who originally chose other groups of majors. Finally, we wanted to know into which majors switchers went once they had left their original majors.

As there were no published national data which compare the switching and persistence rates in S.M.E. majors with those of other majors, we asked the

Higher Education Research Institute to provide us information derived from their most recent C.I.R.P. survey data. From a set of unpublished tabulations from data on the last cohort of freshmen (1987) in the C.I.R.P. surveys for whom the H.E.R.I. had a complete four-year record (i.e., to 1991), we constructed the patterns of switching, persistence, and transfer of majors which are summarized in Tables 1.1 through 1.5.

Table 1.1 shows the pattern of persistence in, and switching from, declared or intended majors by 1991 for those freshmen who entered in 1987.[7] It portrays a continuum of stability to instability in original major choices: beginning in English, where the switching rate is very low (15%), through the social sciences, fine arts, education, history and political science, where the switching rate is 28 percent to 35 percent; through engineering and business, where it is 38 percent to 40.5 percent, to the sciences, computer sciences, and mathematics, where the range is 47 percent to 63 percent; and finally to majors geared to the needs of the non-technical and health professions, where instability is highest (62 percent to 71 percent). The picture for pre-medicine is complex because many freshmen with aspirations to enter one of the health professions initially enter the biological sciences. They may change their minds about this career path before getting to a 'pre-med' declaration.

The most stable major of the S.M.E. group is engineering, which is also the most selective in its screening procedures for applicants: 53 percent of engineering entrants stayed within one of the engineering specialties. The S.M.E. majors most vulnerable to switching are mathematics and statistics, where the loss rate is almost 63 percent. The physical and biological sciences share a similar rate of switching: approximately half of all entrants to these majors (51%) move into non-S.M.E. majors. However, freshmen who begin in the physical sciences are also more likely than those who begin in any other S.M.E. major to stay within the sciences by moving into a different S.M.E. major prior to graduation. The switching rate of 44.1 percent for all S.M.E. majors (i.e., excluding computer science, and the health professions), is very similar to that of 40 percent found by Strenta, Elliott, Adair, Scott, and Matier (1993) for well-prepared and talented students who entered four highly selective institutions in 1988. The S.M.E. switching pattern of the 1985 entrants described in the 1993 C.I.R.P. report (discussed earlier in this chapter) is also very similar to that of the 1987 entrants shown here.

In the humanities and social science groups, approximately three-quarters of the freshmen who entered their original majors in 1987 were still in them in 1992. In English, the social sciences and fine arts, over half of all entrants remained in the major of their first choice. Most of the changes in this group were from one humanities or social science major to another.

TABLE 1.1   Patterns of Persistence in, and Switching from, Declared or Intended Majors by 1991 for 810,794 Undergraduates Entering a National Sample of Four-Year Institutions in 1987.

Based on unpublished tabulations provided by the Cooperative Institutional Research Program, Higher Education Research Institute, University of California, Los Angeles, April 1993.

Original major	% Stayed in same major	% Moved to major in same group	% Stayed in major or group	% Switched to majors in other groups
S.M.E. Majors				
Biological Sciences	42.0	7.1	49.0	51.0
Physical Sciences	29.9	18.9	48.8	51.2
Engineering	51.4	10.5	61.9	38.1
Mathematics/Statistics	34.1	3.2	37.3	62.7
Math (only)	29.2	8.2	37.4	62.6
Agriculture	52.8	0.0	52.8	47.2
All S.M.E. Majors	*46.0*	*10.2*	*55.9*	*44.1*
Humanities/Social Science Majors				
History/Political Science	43.5	21.7	70.4	34.8
Social Sciences	56.0	16.0	72.0	28.0
Fine Arts	50.6	19.5	70.1	29.9
English	56.5	28.4	84.9	15.1
Other Humanities	28.6	40.2	68.8	31.2
All Humanities/Social Science Majors	*48.1*	*26.0*	*74.1*	*29.9*
Other Majors				
Health Professions	29.4	----	29.4	70.6
Computer Science/Technical	46.4	----	46.4	53.6
Business	59.5	----	59.5	40.5
Education	67.7	----	67.7	32.3
Other Non-technical	37.8	----	37.8	62.2

In making these comparisons, we must bear in mind the different traditions of the liberal arts and the sciences. In the humanities, faculty commonly encourage students to experience different disciplines before making a final choice. By contrast, S.M.E. faculty demand early commitment from students in order to build their skills and understanding in linear fashion over time. The acquisition of a broader educational experience is, thus, more difficult for S.M.E. majors. Moving to another major, even within the S.M.E. group, is also more costly in terms of time, money and effort than changing from one humanities major to another. Those who choose the sciences are encouraged to see themselves as entering difficult and demanding majors, and those who graduate as part of an élite. Nor is switching viewed by students and faculty in the humanities and social sciences in the same way as it is in mathematics, science and engineering. As we shall later discuss, we found that students who left S.M.E. majors tended to see themselves either as 'failures' or 'defectors' (depending on the degree of choice in their decision to leave). A student who leaves the social sciences for physics is treated by family, peers and faculty as someone who has done something interesting and worthwhile. A student who leaves physics for the social sciences tends to attract criticism or concern. Thus, not only do the S.M.E. disciplines have a higher rate of switching overall (44%) than do the humanities, social sciences and education (approximately 30%), those who leave them attract negative responses from faculty, family, peers and friends, which is not the case for students who leave the liberal arts.

Table 1.2 shows the final choice of major (by 1991) of those who initially entered S.M.E. majors in a national sample of four-year institutions in 1987. Almost a quarter (24.6%) of those leaving the physical sciences moved into the humanities, social sciences and fine arts, with the highest proportion (14.4%) moving into the social sciences; 17.2 percent moved into non-technical majors which lead to professional or semi-professional occupations (largely, journalism, library/archival science, communications, law enforcement, home economics and military science). A quarter of switchers from the biological sciences (24.8%) also chose the humanities, social sciences and fine arts. However, a larger proportion of former biology majors (10.2%) moved into computer science and other technical majors than from any other group of S.M.E. majors. Far fewer former engineering majors (11.4%) switched into the humanities, and far more switched into business majors (13.9%) than from other S.M.E. majors. The most frequent final choice of switchers from mathematics and statistics majors was either a humanities or an education major (with approximately 17 percent entering each of these). However, the most distinctive characteristic of switchers from mathematics and statistics was the high proportion (8.1%) who were still 'undecided' four years later.

The dominant pattern for all switchers (whether they begin in S.M.E. majors or elsewhere) is to move into the social sciences, humanities and fine arts. This trend is enhanced by the tendency of those who begin in this group

TABLE 1.2 Final Major Choices by 1991 of 148,204 Undergraduate Switchers Entering S.M.E. Majors in a National Sample of Four-Year Institutions in 1987.

Based on unpublished tabulations provided by the Cooperative Institutional Research Program, Higher Education Research Institute, University of California, Los Angeles, April 1993.

Original S.M.E. Majors (Total Entering)	Non-S.M.E. Destination Majors of S.M.E. Switchers							Totals by Majors
	Computer Science	Health	Business	Education	All Humanities & Fine Arts	Other Non-technical	Undecided	
Mathematics/ Statistics (5,651)	5.6 (316)	1.7 (97)	6.2 (350)	17.3 (977)	17.8 (1,004)	6.0 (337)	8.1 (458)	62.7 (3,539)
Physical Sciences (16,325)	0.4 (71)	2.5 (413)	3.2 (525)	1.8 (294)	24.6 (4,013)	17.2 (2,815)	1.4 (230)	51.2 (8,361)
Biological Sciences (38,614)	10.2 (3,957)	1.1 (442)	3.7 (1,418)	5.3 (2,048)	24.8 (9,546)	5.8 (2,258)	0 (0)	51.0 (19,668)
Engineering (82,400)	6.7 (5,480)	1.0 (860)	13.9 (11,428)	1.5 (1,269)	11.4 (9,372)	3.4 (2,797)	0.2 (187)	38.1 (31,393)
Agriculture/Forestry (5,314)	8.5 (443)	0 (0)	0 (0)	0 (0)	28.1 (1,461)	10.7 (558)	0 (0)	47.2 (2,462)
Totals: S.M.E. to Non-S.M.E. Majors (148,204)	6.7 (10,267)	1.2 (1,812)	9.3 (13,721)	3.1 (4,588)	17.1 (25,369)	5.9 (8,765)	0.6 (875)	44.1 (65,424)

of majors to stay within it, though not necessarily in their major of first choice. Within S.M.E. majors overall, 'internal resettlement' accounts for 9.7 percent of all relocations, compared with over a quarter (27.3%) of all such moves in the social sciences/humanities group. Education attracts far more switchers from history and political science (25.3%) than from any other major, except mathematics, which contributes 17.3 percent of its former majors to education.

Overall, the level of transfer into S.M.E. majors from all majors defined as 'non-S.M.E.' (including those who enter as 'undecided') is modest (6.2%). The fields contributing most switchers from other groups to S.M.E. majors are the computer science and technical majors, and health profession majors, who provide 21.0 percent and 26.7 percent respectively. The biological sciences gain 20.4 percent from those originally committing to careers in the health professions. Engineering gains 13.1 percent of switchers from the computer and technical fields. The only other group to make a significant transition (8.8%) into S.M.E. majors are those who enter as 'undeclared'. Transfers into S.M.E. majors from the social sciences, humanities, fine arts, business and education combined are very small (2.8%).

The C.I.R.P. data also allowed us to clarify patterns of persistence, switching and transfer of majors by sex. Of those initially choosing S.M.E. majors in 1987, 73.7 percent were men and 26.3 percent were women. The proportion of women ranged from 14.2 percent in engineering, approximately a quarter in agriculture and the physical sciences, to 45.2 percent and 47.7 percent, respectively, in the biological sciences, mathematics and statistics. There was a striking gender difference in switching patterns in that, across a wide range of majors, women more commonly than men switched to a major outside the group of their choice. The exceptions were: engineering, English and business, where the switching rates of men and of women were very similar; and the physical sciences, fine arts, health professions and education, where the switching rates of men were higher than those of women. Whether in S.M.E. majors or the humanities and social sciences, women were less likely than men to stay in their original major, and more apt to switch to another group of majors altogether. However, switching was much higher among women who originally chose S.M.E. majors than among those who chose majors in the humanities and social sciences (52.4% compared with 35.3%). The majors in which women switchers exceed women entrants by more than 55 percent include agriculture (79.1%), mathematics/statistics (72.3%), the biological sciences (56.7%), computer science (69.2%) and the health professions (60.7%).

In S.M.E. majors overall, men show a higher propensity to persist with their original choice (58.8%) than do women (47.6%), and a lower propensity to switch to a non-S.M.E. major.[8] For almost all S.M.E. majors where data are available, women show a higher propensity than men to abandon their first choices, whether by moving into other S.M.E. majors, or out of them altogether. Women are 26.3 percent of those who choose S.M.E. majors, but

31.2 percent of all S.M.E. switchers; men are 73.7 percent of all those choosing S.M.E. majors, and 68.8 percent of all S.M.E. switchers.

The greatest proportionate loss of women by switching occurs in mathematics/statistics and the biological sciences, where women are 7.3 percent and 5.0 percent (respectively) more of switchers than of those choosing S.M.E. majors. The comparable loss of women by switching from the physical sciences is 3.4 percent, and from engineering 0.4 percent. Persistence in an original S.M.E. major is also weakest among women in mathematics and the biological sciences, although their initial representation is stronger than in other S.M.E. majors. A variation occurs in the physical sciences, where women show more inclination than men to transfer into another S.M.E. major rather than to move out of the sciences completely. This trend is also discernable, to a lesser degree, in the biological sciences and engineering. However, the numbers of such transfers are small. Only around 10 percent of all students who chose S.M.E. majors switched from one science to another.

Tables 1.3, 1.4 and 1.5 reveal a pattern of reverting to gender-related traditions in the final choice of major of those who originally selected S.M.E. majors. While male switchers from mathematics, engineering and the biological sciences are substantially recruited into computer science, few women follow this path. The non-technical professional majors recruit proportionately more men (largely from mathematics and the physical sciences) than women. The humanities and social sciences receive the highest proportion (17.1%) of all switchers. However, they are chosen by more female than male switchers from all S.M.E. majors except mathematics/statistics—from which about one-third of switchers of each sex go into the humanities and social sciences. The health professions also recruit proportionately more women than men, largely from the physical sciences. However, the gender difference in the final choices of S.M.E. switchers is greatest in education, which recruits much more heavily from female than from male S.M.E. switchers. The trend is most marked in mathematics/statistics where 45.2 percent of women switchers opt for an education major, compared with 8.5 percent of the men. However, the preference for an education major is much stronger among women than among men for all S.M.E. switchers. Interestingly, the resurgence of traditional gender-based choices following switching is least marked in engineering, where a high proportion of both men and women switchers chose business majors. Women who are former engineering majors also select a computer science major more often than do women from other S.M.E. majors, and they are slightly less inclined to chose a liberal arts major than female S.M.E. switchers.

Overall, these data reflect the importance of different cultural traditions for the sexes with respect to their academic and career choices. As we shall discuss in more detail in Chapter 5, changes of mind among young women are more culturally supported than changes of mind among young men. This is especially the case where women initially proposed to enter fields which family, peers,

TABLE 1.3   Percent of Men and of Women Who Persisted in and Switched from Declared or Intended Majors by 1991, for 810,794 Undergraduates who Entered a National Sample of Four-Year Institutions in 1987.

Based on unpublished tabulations provided by the Cooperative Institutional Research Program, Higher Education Research Institute, University of California, Los Angeles, April 1993.

M=Male, F=Female, N/A= Not Available

Original major	% Stayed in same major		% Moved to major in same group		% Stayed in major or group		% Switched to other group of majors	
	M	F	M	F	M	F	M	F
Biological Sciences	47.1	35.8	6.6	7.5	53.8	43.3	46.2	56.7
Physical Sciences	30.6	27.7	15.9	28.1	46.5	55.7	53.5	44.3
Engineering	51.5	50.8	10.2	12.1	61.7	62.9	38.3	37.1
Mathematics/ Statistics	39.9	27.8	6.2	N/A	46.1	27.8	53.9	72.3
Agriculture	N/A	20.9	N/A	N/A	N/A	20.9	N/A	79.1
All S.M.E. Majors	*49.0*	*37.7*	*9.8*	*10.0*	*58.8*	*47.6*	*41.2*	*52.4*
History/ Political Science	62.0	31.3	25.5	19.2	87.5	50.5	12.5	49.5
Social Sciences	64.4	52.5	18.9	14.8	83.3	67.3	16.7	32.7
Fine Arts	48.1	53.2	16.7	22.4	64.8	76.7	35.2	24.3
English	57.2	56.2	26.9	29.1	84.1	85.3	15.9	14.1
Other Humanities	30.5	27.8	46.2	37.5	76.6	65.3	23.4	34.7
All Humanities/ Social Sciences	*54.7*	*44.0*	*23.2*	*20.7*	*77.9*	*64.7*	*22.1*	*35.3*
Health Professions	11.8	39.3	-	-	11.8	39.3	88.2	60.7
Computer Science/ Technical	54.2	30.8	-	-	54.2	30.8	45.8	69.2
Business	61.8	56.7	-	-	61.8	56.7	38.2	43.3
Education	44.7	73.1	-	-	44.8	73.1	55.3	26.9
Other Non-Technical	48.7	30.1	-	-	48.7	30.7	51.3	69.3

TABLE 1.4 Of those who Persisted in and Switched from Declared or Intended Majors by 1991, Percent who were Men and Percent who were Women among 810,794 Undergraduates who Entered a National Sample of Four-Year Institutions in 1987.

Based on unpublished tabulations provided by the Cooperative Institutional Research Program, Higher Education Research Institute, University of California, Los Angeles, April 1993.

M=Male, F=Female, N/A= Not Available

Original major	Of all who stayed in same major, % who were		Of all who moved to major in same group, % who were		Of all who stayed in major or group, % who were		Of all who switched to other group of majors, % who were	
	M	F	M	F	M	F	M	F
Biological Sciences	61.5	38.5	51.8	48.2	60.1	39.9	49.8	50.2
Physical Sciences	77.0	23.0	63.1	36.9	71.6	28.4	78.5	21.5
Engineering	86.0	14.0	83.7	16.3	85.6	14.4	86.2	13.8
Mathematics/ Statistics	61.2	38.8	N/A	N/A	64.5	35.5	45.0	55.0
Agriculture	76.4	23.6	N/A	N/A	76.4	23.6	N/A	N/A
All S.M.E. Majors	*78.4*	*21.6*	*73.6*	*26.4*	*77.6*	*22.4*	*68.8*	*31.2*
History/ Political Science	56.6	43.4	46.7	53.3	53.3	46.7	14.2	85.8
Social Sciences	33.6	66.4	34.4	65.6	33.8	66.2	17.4	82.6
Fine Arts	49.3	50.7	44.5	55.6	48.0	52.0	60.9	39.1
English	34.0	66.0	31.0	69.0	33.3	66.7	35.4	64.6
Other Humanities	33.8	66.2	36.5	63.5	35.4	64.6	23.9	76.1
All Humanities/ Social Sciences	*43.4*	*56.6*	*40.9*	*59.1*	*42.7*	*57.3*	*27.9*	*72.1*
Health Professions	14.5	85.5	-	-	12.7	74.7	45.0	55.0
Computer Science/ Technical	77.9	22.1	-	-	77.9	22.1	57.0	43.0
Business	57.0	43.0	-	-	57.0	43.0	51.8	48.2
Education	12.6	87.4	-	-	12.6	87.4	32.6	67.4
Other Non-Technical	50.5	49.5	-	-	50.5	49.5	32.2	67.8

TABLE 1.5 Final Major Choices by 1991 of 142,890 Male and Female Undergraduate Switchers Entering S.M.E. Majors in a National Sample of Four-Year Institutions in 1987.

Based on unpublished tabulations provided by the Cooperative Institutional Research Program, Higher Education Research Institute, University of California, Los Angeles, April 1993.

M=Male, F=Female

Original S.M.E. Majors	Non-S.M.E. Destination Majors of S.M.E. Switchers												Totals by Major	
	Computer Science		Health		Business		Education		Humanities & Fine Arts		Other Non-Technical			
	M	F	M	F	M	F	M	F	M	F	M	F	M	F
Mathematics/ Statistics	24.4	2.0	0.0	5.0	9.4	12.5	8.5	45.2	33.6	32.0	24.0	3.3	99.9	100.0
Physical Sciences	0.0	4.0	1.5	17.8	5.3	10.5	1.8	10.0	47.0	57.8	44.4	0.0	100.0	100.1
Biological Sciences	39.3	1.1	1.9	2.6	8.4	6.0	1.1	19.7	39.9	57.1	9.4	13.6	100.0	100.1
Engineering	18.9	9.0	3.2	0.0	39.1	21.4	2.2	15.5	28.1	42.0	8.5	12.1	100.0	100.0
Totals: S.M.E to Non-S.M.E Majors	20.7	3.4	2.6	3.7	26.4	10.9	2.0	20.5	33.2	50.8	14.1	10.7	99.0	100.0

faculty, or the wider community see as traditional male provinces. Among those whose first choice lies in the humanities and social sciences, women also exhibit (to a higher degree than do men) the liberal arts tradition of 'trying out' different majors before settling into a final choice. The C.I.R.P. data also show young women exercising a greater degree of liberty to change their minds across a broad spectrum of majors. These data also suggest the dominance of conservatism in the field choices of women. The majors in which women show strongest adherence to their original choice are those in which they have a longer tradition of academic involvement, career access, or professional dominance, namely, education, the fine arts, the humanities and English.[9] Women who choose one of these majors are much more likely to remain in it. S.M.E. majors are a less-traditional choice, and women show much less persistence in these than in more traditional majors. Not only do women enter these majors in lower proportions than men, they also leave them in higher proportions. To enter S.M.E. majors at all, women must resist traditionalist pressures. They will be supported or encouraged by the same conservative pressures to leave an S.M.E. major for something more traditional. The final field choice of women who initially chose (non-traditional) S.M.E. majors tends to be conservative.

We are greatly indebted to the Higher Education Research Institute, U.C.L.A., for enabling us to set S.M.E. switching patterns within the wider context of persistence and switching across all majors, and to distinguish the field choice patterns of women from those of men.

Method of Inquiry

Our research design for this study was ethnographic. It's purpose was to derive from students' reflections on their undergraduate experiences a set of testable hypotheses which address our research questions. This method differs from deductive research which tests hypotheses derived from prior studies or speculation. The study was conducted over a three-year period (1990-1993) with 335 students at seven four-year institutions of different type and location. Approximately 75 percent of the data were gathered by personal interviews and the remaining 25 percent in focus groups of three to five members. An additional 125 students (i.e., 460 in total) took part in focus group discussions on six other campuses. Their purpose was to check the validity of our tentative hypotheses. Interviews varied in length from 45 to 75 minutes and focus groups from 90 minutes to two and a half hours. The verbatim transcriptions and field notes from all interviews and focus groups yielded a data set of over 600 interview hours. All interviews and focus groups were conducted in the manner of semi-structured conversations that focused on students' experiences in science, mathematics, or engineering classes, and in other contexts (e.g., high school) with relevance for their decisions to enter, continue in, or leave their original S.M.E. majors. The form and content of interviews was focused upon discovering what factors (whether present or absent) had bearing for S.M.E. attrition and persistence, and what were their patterns of interaction and relative importance.

We asked the institutional records departments of the participating institutions to randomly generate lists of potential informants who, *prima facie*, met our requirements for interview. We included as 'science': the biological sciences (biology, biochemistry, microbiology, botany, zoology and animal science); the physical sciences (astronomy, physics, chemistry, earth science/geology). Mathematics and applied mathematics majors were drawn along with science majors so that, taken together, they represented half of our sample. Engineering majors comprised the other half of the sample, and included aerospace, civil, chemical, electrical, industrial/design, mechanical, environmental and general engineering. Participating institutions were asked to draw approximately twice as many potential interviewees as we ultimately selected for interview, and to provide information on each student's sex, ethnicity, current major, former major (where applicable), year in school, S.A.T. score in mathematics (or equivalent) and local telephone number. We subsequently checked the accuracy of this information with each potential interviewee in a short telephone conversation.

All of the students selected were those who had a mathematics S.A.T. (or equivalent) score of 650 or higher. This performance criterion was chosen on the advice of S.M.E. faculty so as to include in our sample only those students whom they expected to be capable of handling the course work. In order to put the accounts of switchers into context, it was also important to have the perspectives of non-switchers. The sample of 335 undergraduates was designed to include slightly more switchers (54.6%) than non-switchers (45.4%).[10] All switchers were either juniors or seniors and all non-switchers were S.M.E. seniors who were close to graduation.[11] In order to clarify what distinguishes the experiences of male S.M.E. students of color, and all women, from those of their white male peers, and how these differences bear upon their higher rates of attrition, we deliberately over-sampled these groups who, historically, have been under-represented in S.M.E. majors: 52 percent of the sample of white students were women, and 48 percent were men; 88 students of color (46 women and 42 men) were interviewed (26 percent of the total sample).[12] The groups represented were: Hispanic, Latino/Latina and Chicano/Chicana; black; native American and Asian-American (whose ancestries were Japanese, Chinese, Laotian, Cambodian, Filipino, Korean, East Indian and Pakistani). We selected only American-born students in order to compare experiences in U.S. high schools. The composition of focus groups was based on shared characteristics such as sex, type of major, and switcher or non-switcher status. With rare exceptions, we found it more productive to interview students of color individually.

As our purpose was to discover as many factors bearing upon attrition and persistence as our panel of expert witnesses could offer, the use of standardized interview instruments was precluded. During the brief screening interviews (by telephone) we explained the purpose of the study. Those we selected, and who agreed to take part, were invited (prior to their interview or group discussion) to think about factors which had shaped their decisions. Interviews and focus groups were conducted in the manner of a focused conversation: issues from an initial topic outline were explored in an order dictated by the natural structure of the discussion, and those not spontaneously mentioned were raised at natural breaks in the conversation. New issues brought up by participants pertinent to the main research questions were always pursued. Thus, from the outset, our tentative set of discussion questions was continuously refined and augmented by the emphases which informants placed on the factors they discussed. As important new themes emerged, they were explored with all subsequent interviewees.[13]

Some basic information was collected from every student: current and former majors; year in school; mathematics S.A.T. scores, high school and college G.P.A.s; evaluation of high school preparation for S.M.E. classes; and reasons for their initial choice of a major. We asked all participants for a profile of their high school and college grades (their mathematics S.A.T. scores having been provided in advance by their institution). However, restrictions on the disclosure of students records, as well as the difficulty of working with unfamiliar institutional data sets, precluded our collection of other than self-reported data. In addition, all women and male students of color were asked to comment on factors which they felt distinguished their experiences from those of white male peers. Conversely, all white males were asked about any differences they had noticed between their own experiences and those of the female and male students of color who shared their classes. Everyone was asked to describe any differences they had noticed in the nature, difficulty, and teaching styles of S.M.E. and non-S.M.E. classes. Switchers were asked to reflect on the process of deciding to change majors. Non-switchers were invited to describe issues bearing on their own persistence, and to offer explanations for the loss of peers to other majors. We explored the personal strategies and institutional programs which had aided the persistence of non-switchers, and asked all students to discuss their experiences with the advisory systems—both departmental and institutional. Finally, we asked every participant to offer advice to their departments, colleges and schools on how the education they had experienced could be improved, and how more students who were able and interested might be retained.

The study took place on seven campuses in four different geographic areas.[14] Institutions were selected on the basis of their funding (public or private), their mission, the level of prestige accorded their research activities, and the size and composition of their graduate and undergraduate populations.

The scheme used to differentiate types of four-year institutions was a modified version of the Carnegie classification.[15] Our concentration on institutions in which the majority of undergraduates receive their S.M.E. education precluded the choice of historically black or women's colleges, and institutions with highly specialized missions. We are aware, however, that important insights into persistence and attrition within these majors are to be gained by inquiries which focus on these more specialized institutions.[16]

The three private institutions included in our sample were:

*   a small liberal arts college in the West with a strong reputation for its teaching (engineering is not offered)

*   a city-based university also in the West, with a small student body (under 5,000) and faculty focus on teaching rather than funded research. This institution offers an undergraduate degree in engineering, and awards master's degrees and doctorates in mathematics and science

*   a large university on the West Coast with a highly selective admissions policy, and a high degree of prestige related to its research-generating faculty

The four public universities selected vary in terms of the prestige accorded their funded research in science and engineering. They were:

*   a multi-role urban university in the Northeast with large enrollments in undergraduate science, mathematics and engineering, but lacking an established reputation or strong funding for its science and engineering research

*   a large urban university in the Midwest which is well-funded by research grants, particularly in the field of engineering, and with an annual production of Ph.D.s and a prestige ranking for its research which are similar to that of the leading private research university selected

*   a state university in the West with well-established graduate programs in science, mathematics and engineering, and a prestigious, highly-funded research program in engineering. Originally a land-grant college, it has an applied science emphasis, a fairly open admissions policy and a large student intake from working-class families

*   a large state university which is considered the 'flagship' institution for its western state, and has a good reputation for its engineering school and high prestige for several of its science departments

Each of the five large universities in our sample offers graduate degrees in science, mathematics and engineering, has large undergraduate enrollments, and a diverse student population. One-third of our interviewees (N = 112) attended the private institutions in our sample, and two-thirds (N = 223) attended the large public universities. Overall, the institutions we selected can be ranked along a continuum of prestige that takes into account research funding and the number of graduate degrees awarded.

It was our concern to interview sufficient numbers of students in particular racial or ethnic groups to get a clear picture of their distinctive concerns. Therefore, our final choice of locations and institutional types was also informed by the racial/ethnic composition of each potential study site. Thus, at the midwestern university, the predominant ethnic minority group was Asian, many of whom were the children of either first- or second-generation Indo-Chinese refugees. The northeastern university enrolled more black students than are to be found in the western or midwestern institutions. Students in the Northeast who were Hispanic had ties to Puerto Rico or South America, rather than (as in the west) Mexico. At the private university on the West Coast, Asian-American students were not numerically a minority. However, on the western campus, most Asian students were foreign-born and had received their high school education overseas. Our supposition that regional differences in the composition of minority populations (whether on campus, or living in the vicinity of the institution) make important differences in the way that S.M.E. education is experienced by students of differing races or ethnicities was, subsequently, borne out by our findings, and is discussed in Chapter 6.

In order to retain site confidentially, we will use the following abbreviations to indicate the location and prestige ranking of particular institutions in the text, and in tables and figures:

* WCPRI1 = West Coast, private, ranking 1

* WPRI2 = western, private, ranking 2

* WPRI3 = western, private, ranking 3

* MWPUB1 = midwestern, public, ranking 1

* WPUB2 = western, public, ranking 2

* WPUB3 = western, public, ranking 3

* ECPUB4 = East Coast, public, ranking 4

Additional Data and Validity Checks

All ethnography is iterative. Data coding and analysis begin with the transcription of the first set of interviews and continue throughout the study. As dominant themes, then hypotheses, begin to emerge, investigators return to the field to check the validity of their tentative theoretical constructs among comparable groups of informants. Over the three years of this study, invitations to discuss our work at institutions which either parallelled or augmented our set of seven institutional types and four geographic settings, offered the opportunity to conduct additional focus groups with 125 students on six extra campuses. The total number of students interviewed was, thus, 460. This second round of interviewing gave us feed-back, clarification and additional information. It also allowed us to discuss the hypotheses derived from the main site data with students at similar institutions, and to augment our understanding of student experiences in a wider range of institutions and settings. In these discussions, students corroborated our findings from the seven main sites, and thus insure the reliability and validity of the work overall.

Both during site visits, and in presentation of findings on other campuses, we continually discussed the issues raised by our research questions and our emergent findings with deans, faculty, administrators, advisors, special program directors and S.M.E. graduate students. They were a valuable source of information on the structure of particular majors, the cultural climate of campuses, departments and colleges, the local economy, initiatives taken to address aspects of S.M.E. recruitment and retention and the difficulties associated with seeking to bring about change.

Method of Ethnographic Data Analysis

The tape-recordings of interviews and focus groups were transcribed verbatim into a word processing program and submitted to 'The Ethnograph',[17] a set of computer programs which allow for the multiple, overlapping and nested coding of a large volume of transcribed documents to a high degree of complexity. Each line-numbered transcript was searched for information bearing upon student attrition. Most commonly, information was embedded in narrative accounts of student experiences rather than offered in abstract statements. This allowed individual transcripts to be checked for internal consistency between the opinions or explanations offered by participants, their descriptions of events, and the reflections and feelings they evoked. Lines or segments referencing problems of different type and importance were tagged by code names. There were no preconceived codes: each new code name referenced a discrete idea not previously raised. Because answers to the same question were often not of the same character and did not cover the same issues, codes were never developed on the basis of the questions asked, but always by the nature of the responses, and by spontaneously-offered comments, narratives and illustrations. Because participants often made several points in the same statement, segments were often indexed by several different codes, each with a different name. Groups of codes which clustered around particular themes were given domain names, and the whole branching and inter-connected structure of codes and domains was gradually built into a code book which, at any point in time, represented the state of analysis.

Descriptions of the problems experienced by both switchers and non-switchers were coded in separate domains from those identified as having directly contributed to decisions to leave the sciences. Students' theories about switching which were based on observation were also coded separately from those grounded in personal experience. The number of participants who mentioned each issue was counted across the whole data set and for particular groups within it. Student concerns about their S.M.E. majors are expressed in terms of the number of people who mentioned each issue. Throughout our account, we have followed the ethnographic tradition of presenting our analysis through the accounts of the participants themselves.

Overview of Findings

Perhaps the most important single generalization arising from our analysis is that we did not find switchers and non-switchers to be two different kinds of people. That is to say, we did not find them to differ by individual attributes of performance, attitude, or behavior, to any degree sufficient to explain why one group left, and the other group stayed. Rather, we found a similar array of abilities, motivations and study-related behaviors distributed across the entire sample. We also found the most common reasons for switching arose from a set of problems which, to varying degrees, were shared by switchers and non-switchers alike. What distinguished the survivors from those who left was the development of particular attitudes or coping strategies—both legitimate and illegitimate. Serendipity also played a part in persistence, often in the form of intervention by faculty at a critical point in the student's academic or personal life.

In reflecting on their experiences in the first two years of S.M.E. majors, switchers invariably distinguished experiences they perceived as bearing directly on their decision to leave S.M.E. majors, and problems of lesser significance which they needed to accommodate, tolerate, or resolve, in order to stay. Exactly the same kinds of problems prompted some undergraduates to switch majors, were an additional source of stress to students who switched for other reasons, and were troublesome to many who remained in their major. Non-switchers expressed the same kinds of concerns and reservations about their majors as did switchers. With some types of problems, switchers and non-switchers differed little in the proportion of each group who had experienced them. With other problems, non-switchers either experienced them less, or had learned to cope with them better, than had the switchers.

On every campus, we also found a small group of S.M.E. seniors who reported they were planning non-S.M.E. careers following graduation. These post-graduate switchers were 16.5 percent of all seniors when all seven campuses were taken into account.

The issues and concerns of switchers and non-switchers focused around the same set of issues across all seven campuses: there were no major differences between institutions of different type in the nature of the problems described by their students. Although there was some variation in the ranking of problems by institutional type, every category of problem was found on every campus, regardless of differences in size, mission, funding, selectivity, or reputation, and there was little differentiation across campuses in identification of the most serious concerns by either switchers or non-switchers.

Overall, the issues raised by our participants fell into 23 categories, some of which are broader than others. There is, necessarily, some overlap in the boundaries between problem categories because, as a normal matter, people see their concerns as essentially interrelated. Also the ways in which undergraduates define or categorize concerns which they perceive as relevant to attrition or persistence do not necessarily square with the ways in which the causes of attrition are conceptualized by others, including faculty. Throughout our analyses, we followed our informants' definitions and distinctions in assigning significance to their experiences. We have found it useful to represent the relative significance of issues arising from accounts of S.M.E. undergraduate experiences using the metaphor of an 'iceberg'. This idea is intended to convey our most important single finding that problems which contribute most to field switching are set within a group of related concerns which are experienced, to some degree, by all S.M.E. students, whether they leave or whether they stay. Those who switch represent only the tip of a much larger problem. As, apart from those few participants who shared any particular focus group, none of the interviewees knew what any other participant had told us, there was a high degree of concurrence across the whole sample as to the salient issues, and their relative significance for attrition. The iceberg metaphor is employed in this chapter in Tables 1.6, 1.8 and 1.9, and in Chapter 5 (Tables 5.1 and 5.2), both as a way to summarize findings, and in order to compare the relative importance that sub-sets of informants (by sex and type of major) assigned to particular issues.[18] In each table, the first column contains all factors cited by S.M.E. switchers as having directly contributed to their switching decision. Each issue for each switcher is counted only once, although switchers often returned more than once to concerns which had considerable emotional significance for them.[19] Switching decisions were never the result of a single, overwhelming concern; they were always the upshot of a 'push and pull' process over time. This process typically involved reactions to problems with S.M.E. majors, concerns about S.M.E. careers, and the perceived merits of academic or career alternatives. The average number of factors contributing to each switching decision was 4.2.

The second column in each of the 'iceberg' tables includes all the decision-related concerns reflected in the first column, plus mentions of the same issue by other switchers, whether or not they had significance for switching decisions. This information is especially useful for comparison with the third column, which represents the proportions of non-switchers who mentioned each kind of concern as an aspect of their personal experience. Non-switchers mentioned an average of 5.4 concerns, compared with an average of 8.6 for switchers. Thus, one simple (though not especially illuminating) way to distinguish switchers from non-switchers is to see them as people who have rather more problems with their original majors than do non-switchers. The final column shows the proportion of the whole sample who mentioned each type of concern. We feel the information in this column might act as a guide for those deliberating what aspects of S.M.E. education might usefully be changed, whether or not their primary consideration is attrition.

Contrary to the common assumption that most switching is caused by personal inadequacy in the face of academic challenge, one strong finding reflected in Table 1.6 is the high proportion of factors cited as significant in switching decisions which arise either from structural or cultural sources within institutions, or from students' concerns about their career prospects. We also found strong similarity between the concerns of switchers and non-switchers in almost half of all the issues represented in Table 1.6: the four most commonly cited concerns leading to switching decisions were also cited as concerns by between 31 percent and 74 percent of non-switchers. Ranked according to the contribution which they make to switching, these are:

* lack or loss of interest in science

* belief that a non-S.M.E. major holds more interest, or offers a better education

* poor teaching by S.M.E. faculty

* feeling overwhelmed by the pace and load of curriculum demands

Seven issues were cited as shared concerns by more than one-third of both switchers and non-switchers. They include the four listed above, plus (by rank):

* choosing an S.M.E. major for reasons that prove inappropriate

* inadequate departmental or institutional provisions for advising or counseling about academic, career, or personal concerns

* inadequate high school preparation, in terms of disciplinary content or depth, conceptual grasp, or study skills

An additional four concerns were shared by a smaller proportion (20-30%) of all switchers and non-switchers. In rank order they are:

* financial difficulty in completing S.M.E. majors

* conceptual difficulties with one or more S.M.E. subject(s)

* the unexpected length of S.M.E. majors (i.e. more than four years)

* language difficulties with foreign faculty or T.A.s.

TABLE 1.6 "The Problem Iceberg." Factors Contributing to All Switching Decisions, and to the Concerns of Switchers, of Non-Switchers and of All Students (N=335).

Issue	Factor in switching decisions (%)	All switchers' concerns (%)	All non-switchers' concerns (%)	All students' concerns (%)
Lack of/loss of interest in SME: "turned off science"	43	60	36	49
Non-SME major offers better education/more interest.	40	58	32	46
Poor teaching by SME faculty	36	90	74	83
Curriculum overload, fast pace overwhelming	35	45	41	44
SME career options/rewards felt not worth effort to get degree	31	43	20	33
Rejection of SME careers and associated lifestyles	29	43	21	33
Shift to more appealing non-S.M.E.career option	27	33	16*	25
Inadequate advising or help with academic problems	24	75	52	65
Discouraged/lost confidence due to low grades in early years	23	34	12	24
Financial problems of completing S.M.E. majors	17	30	23	27
Inadequate high school preparation in subjects/study skills	15	40	38	39
Morale undermined by competitive SME culture	15	28	9	20
Reasons for choice of SME major prove inappropriate	14	82	40	63
Conceptual difficulties with one or more S.M.E. subject(s)	13	27	25	26
Lack of peer study group support	12	17	7	12
Discovery of aptitude for non-S.M.E. subject	10	12	5	8
Prefer teaching approach in non-S.M.E. courses	9	24	15	20
Unexpected length of S.M.E. degree: more than four years	9	20	28	24
Switching as means to career goal: system playing	7	9	3	6
Language difficulties with foreign faculty or T.A.s	3	30	20	25
Problems related to class size	0	20	11	16
Poor teaching, lab, or recitation support by T.A.s	0	20	11	16
Poor lab/computer lab facilities	0	4	4	4

*Issue raised by non-switchers intending to move into non-S.M.E. field following graduation.

Only four issues which contributed to switching decisions were *not* substantially shared with non-switchers. Three of these reflect underlying concerns about career prospects: that the perceived job options, or material rewards, of S.M.E. careers are not worth the effort required to complete an S.M.E. degree; perceptions of low job satisfaction and/or unappealing lifestyles in S.M.E. careers; and that careers in non-S.M.E. fields have greater appeal. The fourth issue in this group reflects students' experiences of low grades and of curve-grading in their first two years, leading to discouragement, and loss of confidence in their ability to do mathematics and science.

It would be hard to argue on the basis of this evidence, either that switchers suffer from a distinctive set of problems, or that switchers differ in salient ways from non-switchers as individuals. All of the most commonly-mentioned problems of switchers and non-switchers, including those which contribute most to switching decisions, imply criticisms of the practices and attitudes which define and sustain the structure and culture of S.M.E. majors. The economic difficulties cited by switchers, and to a lesser degree by non-switchers, reflect a shared high level of anxiety about career and lifestyle prospects at a time of economic uncertainty, and about the level of satisfaction that careers open to those with S.M.E. qualifications are likely to offer. Expressions of anxiety about career and lifestyle prospects increased over the three years of interviewing. Job-related concerns were more highly ranked by undergraduates interviewed at the last three campuses than at the first four campuses reported on in 1991.

Criticisms of faculty pedagogy contributed to one-third (36.1%) of all switching decisions, and were the third most commonly-mentioned factor in such decisions. However, complaints about poor teaching were almost universal among switchers (90.2%), and were the most commonly-cited type of complaint among non-switchers (73.7%). Complaints about pedagogy cannot, however, be seen in isolation. All of the four most highly-ranked factors contributing to switching decisions reflect some aspect of teaching, or rate the quality of learning experiences offered by S.M.E. faculty as poor, compared with those offered by former high school science teachers, and/or faculty in non-S.M.E. disciplines. The significance of this factor does not end here. In one way or another, concerns about S.M.E. faculty teaching, advising, assessment practices and curriculum design, pervade all but seven of the 23 issues represented in our 'iceberg' tables. Thus:

*   The rejection of S.M.E. careers or lifestyles is partly a rejection of the role models which S.M.E. faculty and graduate students present to undergraduates

*   S.M.E. faculty are often represented as 'unapproachable' or unavailable for help with either academic or career-planning concerns

* Students perceive the curve-grading systems widely employed by
  S.M.E. faculty as reflecting disdain for the worth or potential of most
  under-classmen. Their presumed purpose is to drive a high proportion
  of students away, rather than give realistic and useful feedback to
  students on their level of understanding, or conceptual progress

* Harsh grading systems, which are part of a traditional competitive
  S.M.E. culture, also preclude or discourage collaborative learning
  strategies, which many students view as critical to a good understanding of the material, and to a deeper appreciation of concepts and their
  application

* The experience of conceptual difficulty at particular points in particular
  classes, which might not constitute an insuperable barrier to progress
  if addressed in a timely way, commonly sets in motion a downward
  spiral of falling confidence, reduced class attendance, falling grades,
  and despair—leading to exit from the major

* T.A.s (whether American or foreign) bear a disproportionate responsibility for the teaching of fundamental material in basic S.M.E. classes
  that are over-enrolled given the pedagogical resources available

* Over-packed curricula which lengthen the time needed to complete an
  S.M.E. degree place extra financial burdens on the growing proportion
  of students who must pay for their education by employment or the
  accumulation of debt. Seniors express the suspicion that over-packing
  the syllabi of basic classes is maintained for 'weed-out', rather than for
  pedagogical, purposes

* Curriculum overload (combined with the growing length and costs of
  S.M.E. majors), also supports the perception that the rewards (both
  material and personal) of S.M.E.-based careers are not worth the effort
  and costs required to secure them

Thus, criticisms of faculty pedagogy, together with those of curriculum design
and student assessment practices, constitute the largest group of problems in 'the
iceberg,' both for switchers and non-switchers.

The Loss of Able Students from S.M.E. Majors

The theory that switchers can be distinguished from non-switchers by their
inability to cope with the intrinsic 'hardness' of S.M.E. majors, or their
unwillingness to commit to sufficient hard work, is a traditional way of
explaining attrition rates and reflects a disinclination to see attrition as 'a
problem.' It may also function as a barrier to attempts to address the concerns
of students who persist, as well as those who leave. In Chapter 3, we discuss
what the 'hardness' of science means to students, and how it shapes their

attitudes and behavior. Here we draw attention to the similarities between switchers and non-switching seniors which support our assertion that, on the basis of individual attributes (including academic performance) it is difficult to predict which students are likely to stay, and which to leave.

First, as Table 1.6 indicates, we found a strong similarity between the proportions of switchers and non-switchers who reported conceptual difficulties in one or more S.M.E. subject(s) (i.e., 26.8 percent of all switchers and 25.0 percent of non-switchers). As a factor in decisions to leave S.M.E. majors, conceptual difficulties were reported by a comparatively small proportion of switchers (12.6%) and ranked 14th out of 23 contributory concerns. Non-switchers suffered in similar proportions to switchers from the consequences of high school preparation which they subsequently found to be inadequate for college-level mathematics or science: 40.4 percent of all switchers and 37.5 percent of non-switchers reported inadequate high school preparation. This deficiency was an important basic problem for many students, despite the apparent competence in mathematics indicated by their S.A.T. scores of 650 or more. However, conceptual difficulty was thought less important than 10 other concerns as a final consideration in switching decisions. Where conceptual problems were a factor in switching decisions students, reported that difficulty with aspects of a single subject (predominantly in mathematics or chemistry) most commonly acted as a barrier to further progress.

One-quarter (24.0%) of switchers described difficulty in getting help from faculty and/or T.A.s as having contributed to their decision to leave. However, 75.4 percent of all switchers, and 52.0 percent of non-switchers also described this problem. More switchers (16.9%) than non-switchers (7.2%) reported they had not worked with peer study groups to gain a better grasp of material they found difficult. With hindsight, 11.5 percent of switchers considered this omission to have contributed to their leaving.

Though we did encounter switchers who were unwilling to undertake the heavy work demands and fierce pace of introductory classes, we also found indications that most switchers had worked hard in S.M.E. classes and had invested considerable time, money, and personal commitment in their effort to persist. Earlier in this chapter, we cited national studies which document the higher demonstrated ability of freshmen entering S.M.E. than those entering non-S.M.E., majors. To this, we add our finding that the mean of G.P.A.s reported by switchers just prior to leaving S.M.E. majors was, at 3.0 (range: 1.9 - 3.85) not dramatically lower than the mean of current G.P.A.s (3.15; range: 2.95 - 3.95) reported by non-switching seniors. There were some variations by discipline: the mean exit G.P.A. for engineering switchers was 2.85 (range: 1.9 - 3.65), and the current G.P.A. for seniors was 3.5 (range: 2.95 - 3.95). The mean exit G.P.A. for science and mathematics switchers was 3.3 (range: 2.0 - 3.85), and the current G.P.A. for seniors was 3.2 (range: 3.0 - 3.95). This finding, based on the self-reported scores of our informants, closely follows that of a recent (1992) study of switchers and persisters at the College of Engineering, the University of California at Berkeley.[20] Humphreys and Freeland's study, which examined all first-time engineering freshmen entering in the fall semesters of 1985, 1986, and 1987, found that, "students who persisted and students who switched earned comparable grade point averages (3.10 as compared with 3.07)" (p. 5). This difference was not found to be statistically significant. Engineering switchers were also found to have entered with higher verbal S.A.T. scores than did persisters. The authors note that "students who achieved well academically, both in high school and in the College of Engineering at the freshman level, may choose to switch nevertheless" (p. 5). Our finding is also supported by data provided by the University of Colorado at Boulder, for freshmen who entered S.M.E. majors between 1980 and 1988.[21] The average predicted G.P.A. (P.G.P.A.) for those who persisted was (at 2.93) only slightly higher than for switchers (2.86). Comparison by gender revealed that women entered with higher average P.G.P.A. scores than men (i.e., 3.05, compared with 2.99 in engineering, and 2.84, compared with 2.72 in science and mathematics). Although women entering S.M.E. majors are, in national samples, found to have higher proportionate rates of switching than men, in this analysis, both the women who persisted and those who switched had higher average P.G.P.A. scores than male persisters and male switchers respectively (i.e., 2.95 compared with 2.92 for persisters, and 2.88 compared with 2.84 for switchers).

We were also impressed by the length of time switchers pursued their original intention before finally deciding to leave. The average time period spent in the major before leaving it was, for engineering switchers, 2.6 years (range: 1 - 4 years), and for science and mathematics switchers, 2.1 years (range: 1 - 3 years). This finding underscores our observation from the text data that, for most students, the decision to switch was not taken until they had already expended a considerable amount of time, money and effort in persistence.

Both the accounts of switchers, and those of non-switchers who describe the experiences of room-mates and friends, also offer powerful testimony of the desire to persist, and the efforts made to do so:

> I do work hard, and my average load over these four years—even when I was transferring out—has been 17, 18 hours a semester, plus a couple of night classes sometimes. It doesn't really bother me to work that hard. But when it's a concept I don't understand and I go to get some kind of help from faculty and they just don't give it, that's discouraging. (Male white engineering switcher)

> She was one of those people who all they did was study...Her freshman year, we had to *beg* her not to spend all her time working...I don't think she took a class that wasn't biology or science...And now she's a psychology major. She just got so burnt out. She was pushing herself so hard, and she just wasn't enjoying it. (Female black science non-switcher)

I tried for all these courses. I've thought about just devoting every ounce of my life, but I don't know if that's possible. But that's what I would think about. This Christmas, I went home with my chemistry book and read nine chapters, but when I came back here, I started failing the tests and I just got more and more upset. (Male native American science switcher)

I'd go home and I would cram and study all night long. And the next day, the teacher might take two steps backwards and perhaps cover a tiny bit of what you covered the day before. But in engineering, there's absolutely no time for any falling back. In fact they're always way ahead of where you think you should be. It was just push, push, push—all the time. That's why I kept on pushing myself. I thought, 'I'm just not pushing myself hard enough.' All my friends were dropping out. (Male Asian-American engineering switcher)

We found many switchers whose level of ability and application should have been sufficient, given a more encouraging learning environment, for them to complete their major. We also encountered a smaller number of multi-talented switchers, the loss of whose high abilities from science-based fields may be of particular concern.[22] Both switchers and non-switchers saw their S.M.E. majors as prone to lose students who had both sufficient ability and interest to complete the degree:

What bothers me is the number of people who know what engineering is about, and really have the capability to do well and be good in the field, but end up going a different way for reasons other than lack of ability. (Female white engineering non-switcher)

You could say to them, 'Do you realize that you're pushing talented people away from your major?' (Male white science switcher)

Well, since I've been here, I've gotten As or B+s, so I've done well in math classes here—same with high school—I always got As in high school. (Female white engineering switcher)

I did one of the 200-level Calc III classes in freshman year, just on the side. It was fine—well, actually it was a bit boring because I'd done all of that in high school. (Male white science switcher)

I love the field work, and that's what I would really like to do. I like to think about what's happening, and form theories about it...I got an A in biology. I got an A in chemistry too. (Male native American science switcher)

My G.P.A. has hung right around 3.7 and only went as low as 3.6 in my first block. My physics courses were Bs or B+s, and the math was, I think, A-. (Male white science switcher, entering graduate school in music)

Student explanations for this 'wastage' stressed the counter-productive consequences of faculty's preoccupation with weeding-out, rather than supporting and encouraging, students:

I've friends who were in physics and in engineering who were really good students, and were good students in high school too. They were the A.P. students, and when they suddenly got Cs, they didn't know how to handle it. I mean, a hell of a lot of self-esteem is attached to those grades. So I think they go somewhere else to rebuild it. (Male white science non-switcher)

The students who left were smart enough. They were just extremely overwhelmed and scared to fail. (Female white female science non-switcher)

You get people that would probably do well if they were given half a chance, but there's so much competition, and not a heck of a lot of help. (Female black engineering senior)

It's the way this gentleman teaches. He believes in grading on a curve and slaughtering people in the first exam. You lose everyone 'cause no one's encouraging you to stay—the professor is very unapproachable. I think you lose a ton of good people. Why sit here and get slaughtered when they can go to another department and have some interaction with the professor, and some encouragement? (Male white science non-switcher)

Mostly, you have to be very willing to take the abuse to see yourself through it. The people who leave aren't necessarily any less talented, but they just say, 'Why do this?' (Male white engineering non-switcher)

I think they are losing a lot of intelligent people who would be very good engineers. One of my friends, he's...gonna switch into International Affairs. And my room-mate's a civil engineer with a 3.8 and just one year from graduation. But he's taking next year off: he just can't stand it any more. (Male white engineering non-switcher)

Weed-out classes also had the unintended effect of driving away some highly talented students because they lacked sufficient intellectual stimulation to sustain interest in the discipline:

The first two years in physics are so *dull*. I mean, they have absolutely nothing to do with what you'll be doing later. I'm afraid that's why you might be losing good students from engineering that are really qualified and have the intelligence...There are ways to make the introductory material interesting so that it doesn't drive away good people through boredom. (Male white engineering non-switcher)

Chemistry was something I excelled in and enjoyed. But there's no way of knowing when you get here that you are going to go on enjoying it. When I saw I was losing interest, I was surprised. But, looking back, it's really not that surprising. The first chemistry class was pretty uninspiring. Then I sat in for a few days on the next class, and I knew then it really didn't interest me any more. The idea of going on with that for four years was really unappealing. (Male white science switcher)

There's a great many who have been very good science and math thinkers their entire life, and who have high confidence. Then they get into engineering and find there's no more stimulation—it's just numbers and numbers and numbers. (Male Asian-American engineering switcher)

I don't think that many people who love science, math and engineering leave because they can't handle it, or because it's too hard...More often than not, people that I know have left because there hasn't been the intellectual fulfillment there for them. (Male white science switcher)

Differences Between Institutions in Student Concerns and Reasons for Switching

Our most important finding with respect to institutional types is that we found very little difference between them in the nature and level of problems reported by current and former S.M.E. majors. Table 1.7 shows, for each campus, the five most commonly reported concerns contributing to switching. It also shows the five issues of greatest concern to students overall. Six factors contribute more than all other concerns to switching decisions across all seven institutions. At six of the seven institutions, switchers cited the same factor as the strongest contributor to switching decisions—namely, being drawn to a non-S.M.E. major which held more interest, or offered a better educational experience. This was closely followed by being "turned off science" by their experiences in S.M.E. classes. The only exception to this pattern was the public East Coast university where both switchers and non-switchers ranked poor teaching by S.M.E. faculty as their most serious concern. However, poor teaching was one of the top three concerns of non-switchers and students overall at all seven institutions, and it was highly ranked by switchers at most institutions. Though not as commonly cited as a reason for switching, at most institutions, both switchers and non-switchers placed poorly-founded initial choice of S.M.E. majors and the poor quality of advising, counseling and tutoring services high on their list of concerns.

Some concerns were more common on particular campuses, or groups of campuses. This is not because they indicate the unique 'flaws' of any institution. The same problems are likely to be found elsewhere among students with similar educational or socio-economic circumstances. It is not, for example, coincidental that the East Coast state university whose students were especially concerned about S.M.E. pedagogy was also the institution where we met the greatest confusion about the reliability of high school performance scores as an indicator of readiness for college-level S.M.E. work. More than at any other institution, students (who were largely drawn from the surrounding geographic area) had been encouraged to aspire to science and mathematics-based careers for which they were under-prepared. However, they could not have known the extent of their under-preparation without recourse to better objective teaching standards and measures of comparison. Retrospective concerns about the inadequacy of their high school preparation were also a major issue for non-switchers at highly selective institutions where more switchers and non-switchers cited the experience of conceptual difficulties than at institutions with less competitive entry. Questioning the adequacy of their high school preparation was also evident at institutions where the weed-out tradition was found to be strongest. Loss of confidence and discouragement engendered by low grades were highly ranked as a cause of switching in the two western state universities where traditional competitive assessment practices were strong—particularly in their Colleges of Engineering.

Accounts of financial difficulties in completing S.M.E. majors were almost always raised in conjunction with complaints about degrees which took more than four years to complete. The highest level of concerns about both issues were expressed at the two state universities where we also found the highest proportion of students working to pay for their own tuition, fees and living expenses, and spending the highest proportion of time in paid employment. The other institutions where one or both of these issues were highly ranked were the two most expensive of the private institutions. Concern that the career options and material rewards of an S.M.E. degree were unlikely to be worth the costs (in all senses) of completing it, were most marked wherever a high proportion of students expressed anxiety about the financial costs of their education.

It is also noteworthy that, in the small, private liberal arts college where we expected to find conditions more conducive to good educational experiences in science and mathematics, the main concerns of switchers and non-switchers differed little from those of students in other institutions. Although some aspects of the teaching emphasis traditional in liberal arts colleges were discernable, they were more in evidence in the non-sciences than the sciences, where aspects of weed-out traditions clearly lingered. In one regard, switchers at this institution reported more problems than did switchers in any other institution, namely, those related to curriculum pace and overload. This was a direct consequence of 'the block system' by which students study discrete areas of each discipline intensively for short periods of time. Although switchers found this a valuable way to learn in some disciplines, in science and mathematics they had insufficient time to gain a good conceptual grasp, think about the material, gain insights, or work confidently with abstract ideas too recently encountered. Finding enough time for laboratory work was a general problem in science classes in all institutions. It was even more difficult for students working within the block system, especially for those who were employed.

Differences Between Students Entering Engineering and those Entering Science or Mathematics

Tables 1.8 and 1.9 summarize differences in the concerns of current and former majors in engineering from those in science and mathematics, and their significance for patterns of switching. Although engineering students described the same kinds of problems with their learning experiences as science and mathematics majors, engineering majors suffered from them more acutely. Half

TABLE 1.7 Comparative Ranking by Students at Seven Institutions of: Concerns Contributing to Switching; Concerns Raised by Switchers Overall; Concerns Raised by Non-Switchers; and Concerns of Students Overall.

INSTITUTIONS: 1 = MWPUB1, 2 = MWPUB2, 3 = WPUB3, 4 = ECPUB4, 5 = WCPRI1, 6 = WPRI2, 7 = WPRI3

MWPUB1 = Midwest, public, ranking 1; WPUB2 = West, public, ranking 2; WPUB3 = West, public, ranking 3; ECPUB4 = East Coast, public, ranking 4; WCPRI1 = West Coast, private, ranking 1; WPRI2 = West, private, ranking 2; WPRI3 = West, private, ranking 3; WPRI3 = Southwest, private, ranking 3; with ranking according to a modified version of the Carnegie Classification of Institutions (cf., Chronicle of Higher Education, July 8, 1987).

Issue	Contributed to Switching Decision — Institution							All Switchers' Concerns — Institution						
	1	2	3	4	5	6	7	1	2	3	4	5	6	7
Non-S.M.E. major offers better education/more interest	1	1	1	5	1	1	1		3			2	1	1
Lack of/loss of interest in S.M.E.: "turned off science"	5	2	2	3	2	2	3		4	4			2	2
Rejection of S.M.E. careers/associated lifestyles	3	3	3	4			2	5		5	5			3
Shift to more appealing non-S.M.E. career option	2			2	3		4							
Poor teaching by S.M.E. faculty			5	1				1	5	2	1	1		
S.M.E. career options/rewards felt not worth effort to get degree	4	5	4		4	3							5	
Discouraged/lost confidence due to low grades in early years		4	4											
Prefer teaching approach in non-S.M.E. courses					5	4								

TABLE 1.7 (continued) Comparative Ranking by Students at Seven Institutions of: Concerns Contributing to Switching; Concerns Raised by Switchers Overall; Concerns Raised by Non-Switchers; and Concerns of Students Overall.

INSTITUTIONS: 1 = MWPUB1, 2 = WPUB2, 3 = WPUB3, 4 = ECPUB4, 5 = WCPRI1, 6 = WPRI2, 7 = WPRI3

Issue	Non-Switchers' Concerns							All Students' Concerns						
	Institution							Institution						
	1	2	3	4	5	6	7	1	2	3	4	5	6	7
Non-S.M.E. major offers better education/more interest					3				4	5	5	2	2	2
Lack of/loss of interest in S.M.E.: "turned off science"				5			3		5			5		
Rejection of S.M.E. careers/associated lifestyles								5						5
Shift to more appealing non-S.M.E. career option														
Poor teaching by S.M.E. faculty	1		1	1	1	2	1	1	1	2	1	1	3	1
S.M.E. career options/rewards felt not worth effort to get degree				5				4						
Discouraged/lost confidence due to low grades in early years														
Prefer teaching approach in non-S.M.E. courses														

TABLE 1.7 (continued) Comparative Ranking by Students at Seven Institutions of: Concerns Contributing to Switching; Concerns Raised by Switchers Overall; Concerns Raised by Non-Switchers; and Concerns of Students Overall.

INSTITUTIONS: 1 = MWPUB1, 2 = WPUB2, 3 = WPUB3, 4 = ECPUB4, 5 = WCPRI1, 6 = WPRI2, 7 = WPRI3

Issue	Contributed to Switching Decisions Institution							All Switchers' Concerns Institution						
	1	2	3	4	5	6	7	1	2	3	4	5	6	7
Curriculum overload, fast pace overwhelming							5							4
Conceptual difficulties with one or more S.M.E. subject(s)						5							4	
Reasons for choice of S.M.E. major prove inappropriate								3	1	1	2	3	3	5
Inadequate advising or help with academic problems								2	2	3	3	4		
Inadequate high school preparation in basic subjects/ study skills											4	5		
Financial problems of completing S.M.E. majors								4						
Unexpected length of S.M.E. degree: more than four years														
Language difficulties with foreign faculty or T.A.s														

TABLE 1.7 (continued) Comparative Ranking by Students at Seven Institutions of: Concerns Contributing to Switching; Concerns Raised by Switchers Overall; Concerns Raised by Non-Switchers; and Concerns of Students Overall.

INSTITUTIONS: 1 = MWPUB1, 2 = WPUB2, 3 = WPUB3, 4 = ECPUB4, 5 = WCPRI1, 6 = WPRI2, 7 = WPRI3

Issue	Non-Switchers' Concerns							All Students' Concerns						
	Institution							Institution						
	1	2	3	4	5	6	7	1	2	3	4	5	6	7
Curriculum overload, fast pace overwhelming						4								
Conceptual difficulties with one or more S.M.E. subject(s)	5	5			4		2							
Reasons for choice of S.M.E. major prove inappropriate	3	4	2	3			4	2	2	1	2	3	5	4
Inadequate advising or help with academic problems	2	3	3	4		3		3	3	3	3	4	4	
Inadequate high school preparation in basic subjects/ study skills	3	3	5	2		1				4	4		1	
Financial problems of completing S.M.E. majors	2				2									
Unexpected length of S.M.E. degree: more than four years	4		4				5							
Language difficulties with foreign faculty or T.A.s						5								

TABLE 1.8 "The Problem Iceberg: Engineering Majors." Factors Contributing to Switching Decisions of Former Engineering Majors, All Concerns of Engineering Switchers, of Non-Switchers and of All Students.

Issue	*Factor in switching decisions (%)*	*All switchers' concerns (%)*	*All non-switchers' concerns (%)*	*All students' concerns (%)*
Lack of/loss of interest in SME: "turned off science"	50	66	41	49
Curriculum overload, fast pace overwhelming	45	55	52	54
Poor teaching by SME faculty	41	98	86	93
Non-S.M.E. major offerrs better education/more interest	37	57	35	48
S.M.E. career options/rewards felt not worth effort to get degree	31	43	18	32
Shift to more appealing non-S.M.E.career option	30	36	14*	27
Inadequate advising or help with academic problems	26	81	53	69
Discouraged/lost confidence due to low grades in early years	25	40	14	29
Rejection of S.M.E. careers and associated lifestyles	24	44	29	38
Reasons for choice of SME major prove inappropriate	20	94	52	76
Financial problems of completing S.M.E. majors	18	32	29	31
Morale undermined by competitive SME culture	16	30	9	21
Conceptual difficulties with one or more S.M.E. subject(s)	15	32	29	31
Lack of peer study group support	14	19	12	16
Inadequate high school preparation in subjects/study skills	10	38	37	37
Unexpected length of S.M.E. degree: more than four years	10	29	38	32
Discovery of aptitude for non-S.M.E. subject	10	11	3	8
Prefer teaching approach in non-S.M.E. courses	6	24	4	18
Language difficulties with foreign faculty or T.A.s	4	34	18	27
Switching as means to career goal: system playing	4	6	0	3
Poor teaching, lab, or recitation support by T.A.s	0	22	14	18
Problems related to class size	0	20	14	17
Poor lab/computer lab facilities	0	3	6	4

*Issue raised by non-switchers intending to move into non-S.M.E. field following graduation.

TABLE 1.9 "The Problem Iceberg: Science and Mathematics Majors." Factors Contributing to Switching Decisions of Former Science and Mathematics Majors, All Concerns of Science and Mathematics Switchers, of Non-Switchers and of All Students.

Issue	Factor in switching decisions (%)	All switchers' concerns (%)	All non-switchers' concerns (%)	All students' concerns (%)
Non-S.M.E. major offers better education/more interest.	44	60	29	45
S.M.E. career options/rewards felt not worth effort to get degree	40	52	22	38
Lack of/loss of interest in S.M.E.: "turned off science"	37	53	31	43
Rejection of S.M.E. careers and associated lifestyles	34	42	15	29
Curriculum overload, fast pace overwhelming	25	36	34	35
Poor teaching by S.M.E. faculty	32	83	64	74
Shift to more appealing non-S.M.E. career option	30	29	19*	24
Inadequate advising or help with academic problems	22	70	51	61
Discouraged/lost confidence due to low grades in early years	21	28	12	20
Inadequate high school preparation in subjects/study skills	20	44	38	41
Financial problems of completing S.M.E. majors	16	27	19	23
Morale undermined by competitive S.M.E. culture	13	27	9	18
Prefer teaching approach in non-S.M.E. courses	12	24	20	22
Unexpected length of S.M.E. degree: more than four years	8	12	20	16
Conceptual difficulties with one or more S.M.E. subject(s)	10	22	22	22
Discovery of aptitude for non-S.M.E. subject	10	12	6	9
Switching as means to career goal: system playing	10	12	5	8
Reasons for choice of S.M.E. major prove inappropriate	9	71	30	51
Lack of peer study group support	9	15	4	10
Language difficulties with foreign faculty or T.A.s	2	25	22	24
Problems related to class size	0	20	9	15
Poor teaching, lab, or recitation support by T.A.s	0	17	18	13
Poor lab/computer lab facilities	0	5	2	4

*Issue raised by non-switchers intending to move into non-S.M.E. field following graduation.

of engineering switchers (49.5%) cited loss of interest in the major, almost half (45.1%) cited curriculum overload and over-fast pace, and 40.7 percent cited poor teaching, as having directly contributed to their decision to leave. The comparative percentages for science and mathematics switchers are much lower (i.e., 37.0%, 25.0% and 31.5% respectively) and no other teaching and learning issue is as highly rated by science and mathematics switchers as it is by engineering switchers. Despite greater selectivity in the admission of engineering freshmen, more engineering switchers (15.4%) than science and mathematics switchers (8.7%) cited conceptual difficulties as contributing to switching decisions. This again points to the higher level of difficulty that engineering students experienced with the pedagogy, curriculum pace and assessment practices of their majors. Although the pedagogy in some science departments encouraged strong competition for grades, current and former engineering majors unanimously reported their classes to be highly competitive. As a consequence, failure to develop collaborative and supportive study groups contributed to the switching decisions of more engineers than non-engineers, and was a generalized problem among all engineering students.

The concerns leading to switching among former science and mathematics majors focused more on disappointments and anxieties about career prospects than those of engineers. Science and mathematics switchers more commonly left their majors because neither the career options and material rewards, nor the personal satisfactions of careers open to them, appeared sufficient to justify the effort involved in graduating. (The comparisons for these two issues are 40.2 percent and 33.7 percent for science and mathematics switchers, and 30.8 percent and 24.2 percent for engineering switchers.) This was not because students in science and mathematics majors were more materialistic than engineering majors. Indeed, the contrary is true. More engineering (19.8%) than science and mathematics switchers (8.7%) cited inappropriate choice as contributing to their switching decision, and the ill-founded choices of engineering switchers more commonly included a predominantly materialist motivation, insufficiently supported by interest, than did the choices of other switchers. Engineering students entered their major expecting more in material terms from their future careers than did science and mathematics freshmen (though they did not necessarily know more about the nature of the jobs they might undertake). The discomforts of the weed-out system, including the competitive ethos, were also greater in engineering (and other classes and majors preparatory to professional qualifications, especially pre-medicine). Engineers were, however, more prepared to tolerate these discomforts than other S.M.E. majors, so long as they saw themselves as likely to have good salaries and career prospects following graduation. They were also more likely to see the process of gaining a degree in 'commodity' or 'investment' terms—that is, as a calculated risk in expenditure of time, effort and money to gain a profitable outcome. Engineering students overall expressed more anger than non-engineers that their degrees took longer and cost more than their advertised length of four years. Science and mathematics majors were also dismayed when degrees took longer than they had expected, but did not share the feelings of betrayal which engineers expressed towards their colleges. Engineering seniors also expressed more financial concerns (28.8 %) than science and mathematics seniors (18.6 %), but it is not clear from the text data that they actually experienced more financial difficulty than other students in completing lengthy degrees.

Although science and mathematics majors were less materialist in their first or subsequent choices than engineers, they expressed much more anxiety about the availability of jobs. As freshmen, they were also less clear than students entering engineering about the career path they wished to follow, had less knowledge about the careers open to them, and were more fearful about the prospects of getting any job. Mathematics majors were the least certain about the careers open to them, or what they would do after graduation. Science and mathematics majors were more likely than engineers to consider graduate degrees, both as a traditional career path in their disciplines and (increasingly over time) as a way to cope with deteriorating employment prospects for science and mathematics baccalaureates. They were also less willing than engineers to tolerate teaching practices that reflected the weed-out system because they had less to gain, in career terms, by doing so. With the exception of students intending to enter the medical professions, science and mathematics majors were less instrumental than engineering students in their reasons for choosing S.M.E. majors, and in their evaluations of the quality of their undergraduate education. Both switchers and non-switchers in science and mathematics were more likely than engineering students to criticize faculty for failing to provide a satisfying educational experience, and to consider alternative majors for educational reasons. With the exception of 'pre-med' majors, who show a pattern of strategic switching to improve their chances of getting into medical schools of their choice, science and mathematics switchers left for reasons which reflect a concern to find work that is satisfying in nature, context, or purpose.

In the chapters which follow, we discuss each of the issues which contribute to 'the problem iceberg' broadly in the order in which students encounter them. We also group together problems which students see as interrelated. The ordering of the chapters does not, therefore, follow the rank order of problems in terms of their contribution to switching decisions. We also present the insights we have gained about S.M.E. students' concerns, including those which contribute to switching, using their own words. Issues are summarized between sections of quotations, but there is much to be learned by hearing the authentic voice of the students themselves.

Notes

1.   The American Freshman studies are conducted by the American Council on Education and U.C.L.A.'s Cooperative Institutional Research Program at the Higher Education Research Institute.

2.   S.M.E. majors vary in the proportion of 'top' students each group attracts: between 1978 and 1988, engineering drew an increased share of A and A- students (from 14.1% to 17.4%); the share of life sciences remained steady at 7.9%; that of the physical sciences and pre-medicine majors dropped (by 18.2% and 10.5%, respectively); and the share of the social sciences rose slightly (8.8% to 9.8%).

3.   Their estimates exclude graduates for whom a terminal baccalaureate is appropriate—as in engineering.

4.   Retention among black, Hispanic, and native American students in S.M.E. majors has remained low, despite improved enrollments (cf., Collea, 1990; O.S.E.P., 1987a; N.S.F., 1988, 1989a, 1990b, 1994; O.T.A., 1989). Women's enrollment shows a twenty-year decline, despite enhanced recruitment efforts; and the retention rate of high ability entering women remains poor (cf., O.S.E.P., 1987b; Vetter, 1988; N.S.F., 1988, 1989a, 1990b, Green, 1989a, 1989b).

5.   A discussion of their findings on the causes of attrition is included in the N.S.F. Report, "The State of Academic Science and Engineering" (1990a).

6.   This follows the precedent set in some earlier studies, most notably: O.T.A., 1985; Lee, 1988; Tobias, 1990; and the series of American Freshman survey reports of the Higher Education Research Institute, U.C.L.A. In institutions where undergraduates are not required to declare a major until sophomore year or later, we initially estimated each student's incoming intention to declare an S.M.E. major by their concentration of classes in mathematics and science taken as freshmen and sophomores. Confirmation that this had been their intention was sought from each potential participant in a short telephone interview before inviting them to take part in the study.

7.   Figure A.1, *Appendix A*, indicates the disciplines included in each group of majors in the C.I.R.P. data.

8.   These persistence rates closely match those found for men (66%) and for women (48%) by Strenta et al. (1993).

9.   In the health professions the pattern is less distinct because this group includes majors which lie at both extremes of traditional male and female professional predominance, namely, pre-medicine and pre-dentistry on the one hand, and nursing and the therapeutic professions on the other.

10. The reason for this is that, as one approaches the end of data collection in an ethnographic study, though there is always the possibility that new information will emerge from those who have experienced the problems being discussed, those who have survived them increasingly act as a source of validation rather than of new information.

11. In *Appendix A*, Figure A.2 shows the number and percent of switchers and non-switchers in our sample who were in engineering, and in science or mathematics.

12. In *Appendix A*, Figure A.3 shows the profile of switchers and non-switchers at each institution by discipline, sex and race/ethnicity. Figure A.4 shows the profile of non-white switchers and non-switchers by discipline and racial/ethnic group.

13. The topical outline produced by this process is included in *Appendix B*.

14. The study was undertaken in two phases, beginning with four institutions of different type in our own state.

15. Cf., Carnegie Foundation. 1987. Carnegie foundation's classifications of more than 3,300 institutions of higher education. *Chronicle of Higher Education, 33*: 22.

16. For evaluation of programs at women's colleges, see: Blum, L., & Givant S., 1982, "Increasing the Participation of College Women in Mathematics-Related Fields," in *Women and Minorities in Science: Strategies for Increasing Participation*, S.M. Humphreys, ed., Boulder, CO: Westview Press; Mappen, E.F., 1990, "The Douglass Project for Rutgers Women in Math, Science, and Engineering: A Comprehensive Program to Encourage Women's Persistence in these Fields," in *Women in Engineering Conference: A National Initiative* (conference proceedings), J.Z. Daniels, ed., West Lafayette, IN: Purdue University; Rayman, P., 1992, "Opportunities for Women in Science: The Undergraduate Experience." Paper presented at the National Research Council conference, Irvine, CA, Nov.4-5. Published proceedings: *Science and Engineering Program: On Target for Women?* 1992. Washington, D.C.

17. Seidel, John V., Kjolseth, J. Rolf, & Elaine Seymour. 1988. *The Ethnograph: A User's Guide*. Littleton, CO: Qualis Research Associates.

18. Tables 5.1 and 5.2, which compare the concerns of male and female switchers and non-switchers, are presented and discussed in Chapter 5.

19. All figures in the "iceberg" tables are rounded to the nearest whole number: those in the text are given to one decimal point.

20. Humphreys, Sheila M., & Robert Freeland. 1992. *Retention in Engineering: A Study of Freshman Cohorts*. Berkeley, CA: University of California at Berkeley, College of Engineering.

21. McClelland, L. 1993. *Students Entering Science, Mathematics, and Engineering Majors as Fall Freshmen, 1980-1988.* Unpublished data provided by the University of Colorado, Boulder, Office of Research and Information.

22. These observations are consistent with those of Sheila Tobias in her 1990 report, *They're Not Dumb, They're Different,* and in a number of articles arising from her work.

2

Entering S.M.E. Majors:
Choice and Preparation

Choosing S.M.E. Majors and Careers

Many faculty, deans and advisors are concerned to understand what reasons for choosing an S.M.E. major make persistence more likely, and which hold up less well during the rigors of the freshman and sophomore experience. We therefore explored the reasons given by students for their initial choice of major, the significance of their motivations for the kinds of difficulties they experienced and for patterns of switching and persistence. Tables 2.1 and 2.2 summarize the responses of switchers and non-switchers to the question, "Why did you choose a science, math, or engineering major?" Their answers to this question were grouped into the 12 categories shown as "Reasons Given" and are described below.

As can be seen in Table 2.1, most students gave more than one answer to the question, with switchers giving almost twice as many answers as non-switchers. This is not surprising. Switchers have more reason than non-switchers to reflect on the part played by their reasons for choosing a major in their decision to leave it. Many switchers felt that they had chosen their S.M.E. major largely because they saw themselves as good at mathematics and/or science in high school, whether or not they understood what was entailed in these majors or the careers to which they might lead. Fewer non-switchers spontaneously mentioned their competence in high school mathematics or science, or their lack of prior understanding about the nature of the major, unless these subsequently created problems for them. Generally speaking, choosing a major for reasons that subsequently proved inappropriate or insufficient did not (at 14.2% of mentions) contribute significantly to switching decisions (cf., Table 1.6). However, ill-considered choices created some degree of problems for most switchers, and choosing an S.M.E. major for 'the wrong reasons' was the second most commonly cited choice-related problem described

TABLE 2.1 Reasons Given for Choice of Original Major by 335 Current and Former Science, Mathematics or Engineering Undergraduates on Seven Campuses (1990-1992).

Reason Given	Switchers	Non-Switchers	Totals
	% All reasons given	% All reasons given	
	(% Switchers or non-switchers who gave this reason)	(% Switchers or non-switchers who gave this reason)	
Intrinsic Interest	7 (11)	10 (28)	17
Active Influence of Others	13 (20)	5 (13)	18
Pragmatism/Materialism	11 (17)	5 (14)	16
Good at Math and/or Science in High School	9 (13)	3 (9)	12
Uninformed Choice	9 (13)	2 (6)	11
Means to a Desired (Career) End	5 (8)	3 (7)	8
Following Family Tradition (Passive: Not Pressured)	4 (5)	2 (7)	6
Negative Choice or Compromise	3 (5)	2 (6)	5
Altruism	1 (1)	1 (5)	2
One of Several Viable Options	2 (2)	0 (1)	2
Recruited	2 (3)	1 (3)	3
Scholarship Money Available	1 (1)	0 (1)	1
All Reasons Given	64	36	100

TABLE 2.2 Reasons Given for Choice of Original Major by 335 Current and Former Science, Mathematics or Engineering Undergraduates on Seven Campuses (1990-1992), by Gender.

	M=Male, F=Female					
Reason Given	*Switchers*		*Non-Switchers*		*Totals*	
	M	*F*	*M*	*F*	*M*	*F*
	% Own gender who chose for this reason		% Own gender who chose for this reason			
	(% All switchers or non-switchers who chose for this reason)		*(% All switchers or non-switchers who chose for this reason)*			
Intrinsic Interest	7 *(12)*	7 *(10)*	10 *(24)*	10 *(31)*	17	17
Active Influence of Others	7 *(13)*	17 *(25)*	4 *(8)*	6 *(18)*	11	23
Pragmatism/Materialism	9 *(16)*	13 *(18)*	8 *(19)*	3 *(9)*	17	16
Good at Math and/or Science in High School	10 *(17)*	7 *(10)*	6 *(13)*	2 *(6)*	16	9
Uninformed Choice	9 *(15)*	9 *(12)*	3 *(8)*	2 *(6)*	12	10
Means to a Desired (Career) End	5 *(9)*	5 *(7)*	3 *(8)*	2 *(7)*	8	7
Following Family Tradition (Passive: Not Pressured)	4 *(7)*	3 *(5)*	4 *(9)*	1 *(5)*	8	4
Negative Choice or Compromise	2 *(4)*	4 *(5)*	2 *(6)*	2 *(6)*	5	6
Altruism	0 *(1)*	1 *(1)*	2 *(5)*	1 *(5)*	2	2
One of Several Viable Options	2 *(4)*	1 *(1)*	0 *(0)*	1 *(2)*	2	2
Recruited	1 *(1)*	2 *(3)*	0 *(0)*	2 *(6)*	1	4
Scholarship Money Available	0 *(1)*	0 *(0)*	0 *(1)*	0 *(0)*	1	0

by switchers (82.5%). However, a high proportion of non-switchers (approximately 39.0%) also appeared to be making the best of choices which, with hindsight, they judged as poorly founded. Although the different components of undergraduates' choices are relatively easy to recognize in their accounts, the total rationale for each choice tends to reflect several interacting factors. Some reasons for choice regularly appeared in conjunction, and particular combinations proved a more stable basis for entry to an S.M.E. major, while others were more difficult to sustain. We will clarify this observation in what follows.

The Active Influence of Others

The most commonly cited choice factor (mentioned by 18% of all informants) was the active influence, pressure, or persuasion of people significant to the students. This was particularly discernable in the accounts of women switchers, 23.5 percent of whom cited the active influence of others as a major factor in their original choice of a major (cf., Table 2.2). No other motivating factor for any other subset of our sample approached this degree of importance. Much of this influence came from family members, especially those students whose parents were financing their undergraduate education. However, the influence of peers, high school teachers and counselors, college advisors, and family friends (including role models and mentors) was also described. Much of the family and peer pressure students described focused on attaining a financially-successful, socially-prestigious career, or consisted of warnings against the risks of poor pay, low status and unemployment resulting from the choice of a non-S.M.E. major:

> My dad specifically told me his friend had a son who was making $70,000 in his first year with a computer science degree. I heard that, and said, 'Well I guess I can't drop the computer science part of the major.' (Female white engineering switcher)

Some students who had entered an S.M.E. major reluctantly and who had considered switching because of greater interest in another field, reported that parents had ridiculed their non-S.M.E. interests and over-ridden their choices:

> Well, my dad's an engineer...I really liked physics, but I thought about changing to linguistics once, and he said, 'How will you ever get a job with *that*?' (Male white science non-switcher)

> I just thought my dad was pushing me too much. He and my mom are both at I.B.M. and really wanted me to go into computer science. I mean my father really *pushed* computers. I've always been a liberal arts person, right back to elementary school. And I knew when I signed up for a Pascal course, and the first day I didn't understand anything. And I tried myself out in the liberal arts, and I really loved it. (Female white science switcher)

Students in this situation commonly encountered the argument, "You can always do something else later, but you can't move into the sciences if you start out in something else." Some families also brought financial pressure to bear:

> I am not sure my parents would pay for anything but a science degree. (Male white science non-switcher)

> I felt obligated to do what my father wanted because he was paying for my education. It was his idea that pre-med was the only way to go. In fact, he wanted me to graduate early so that I could get into medical school early, and finish a medical degree early. I tried talking to him, but it was hopeless. (Female Asian-American science switcher)

Some students felt they had been pressured to re-live a father's (sic) thwarted or incomplete ambition:

> I called home and said, 'Maybe I shouldn't do this,' and he said, 'No way.' Maybe that's because he wanted to be a medical student, and look what he's doing now—teaching somewhere. Maybe it's because he felt like he missed out on something. (Female white science switcher)

Others described the power of unspoken family pressure:

> He never really said to me, 'Go do this.' But he kinda influenced me silently. (Male white engineering switcher)

> I was doing math because I thought my parents would think, 'Math: that's all right.' (Male white mathematics switcher)

> My father was very instrumental—not that he ever exactly pushed—but my sister was not mathematically-inclined; and my brother started out in engineering, then he changed. It was not his cup of tea. So I kinda had this pressure that I put on myself. (Female white mathematics switcher)

However, the direct pressure which some family members exert can be very powerful:

> My father, being an engineer, ground into me the fact that I should be an engineer too. (Male white engineering switcher)

> I had a lot of pressure from my grandparents and from my parents to get into a field I could get a job in. And I probably would have ignored them, 'cause I feel like, 'Well, it's my life. I should be able to do what I want to do.' But, back then, I wanted to do what they wanted me to do. (Female white science switcher)

> My father was an engineer; then he went to law school. He's always been plugging that since we were babies. (Male white engineering switcher)

Students also yielded to pressures to choose something prestigious which came, more diffusely, from people in their social environment:

People asked you what you wanted to be and you had to think of something good. You couldn't really be honest. I always said, 'A vet,' because anything in science has very high status. I don't think it was very realistic; it was just a status thing. (Male white mathematics switcher)

Where high school friends were caught up in a collective sense that 'everybody's doing science', peers mutually reinforced the pressures they felt from other sources:

I think my friends also felt pressured about going into science. My best friend from high school went into M.I.T, and that was the thing his family expected him to do. (Male white science switcher)

I think that was the main reason that my friends and I all went into science. Everyone who was in the top 15—I was 10th in my class—they all went into science. And I felt pressured to do that as well. (Male white science switcher)

In the uncertainty of the early college experiences, the latest peer folklore about the perceived career possibilities of different majors was also influential:

Well, actually I entered the university as a biology major, and that's what I liked better in my high school. But, talking to people when I got here, everybody said, 'You can't do anything with biology: you'll end up testing sewer systems or something. You can do more with a chemistry major. And there's just more money.' I didn't like chemistry as much, but, in my naivete, I thought, 'Well, it's almost the same thing.' (Female white science switcher)

Young men worried about what might happen if they did not take into account the practical considerations that family and other significant people presented to them. However, in their final decision, young women were much more influenced by the opinions and preferences of others than were young men. From a focus group of female white engineering switchers:

My dad's an engineer, so I kinda had the idea that the only worthwhile majors were technical majors. I was always good at math and science, but I hated it. I just figured that's the only respectable major to go into.

I had that impression too—that I had to find a respectable major. And a lot of it was my parents' decision. I'm still not majoring in English because my parents would not find that respectable.

In engineering, especially, women often felt pressured to follow an engineering father into the field:

My father's an engineer. I think you'll find that every single engineering woman on this campus has a father who is an engineer. I can only think of a few exceptions. For some reason, it doesn't seem to be a major that women go into by themselves. I mean, I know plenty of guys who go into it just because it sounded interesting, but it doesn't work that way for most women I've met. I can't say that dad exactly pushed me, but I really couldn't think during high school what else I could possibly do. (White woman engineering switcher)

My dad's an engineer, and he kind of pushed me into it telling me how much money I would make. So I figured I might as well try it because I was always good at math. I passed all of the math modules, but I didn't like it as an engineer. My heart wasn't in it because it was kinda something put on me. The money was intriguing. (Female white engineering switcher)

Most family pressure on young women came from their fathers, but for that smaller group of women with professional mothers, this too was a strong influence:

I really didn't have any set goals and was a little confused about what I wanted to do. But my mother, she was really pushing me. (Female white mathematics switcher)

My mother really wanted me to do science, and she is still disappointed that I didn't stay with it. (Female white science switcher)

My parents are both teachers, and they've seen a lot of people getting transferred out. So they kept telling me not to be a teacher, or anything in liberal arts. 'Do math and science and you'll always be safe,' they kept saying. (Female white science switcher)

She's an obstetrician, and I take her suggestions very seriously...Like, she's a guide. She's very influential. (Female white mathematics switcher)

Where women (and especially women of color) showed facility with mathematics and science at high school, family pressure was especially hard to resist, regardless of other skills or preferences:

I always wanted to be a vet. I worked for a vet for about three years before I entered college, and had applied to vet school. But dad talked me out of it, saying there's too many people doing it; too much competition. He persuaded me to try engineering—he's an engineer. (Female white engineering switcher)

I always wanted to go into pre-med because my father wanted me to...I was one of four daughters, and was considered the brightest—the one with the best chance to do well. But I've always been better in writing. My S.A.T. scores showed that. I was editor-in-chief of my high school newspaper. But I felt this pressure from my family—you know, I really should do this because my dad's depending on me, and my mom thinks I should too. So I enrolled in a biology major. (Female Asian-American science switcher)

The big push was from my parents, because my good grades were in the sciences. And I didn't know exactly what I wanted to do. So I thought, 'I always have the option to do what I want to do later,' and I just went along with it. (Female black science switcher)

It was my father's decision, more than both my parents' decision. He said this would be the best profession for me. My last few years of high school, I really enjoyed my government and politics classes, although I did fine in my science classes too. But I didn't really want to go into biology or pre-med. (Female Asian-American science switcher)

Women left high school with less clear ideas of what they wanted to do than did their male peers, and were more apt to choose a major to please important people in their lives. However, as we shall discuss in Chapter 5, women also felt more at liberty to abandon choices which had been pressed on them if they became unhappy with their initial choice:

My father's a professor of chemistry here at the university. I came here with a real liberal arts background, but no idea of what I really wanted to do. My parents said, 'You can never go wrong with a science background,' and I could always go from there into any other major, and it wouldn't be thought of as bad. (Female white science switcher)

Some of the consequences of choosing an S.M.E. major in response to family pressure were described as: failure to gain focus in the academic work, feeling little motivation to work, frustration at the denial of other talents and interests, diminished confidence and self-respect, and uncertainty about identity:

My best subject's always been English. I think what finally happened was, I had to decide whether or not I'm simply going to be a shadow of my father, or if I was going to be the person that I am, which is a creative, drawing, writing kind of person. And, finally, I decided it was *this* voice that was speaking to me, and not the desire to succeed in a major that was just a manifestation of my father's identity. A very big part of me had to take second place, and my identity was getting lost as long as I went on trying to pursue engineering. (Female white engineering switcher)

I've always been medically-oriented, and I'm fascinated with physiology. So I tried to shove in some anatomy classes here, and some biology there. But I was always swallowing my own interests because my dad was kinda stubborn. He thought a woman probably couldn't make it through med school. (Female white engineering switcher)

There was no possibility of taking the time to do some of the classes I enjoyed. Like, I couldn't find time for a foreign language. There just wasn't any opportunity for it. You start to realize that you really don't want to go on doing this, because it's not exciting enough to allow you to put on blinkers as far as the rest of the world goes. (Male white mathematics switcher)

Students who felt they had been pressured into S.M.E. majors by their families were among those expressing the strongest desire to switch. They employed a number of extreme tactics in order to force parents to allow them to leave majors they had not wished to enter, and found increasingly intolerable. These included, provoking failure in critical classes by refusing to work for them, and procrastination in declaring an unwanted major:

So I just waited two years and when it came to a point where I *had* to pick a major, I switched and went to liberal arts. (Female white science switcher)

So I started skipping classes and skipping exams on purpose. I knew when I had an exam. I wouldn't study. When I did try, I would just open the book, and just leave it in front of me, and just sit looking at it. I thought, 'This is all a bad dream. It's going to go away, and I'm going to end up doing what I want.' (Female Asian-American science switcher)

High school mathematics and science teachers were also cited as influential in the choice of an S.M.E. major. Their influence was of several kinds. First, good teachers are critical to the development of a strong interest in mathematics and science, and to a good grounding in basic knowledge and skills. The teacher who dazzles, excites and promotes their discipline, is often the primary inspiration for the student's choice of an S.M.E. major or for their desire to teach science or mathematics:

I've had some teachers in high school, and before, that were real influential in my choice, just by encouraging me. I would say that's where it started. (Male white engineering non-switcher)

I had incredible math teachers in high school. Very organized—which I loved. My calculus teachers would have the all the homework that you would have to do for the whole year all laid out in advance, so you could plan your work ahead of time. I really learned from that. She was *amazing*. And she really made it fun. I don't know how she did it. It was just like she was excited about it and she made you feel the same. (Female white engineering switcher)

It mattered that I had some really good teachers that turned me on. That's how you find things in the subjects that you like. You enjoy it, and so you continue. I had math and science teachers in junior high that got me interested. And then in high school I had a couple of really good biology professors. One of them came here, which is one of the reasons I applied. (Female white science non-switcher)

For students whose passion for mathematics and science is kindled at this flame, then focused and refined by Socratic dialogue, the influence of good teachers continues as a source of support and strength through times of academic difficulty:

I think two reasons why I kept going in physics is because I had brilliant physics and chemistry teachers in high school—just excellent. That really kept me going. We had much more interaction and participation in class time, even in larger classes. (Female white science non-switcher)

My biggest inspiration towards math was my 10th and 12th grade teacher. He really got me into math. I never really liked him, but what he did was to get me interested. And he did it in a way that helped me to learn. That's why I feel I've got a good grasp on mathematics. (Male black mathematics non-switcher)

This influence was reinforced where students were drawn into interesting extra-curricular activities devised by teachers who made them feel part of an élite group who could make a contribution to the future of science or mathematics:

> We had a really good high school science program. We had some students go to the Soviet Union to study science over there...We had accelerated classes which included people who are seniors here right now. From the 13 in our group, six or seven have already been accepted into med school. We all had strong interests as a group—and I still carry that over. (Male white science non-switcher)

> In our high school, the sciences were far superior to the rest in terms of the quality of the teachers. And if you were seen as one of the brighter kids, you were encouraged to go into the sciences. I'd say a lot of my interest in science came out of being part of those science groups. (Male white science switcher)

However, we noted in the accounts of switchers the danger of confusing admiration for good high school mathematics or science teachers with a genuine personal interest in the subjects they taught. The confusion is compounded for those women and students of color whose teachers had encouraged them to be 'standard bearers' for increased gender or racial/ethnic representation in the sciences:

> We had a biology teacher who was wonderful. I mean, he was my favorite teacher to this day. He took the time to make sure you understood everything. He was tough; he made you work. You felt like you wanted to do your best for him. (Female Hispanic science switcher)

> My high school calculus teacher still sends me information on math, including jobs. He really pushed me. He's a great guy. I mean, we really got along well. And he's the one who kinda pushed me into math in college, and said I had the mind for it, and that there's a wide open field with lots happening, and good money. (Female white mathematics switcher)

> I had excellent teachers. That was really the defining thing for my interest. I just loved my high school math teacher. He was just unbelievable. He really instilled a love for the math. I just loved to be around him. And he taught so we understood it. So then, of course, that made you feel good. Yeah, that definitely was a *huge* influence on my decision. Because I ended up picking a major based on what I liked in high school, and that all goes back to the teacher. (Female white mathematics switcher)

Where interest in the sciences was based largely on the enthusiasm of particular high school teachers, or was over-dependent on their personal encouragement, students were at risk of discovering their lack of interest only after college entry. Unless love for the subject is effectively disentangled from love for the teacher, and from the seductive idea of becoming a part of an élite, interest in the subject withers once the teacher who engendered it is no longer present. This was a particular danger for women and students of color:

My high school teacher, he loved us. I mean, he loved the girls, and he was always encouraging and pushing us. I think he recognized there was a lack of girls in science, and that things really hadn't changed...maybe just a few more would help. (Female white science switcher)

I feel my teacher encouraged me in science a lot more just because I was female, you know, and they want more females involved in the sciences. But I came across problems with that. (Female white science non-switcher)

It kinda was a pressure at high school that I should try to be one of the different people, and get through it as a female—which wasn't a good idea at all. (Female white engineering switcher)

Many teachers also pass on to their students the idea of mathematics and science as accessible to all, and/or as 'fun'. Students who confused the fun of hands-on science fairs, camps and competitions with a profound intrinsic interest in science, found the experience of science as 'fun', by itself, to be an insufficient basis for the choice of these majors. Their interest proved to be extrinsic—that is, contingent on the charisma and skills of particular teachers:

In high school, my chemistry teacher made chemistry fun and easy. I wasn't ever really strong in math, but I always kind of enjoyed the sciences. And my junior and senior year teacher made it enjoyable. It was fun to get hands-on experience. I guess I chose chemistry because I wanted to be a teacher, and make chemistry fun for other kids like my teacher did. (Female white science switcher)

In 10th grade, we were required to take a biology class. And, up 'til that point, I wasn't really good at science. I wasn't really interested. But I enjoyed that class, and I started to get more and more interested. My teacher encouraged me a *lot*. By the time I reached 12th grade, I was really involved in science clubs, and in my science classes. I still wasn't really great at science. I was good at biology, but the chemistry and math still stumped me. But I just kept going, and, when I came to college, I decided to stay with something I enjoyed. (Female black science switcher)

The influence of particular high school teachers was critical in inspiring some students to wish to follow them into teaching mathematics or science:

I had a great teacher and that's why I thought, 'Maybe I could teach physics too.' (Female white science switcher)

There was one math teacher I really liked. He had a great sense of humor, and he'd make class a lot of fun. And I'd always liked math, but had a lot of dry, really boring teachers—and that makes it harder for some kids to learn. But he kind of inspired me to want to teach math. And I'm actually going to do it. I want to make classes fun so that kids really enjoy math. (Female white mathematics non-switcher)

> Originally, I thought I would go into teaching math, and that's why I chose the major. There's a shortage in the high schools, and yet I was so impressed by my teachers. They were just incredible. I think I was really spoiled. (Female white mathematics switcher)

Interestingly, a negative experience of teaching in a subject that is otherwise enjoyed may also prompt a desire to teach:

> I am, hopefully, going to teach in a completely different manner from my own math teachers, just because they were all so boring. I want to make my classes fun, so that kids will enjoy math. (Female white mathematics non-switcher)

Other sources of active influence, usually connected with family or high school, were role models whom students admired and sought to emulate, and mentors, whose advice on education and career direction was influential in their choices. It is usually assumed that, for a young person to be guided by a more experienced person whom they trust and admire is inherently 'a good thing'. However, whether the role pattern or advice followed is actually 'good' depends on the relevance of the message for the recipient. As with high school teachers who stressed science at the expense of students' other interests, some switchers regretted having followed the lead of people whom they saw as role models or mentors when younger:

> A good friend of our family was high up in Amoco, and had a daughter who I thought was just great. She was a lot older than I am. I think the fact that they were both women doing well in a very male field influenced me a lot. (Female white engineering switcher)

> I was working with a really great counselor who really wants girls to succeed in engineering. Even though my grades were low, she knew I could get a job as a woman, and she kept saying, 'You can do it.' And I felt it was kind of a challenge. Now, I wish maybe she'd said, 'Why aren't you doing so well?' If she hadn't been so good, I think I would have dropped out a lot faster. (Female white engineering switcher)

> My youngest uncle had some influence on my choice. He's got a nice job. He's got a big office. And he's doing *real live* things that actually change the world. He's working on Star Wars, and burying nuclear waste, and he really gets into his work. And I wanted a job like that. (Male white engineering switcher)

> My mentor was a mechanical engineer and he was always trying to get me to go into that. I was a pretty good student, and I was thinking about aerospace, but he talked me out of it. (Male white science switcher)

Given the nationwide effort of the last decade to recruit more under-represented groups into science majors, we were surprised to learn how few students (2.6% of our sample) chose their S.M.E. majors in response to programs targeting women and minorities. The kinds of active recruitment most often mentioned were: Minorities in Engineering and Science clubs at high or junior high school; R.O.T.C. scholarship programs; and summer outreach programs organized by colleges or universities for local school children. However, the idea that it is socially desirable to increase the representation of women and students of color in the sciences was clearly being disseminated, particularly by high school teachers and counselors, college advisors, and high school science clubs. An even smaller proportion (0.5%) of those formally recruited had been offered scholarships on entry to an S.M.E. major. There was no difference between switchers and non-switchers in the degree to which they had been recruited or offered financial assistance.

Finally, we noted some critical qualitative differences between the kinds of family influence which pressured their young to become square pegs in round holes, and those which fostered well-founded major choices, consistent with temperament, talent and preference. Students' accounts of the kinds of influence that helped them make appropriate choices and to persist in their majors contain consistent themes. Appropriate decisions are encouraged where parents, siblings other family members:

* play at science, math, or technical problem-solving with their children

* discuss scientific and mathematical issues, and their applications, with their children as part of everyday family life

* include their children in a hands-on way with technical domestic tasks, and in aspects of their own work

* discuss what they do at work, what part their work plays in the world, and what they like about it

* recognize and foster their children's interests and abilities in school without bias or pressure towards particular subjects or careers

* offer practical help with conceptual hurdles and emotional support through academic difficulties

* encourage their children to develop realistic aspirations, and (for girls especially) not to under-estimate their potential or options

* are active in ensuring that the quality and level of high school science and mathematics are adequate for college preparation

* offer themselves as a source of information and advice, and give plenty of opportunities to talk out the options, clarifying the pros and cons of particular majors or career paths even-handedly

It will be a relief to most parents to know that no single student ever described such perfect parenting. However, it was notable that non-switchers who were happy with their initial choice, mentioned several of these elements in stories of how they had come to choose their major:

> I had a mom who was always setting up little experiments around the house. I remember playing in bath tubs with water and seeing why things sank, or why they didn't. She always kind of kept you asking, 'Why?' (Female white science non-switcher)

> Dad and I would always talk science and math any time we were together, and I really enjoyed that. (Female white engineering non-switcher)

> My brother was a very strong influence on me. He was just part of an environment that got me into science, and kept me there. He did a double in biochemistry, and just gave me a sight of the future that really helped me stay with it. And he would help me sometimes when I got into problems with my studies. (Male white science non-switcher)

> I've always enjoyed helping my father. He's Mr. Homemaker—he fixes everything. So I was always there working alongside him from being a little kid. Just that experience interested me. Then, in high school, I had the same good teacher for four years. He made a strong impression on me also. I was strong in math and the sciences in high school, but we'd always talk about things that were happening in science and technology. So all of that together got me in and kept me interested. (Male white engineering non-switcher)

> Well, my dad's a mechanical contractor. And that's where I really got my interest—working alongside my dad. (Male white engineering non-switcher)

> He would bring home designs that he was working on. Things like that. And being the one who designs and produces things, that became very important in my eyes. (Male white engineering non-switcher)

> I talked to my dad a lot before I made my choice. We discussed all the goods and bads of different colleges and different options. Just to keep talking it through until you can see what you want more clearly makes for a better decision, I think. (Female black science non-switcher)

> Ever since I was a little kid, I always told my mom I was going to be a nurse. Finally, she asked me, 'Why don't you want to be a doctor?' And I said, I didn't think girls could get to be doctors. And ever since she said I could do this, it stayed in my mind—right through high school. (Female white science non-switcher)

> My parents always encouraged me. They were, basically, always my best supporters. (Female white science non-switcher)

Intrinsic Interest

As the information in Table 2.1 makes clear, the best foundation for survival and success is to have chosen one's major because of an intrinsic interest in the discipline and/or in the career fields to which it is leading. The sharpest difference in the choices of switchers and non-switchers was that non-switchers cited intrinsic interest as a prime source of motivation more than twice as commonly (27.8%) as switchers (11%). Feeling free to choose on the basis of personal interest was important because it encouraged bonding to the major, a sense of direction and feelings of resolve through times of difficulty. As several seniors explained, it is hard "to be focused" unless you have a clear sense of where you are going, and why:

> I want to go into bio-medical engineering, and I used my hobbies and interests outside of school to bring me in that direction. This has really helped me to focus and study a lot more. (Female white engineering non-switcher)

> I would have dropped out of engineering in a heartbeat. I hated it sometimes. It's just that I love airplanes so much. That's the reason I stick with it. (Female white engineering non-switcher)

Some of those with a strong interest in their major owed their sense of direction, in part, to particular teachers, family members, role models, or mentors. However, these were students who, while bearing in mind the counsel of people whose opinion they valued, felt free to choose their own paths:

> I've always been interested in the way things work. My father is a machinist, and I've had some high school teachers that were real influential in my choice just by encouraging me. (Male white engineering non-switcher)

Some switchers who also chose an S.M.E. major on the basis of intrinsic interest were disappointed that this had been dissipated by the poor quality of their freshman or sophomore learning experiences. Dullness of the curriculum or pedagogy and lack of hands-on science experiences were described as having undermined their incoming interest and had prompted their search for more stimulating academic experiences. (This issue is discussed further in Chapter 3).

For some students, interest in mathematics and science began at an early age, as did the career ambitions related to them:

> I can't even remember when I wasn't interested in science and math. I think my mother, being a big feminist, always encouraged me in this, rather than in the more typical feminine pursuits. I went to science camp when I was young, and when I graduated from high school I knew I wanted to go into engineering. It was in high school that I started understanding the difference between being a scientist and doing research, and being an engineer, and developing applications. As it happens, I'm much more interested in the applications of science. (Female white engineering non-switcher)

> I chose biology because I just love science. And it's something I feel I can handle. I've always wanted to be a doctor, ever since I was little. I never thought of anything else. I just can't imagine what else I would ever want to do. Nothing else remotely appeals. This is just me. (Female black science non-switcher)

There is, however, an important qualitative difference between early interests—which were refined and enhanced over time, and those based on romantic fantasy—which we found to be a poor basis for the choice of a major.

Interestingly, not all those who enjoyed science had developed their interest at an early age. On each campus, we encountered a small number of S.M.E. seniors who had not become interested in mathematics or science until junior high or high school, or until their first year of college:

> It was definitely in high school. Before that, I had much more artistic goals in either music, dance, or theater. But, when I got into my chemistry class, then my advanced math track—and maybe even a little before that in trigonometry and advanced algebra—that was what clicked with me. (Female white engineering non-switcher)

> In the 10th grade, we were required to take a biology class. And, up to that point, I wasn't really good at science. I wasn't really interested. But I enjoyed that class, and I started to get more and more interested. My teacher encouraged me a lot. By the time I reached 11th and 12th grades, I was really involved with the science clubs, and with my science classes. So I just decided I wanted to stay with something I enjoy. (Female black science non-switcher)

We feel that examples such as these are especially interesting because they contradict the common assumption that interest in, and the discovery of facility with, mathematics and science-based subjects tends to emerge early. Thus, the loss of interest in mathematics and science during adolescence often found among girls who were interested in them at an earlier age, may not be irreversible.

Altruism

An element in initial choice that is closely interwoven with intrinsic interest is the desire to enter a particular field because of commitment to a wider social purpose—a motivation we have labelled 'altruism'. Attaching one's career goals to a clear social purpose in some practical form appears to sustain interest and momentum through periods of difficulty. Certain themes recur in the kinds of socially-directed careers which students were seeking: service to others (including adaptation of particular skills or technologies to help groups with special needs); protection of the environment (wildlife, eco-systems, climate, air, water etc.); and the promotion of international peace:

> I'm going to work in environmental engineering—in alternative energy, or on water pollution control. I feel it's very important work, and because of the technical background I have, I think I can be a bit more effective, and more practical in helping with what needs to be done. (Female white engineering non-switcher)

> It's neither the prestige, nor the money. It's the contribution I could make. I want to get into work that's satisfying; that I can feel good about doing—and

in the hope of benefitting animal conservation. (Female white science non-switcher)

There's a lot of tension world-wide, and I think there's a need for people who are interested in science to help with that. (Male Hispanic science non-switcher)

I've decided to go into environmental and land-use development law. And with my background in civil engineering, I can perhaps speak with more authority than people who have to depend on someone else to explain the technical issues. (Male white engineering switcher)

And all my friends said I should get into something with immediate economic gain, and certainly not anything related to wildlife and the environment. It's well known that the jobs are hard to find, the salaries are very low, and the advancement minimal. But I said, 'Well, I've got to do what I *want* to do, and the hell with what everybody thinks.' (Female white science non-switcher)

Altruistic reasons for choosing S.M.E. majors are predominantly expressed (90.9%) by women and students of color. As indicated above (and as discussed further in Chapter 5), women are more likely than men to rank materialistic goals below the desire to work at something they care about, either as a matter of personal fulfillment, or in pursuit of a valued social cause. The goals of students of color, which often include making a long-term contribution to their families and communities, are discussed in more detail in Chapter 6.

The Uninformed Choice

With the benefit of hindsight, 13.1 percent of switchers, and 9.3 percent of non-switchers, realized that they had chosen a science-based major because it seemed (or was presented to them as) a logical extension of doing well in mathematics and/or science classes at high school:

I was always told I was good at math. I got all As, and my S.A.T. scores were really high, so, everyone I talked to—my parents, counselors, everyone—was saying, 'Go into engineering. It's a lot of money, and women are really needed.' And I got caught up in all the hype, really, based on the idea that, if you are good at math, this is what you do, right? (Female white engineering switcher)

I was good at math, and people told me that a good combination might be the engineering sciences, or maybe chemistry. So I just dived in, which was foolish, because, right away, I found out I did not like chemistry at all, and that having an ability in math does not really mean that you're going to like engineering. (Female white engineering switcher)

As is clear from these extracts, some students realized they had confused good grades with interest and aptitude for science and science-based careers. This confusion was compounded where students discovered that the curriculum or assessment standards used in their high schools were lower than those of many freshman peers, although their high school grades were comparable:

> High school's nothing like college. Even though I finished all the way through calculus in high school, I still might not be ready for a college-level math course. The placement test is good. I mean, it works for most people. But there's no way you can look at someone's high school background and know if they are good enough, or ready—especially if you are judging mostly by high school scores. (Female white science switcher)

Such discoveries have negative ramifications for self-confidence and persistence. Some choices that subsequently proved ill-founded were based too narrowly upon students' perceptions that they had good ability in mathematics or science. Once in college, 13.3 percent of switchers, and 6.5 percent of non-switchers, found they had entered with insufficient knowledge of what was entailed in the major or in the career fields to which they aspired:

> I think a lot of people now admit that they really had no clue about what they were getting into. (Male white science non-switcher)

> I originally wanted to go to medical school, and I didn't know what major I wanted. And then, at preview, they said microbiology would be a good major. So that's why I took it. I went with the career rather than the subject. I didn't know anything about microbiology. (Female white science switcher)

> I still didn't really know, going into it, what it meant to be an engineer, like, after you graduate. You hear that you make a lot of money, and there's good jobs. But, just having some interest in math and science—you need a little more than that. (Male white engineering switcher)

An interesting variation on the under-informed choice was offered by those who had followed through on a childhood dream. The career arenas in which this group reported they had most often imagined themselves were: space exploration, flying, or aerospace design; work with animals (either in a veterinary or wildlife context); and some branches of medicine. Many non-switchers had built their choice of major on long-standing aspirations, and had expanded their knowledge and experience in pursuit of these goals, whether at school, in hobbies, contact with people already in the field, or in part-time work. We, therefore, counted these accounts as indicative of 'intrinsic interest'. However, some childhood ambitions remained in the realm of fantasy and had never been developed by reading, inquiry, or hands-on learning. With hindsight, students realized unexamined dreams had proved a poor basis for their choice:

> I changed from microbiology, 'cause, when I was a kid, I wanted to be an immunologist. I'm not exactly sure why. (Male white science switcher)

> I always thought I'd be a vet, so I had pretty much decided to start in biology. But then I found I didn't really like biology that much. (Male Hispanic science switcher)

I really liked whales, and I thought I would go into something related to them. My dad was born on a Pacific Island, and used to scuba dive; and so did I once in a while. So I thought marine biology was the thing for me. (Female white science switcher)

I thought I'd go into aeronautical just because I was interested in space, and hoping, you know, that we would have contact with something out there—you, know, build colonies in space (laughing). (Female white engineering switcher)

I got my interest in flying from my dad, who was a private pilot. And it seemed like aerospace engineering was the way to go...In retrospect, I didn't really know what I was getting into. (Male white engineering switcher)

Another version of the 'blind' choice (evident in 7.7% of switchers and 7.4% of non-switchers) focused more on a desired career goal than on the academic disciplines leading to it:

More than anything, I wanted to go to med school, and I figured it was kind of the path I needed to take to do that. (Male black mathematics switcher)

I was real clear on the motivational component. I wouldn't come to school just to learn. That wasn't what it was about. I just knew what kind of work I wanted to do. (Male white engineering non-switcher)

A different kind of uniformed choice, following a family tradition, was reported by 5.6 percent of switchers and 6.9 percent of non-switchers. Such choices were rarely made in response to direct family pressure, but were a consequence of following, in an unquestioning way, what seemed the most obvious path. In engineering, following in family footsteps was reported to be the norm, especially for women:

People in high school, they just assumed I would go into engineering, because it was kinda the family tradition. My father's got an engineering firm, and all of us kids worked in it. And so it's kind of been a big part of our entire life. (Female white engineering switcher)

Support for a family career trend was sometimes given by high school teachers who failed to notice other interests or talents. The following extract illustrates both this and several other elements common to blind choices:

I was doing fine in math and science, but I didn't really like it. I just kinda did it, and they assumed I was good at it. And all my teachers knew the rest of the family so they assumed that since they did math and science I would do math and science. I never really was an individual person that they had to deal with. I think that was a big part of it. I really liked languages. I took German and Spanish in high school. But it was just an assumption that was made for me, and I couldn't come up with anything else. And I thought, 'Well, there's always a job in engineering,' so I went along with it. (Female white engineering switcher)

This group of factors combined to produce many uninformed choices that proved highly unstable unless buttressed by other factors favoring survival.

Too Little or Too Much Choice

A small number of students appeared to be at opposite ends of the same spectrum: 4.9 percent of switchers and 6.0 percent of non-switchers felt they had not actively chosen their major, but had entered it for negative reasons—against their wishes, as a compromise, or because they found non-science alternatives difficult or unpalatable:

> I had no idea what an electrical engineer did when I came in, but you have to chose a specialty. So what you do is to make a list of all the different specialties, cross out everything you hate, and what you're left with is what you are gonna be doing. (Male white engineering non-switcher)

> My last summer at school, I took chemistry and English. As for the chemistry, I didn't study that much, you know, and I enjoyed it. But, for the English class, I spent every waking hour reading books. And I hated that. So I guess I like science better. (Male white science non-switcher)

Conversely, 2.3 percent of switchers and 0.9 percent of non-switchers reported that entering a science-based major was just one of several options open to them given their range of interests, abilities and high school preparation:

> I finally ended up with economics, and decided to drop everything else in the humanities that wasn't related to math and science. I'm doing quantitative economics, so the mathematical stuff fits very well with my background. (Male white science switcher)

> I had the highest test scores in my high school for math, but I didn't want to be tied down until I had the chance to sample other things. I was happy to come to college and discover what I wanted to do with my math as I went along. (Male white mathematics switcher)

As we note throughout this report, on every campus we encountered a group of multi-talented switchers who felt under-stimulated by their freshman or sophomore intellectual experiences and who were drawn to explore other interests. Some found ways to blend their interests in science and mathematics with other disciplines; others left with regret, but with an ongoing interest in science and mathematics. By any measure, they represent a real loss to the fields of science, mathematics and engineering.[1]

Materialism and Pragmatism

The reasons for choosing an S.M.E. major we have labelled 'materialist' are, broadly, of three kinds. First, some freshmen saw particular majors as the key to desired levels of remuneration (both in terms of starting salary and long-term salary prospects), and/or prestigious career paths:

There's also the lure of earning a lot of money as an engineer—the glamour and the money if you're a doctor. And I think some people are misled by that. (Female Asian-American science switcher)

There's a lot of people, like me I guess, who try to go through it 'cause it's good money. And there's only a core of people who are really into engineering as a passion. (Male white engineering switcher)

People go to college and choose what they want to do, because it has some rewards in the future. It must at least be on the back-burners in high school—students talk about money and jobs a lot. (Female white science switcher)

The pressures from materialist peer culture, and from the wider social world of the high school senior, may prove hard to resist:

Everyone you know says, 'Go to school to get an education to get a good-paying job.' They don't say, 'Get a good job.' They always say, 'Get a high-paying job'—one that pays well, not necessarily one that you love. (Female white science switcher)

A lot of people told me I would make a lot of money, particularly as a woman in chemical engineering. And it all *sounded* good to me, especially since a lot of my friends from high school were going to places like Princeton. I felt I had to live up to that. And what I really wanted was to teach math and science, but I didn't want to say, 'Oh I'm going into an education major.' (Female white engineering switcher—to education)

Some well-prepared students who considered entry to mathematics or a particular science on the basis of ability or interest, but who were diverted into career-focused majors for material reasons, ended up outside of the sciences altogether:

I was good in chemistry, and I heard that engineers made more money than chemists. So I figured, well, chemical engineering, and that sounded good to me. But it was obviously a big mistake, because, as I started taking the real engineering classes, I realized that I hated what engineers do, and, before that I had no idea. (Female white engineering switcher)

I chose engineering because I liked math. That was my favorite subject all through high school...But I didn't wanna major in math because engineers make more money. (Female white engineering switchers)

Since I was a little kid, I've had a fascination with wanting to be an architect. So that got sort of suppressed, I guess, throughout high school when I started to think practically, like, 'How much money am I going to make when I get out of school?' And that got me thinking of choosing a major that was gonna get me a good job when I got out of school, rather than doing something I really wanted to do. (Male white engineering switcher)

A relatively rare form of 'materialism' was evident in choices which were influenced by a concern to make a solid financial contribution to the student's family or community. This type of motivation was most discernable among students of color and is discussed in Chapter 6.

Pragmatic elements in choices were highly interwoven with material considerations, and reflect the concept of the major as a commodity:

> I think people think about this a lot: 'Will I have a good job?...In four years, five years, this will be over, and I'll be out, and it will be an easy ride for the rest of my life.' (Female white science switcher)

> I was originally going to do architecture in high school, and I changed my mind and decided that mechanical engineering would give me the broadest background in four years. (Female white engineering non-switcher)

> Well, actually, I always wanted to be in International Relations. I always did really well in math though: I took calculus, chemistry and advanced chemistry and physics in high school. And I didn't think there was a future in liberal arts at that time, so I decided to go into physics. Very pragmatic. (Female white science switcher)

Pragmatic considerations also included: looking for the best long-term value for the time and money to be invested in a major; seeking a field which would offer a competitive edge in a rapidly changing job market; and 'hedging your bets' by choosing a major with a reputation for 'hardness' in expectation of less competition over the long term. A fall-back position was often added in case the major proved 'too hard.' Switching as a form of system playing (mentioned in the overview and discussed further in Chapter 4) also included students who entered, and then left, S.M.E. majors for pragmatic reasons:

> I'll make a lot more money, and have a lot more choice of areas to get into. And I feel finance is a lot more prestigious. I mean, teaching is known as a low-paying job, and research too. And I'm not interested in it. This was one of the key factors in changing, you know, the idea of making more money...Now I can make more, and have a lot more prestige in a finance-related career. (Male white science switcher)

> This may sound terrible, but I'm in college to make some money. I'm not here to get the degree. I didn't think I was going to make it in any of the science fields that I wasn't happy with over there, so I looked around. (Female white science switcher)

Interestingly, pragmatic motivations of this kind, which were very prevalent (among engineers especially) in many of the earlier interviews, were less commonly encountered in later interviews. They were increasingly displaced by concerns about securing *any* employment beyond graduation, and about the future prospects in particular career fields or specialties. The issue of, How much can I expect to earn? was increasingly replaced with, Will I get a job at all? and, How secure a future will it offer? This shift, reflecting the high sensitivity of undergraduates to changes in the economy, was most discernable in physics, mathematics, geology and in the engineering specialties most closely linked to the military-industrial sector. This trend has increasing relevance for switching decisions because over the three years of data gathering we increasingly found students weighing the time and money they had invested in particular majors, and the costs and benefits of graduate school, against their perceptions of career prospects:

> My middle brother went to Yale and did art history and is unemployed. So that was a factor. I've always had this sense that you would be able to get a job if you did engineering—which is a consideration nowadays. (Male white engineering switcher)

> You can get a management job that might be technically-oriented, and step into positions above humanities majors. Engineering majors, if they've done well academically, are much more competitive than other students. (Female white engineering non-switcher)

> I think there's a lot of opportunities for women engineers. I knew there were jobs, but I don't know if I knew what I'd be doing in those jobs. When I got here, I realized this isn't really what I want to do at all. I don't think engineering even really interested me. I would have had a job right after I graduated, and I wouldn't have had to worry about it, but I wanna make sure that I like what I'm doing. (Female white engineering switcher)

> This school is so expensive that you want to be able to get a job when you get out. You're guaranteed a future with engineering coming to a place like this. You're *going* to get hired. And that was very attractive to me. (Female white engineering switcher)

> I think the liberal arts really scared me. They were what I really loved, but I thought, 'I need to do something concrete with my life. I can't just graduate with a major in history. What am I going to do with that? There are no job opportunities.' And I'm a woman. I have to have an area that I can do something definite in and prove myself. (Female white science switcher)

The accounts of switchers whose choice of major was based partly on pragmatic considerations resonate with regret. Unless accompanied by strong disciplinary interest, unsupported materialism or pragmatism tends to break down under pressure. Switchers describe their error as: "giving up the present for the future," "squandering the chance to work at something you will enjoy," and "ending up in a job you don't like." For these switchers, money and prestige came to be seen as a poor recompense for loss of enjoyment of one's work, or a congenial quality of life, a perceived loss of integrity, or a diminished sense of identity. Some of these realizations are evident in the following accounts:

How could you go through that much stuff and not even like it—just doing it for the money? There's a lot of them still in there—they're in it for the money. They don't like the material, but you can get a good job. One friend of mine, he's in electrical engineering because of the money. He really likes business, but he's sticking with engineering. (Female Hispanic engineering switcher)

You can't do your best by staying in an area that you're uncomfortable with, or you *do not* like—you're never going to do well. Maybe they will earn some money, but think of what they could have done with something they really liked. (Male Asian-American science switcher)

And it's pretty hard to stick to something when all you're looking for is four years down the road—not there for yourself at the moment, but for something in the future. And you're not enjoying the experience right now because the money and prestige doesn't come until then. (Female white science switcher)

I had my heart set on pre-med because I thought, 'Neat. I can put my brains to work and make a lot of money.' And that's what I was originally thinking. I gradually realized my priorities were really out of whack—that I wouldn't enjoy what I was doing. (Male Hispanic science switcher)

It was held up by everyone as something that was prestigious and well-paying. And I think that kept me going for the first couple of years. But those goals began to seem meaningless if you don't care for the work involved. (Female white engineering switcher)

Non-switchers who described the experiences of their class peers and room-mates also reflected upon the inadequacy of pragmatic and materialist motivations:

A lot of people make the mistake of going into engineering to make $60,000 when they get out of school without realizing the kind of work that goes into it. You've got to *love* engineering, or be extremely tolerant of it, to get through. (Hispanic male engineering non-switcher)

My room-mate was doing pre-med because of the money, and the prestige of being a doctor. It's pretty scary if that's what you're basing your happiness on. (White female science non-switcher)

Lots of people go into engineering—especially the ones who drop out—strictly for the job prospects. But most of those people are gone by the time you graduate because, really, it's not worth it! (Laughs.) The ones that I know who are going to graduate did it just because it was interesting, and it's what they want to do. I don't think too many people who want it initially for the money or a good job really stick with it, because, in the end, it wouldn't be worth it. (Male Hispanic engineering non-switcher)

As Table 2.1 makes clear, materialist (or pragmatic) motivations were not confined to switchers, and 13.9 percent of non-switchers (largely engineers) also included them as factors in their choice:

Money is important to me. Other people may not care. But, I've grown up in a comfortable setting, and when I start my career that's not going to be there any more. But I wanna get back to my standard of living—the way I enjoy it. (Male white non-switching engineer)

The reason I chose engineering was because it was up there. I happened to be looking through a magazine, and it was, like, $40,000 or $50,000 early in your career. (Female black non-switching engineer)

However, switchers were more likely than non-switchers to have been influenced by considerations of money, career options and prestige. Non-switchers tended to combine these motivations with other, more stable, reasons for their choice. In some ways, the materialist and pragmatic emphases in the initial choices of 16.2 percent of all students in our sample might seem depressing to many educators. There was, however, clear evidence in many accounts that materialist motivations had been replaced by intrinsic interest as the basis for career goals. This was especially clear in switching decisions where the greater interest afforded by the new major or careers was an important element. This observation gives grounds for optimism that the college experience continues to encourage self-discovery and the development of independent criteria for life priorities.

Gender Differences in Reasons for Choosing S.M.E. Majors

The most marked difference between the sexes documented in this study lies in the reasons for their choice of majors. Women were about twice as likely as men to have chosen an S.M.E. major through the active influence of someone significant to them. Among switching women, this factor accounted for 25.3 percent of all reasons given for their choices (cf., Table 2.2), but was also strongly discernable among women who persisted. For both groups of women, the influence of significant others on their choice of major was greater than was the case both for switching and non-switching men.

By contrast, men were almost twice as likely as women to cite 'being good at mathematics and/or science in high school' as a reason for choosing an S.M.E. major. Whether they were actually better prepared or skilled than women entrants is not the issue. What matters is that many more young men than young women felt confident in their readiness to undertake higher level science and mathematics. Switching men stand out, both against non-switching men and against all women, as more apt to make this the basis for their choice. Choices based largely on perceptions of aptitude for science or mathematics proved particularly unreliable when coupled with inadequate prior understanding of the nature of their major.

The contrasts between switching and non-switching women are also interesting. As well as being more open to the influence of others in their choices, switching women were more likely to have chosen an S.M.E. major for materialistic reasons and to have a lower level of intrinsic interest in science than women who persisted. This distinction is greater among female than among male switchers and persisters. However, women persisters stand out as more highly motivated by interest than any other group. Women persisters also appear to be the least (and women switchers to be the most) driven by material or pragmatic considerations.[2]

Reasons for Choosing S.M.E. Majors: Significance for Persistence

It is clear that students who persist in their original choice of an S.M.E. major are more likely than switchers to have chosen their major (and/or their career path), at least to some degree, by reason of their interest in it. In only one other category—altruism (which is cited much more rarely)—is the distinction between switchers and non-switchers so clear. Switchers were much more likely to have made their choices for reasons not directly connected with the nature of the academic work entailed in the majors they chose. Notable among switchers' reasons for choosing S.M.E. majors were: the active influence of others; materialistic and pragmatic considerations; feeling their choice to be the logical extension of doing well in math and/or science in high school; and choosing with little or no knowledge of what the major might entail (either in terms of the course work or career alternatives). There was surprisingly little difference between switchers and non-switchers in most other factors found to influence choice. The choices of non-switchers were also commonly prompted by instrumental considerations, by the pressures of people close to them, by compromise and by a limited understanding of what might be entailed. However, non-switchers were consistently less driven than switchers by factors other than intrinsic interest. It would seem, therefore, not to matter too greatly what other reasons students have for their choices, so long as one strong element in their decision is an intrinsic interest in the academic disciplines which comprise the major and in the kinds of work to which they lead.

High School Preparation

All seven institutions took mathematics scores (S.A.T. or A.C.T.) into account for admission purposes, enrolled freshmen in introductory S.M.E. classes on the basis of mathematical placement tests, and considered the S.A.T. (or equivalent) mathematics scores targeted for our sample (i.e., 650 or more) as adequate for entry to an S.M.E. major. If S.M.E. freshmen displaying mathematical competence at this level or above are expected to be capable of understanding the material presented in introductory S.M.E. classes, the quality of high school mathematics preparation should not have created difficulties serious enough to contribute to switching decisions for most of the students in our sample. Neither should we have found many students who had switched because of serious conceptual problems in these classes. This proved to be the case: neither inadequate high school preparation (which contributed to 14.8% of switching decisions), nor serious conceptual difficulties (which contributed 12.6%) were major factors in switching decisions. However, the effects of inadequate high school preparation were the most common contributor to early decisions to switch. Approximately 40 percent of both switchers and non-switchers reported some problems related to high school preparation, and around 25 percent of each group reported conceptual difficulties. Both types of problems were disproportionately experienced by students of color in our sample: 25 percent (compared with 10.7% of white students) reported inadequate high school preparation; and 30.8 percent reported conceptual difficulties with one or more S.M.E. classes (compared with 5.3% of white students). We also discovered in drawing our samples that all seven institutions had admitted some students of color with mathematics performance scores below 600 S.A.T. (or equivalent). The consequences for these students are discussed in Chapter 6. In this section, we discuss the nature of the under-preparation difficulties recounted by students. The nature of their conceptual problems are discussed in Chapter 3.

Students' accounts of under-preparation were broadly of two types: deficiencies of curriculum content and subject depth, and failure to acquire appropriate study skills, habits and attitudes. However, both facets of under-preparation were, in reality, inter-connected. Some switchers and non-switchers had received no high school teaching in calculus, or described the content and depth of their high school science or mathematics as insufficient for their first college classes:

> I never had a calculus class before I got here. What a shock it was! And our physics was calculus-based too. I was really struggling: What's a derivative? What's an integral? (Male white mathematics non-switcher)

> I was seen as a very, very good student at high school because I was a natural in math. But when I had to retake both semesters of calculus, I realized that my math preparation hadn't been all that good. (Female white science non-switcher)

Other dimensions of deficiency in content or depth were: lack of laboratory experience or exposure to computers; no introduction to theoretical material, or to analytic modes of thought; lack of opportunity to take college preparation classes (including Advanced Placement); and uneven quality in the science and mathematics classes in the same school:

> Coming out of high school I'd never seen a chemistry lab; never seen a good scale, or handled any of the apparatus you're expected to use right off. (Male white science non-switcher)

> I'm going to graduate in aero this year. But when I came in, I'd never seen a computer. I had to ask where the 'on' switch was. And I was with people who had been working with computers since they were kids. (Female Hispanic engineering non-switcher)

One day in class there was an announcement: 'Anybody who wants to go to college should see their counselor and take the S.A.T. or A.C.T.' This was my senior year, and that's how I learned about college entry. I didn't do well on the tests. (Male Hispanic science non-switcher)

The only thing I was good for was calculus. I had a very good calculus teacher. But everything else was new. I was very upset: I don't think they prepared me for college at all. There was A.P. chemistry, but all we did was play cards and make ice cream. (Female Hispanic engineering switcher)

Complaints of these kinds were not confined to undergraduates at the more open-entry state institutions: we heard similar complaints at the competitive-entry, private research university:

I don't consider myself to have been well-prepared at all. My math background wasn't as strong as it could have been, especially compared to a lot of the people around me. And my physics preparation—god, that was just a nightmare...I had no calculus in high school. I mean, I enjoy math—but the speed of the first class was incredible. (Male white engineering switcher)

My high school chemistry class had no labs...It was all from books. (Male white science switcher)

Everybody got done with math in their high school freshman year; the highest we got was pre-calculus. There wasn't much help if you were working to a higher goal. (Male white engineering switcher)

Reading students accounts of under-preparation without information about the speakers, it would be hard to guess which were switchers and which persisters. Indeed, that some S.M.E. seniors were able to overcome these problems seems less predictable than that they would become discouraged and leave. However, as seniors made clear, the consequences of poor high school preparation are serious and long-lasting:

I suffered all through college for things I didn't do in high school. I took algebra, which is all they required, and never took math the next three years. I blew off a lot of the really significant stuff, and then I had to come here and redo it. I had no real background. I had no math. I am still real sketchy about much of it. I do well as long as I have time to work it all out. (Male white science non-switcher)

I was left with a lot of conceptual holes. There were a lot of times when I somehow got through things without knowing how. But right from the beginning, they added up. When I looked back, I realized that there were pockets of things I did not know, and had never known—and probably never will. (Female white engineering non-switcher)

It all came too easy in high school. I thought I didn't have to study here either. I struggled all the first year to get the whole study thing. I never did quite recover. (Male white engineering non-switcher)

A more subtle form of under-preparation was having to unlearn a tendency to see material in modular form, without transfer, connections or framework:

> They don't encourage you to think about the material. You work for a test, and then for the next test. And working for tests doesn't teach you to continually review what you know—which I think is one of the keys to learning in college. (Male black engineering switcher)

Students were often shaken to discover how poor their high school preparation had been by comparison with that of other freshmen. Their above-average performances in standardized tests gave them little indication of their actual level of readiness for college work. Appreciation of their deficiencies in study skills and habits came with their very first freshman classes:

> I went to such a small high school. Teachers weren't all that great, and there were no advanced math or college prep classes—just the basic core classes up to pre-calculus—which meant that I had to start at the beginning in engineering. My room-mate, who went to a large, suburban school in a wealthy area, started with the second year of calculus, and circuits too. I had other friends who were way ahead of me—just because of the better education they had had in high school. (Female white engineering non-switcher)

> I just kicked back and got straight As—with zero effort on my part. And I came here thinking I was going to coast through college like that. In the very first week, I had a terrible eye-opener. There were students sitting all around me that *knew* what was going on, and I had absolutely no idea what they were talking about. I was completely lost. I was expected to *be* at that level the very first day. I realized I hadn't had any of the stuff at high school that I needed—like physics. I'd never even seen a computer. (Male white mathematics non-switcher)

> The teachers that did the worst job were, I think, oblivious to the fact that they were not giving us good preparation for college...I think the problem might also have been with the resources that my district didn't have. (Female white science switcher)

It is difficult to generalize about the types of high schools which are more likely to under-prepare students for college mathematics and science in terms of curriculum content or depth. However, students from small rural schools, large inner-city schools, reservation schools, and poorly-endowed schools located in working-class areas (white or minority), were those who most often cited insufficient resources and limited access to well-qualified teachers as salient features in their high school science and mathematics education:

> A lot of it comes from the shortage of teachers with real degrees in math and science. My math classes were taught by someone with a master's in Phys. Ed. I think she had some sort of bachelor minor in math. She was worse at algebra than we were. (Female white mathematics science non-switcher)

The high school I went to was backwards, to say the least. It was a small
school in a farming area in South Texas. Maybe two or three people each year
went on to college, and they weren't prepared for anything. The highest level
of math I got to was trig, and a few weeks of pre-calculus, and one year of
basic high school physics taught by a coach. I had only one math teacher who
wasn't an athletics coach in my whole time there. (Male white engineering
non-switcher)

I came from the worst high school in the city. My physics teacher used to be
a bus driver. He was an interesting man, but he wasn't a physics teacher. A
good 40 percent of the time we watched navy recruitment films. It was
supposed to be an honors class, but we just kind of hung out together and did
assignments. (Female white science switcher)

With my high school, it was more of a funding problem. They just didn't have
the money to offer calculus and A.P. math. I think revenue-sharing will be a
big help in the rural Midwest. (Male white engineering switcher)

As we shall discuss in Chapter 6, the consequences of poor content preparation
were especially serious for freshmen of color from high schools with limited
resources:

There was just so much that I didn't know...I felt like I wasn't even in the
same game as everyone else. (Male black engineering switcher)

Poor high school preparation was also experienced as a form of gender
discrimination by some of the women in the sample:

We were the only two girls in our high school physics and chemistry classes,
and the only two who ended up coming here. And we were really discriminated against by our teacher. In all the experiments, he wouldn't let us touch
anything—especially in physics. I mean, it was totally hands-off to us. I still
liked it, but I wasn't learning enough. I was totally lost in physics when I first
got here. Chemistry was more equal, but we didn't have enough equipment.
Only certain people got picked to do the experiments, and we lost out on that
because we felt a little timid. We didn't feel good about being there. I didn't
say anything to my mother, because at the time, it didn't occur to me that
anything was wrong. (Female white science non-switcher at a competitive-entry
research university)

Even with good teachers, an able student at a school with multiple social,
financial and educational problems was still at risk:

I didn't really have to do anything to get good grades. When they have kids
that have difficulty even getting to school, it's hard to cater to the upper level.
So they didn't push you; and they didn't prepare you to be self-motivated to
study. (Female white science switcher)

All of these students knew they had received a sub-standard education and
most knew it while they were in high school. They felt that the communities

from which they came, their parents, and the schools themselves, often had limited understanding of their schools' inadequacies. However, some students who, in retrospect, saw their high school preparation as having been inadequate had attended private schools, had been included in special programs, or were the recipients of awards for science:

> I'm sort of against my high school because they made a lot of promises to us. They told us we were a nationally-acknowledged high school, and it turned out that no one here recognized the school at all. I graduated with a 3.8, but it didn't turn out to be as good as someone who had taken A.P. courses at the neighborhood school. (Female white engineering switcher)

> It was tremendously overrated I think, you know, with hindsight. They looked at my G.P.A., and at the fact I was a Merit Scholar. But I found the level of work here completely different from what I'd been used to, and I was totally blown away. (Male white engineering switcher)

> I won a science fair in the 12th grade, and had gone to New York, and thought I was the scientist of the world—or at least, very bright. And then, when I didn't do very well in the first engineering classes, I completely lost faith in myself. Because I really believed, for the very first time, that I was stupid. (Female white engineering switcher)

> I found you couldn't look at how you did in high school, and then transpose that onto college. I don't place much merit in S.A.T. scores. I was National Merit commended, but my scores didn't mean anything. I took a math class to improve my scores, but all they did was teach me little tricks. I raised my score by 100 points, but it didn't mean anything—except that I was good at taking tests. (Female Asian-American science switcher)

Students who had moved around the country during their high school years knew from personal experience that there were wide variations between schools in the quality of the mathematics and science classes offered for college preparation. Those who had experienced high school mathematics and science in other countries were sometimes uncomfortable in acknowledging they had found standards in U.S. high schools to be lower:

> Going back to my family's home in the Philippines, I realized that my peers there were doing more science than I ever did. And, you know, they live in the provinces and go to these dinky little schools. It was kind of alarming to admit. (Male Asian-American science non-switcher)

> The teachers in my school in Switzerland were really into teaching. They really pushed you hard...I remember once I had a class I wasn't doing very well in, and the vice-principal called me in to talk about it. That wouldn't happen here. But I guess they don't have the same standards here. (Male white mathematics non-switcher)

However, most students who felt that they had been under-prepared were angry that they had no way of knowing this was the case until they arrived in their first college mathematics or science class.

Failure to Learn Good Study Skills and Habits

One of the reasons why students' scores in standardized mathematics tests may not be useful in predicting who will remain and who will leave, is that students with a good natural aptitude for mathematics may have failed to learn the study skills, habits, and discipline needed for college-level work. Looking back, some informants saw how elements in the culture of school, home and peer group had mitigated against their acquiring these aspects of college preparation. A common story of this type was recounted by students who had always found mathematics and science easy, 'scored' high grades in these subjects with little effort, and were accustomed to praise from teachers, family and peers. Rarely had their teachers made appropriate demands on their abilities. Achievement targets had been set well below their capability, and they had been neither stretched nor challenged. They did little homework, or did it hurriedly at the last minute, and were often left to their own devices while teachers worked with the rest of the class:

> I breezed through high school very easily with high grades. I think a lot of kids that did well in high school are gonna come in and use the same study habits and just get blown away. That's what happened to me. (Male white mathematics non-switcher)

> I just really didn't know how to study, so I had to train myself how to do that here. In high school, I didn't really have to try that hard to get good grades. (Male white mathematics switcher)

> I got through high school very easily. I think it was probably a pretty poor high school, because I finished with a 3.98, was fifth in my class, and yet I hardly studied at all. I always worked the night before—that's how I got through high school. It always worked—piece of cake. I think this was a problem a lot of us experienced. (Male white engineering non-switcher)

> I came out with close to a 3.8 without ever having to put much effort into it. And so I never learned the in-depth study skills that are required to do well here. (Male white science non-switcher)

Being singled out as 'talented and gifted' could also be counter-productive to learning good study habits:

> I got a state science scholarship to come here, but I had problems in my first year. I hadn't ever really studied. If I need something during a test, I derive it. (Female white science non-switcher)

> Having the 'talented and gifted' tag put on you is a huge handicap. You have too much free time, but no one ever teaches what to do with it. I mean, I

never really learned to study, or how to approach problems. I suppose they thought I just knew. (Male white engineering switcher)

When I was young, I was in all these 'talented and gifted' classes. I used to be impressed by it, but I'm not any more. I never opened a book in high school—my father says he didn't either. After class, we went home, played basketball, ate dinner and screwed around. I probably never did any home-work. My teachers didn't like it that I didn't work, but I kept scoring high on the tests, so they couldn't say anything to my dad. And I still came out of high school with a 3.7 average and over 700 in my math S.A.T. Six years later, I'm still learning how to study. (Male white engineering switcher)

Students who were mathematically gifted, but who had learned to under-achieve, were at high risk of abandoning their plans for S.M.E. majors at a very early stage—that is, soon after their first experience of having to produce large amounts of work at speed, and of receiving the first non-A grades of their lives. They described an ego-crisis soon after college entry, in which they felt angry toward their high schools, and began to question their interest or ability for college-level work:

I was very ill-prepared. I had gotten really disenchanted with high school and just stopped trying. Here you immediately hit a sheer change in the way you have to work. You need organization, way more organization skills. God, that's the biggest thing. (Male white science switcher)

I didn't know I would have to work that hard. I'd never had to. Nothing had prepared me for this. In fact, I didn't *know* how to work. Once I fell behind, I had no idea what to do. (Male white science non-switcher)

I did well in math through high school and got all As, and always felt confident about it. And then when I took calculus here, it was a nightmare. (Male white science non-switcher)

I studied minimally, and graduated at the top of my class of 270 students. And I thought, 'Hey, I'm ready to take on the world.' And I was from New York, and when I got here my head just spun. I mean, I couldn't believe all the work they expected. (Male white science non-switcher)

That's one of the things I kinda resent about my high school. Calculus was so easy—everything was so easy. If I had had more challenge in those classes, I would probably not have decided to pursue it, because I would have found out earlier that I had no real interest in science—just in the good grades. (Female white science switcher)

A lot of kids come here like I did with upper-700 math S.A.T scores and straight As, and everyone in high school building you up as someone special. And then you hit college, and its suddenly very humbling. Some people never get off their knees. (Male Hispanic engineering non-switcher)

Again, from the content of under-preparation stories alone, it is hard to guess which students had switched, and which had stayed in their major. This also illustrates our contention that there is little to distinguish switchers and non-switchers at this level of ability in terms of objective 'risk factors'.

If we consider attrition as a process (as opposed to a static phenomenon without context or chronology), it becomes clear that one of the first groups of students to be lost are those who have internalized the attitudes of teachers, parents and peers who confuse talent with achievement. As bright, but undisciplined (and/or academically under-prepared) freshmen, they almost immediately discover the gap between their incoming expectations and the reality of their capacity to perform as required:

> I came to university thinking, 'I know how to do physics and calculus,' and I'd be able to breeze through the classes without really studying. And I know it really hurt me having that background. (Male white engineering switcher)

They may complain, with good reason, that they had no way to know how poorly they had been prepared. Having learned to judge themselves extrinsically by the high grades they received, they have no psychological defenses against lower grades. Viewing grades as an acknowledgement of their talent, rather than as feedback, a guide to progress or a reward for effort, they had little experience of coping with frustration or set-backs, compared with less talented peers who always had to work. Thus, students with strong ability in mathematics may, paradoxically, become early casualties of the weed-out system:

> I knew a gal from a small town who was a super-star in her local high school. And she and I were both struggling in this calculus class—but I hadn't had math for 10 years. She was really getting down on herself because she wasn't pulling As when she thought she should be...I don't know what happened to her. (Female white engineering non-switcher)

> Some people thought their high school preparation was very good. And then when they got here, they realized it wasn't. I had the exact opposite—I knew I had a terrible math background, but I worked myself to death. (Male Asian-American engineering non-switcher)

> A lot of people that go into engineering are straight A students. And then they get the first exam back with a 40 or 50 grade on it—and it's devastating. These are people that have never seen anything below a 95. (Female white engineering switcher)

Almost one-quarter (24.2%) of our whole sample, 33.9 percent of switchers and 12.5 percent of non-switchers, reported a fall in their level of confidence caused by expectation of high (or easy) grades, and their shock at receiving the lower grades that are traditional in introductory S.M.E. classes. Twenty-three percent of switchers reported that this had contributed to their decision not to continue in the sciences. The survivors described their struggles to overcome the blow to ego:

> High school was a piece of cake for me. I mean, it all came naturally, and I did good, you know—and it tells me I'm smart. And I came here and failed my first exam. I'd never failed a test in my whole life. I'd never failed anything. I went home and cried—over a stupid test! I got As on the rest of them, but I still got a C because I failed the first one. I went and talked to the instructor and said, 'Are you sure you can't give me a B?' He said, 'It's not that you don't deserve one, but the numbers don't work out.' I was really upset. But you gotta stand back and say, 'Well, I just choked on one test.' But you can imagine, if you're 18 and you get to college and you get a C when you're used to getting As...And there's no one there to say, 'Well, five years from now, it's not going to matter.' (Female white engineering non-switcher)

> Your self-esteem takes a hell of a beating. But, eventually, you just laugh and say, 'I used to be smart: now I'm a C student.' (Female white science non-switcher)

Learning not to interpret grades as personal criticism was critical to surviving the discovery that high school had not adequately prepared them for college—intellectually, or in terms of work skills, discipline, or grade expectation. Although failure to recover from the shock of under-preparation, per se, contributed to only 14.8 percent of switching decisions, approximately 40 percent of both switchers and non-switchers described a struggle with problems created by under-preparation, usually from the very first week in college. Those who dropped out or failed classes because of under-preparation—many of them mathematically-able—were in the first wave of attrition. Some of those who survived to become seniors reported that they were still coping with aspects of under-preparation from high school.

Notes

1.   These observations are supported by Humphreys and Freeland's findings from their 1992 study of retention among freshman engineers at Berkeley: that students who switched from engineering entered their major with significantly higher verbal scores than non-switchers.

2.   As a group, female switchers contained both the highest proportion of students who chose S.M.E. majors for materialistic reasons, and who either chose or switched majors in pursuit of altruistic goals. However, there was no instance of a female switcher or non-switcher who reported both types of motivation.

3

The Learning Experience
in S.M.E. Majors

The 'Hardness' of Science

In this chapter, we present four aspects of our findings that describe the character of the experience of S.M.E. undergraduates as learners. We discuss: what makes the sciences 'hard'; the nature and consequences of traditional 'weed-out' processes; the role of advising, counseling, and of the teacher-learner relationship in persistence and switching.

The Nature of Conceptual Difficulties

It became clear at an early stage in our inquiry that students referenced a number of different facets of the learning experience by the terms "hard" or "hardness." Switchers sometimes described aspects of their S.M.E. major as "too hard," and some non-switchers spoke of the "hardness" of their discipline when explaining the loss of class-mates. Throughout the interviewing process, therefore, we sought to clarify exactly what our informants meant when they used these words. Feeling overwhelmed by the sheer volume of material, coupled with the pace at which it was presented, and by conceptual difficulties were the commonest kinds of problems glossed as "hardness." They contributed to 34.9 percent of switching decisions and were mentioned as a problem by 45.4 percent of switchers and by 41.4 percent of non-switchers. Conceptual difficulties (of several kinds) contributed to a smaller proportion (12.6%) of switching decisions. They were 26.8 percent of all switchers' concerns, and were described by a comparable proportion (25.0%) of non-switchers.

The experience of conceptual difficulties, and of problems related to curricular pace and load, was often linked to inadequacy in high school preparation. Students who were substantially under-prepared reported more conceptual problems and feelings of being overwhelmed in the early stages of their major. We met students in this predicament on every campus. Also on every campus, we found remedial arrangements that were intended to allow these students to catch up with their peers. Wherever this involved students trying to acquire material not previously encountered, at the same time as undertaking introductory class work in which the same knowledge and skills were assumed, the outcome was usually disastrous. Not only did most of these students abandon their ambition to continue with an S.M.E. major, they also suffered emotional damage by attempting what proved an impossible task:

> If you have a cruddy background in math and science, you're not going to be able to suffer through what you're gonna have to suffer through to learn what you should have learned before you came into school. And then, on top of that, trying to do the same work as everyone else who was better prepared than you. (Male white science switcher at competitive-entry private research university)

> I tried to take that remedial math class at the same time that I was taking the first level mainstream class. Then I took the intro class again, and this time, I thought I would try to teach myself the material I didn't have. I also had to take differential equations that semester to keep up with the sequence. In the end, I withdrew from that and stopped going to the math class half-way through. I'd failed several tests by then. It was just too discouraging to start from so far behind. There's no way you can catch up if you don't come in ready to go, I don't care how smart you are. (Male white engineering switcher)

Students with this kind of experience were prone to early switching decisions. They sometimes described their difficulties as "conceptual," but they are more properly seen as the result of high school under-preparation on the one hand, and failure to devise realistic bridging programs on the other. Bridging programs can be negotiated between college S.M.E. departments and junior or community colleges and offer guaranteed college entry once students achieve an agreed level of competency in college mathematics and science.

If we lay aside the accounts of students in need of a bridging program, and consider accounts which focus on pace and load issues, we are left with a smaller number of accounts (26.0% in the sample overall) which explore difficulties which can properly be called 'conceptual'. Students describe conceptual problems as arising from a number of sources. The abstract or theoretical nature of the material (especially as students move further into the discipline) is an important type of difficulty. Students who recount this kind of problem become stuck at the point at which they can no longer 'see' what is being discussed, nor relate it by analogy or metaphor to something 'real' in the world:

> People have a hard time with organic chemistry because they have a hard time visualizing it. It was hard for me at first too because you can't see it, touch it

or feel it—it's not real. And taking it on trust is just one of those big steps you have to take in any science. (Female white science non-switcher)

I had trouble visualizing calculus after a certain level. I mean, once you're in the third dimension, you're not working on paper any more. And then it shifts into a fourth dimension—that's entirely beyond your imagination. (Female white mathematics switcher)

A second kind of problem arises from the sequential way in which an understanding of mathematical or scientific principles is built up. At every stage, the presentation of new material poses the risk that it cannot be comprehended unless sufficient prior learning has taken place:

I was never really comfortable with any of it. In fact, my entire life, I've kind of slid through science. When I was doing experiments, I didn't really know what was going on. I somehow managed to fake my way through about 17 years of math and science. Eventually, you hit a point where you just can't go on without that solid understanding to pull on. (Female white engineering switcher)

Sometimes, teachers misjudge the distance students can leap from one level of comprehension to the next. Students for whom this gap is too great may be in jeopardy unless tutorial help is at hand:

The junior year was just intense. It was too great a step up for me from sophomore work. The gap between the physics and chemistry foundation layer, with all the labs and the calculus, then up to the first chemical engineering classes, was a huge jump. Luckily for us, so many people had dropped out by that stage we were able to get some help. (Female white engineering non-switcher)

Another kind of conceptual difficulty related more to teaching methods than to the nature of material, *per se*, is finding the class work (including the home-work) comprehensible, but not the problems presented in tests. (The issue of 'fit' between class content and tests is discussed later in this chapter.)

Students commonly visualize their conceptual progress as a linked series of insights that are strengthened by regular problem-solving. Insights are usually described as "getting it." Some students break through to insight by working a large number of problems that exemplify the phenomena to be mastered. For others, insights 'just happen'; they are seen as a mysterious and inexplicable gift:

You can be taught to manipulate numbers, and be able to use them. But you can't be taught the process that allows you to come up with the answer just like that. (The speaker snaps his fingers.) (Male white engineering switcher)

Students were divided over the issue of whether or not it was possible to succeed in an S.M.E. major without a level of natural ability greater than that required to enter the major. Some saw insight as gained mainly by determination and effort:

> I think, basically, everybody that has acquired the necessary skills to come here has the ability to survive. Then it's a matter of being willing to get through the day-to-day ritual of the hard classes. (Female white science non-switcher)

Others saw insight as a matter of having sufficient time to absorb the ideas presented to you:

> When I was doing physics, I tried so hard, but just couldn't seem to get it. Then, the other day, just for curiosity, I sat and worked out some of my old problems. And I could do them all. I think it was just a matter of time to think about it. So now I kind of wonder if I went back into engineering if I could maybe do it—and even do well. (Female white engineering switcher)

However, for those who could only 'get it' by devoting enormous amounts of time to the process, their slowness to grasp material compared with the rest of the class became an absolute barrier to continuing in the major:

> I had to get it more from reading the book over and over, I wasted a lot of time reading and reading. I could understand the book, but not the classes. I felt the professors were just sloppily throwing it up on the board. If one day in lecture I was totally lost, I'd go home and study all night, and come back to class the next day. And maybe the teacher would go over a little bit of what she'd covered the day before, and that would help me catch up too. (Male Asian-American engineering switcher)

When students who are struggling to understand material at a pace which is faster than they can absorb it, and encounter this difficulty in more than one subject, they are likely to leave:

> I switched because I couldn't get either the math, or the physics as quickly as a lot of the other people. (Male white engineering switcher)

Students imagery of conceptual progress often includes the notion of mental blocks. These were portrayed as fairly predictable crisis points in understanding which many learners expected to encounter and overcame with insight—however gained. Students were again divided into two camps of opinion—one élitist, the other democratic—about the nature of conceptual barriers. One group believed everyone had natural limits to their ability: people who failed to overcome intellectual crises, despite determination and effort, had probably reached their own particular conceptual wall:

> Being in the gifted and talented program, I got a good basis. But then, I just dead-ended. That's as close as I can come to explaining it. You really can't expand your mind any more than up to a certain limit. I hit a stage where

anything was difficult, and where I realized this was as far as I would go. (Male white engineering switcher)

> As it got more and more removed from reality—more theoretical—I lost that feeling of discovery and understanding of the world. And, at the same time, I was struggling with the math. I was still getting Bs, but I would feel like the insights weren't coming any more. (Male white science switcher)

The other group believed that all, or most, conceptual barriers were surmountable—given a certain level of ability and academic preparation, decent teaching, sufficient time, and help from faculty, T.A.s, or peers. Seniors recalled their struggles with particular mental blocks. Though, at the time, mastery had seemed impossible, once the insight was gained, the concepts seemed obvious and familiar:

> Some of the stuff is just plain hard. It's obvious that the professor understands it very well. And later on, you do too. But, at the time, it's like being in third grade trying to understand multiplication. In the third grade, that multiplication's a hard concept. And the professor has forgotten that it was once difficult for him, and he doesn't remember why you find it so hard. (Female white science non-switcher)

Though the nature of conceptual barriers and the ways in which insights are gained were discussed by students on every campus, on only two campuses did they offer the theory that everyone has their own absolute conceptual wall which, sooner or later, blocks their progress. One of these was the large East Coast state university where we also found the greatest variation in high school preparation among freshmen, and the most unworkable remedial programs for those who entered under-prepared. The other was the private research university with competitive entry where students were well-aware that, though they could have been high-achievers at their own state institution, at this university they were pitted against class-mates with abilities greater than their own. Though we can offer no evidence one way or the other to support or refute the reality of absolute conceptual barriers to intellectual progress in science or mathematics, we note that belief in the existence of such barriers has consequences—both for the philosophy on which faculty base their pedagogy and for students' responses to blocks to conceptual progress. What we can assert on the basis of these data is that conceptual barriers, *per se*, are not a major cause of switching among students at this level of ability.

Problems of Curriculum Pace and Work Load

When students speak of the 'hardness' of S.M.E. majors, they are referring, more than anything, to the large volume of work required of them, coupled with the high speed at which it must be completed. Over one-third (34.9%) of switchers included this aspect of S.M.E. curriculum structure among their reasons for switching; and similar proportions of both switchers (45.4%) and non-switchers (41.4%) found the pace and work load of their S.M.E. majors 'hard' in this sense. Those whose high school preparation and study habits were insufficient for college-level work were among the earliest victims of work demands which seemed impossible to meet. However, even those students who were well-prepared were shocked by the speed at which faculty presented, and expected them to absorb, material:

> I was just astounded at the quantity of work—overwhelmed would be a good word for it. I was just stunned. (Male white engineering non-switcher)

> I think, in people's minds, chemistry is a hard subject. Once you get over that, you are still faced with having to take in an enormous amount of material. I mean, the discipline it takes to study and keep good grades in chemistry was the incredibly big jump I had to make. (Male white science non-switcher)

> I guess what makes it hard is both the intellectual grasp needed, and the tremendous volume of work—especially coming from high school. It's just like drinking from a fire hose—all this stuff you've never seen before in your life. And there's none of the personal attention you're used to in high school. The pace is just incredible. You either sink or swim: and a lot of them end up sinking. (Male white science non-switcher)

When students speak about "overload," they reference several different aspects of curriculum demand, as well as the practices and attitudes which support them. In their first year, many students found they had undertaken too many courses in mathematics and science. This happened because they did not know what was involved, and followed the suggestions of advisors, or the ideal timetable laid out in the course sequence guide, before checking these recommendations against the experience of other students:

> They make you take too many courses. If I hadn't had such a heavy load in my freshman year, and struggled so badly with just the weight of it all, I'd probably still be in engineering today. (Female white engineering switcher)

> I was trying to take too big a load—18 credits. My advisors pushed me. You just felt kind of crummy if you didn't take at least 17 credits. (Female white engineering switcher)

Students quickly learned that the challenge facing them was not only intellectual; it was also physical and moral. To survive the constant round of assignments, problem sets, tests, lab work and reports required by several courses simultaneously, class work had to take precedence over all other educational interests, personal relationships, athletic commitments, social life, paid employment, leisure and sleep:

> It was just constant. You always had to prepare for class, or you'd lose it. It was constant quizzes and checking that you were on top of things. If you missed a day of lab, you couldn't make it up. You just had to work all the time, and you never got a break. (Female Hispanic science switcher)

I value my sleep. And I found this physics class was keeping me up until 3:00 a.m. every night, just to get everything done. When I finally dropped it, it was the happiest day of my life. (Female white science switcher)

Students discovered that the curriculum structure did not accommodate mistakes in deciding what classes to take, the sequence in which to take them, or the retaking of classes which had proved difficult:

I came in with a good G.P.A., and a math S.A.T. score of 740. But I ended up taking the second physics class over because I'd got a C. It was a passing grade, and I could have gone on to the next level, but I didn't feel adequately prepared. I got a B the second time, but by then I was a year behind and looking at a five year schedule—that's if I stayed on schedule the rest of the time, which I began to doubt. (Male white engineering switcher)

Once you have to retake any course in engineering, you're doomed. There's no way you can ever catch up. (Male white engineering switcher)

In my sophomore year I dropped circuit theory, which immediately put me a year behind. They have fall courses and spring courses. If you miss any one of 'em, you're a year behind. So that's when I first started to think about switching. (Male white engineering switcher)

There was also no allowance for illness, accident, or the death of a family member.

Students who needed more time than was allowed to think about class material were exasperated more with the pace than with the amount of the work:

Vertebrate zoology asks just as much as chemistry. It takes just as much time and comprehension, but I understood it and put as much effort into it. But with chemistry, they took it way too fast. It wasn't the amount of work. I don't mind working hard. But I want more time to absorb it. They are both hard subjects, but I can't see why one had to go so much faster than the other. (Female white science non-switcher)

They allow you one semester under 12 hours—and that's your whole career. There's some people who take 17 or 19 hours. I think they're crazy. They try to juggle, but eventually they burn out. I'm not willing to do that. I want time to think about what I'm doing. (Male white engineering non-switcher)

The suspicion that the pace in some classes was made deliberately faster than was really necessary was fairly widespread:

There's just too much work the first two years. The amount of pressure they put on you is mostly to see if you can stand up to them, not to make sure you understand what you're doing. I think it's kind of designed that way to weed people out. It's all a big test. (Male white engineering non-switcher)

However, seniors also accepted that at least some of the high volume of work demanded by their disciplines arose intrinsically from the nature of the task at hand. They could often clarify the different kinds of 'hardness' they had encountered in particular subjects, classes, or types of material:

> Calculus is the kind of thing where, unless you do the problems over and over again, you're not going to get it. It's not just memorization: you have to know how to do it. Genetics is a hard class too—for many of the same reasons. You just have to do so many problems just to understand it—that's mostly what makes those classes hard. (Female white science non-switcher)

> You can call analytic chemistry a weed-out course. But I don't think it's as hard as animal cell physiology. That's a harder class conceptually...Now, with organic chemistry—if you just put your mind to it, it's a lot of time more than anything else. (Male white science non-switcher)

Curricula designs were faulted for creating unnecessary 'hardness' where material was not presented in a logical sequence, or more commonly, where there was insufficient co-ordination with the syllabus structures of supporting disciplines—often mathematics:

> It's very difficult to do the physics when it's making use of material that you're not going to get for another month in calculus. (Male white engineering non-switcher)

Beyond basic classes, the pace and volume of class work continued to make the experience of S.M.E. majors 'hard' right through to senior year:

> You think you've been working hard as a freshman (laughing), but now you walk into 300-level classes and they're moving three to four times as fast, and covering information which you're expected to get out of a book. And you're covering two or three chapters a day. I mean, I don't want to be spoon-fed, but I also don't want to be so overwhelmed and so frustrated when I get behind, that there's no time to think about what you're doing—or why. (Male white science non-switcher)

> He's tremendously overworked—and has been for all four years. You know, I'll go to bed, and wake up, and he's still working. He had eight all-nighters recently. Last semester seemed to be worse. He'd get maybe three hours' sleep, and then the next night, he's got another project, so he'd have to manage with three hours again. And it's never abated right to this semester—which is his last. (Male white engineering switcher, speaking of his engineering room-mate)

We asked students to give examples of what exactly they found unreasonable about their work load. Their answers included the following:

> In my first engineering class, we were required to do 18 programs and three different languages over the semester. We were given algorithms to use for each program and just one week to complete each of them. And, though we went to all the labs, we weren't given any material. We were just expected to

know so much that, if someone wasn't willing to explain it to you, then you couldn't do the programs. (Male black engineering switcher)

Some profs will say, 'This is the textbook for this class, but you should also go and read these five or six reference books.' And that's asking a bit much when you've got six other classes. If they all did that, you'd have 30 to 40 books a semester to read. (Male white engineering switcher)

In physics, they will test us for the few things that they think are important—but they don't tell us what those are until after the test. I suppose they want you to see all this other stuff in case you go on to get a Ph.D. Once you've seen it, it's easier the second time around. But what about the rest of us? This is supposed to be an undergraduate degree. (Male white science non-switcher)

The main foci of their complaints were: doubts about the logic behind the choice or balance of particular materials in the curriculum; failure to teach (or to test) what had been chosen; failure to distinguish between materials of various degrees of significance; and, failure to co-ordinate with colleagues in planning either the sequence of presentation, or a coherent assignment and assessment strategy. In the view of undergraduates, all of these resulted in unnecessary overload:

I mean, there's too much material in 100-level classes. Does it *all* need to be covered—or covered in such detail? A lot of it is just syllabus stuffing. I'll give you an example. In the first inorganic freshman chemistry class for engineers, they quickly ran over some stuff. Later, in an honors organic with a professor who adored quantum mechanics, I realized that those equations we had scurried over as freshmen were actually related—in a very distant way—to the quantum mechanics he was teaching. If I hadn't just happened to have a professor interested in this field, would I, in a zillion years, ever have used that little corner of knowledge? The answer is, 'No.' And there were a whole lot of things like that—things which you never use—that they just tried to cram in. (Female white engineering non-switcher)

However, by far the commonest type of complaint, whether from switchers or non-switchers, concerned the relationship between classes and laboratory work, particularly the disproportionately small amount of credit labs received, given the large amount of time they took to complete:

Labs, labs. That's the key thing. *That's it!* They're just terrible. The field geology course gives only four credits, but people spend 40 hours a week on it. (Female white science non-switcher)

One reason for changing my major is that I spend more of my time preparing for labs than I do for lectures or assignments. But they are only one credit for a three-hour lab. (Female white science non-switcher)

I've spent more time in those one- or two-credit lab classes than in all the other classes combined. It's a big commitment of time for a small amount of credit. I think they do that so they can stay underneath the 45 credit-hour limit. Last semester, I took a one credit two-hour lab and spent very little time outside the lab—and that's what they encourage. The professor knows it's unreasonable. He says, 'This should be an eight-hour class; but there's all sorts of politics involved.' (Female white science non-switcher)

And it doesn't even make any sense. In engineering at the 300- and 400-level, there's so much variation between courses about what they expect for exactly the same credits. Just incredible amounts of work in some—like a 32 page report every week—just unnecessary work loads. (Male Hispanic engineering non-switcher)

Physics 429—atomic physics—it's insane the amount of work you have to do. It's supposed to meet five hours once a week, but it doesn't. It takes all of your time—all for three credit hours. And you have to produce two papers and submit them for publication. It's one of the reasons I finally dropped out of physics. (Male white science switcher)

Faculty were faulted for running labs on a syllabus different from that of the class, and for expecting their research assistants to teach extra syllabus material:

In organic chemistry, the profs look at them as two separate classes...You're trying to learn techniques which are totally different from the course material. There's some overlapping material, but the T.A. is supposed to cover both. And he can't. He's already got to cover the information for the lab. So now you are out on your own—sink or swim. I think that's the biggest problem. There's where we really started to lose people. (Male white science non-switcher)

There were three aspects of work demands which contributed most to switching. First came feeling overwhelmed (experienced by students who were well-prepared, and more acutely, by those who were not). Second, students experienced a downward spiral out of the major (usually within two semesters) which began by their falling behind in a particular class and attempting to repeat it. The third factor was a growing awareness that staying in the major involved making a choice about the kind of educational experience they really wanted. The volume and pace of early classes also conveyed the message that to follow science entailed giving up whatever else in life students valued, including full participation in college life. The inherent imbalance of S.M.E. curricula was critical in the decisions of these switchers:

It's really rough when they won't let you add a class outside of your field because you can't get the dean's approval. I couldn't believe that I wasn't required to take *any* kind of English class. I wanted to take it, and they kept refusing me. I think that's one of the things that pushes people like me away. (Female white mathematics switcher)

I'm more comfortable taking a 15 credit-hour load, working a 20 hour week, and having a little time for a few other things. It's having more of a sense of balance, and getting a fuller education. If all you're doing is studying one thing for four or five years, how do you know who you are when you're done? (Female white engineering switcher)

With all the classes that are gonna be required for you to graduate, you start to wonder if you are ever going to fit in anything that you want to study. That's when it becomes overwhelming. The people who finish get good jobs, but you wonder how much of a life they have...I think, unless they give you more freedom, they're just gonna lose more good people. (Female white mathematics switcher)

As these extracts suggest, the perception that one could only stay in the sciences at the expense of other valued parts of one's life was significant in the switching rationale of many women. Why this should be so is discussed in Chapter 5.

Every concern reflected in 'the problem iceberg' was presented in our informants' accounts along with a set of interrelated concerns. In all descriptions of the factors leading to the decision to leave or to stay, we found a 'push and pull' thought process at work. Feeling overwhelmed by curriculum demands was often the beginning of a process in which students questioned the wisdom of their initial choice, and began to think about other possibilities. The debate with self, and with others, about whether or not this was the right career path might continue for two semesters, or two years. However, it was always a complex matter, and involved issues of identity and a weighing of costs, benefits and alternatives. This process was almost always mediated by others: indeed, the need for an informed mediator was often the impetus to seek help from faculty or advisors. The final decision was often shaped by deadlines in the course calendar, provoked by a 'last straw' incident, or settled by the critical intervention of another person. The typical shape of the decision-making process (initially prompted by feelings of overload) was that of a downward spiral which, unless effective help and advice were found, brought a quick end to the agony:

Most people, once it spirals, it just gets worse and worse. Not that they can't stop it. They can. I mean, if somebody intervenes in that process to help you. But, usually, it just accelerates...In three quarters, you can be finished forever. Its kind of terrible. It's really up to you to take the initiative to try to talk to someone, but then comes the question, 'What do you really want?' Then comes the second quarter, and if you still don't do so well, you're on probation. So by the third quarter, you could be finished—if you don't want it bad enough. (Male black engineering switcher)

Whether one "wants it bad enough" is one of a number of critical issues usually included in reflections on curriculum overwhelm. Other inter-connecting questions are: will the effort of getting an S.M.E. degree ultimately be worth it; what kind of a lifestyle do careers imply; will there be support through other difficult times; how long will it take to graduate, and how to manage this financially. Wanting more out of life in college, and beyond, than seems possible with an S.M.E. degree, students caught in this downward spiral struggled to reconcile their low grades and feelings of overwhelm with a depleted sense of self-worth or began to recast their career options in the light of other talents or interest.

Engineering students were at greater risk of switching than other S.M.E. majors for reasons related to curriculum overload. Pace and load issues were a factor in 45.1 percent of the switching decisions of engineering students (compared with 25.0 percent for science and mathematics majors), and ranked second among reasons contributing to switching among engineering majors. They were raised as issues of concern by 55.0 percent of all engineering switchers (compared with 35.9 percent for science and mathematics switchers), and half (51.5%) of all engineering seniors (compared with 33.7 percent of science and mathematics seniors). Current and former engineering majors often described their colleges as guilty of tacit dishonesty in representing engineering as a four-year degree, both in official literature, and in the formal rhetoric of deans and advisors:

> To make it look like you can do this in four years, and to have all that pressure on you to make it happen, that's why people are so angry. They come in thinking they can do it in four years. And it's impossible for most people—without having a break-down. They build the argument that it's do-able on the exceptions, not the norm. (Male white engineering non-switcher)

> It's a matter of, 'We want you to take all these classes, and this is how we schedule all of it into four years.' I don't think that's right. It creates havoc. (Male white engineering non-switcher)

It is important to emphasize, that students do not suddenly discover their 'true vocation' as a consequence of struggling in the 'wrong' major for a semester or two. Students who had a facility with mathematics, and an interest in the sciences, but who were under-prepared for the freshman experience, or had set-backs in early classes, reported they could (or would) have persisted if help with these relatively common problems had been more available or better organized. Their search for an alternative major began *only after* the downward spiral was set in motion.

Other Perspectives on the 'Hardness' of S.M.E. Majors

Broadly, undergraduates distinguish between aspects of subject matter they see as inherently difficult to understand, and those which they see as made unnecessarily hard so as to perpetuate the image of science as 'hard majors'. Again, students often use 'hardness' to reference several different, but related, ideas in the same conversation. Seniors reported that the most frustrating attribute of some subject content was its illusiveness: regardless of level of effort expended in trying to grasp certain concepts, the leap to comprehension could seem entirely intuitive. The problem of how to "get it" was what made some parts of science and mathematics intrinsically hard:

> You grasp a concept, and then, it's *so* easy. And you can't explain it to the next person who doesn't get it. (Female Asian-American science switcher)

The ability to grasp concepts intuitively and quickly made survival at the early stages of the major more likely. Seniors also discussed the haunting sense of ideas which were "out there" just beyond their intellectual grasp: the more they understood, the more this illusive matter (which they sometimes referred to as "the real stuff") seemed to move further away:[1]

> You get through one theory, and you think you finally understand it, and then some joker says, 'Okay. That was the watered down part. Now, here's the real stuff.' They will always pull that rug from under you. Presumably, when you get to graduate school, they're finally gonna give you the real stuff. (Female white science non-switcher)

From a focus group of male and female science seniors—

> You've gotta kind of keep the faith—and that's hard to do.

> Yeah, hold onto that bible. (Laughter.)

> You know, eventually, you think you're gonna get this stuff. And in a form where you can do a good job with it—in research or whatever.

> What happens occasionally, I'll see something I've seen a thousand times before, but suddenly, I know what it is.

> Right. And, suddenly, you understand an awful lot more about the whole thing because some little piece of it just made sense.

> And, between times like that, you just do it, and do it.

> Yeah, it's a tease.

The suspicion that faculty make these insights harder to achieve by deliberate mystification was echoed in the concern that, notwithstanding the emphasis on proof, one is often expected to accept theoretical material as a matter of faith:

> With science, there are some things you are just asked to take for a fact— they're just given. But a lot of people can't accept that. They question what it means when you speak of 'a force.' (Female white science switcher)

> You never really know whether molecules exist. When I began organic chemistry, I kept thinking, 'How long did it take people to make up these stories?' You don't hear any kind of proof, and yet, you're supposed to look for proof to support an argument. You're taking a whole lot more on trust than

seems reasonable. It's sort of like hearsay. (Female white science non-switcher)

The highly abstract, theoretical nature of some of the material also made aspects of science and mathematics 'hard', as did the apparent paradox of working simultaneously with both the abstract and the concrete:

> The work doesn't get any easier as you get further in. It isn't until junior year that you start to get all the theory. (Male white engineering switcher)

> With chemistry, there's always a definite answer that you're looking for. It's almost easier, but its harder at the same time. (Female black science switcher)

Encountering intrinsically hard aspects of S.M.E. majors was made all the more frustrating when students observed the intuitive way in which some class-mates grasped abstractions which they could not seem to 'get' with any amount of effort:

> This friend of mine, he never studied. I would be there late at night trying to work on a problem. And I wouldn't get it. And I would try all night, every night, all week long, but he wouldn't even open a book. When we would meet him in the cafeteria at 9:00 p.m. the night before the assignment was due, he'd just be starting to work on the problem. And we'd all huddle around him to see how he did it. And he ended up with an A in that class. It was just natural talent. (Female white engineering switcher)

> He was getting the same grade as I was, but he was doing half the work. (Male white engineering non-switcher)

> I think it's like innate or inherent in you. It's kinda like people who don't understand calculus. It's not always something that can be learned with lots of studying. I didn't feel that engineering was difficult, or more difficult than any other major. It was just different. (Female white engineering non-switcher)

This discovery made it particularly painful for switchers to bear the common presumption that those who didn't do well, or who failed tests, did so because they were not working hard enough. The anger generated around this issue illustrates the conflict between the democratic norms of U.S. education, and the élitist norms of science as a transnational institution. That some people appear to have an 'aptitude' or 'gift' which allows them to grasp the abstractions of science and mathematics intuitively and succeed without trying, flouts the learned expectations of freshmen that they will succeed if only they try hard enough. The 'Little Red Engine' prescription for success is learned at an early age from family and teachers, and continues to be reinforced throughout pre-college education. Hard work remains the dominant explanation for success at college and is reinforced by parents, peers and S.M.E. faculty. By this usage of the term, science and mathematics are seen as 'hard' because they are seen as 'unfair'. Rewards seem to be given to people who do not necessarily try very hard, while faculty blame 'less gifted' students for not trying hard enough. This aspect of college science is especially demoralizing for all students who have been rewarded by high school teachers for 'effort' as well as for performance.

Another 'hard' aspect of science and mathematics is that comprehension and skills must be built sequentially, as in the acquisition of fluency in a foreign language:

> Engineering is an unforgiving major. You have to know your stuff...You can't just memorize, or think about how to solve this. You have to learn it to know how to do it. (Male white engineering non-switcher)

> Everything you learn is based on what you learned before, and if you don't understand a certain concept then it's gonna make it much more difficult to understand the succeeding concepts. In some other classes I've taken, if you miss one part, it's not really going to affect your understanding of another part. They're not so interdependent. (Male white engineering switcher)

Building this mental structure, and being able to use it effectively, are 'hard' partly because of the amount of work required:

> It's the kind of thing where, although you can memorize the formulas, unless you also do the problems over and over again, you're not going to get it, or know how to do it. Those are the harder classes. (Female white science non-switcher)

However, this intrinsic difficulty is increased if faculty fail to structure the material in a way that allows students to build these steps, and make the necessary conceptual connections. In this sense, science and mathematics are 'hard', both intrinsically and non-intrinsically, because so much depends on the efficacy with which faculty structure the presentation of materials:

> If you have a class that deals with things you've never had in any other class—just completely unrelated concepts—and you have to pick them up right away, because the whole class is based around them—that's difficult. I can think of a couple of classes like that, and it was one of the things that really bothered me. (Male white engineering switcher)

From a focus group discussion among male and female senior science majors—

> In any class, I see how much there is, and how much I actually got out of it, and how much he tried to present that I didn't understand. Or, I'm looking through the book and I see all this other stuff that is meaningless to me....

> Or, you walk into a class, and they start lecturing on things you didn't know existed.

> And then they say, 'We're gonna have a test on this.' And you're thinking, 'Really?'

> I think that's disturbing to a lot of people. It's disturbing to me.

Students also understood that acquiring the competence to do science well involved a great deal of repetition in the working of problems and in memorization. This too was seen as hard. They were dubious, however, whether repetition and memorization were necessary to the degree to which faculty demanded them:

> The way they teach in engineering is basically through repetition. They show you something in class, and then you do homework problems on it. (Male white engineering non-switcher)

> And when you're an engineer, you'd darn well better know how to memorize. I guess I had an advantage, 'cause I do have those memorization skills. Other people might think it out—use their heads—use common sense. But engineers aren't into common sense! (Female white engineering switcher)

> All I remember about organic chemistry is memorizing these high reaction processes. All of that good stuff, just forgotten. (Male white science non-switcher)

Undergraduates accepted that some of the subject matter and skills needed to do science are inherently 'hard'. However, they constantly questioned whether faculty conspired to make their learning experiences harder than they needed to be. Nowhere is this questioning more evident than in students' use of "hardness" to describe the all-demanding nature of S.M.E. majors. Persistence was portrayed, in large part, in terms of moral fiber, physical stamina, and the capacity to tolerate frustration, loneliness and self-doubt:

> Science is hard, tense, always focused. Just to use another part of my thoughts is relaxing. (Female black science non-switcher)

> You can never sit down and read a book that's not related to school—that's a luxury. (Male white engineering non-switcher)

> It's a hard field. It's risky to study it, I think, for your ego, and friendships suffer. (Female white engineering switcher)

> You usually have nobody to help you, or discuss it with you. You're out there on your own...And you have this pressure on you the whole time. It takes everything from you. It takes all the time you've got. I think I had one Saturday off the whole semester. I left my apartment at 8:00 a.m. every morning, and I was never back before 11:00 p.m. at night. And I was jogging in the middle of the day, because if I didn't do that, I couldn't keep it up. (Female white engineering non-switcher)

> You can spend hours—I mean, 10 to 12 hours—just trying to figure out what's going on, and not even get to a point where you can solve it...It's hard just because of the amount of time required. (Male Hispanic engineering non-switcher)

> I have a friend who managed to complete a civil engineering degree in four years—one of the few who could pull that off. But it cost him his girl friend—quite literally. 'Cause I've seen him look at his watch, and say, 'I haven't talked to her in a month.' He'd wake up and realize it had been that long. Eventually, she said, 'Sorry, I don't remember what you look like anymore.' (Male white science non-switcher)

The moral challenge which makes S.M.E. majors 'hard' is partly created by living alongside non-S.M.E. undergraduates whose time is not totally consumed by class work, who seem to do less work for more credit, and whose majors require fewer credit hours for graduation:

> I was living in a dormitory where everyone else was a liberal arts major. And they seemed to have much less work to do and were getting As, while I was struggling for Bs and Cs—which I thought was terribly unfair. (Female white engineering non-switcher)

The 'cruel mistress' paradox of science and mathematics described by seniors is that only by total immersion in the discipline and willingness to submit to all its demands, does one find the excitement of science which most students who entered it hoped to experience:

> Science can be so scary, because so many people rely on it, and there's something new being discovered every day. It changes constantly, and it's so tough to learn. There's so much to know. But that's what makes it exciting for me. It's a challenge. And a lot of people see it as too much of a challenge, or get scared by it—like with organics, which is one of the toughest classes, because you have to eat and sleep organics. (Female white science non-switcher)

By contrast, some students perceived their major as more demanding than the discipline itself required:

> It teaches you to learn things quickly, and how to survive. And those skills aren't necessarily relevant to what I consider a good engineering curriculum...A good engineer and a good survivor aren't the same thing. I shouldn't have to worry about how to get an A. I should be going into class to learn what's important. (Male Hispanic engineering non-switcher)

Students also wondered if developing an ability to cope with an over-demanding major might not become addictive. They described the appeal of being seen as the kind of person who can "hack it." The respect this brings from peers or outsiders can become a reward for persistence in and of itself. It also helps to perpetuate the image of the 'hard' S.M.E. major among other undergraduates:

> Most of my engineering friends think engineering is hard. But they are always telling each other, 'This is so hard.' They pull all-nighters and abuse their bodies with caffeine and lack of sleep. They get through it because they want

to, or because they feel they need to be someone. You have to be a really driven person to do it, I think. (Female white engineering switcher)

The fortitude shown by survivors reinforces the self-doubts of those who leave. As is hinted in the extract above (and as we shall discuss in more detail), women in these majors often find demonstrations of 'hard men doing hard things' off-putting, alarming, or fuel for further self-doubt:

> It's all hard core, and it's largely male. (Female white engineering non-switcher)

> I think the general feeling is that I just couldn't hack it. (Female white engineering switcher)

> It's immediately assumed that you either weren't bright enough, or that you weren't capable of handling it. And I do feel inferior—like I wasn't capable of handling it—although I really doubt that too. (Female white engineering switcher)

Subtly, the argument that some aspects of the subject matter are intrinsically 'hard' is transformed into the basis for moral judgements through the ways in which curricula are constructed, taught and assessed. Not only is the 'aptitude' or intelligence of switchers in question, so too is their moral worth (which faculty define largely in terms of their capacity for hard work). However, as many seniors point out, the amount of work demanded by faculty may, or may not, be dictated by the intrinsic hardness of the material they are teaching, and high rewards are often given to those who do not work particularly hard but who have a good intuitive grasp of the subject. Part of the 'hardness' of S.M.E. majors, therefore, includes the projection and perpetuation of an *image* of 'hardness'. It functions to reward those who persist with an enhanced self-image and social reputation. Latently, it protects the non-intrinsic, socially-constructed aspects of 'hard' majors from arguments favoring changes in curriculum design or pedagogy. Students often suspect that there is something slippery about the ways in which faculty speak of the 'hardness' of their discipline. They make their own distinctions between what is and is not inherently hard about subject material, and question the rationale for the inclusion of particular subject content, and for some teaching and assessment methods:

> This ridiculous computer programming and graphics stuff needn't have been so heavily emphasized in the first semester. A lot of it was really bogus. (Female white engineering non-switcher)

> I don't think the fundamentals of chemistry are that difficult to grasp. It's very logical. But I think they do *make* it harder than it needs to be. (Female Asian-American science switcher)

One 'hard' aspect of S.M.E. majors which students see as entirely socially-constructed is the encouragement of competitive, rather than collaborative, learning. This is especially puzzling to students who discover that working together on problems and projects enhances comprehension, provokes intellectual debate, and provides the emotional support necessary to persist. Seniors almost universally cited collaborative learning strategies as an important way to address intrinsically hard material:

> A lot of the students felt threatened—felt they had to compete against the other students. They would not even associate with other members of the class as far as getting the homework or programs done. (Male black engineering switcher)

> It's very important to sit at a table together and to be able to make little jokes about the work, just to get a strong sense of support from people who understand you can spend four hours on one problem. It's just very important to be around other people who are making the same type of commitment. (Female black engineering switcher)

Discussion in a focus group of female engineering switchers—

> It seemed in a lot of classes you were actually discouraged from working together—'You *can't* work together on homework,' is how it was put.

> Yeah, they make a point of being anal-retentive about the plagiarism rules. They make a lot of students look at studying together as one possible way of getting busted—even if its not a violation of the rules.

> Yeah. It has a very chilling effect.

We shall explore the significance of 'the competitive S.M.E. culture' and peer group learning further.

The Significance of Grades

Almost one quarter (23.0%) of switchers reported that problems with grades, especially in early classes, were a factor in their decision to leave the major. A third of all switchers cited grade-related issues as having caused some level of difficulty. By contrast, 12.5 percent of non-switchers cited grades as having been, or continuing to be, problematic. Although switchers and persisters do not experience the same level of difficulty with grades, it is surprising that the difference between them is not greater. On the basis of conventional wisdom, we expected grade-related problems to figure rather more than they did in switching decisions, and rather less in the accounts of persisters. In this section, we explore some aspects of the relationship between grades and attrition as illuminated by our data.

In our overview of findings, we presented data to support our hypothesis that differences in performance scores of switchers and non-switchers at this level of ability are insufficient to predict which students are likely to stay and which to leave. We have also argued that women who, as a group, have been identified at high risk of switching, often leave S.M.E. majors with grades which are as high, or higher, than the average grades of men who remain. We also illustrated our contention that students competent to complete S.M.E. majors are often lost, and that these losses include some highly talented students. Finally, by drawing our selection line at 650, or above, in S.A.T. mathematics (or equivalent) scores, the students included in our sample should have reported fewer problems with low grades than would a less selective sample of S.M.E. freshmen and sophomores.

Predicting which students are more or less likely to leave S.M.E. majors by establishing statistical relationships between performance scores and persistence outcomes is difficult, partly because the 'fit' between the two is always imperfect, and partly because this relationship does not take into account how people respond to the grades they receive. Grades are not objective, neutral, facts about people; they are labels to which people react emotionally, and in terms of behavioral and identity adjustments. Our data offer some insights into the relationships between grades, feelings, identity, and action which have relevance for attrition and persistence.

Some students abandon their original intention to major in an S.M.E. discipline for grade-related reasons: their preparation is not as good as their high school grades would suggest; they are admitted, or allowed to take basic classes, despite marginal grades; they get poor grades because they do not settle down to college work quickly enough, or simply do not work hard enough. Our data provide examples of students for whom one or more of the above statements would, by their own accounts, be accurate. However, at this level of demonstrated mathematical ability, we did not expect, and did not find, these to be dominant factors in our informants' relationships with grades. For example, we encountered students who chose to leave S.M.E. majors although their grades were as good, or better, than those who remained:

> I got quite a negative reaction when I quit—just from the fact that I was still doing fairly well in classes when I made the decision to leave. (Female white engineering switcher)

> My first year, I did really well—like 3.8. And it was a real surprise to people, like my mother, that I wanted to change my major—because I was doing so well. And I told her, 'It's not that it's hard. I just don't want to do it.' After that, my grades dropped off a bit, because I wasn't sure what I wanted to do—and that was purely through lack of interest. Last semester, after I had officially changed my major, they went back up to a 4.0. (Female white mathematics switcher)

We also encountered students whose grades (and whose decisions based upon them) were seriously affected by illness or a family crisis. The effects of such emergencies are exacerbated by a curriculum pace which makes no allowance for them, and by lack of good advising:

> I got an A in calculus, and a B in chemistry, then, in the winter, I got very ill and missed about two weeks of class. Instead of just dropping out, I tried to catch up. And I couldn't do it. I didn't fail, but I didn't do well either. At that point, I just thought, 'Oh, forget it,' and transferred out. If I had dropped out for that quarter and started again in the spring, I think everything would have been okay. Right now, I would probably be thinking about teaching chemistry, or being a chemical engineer. (Female Asian-American science switcher)

However, by far the commonest way in which grades affected switching decisions was through the shock to ego caused by introductory class grades which were far lower than those to which students had been accustomed in high school. This issue has already been raised as one facet of the way that high schools under-prepare students for college. Here we describe how that experience translates into an attrition risk. Typical early grade-shock accounts read as follows:

> You've been getting As and Bs, and you don't have to do any homework, and you just coast through and get good grades. Then you hit college, and it really, really slaps you up to get your first Cs. (Male white science switcher)

> I was always at the top of my class in high school for math and science, but when I got into college science classes, I was only getting mediocre grades. I think that was the biggest problem. I could do the work okay, but I didn't feel comfortable being in the middle after always being at the top. (Male white science switcher)

> By my second mid-term, I was still pulling around the mean—which is okay—even pretty good. But I was still a B- or C+, which is horrible for someone who does well in high school and is accepted into a school as good as this. I mean, I never got a B until I got to college. It was very discouraging. (Female Asian-American engineering switcher)

These accounts raise the question of what it is that allows some people to persist despite the discouragements wrought by the experience of low grades in basic classes, while others, whose grades may be similar or even better, do not. The following account gives some of the clues:

> I think the hardest thing is, you're used to getting As and Bs. And then you come to college and you're, like, an 'A' or a 'C'. It's really a kick in the head...And it's hard, because you're working just as hard and applying yourself just as much, and you're still a 'C'...It makes you feel awful. You can't focus on what you're doing: you always have to look at everybody else. (Female white engineering non-switcher)

The key problem is that, throughout their pre-college education, students have been encouraged to use grades as an extrinsic measure of comprehension, progress, and self-worth. Over time, students come to see a person who receives A grades as an 'A' kind of person. The grade becomes detached from its origin in particular teachers' judgments of particular pieces of work and becomes a defining element in identity and self-esteem. As with all extrinsic measures of self-worth, the self-image becomes vulnerable to external evaluation: if receiving A grades over time bestows the feeling one must be worthy of them, by the same logic, receiving Cs and Ds implies a much lower level of personal worth. A policy of tough grading for freshmen and sophomores accomplishes more, therefore, than bringing lazy high school graduates face to face with the hard realities of academic work. It also has the potential to undermine the sense of self-worth of students with good study habits and a wide range of abilities:

> A lot of people let their self-esteem get caught up in their grades. So when their grades are going down they are pretty miserable. (Female white engineering switcher)

Survival requires that students redefine the purpose of grades, and re-evaluate their criteria for self-esteem. In the following example, a non-switching senior describes how close she came to switching as a freshman. Receiving just one D in a steady record of As was sufficient to make her question whether she was good enough to be in college at all:

> You look at all these As, and then there's freshman biology—a D. I have no idea what happened. It was terribly frustrating. And I seriously thought that whole terrible semester, 'Why am I here?' I really questioned whether I should be here. (Female white science non-switcher)

Students also arrive in college having learned to detach grades from the processes of comprehension and skills acquisition:

> You're conditioned from age five, or whenever you start school, that you work for a grade. You don't work to learn. (Female white engineering non-switcher)

Students have learned to use grades as an indication that they understand the material and/or are interested in it—whether or not this is true. As objects detached from their purpose, grades become more important than the knowledge used to acquire them or than the student's awareness of how well they understand the material:

> When I came to college, I felt like I came for the grade, not the knowledge—for the grade—just any way you could get it. (Male white engineering non-switcher)

> A lot of the people in the class are very disappointed with the average. They don't think they are learning anything because the average is so low. (Female white engineering switcher)

> If I hadn't felt perfectly comfortable that I was grasping everything, but I was still getting good grades, I would have felt reassured that I was getting what I was supposed to out of it. If I had been getting good grades, I would have been comfortable with the material. (Female white engineering switcher)

As we discussed in the section on conceptual difficulties, 12.6 percent of switchers left partly because they felt they did not understand salient parts of the curriculum. Here we are concerned with students who used their grades as their main indication that they had insufficient understanding to stay. The habit of judging oneself by the grades one receives, and of focusing on getting particular grades, more than on understanding the material, does not necessarily fade in college:

> It seems like a lot of people don't care if they are getting it or not—in the sense of understanding it. And that's how I was at 19 just out of high school—surviving just by hook or by crook. (Male white engineering non-switcher)

> I've a friend in my classes who wants his As, and gets pissed if he gets a B. He hasn't gotten a B since the second grade. He might get one this semester, and it's upsetting him a lot. (Male white engineering non-switcher)

> When I first got to college, I just got this big fear that I was never gonna get As again...But, I'm like back in gear, and I get 'em now. And it means everything to me. I can't stand getting anything lower than a B right now. (Female white engineering non-switcher)

> I was getting low Cs for my programming grades, and I didn't think that spending that much time for such a low grade was worth my effort. So that's when I decided to change my major. I changed to business, and since then, I've been getting a 4.0 G.P.A., and I've been *extremely* happy with where I am. (Male white science switcher)

Not only does seeking to define oneself as a winner, rather than as a learner, persist in college; it continues to be reinforced by people significant to students—their peers, parents, employers, program directors, and faculty:

> It is very competitive, but they only look at the top grades—and the rest are kind of lumped together over there. They just write them off. They just look at the top, and everyone else has to fend for themselves. And that made it very difficult—I mean, it definitely lowers your self-esteem—to be just forgotten about as one of the lesser beings...I mean, if someone had given me some indication that, even with a C, I could pull through, I think I'd have had a better chance. (Female white engineering switcher)

> I was really disgusted when I would get my report card, and find my G.P.A. ran to four decimal places. My whole life was based on this G.P.A. That was just hammered into me by R.O.T.C. The attitude was, 'We don't care what you do, just so long as you get your G.P.A. up.' I feel like I'm over the hump. I can't say I don't go through the emotional swings any more, but they're not as wild and wide as they used to be. (Male black engineering switcher)

> When you're a pre-med student, it's very rough, because they're always comparing how you're doing with everyone else the whole way along. The

people who know who else is going to med school talk about it all the time. (Female white science non-switcher)

In my department, which is small, you can get tagged as a B student or an A student. The professors talk about their students, and they're either subliminally or consciously influenced as to what kind of student you are expected to be from the first day of class. (Male white science switcher)

As some students clearly appreciated, traditional assessment practices also help to perpetuate the use of grades as extrinsic measures of self, and as the central objective of class participation. Curve-grading, especially, functions to reify grades and detach them from their pedagogical purpose:

And something is wrong with the test; something's wrong with the teaching; something's wrong somewhere. I've taken so many courses where the class average was below 50, and you get that feeling of hopelessness. And, yet, I know I'm above average, and I'll get a B overall. It's a game, I think. But what worries me about it is, three or four years down the road, am I really gonna understand the material I just crammed for a test, and didn't know one word of? (Male white engineering non-switcher)

In the weed-out courses, they make the exams so needlessly difficult that people just drop out. They study as hard as they can, go to class every day, try to get their homework, and then they take the exam and get a 65 on it—and the class average is 63. And it makes you feel terrible. But, even if you get wise, and realize that you're going to get a B out of it, what's the point, if I feel like I learned nothing from the course? (Female white engineering non-switcher)

It is difficult for students to break old ways of thinking about the relationship between grades, educational objectives, and self-esteem, as long as faculty assessment systems continue to reinforce them. The commonest criticism of existing assessment practices was the lack of fit between the grade awarded, and the level of comprehension which students felt they had attained, the standard of work they had demonstrated, or the amount of effort they had expended:

My boyfriend, he's going crazy, and this is his fourth year. Because the classes are so hard. He gets a 56, and the average is 54 or something. It's *very frustrating*. The professors need to do something with the exams so they test understanding of what needs to be learned. I feel students should leave with a sense of accomplishment—feel that they learned something—so that, when they go on to the next course, they'll say, 'Oh, I remember that from before.' (Female white engineering switcher)

Seniors also expressed concerns about the contrary situation whereby the grading structure allowed students who knew they did not really understand the material to end up with a reasonable grade:

> I've handed in bad papers and gotten good grades. And that really bothers me, because I feel like they're not grading hard enough. I want my grade to reflect what I understand and what I don't. (Female white engineering switcher)

> I ended up getting a good grade, but not knowing *anything* about FORTRAN. I totally bombed the final on that section, and I still got a B. And it was like, 'How come I should get a B when I'm not getting it?' (Male white engineering switcher)

Curve-grading allows a high degree of separation between comprehension and performance on the one hand, and reward on the other. It can also make grades seem totally arbitrary:

> Something new this last year that was totally shocking to me was that, in most classes, the instructor has a grade quota. He has to give out so many As and Bs. (Female white engineering switcher)

Students also questioned the purpose and ethics of grade manipulation which made freshmen feel useless, hopeless, and incompetent:

> You feel terrible your first year, and you just repeat that old thing, 'Well, everyone does badly their first year.' But *why* does everyone do badly in their first year? I suppose the idea is that they can look back and say, 'Now I see what I should have done.' They work real hard and by the end they're okay. But, you lose good people. People should do well in their first year. And that way, I bet they'd do well all the way through. (Male black engineering switcher)

One of the counter-productive consequences of the weed-out approach is that it reinforces the tendency to focus on tests (and on how to pass them), and upon 'getting' the material as a by-product of getting the grade. Freshmen develop resentments about the 'unfairness' of S.M.E. majors because trying hard doesn't necessarily lead to success, and goes unrecognized by faculty:

> His first D was a real shock to him, because he had been used to working hard—not just kicking back and passing classes easily—but working hard and doing well. And he believed that the working hard went with the doing well. But when he worked hard here and still got a D, he couldn't understand that. He was very angry and upset. (Male white science switcher)

In the face of poor early test grades, freshmen fall back on the same strategies for getting good grades that they learned in high school: they try harder, they cram, they try to work out what it is that the teacher 'really wants to know', and they cheat:

> People just kind of became discouraged. Instead of learning—they just tried to manipulate the tests. (Male white mathematics switcher)

> The second semester chemistry professor went pretty quickly, and gave really long assignments, and people would get frustrated and give up trying to do it.

So if they wanted to pass the tests, they felt cheating was the only thing they could do. (Female white science non-switcher)

The people sitting at the back? Well, there's a couple of possibilities. Their homework's not done and they're doing it; or their homework's not done, and they're copying it!—(laughing)—which happens. I mean, it happens quite a bit. (Male white engineering non-switcher)

I do find a lot of cheating in the College of Engineering. They'll give you a three-part homework, and one person will each take a part, and the other two copy their answers. And that's something I'm not used to...There's always that weed-out pressure for you to get on, or get out. (Male white engineering switcher)

From a focus group of male white engineering seniors—

They'll copy it—I mean, that happens quite a bit.

And who knows if the professor knows—if your work is correct.

Sometimes the T.A. realizes it, and they'll ask you to come in...But it's hard to differentiate whether it's your own work or if it's copied, as everybody's work should be the same.

Interviewer: Is cheating an accepted way of surviving?

Maybe—through the unwritten code.

I'm not sure. I mean, I've done it in a jam, and it's like, I know I'm not gonna get caught because the chances are one in a 100.

And, if I don't get the 10 points, it just shoots my grade way down at the bottom of the list...because everyone else is doing it—you know, getting together to get it all done.

So if you don't do it, you lose...So if I get the grade, but not the education, well, one out of two is better than none out of two.

Interviewer: Is that a fairly common way of looking at it?

Yeah.

Because you're competing, and you don't know what the standard is.

In classes where work demands seemed unreasonable, and the assessment system implied that the main objective was to beat class-mates to a good grade, cheating was discussed as logical and predictable. It was not, however, legitimated, because, in an arbitrary (curve-grading) situation, it gave one's competitors an edge.

How undergraduates respond to their first experiences of grades that are much lower than those to which they are accustomed is critical to their survival in the major. This is as critical for students with good potential as it is for those who are academically marginal. It is as true for students who are doing reasonably well as it is for students who are doing worse than average. Throughout this section, we have sought to explain why this should be so. Where feelings of disappointment, frustration, anger, faculty unfairness, and above all, plummeting self-esteem, are not countered by redefinition of the task and affirmation of self, these affective responses to low grades accelerate the downward spiral out of the major. Typically, this process begins with discovery that one is under-prepared (in any sense) for the level of understanding or work demanded in early S.M.E. classes; it continues with the ego-shock of grades by which students—who had defined themselves as 'good' (or at least competent)—redefine themselves as 'incompetent'. When old high school strategies, including trying harder, seem much less effective than hitherto in securing higher grades, self-doubt, panic and depression increase. Some students seek help; many do not—or do so at too late a stage, because they believe they are supposed to "hack it" alone. (This response is reinforced in classes where working collaboratively is defined as plagiarism.) Some find the guidance and reassurance they need; most do not. As their sense of hopelessness increases, students begin to skip classes, isolate from peers, do less work, understand less and less, do even worse in exams, fail and leave:

> Once you get a little lost, then there's that dread of going to class and just sitting there, and not knowing what's going on. It just made it easier for me not to go. (Female white science switcher)

> I gradually came to dislike it...And I hated going to class because I felt I didn't know anything. After that, my grades got so poor, I just got into that downward cycle. (Male white engineering switcher)

> Anybody who's smart enough can muddle through anything. But when you get failing grades, and you're getting depressed, you lose interest. Once you stop going to classes, that tends to get you outta there *fast*. (Female white engineering switcher)

It is precisely because the relationship between students and their grades is reactive and cumulative over time that it is difficult to explain why some students leave and others do not by examination of their grade patterns alone. Once a student's negative reactive spiral begins, their grades and self-assessments chase each other downwards. Switching becomes a means to escape from a situation in which students continually feel badly about themselves. Seniors accounts of their early grade-related crises often stress how closely they came to switching, and how a timely intervention by faculty, senior students, or peers was critical to their decision to stay. For those who find the kind of academic or personal help they need at the right time, the downward grade spiral can be reversed.

Seniors described it as essential to re-focus their learning objectives, accept an average grade and trust their own judgement about how well they understood the material. Making this attitude shift, after years of socialization in the opposite direction, may not be easy:

> I try to look at it my sister's way, 'cause she's always telling me that if you've got a low grade, but you really got something from the class, then it's okay. I keep trying to tell myself that when I don't do well, but it's hard for me. I've thought about transferring, too—it's a hard decision. (Female Hispanic science switcher)

> I think that's the only thing that saves people—at least in physics and math—is to say, 'At least I'm doing average. Everyone else is right along with me.' (Female white engineering non-switcher)

Survival techniques varied, but most included some unlearning of attitudes towards grades. Students reframed faculty grading practices as a game which they had also learned to play; took time out from college to gain perspective; and overcame despair by focusing on their interest in the discipline. They cited employers, former teachers, older students, and faculty who had helped them distance their grades from their self-image, and valued faculty whose methods emphasized comprehension over performance snap-shots:

> I was nervous 'cause he didn't give quizzes and tests. We did some assignments, but they weren't graded. What we did was to read, and come to class to discuss the material. And Dr. J--- really taught us. He stressed that we should understand it really well, and be able to apply it. I was nervous the whole semester because I didn't know what my grade was. But I gradually began to realize that he wanted you to concentrate on learning. The second class I had from him, I just loved it. Right from the start, I went in there to learn...I'd love all the classes to be taught like that. But I suppose it's not possible, because for most people, the grade's the motivating factor, not the learning. (Female white engineering non-switcher)

A totally different way of coping was not to reverse the instrumental attitude to grades, but to extend it to the point where grades are seen simply as a commodity—as the main return for the cost of a college education. If S.M.E. faculty fail to deliver the kinds of grades one needs for career purposes (entry to a good medical school, or a well-paid job with an employer who is grade-conscious), then it makes sense to switch before too much damage is done to one's G.P.A. Switching as a form of 'system-playing' (discussed in Chapter 4) was reported in 7.1 percent of switching decisions.

The Competitive Culture

The degree to which an instrumental attitude towards education is reinforced depends on the culture of particular S.M.E. colleges and departments. The strength of the competitive atmosphere in S.M.E. majors varied between campuses and disciplines. However, it varied much less between campuses than we had expected. We were surprised to find evidence of competitive cultures in the science and mathematics departments of smaller institutions whose philosophy stresses collaborative learning and a well-rounded educational experience. Though the competitive pressure was less than in the research universities, it was strong enough for students in these smaller institutions to make invidious comparisons with disciplines which they felt better exemplified the traditions of liberal education.

We suggest that the national, possibly international, norms of science education favor individual competition rather than collaborative learning in the early stages of undergraduate education. These traditions may transcend the liberal culture of particular types of institutions or individual campuses. In the two smaller campuses in our sample (including the private liberal arts college), the competitive atmosphere experienced by students in science and mathematics classes was less than that experienced by their counterparts in other types of institutions. However, compared with classes in other disciplines, S.M.E. classes followed the same competitive tradition as other institutions.

This tradition may have grown out of two essentially unrelated beliefs: that the ability to do science and mathematics is relatively rare, and that those who possess it are of stronger moral character than those who do not. The competitive ethos of science may be especially strong in the United States, partly because of its tradition of rugged individualism, and partly because of its highly local system of education. A generalized nervousness about adopting mandatory national curriculum standards, or developing statewide assessment systems (on other than a voluntary basis)[2] as the criteria for entry to higher education is one reason for large intake classes that must be reduced to fit departmental resources. This reduction process also meets faculty's need to identify that small number of 'good' students which they expect to find among the larger number of freshman entrants they must initially accommodate. These essentially non-educational objectives support the competitive culture found in most S.M.E. departments.

Dislike of the highly competitive approach to education found in S.M.E. classes was a factor in 14.8 percent of switching decisions and a source of complaint for 28.4 percent of switchers overall. It was not a major problem for seniors, of whom only 9.2 percent mentioned it as such. This finding squares with seniors' observations that the uncomfortable competitive atmosphere usually only lasts for the first two years. Early in their junior year, students reported a dramatic change in faculty's approach to teaching, in attitude toward collaborative learning, and in personal behavior towards undergraduates:

> The toughness and pace of those classes is probably part of the system, because, when you get past them, suddenly, they make the material more interesting. You get to review things, and sometimes the professor even bucks you up: 'You're not doing well—come on, get with it.' They start to give you just a little bit of encouragement. (Female white science non-switcher)

And, all of a sudden, you're working in a group. And it seemed like something totally new, and we weren't used to co-operating with everyone else to get something done. (Female white engineering non-switcher)

Students who resisted these new norms of collegiality became the new deviants:

After that point, there develops a kind of camaraderie. But there are still the other people—the curve-breakers. There's one female physics major in our graduating class. She's incredibly smart, and she won't share her information with anybody. (Male white mathematics non-switcher)

Seniors, therefore, concluded that the competitive atmosphere of their introductory classes was not a 'natural' phenomenon, but had been socially engineered. Many switchers had also come to the conclusion that students were deliberately set up to fight the curriculum, the professor and each other:

The competition in these classes is so great because professors only want to give out so many As, Bs, and Cs. Otherwise, it makes them look like their class isn't challenging enough. They want to disperse the grade across the curve. (Male white science switcher)

The teacher sets the level of competition by his own grading policy. In chemical engineering, people didn't want to help you unless you were gonna be able to help them. (Female white engineering switcher)

They noticed that competitiveness was usually greatest in majors leading directly to a professional career, mainly engineering and the 'pre' health majors. For some students who had intended to pursue these careers, the competitive atmosphere became a factor in their change of mind; for those in other S.M.E. majors, who shared classes with profession-bound students, it diminished their educational experience:

I really didn't like the entry bio core class I took last year, because it was so cut-throat. The whole point of it is to make sure that only a certain percentage of the pre-meds get good enough grades to get into med school. I'm glad that's the last course that I have to take with pre-meds. (Female white science non-switcher)

It would have been easier if there hadn't been such competition between all the pre-meds and the engineering students in our classes. It was just *intense*. (Female white science switcher)

The word 'pre-med' conjures up a lot of fear in a lot of other people: 'I guess I'm outta this class, because I don't want to be swamped by pre-meds.' Because these people are gonna raise the competition level. (Female white science switcher)

Students also observed that competition was not an inevitable function of large class size. Large classes in other disciplines were not necessarily competitive:

> Civics was a huge class. But it's required, and you feel you're in it together,
> It seems to induce co-operation. So size isn't what creates competition.
> Philosophy was a huge class also. I assume it's how important you think the
> class is to your future. (Male white science switcher)

It was also thought likely that external economic factors encouraged competitive learning environments:

> They don't come out and say it, but the better your grades, the better your
> placement in graduation, the better your job offers. And everybody's always
> scrambling for the best job available. (Male Hispanic engineering non-
> switcher)

> People don't want to become friends, because they're worried about someone
> calling them up, asking about notes, and this or that question, or wanting help
> in the lab...In a business class, you always have someone you can call on, and
> they're always willing to give notes, because in accounting there are lots of
> jobs. So they're not so worried. But in zoology, you're always worried about
> getting into med school—and it's just gonna get worse. (Female white science
> switcher)

Curve-grading is the engine which drives the competitive atmosphere in early S.M.E. classes. It is this, above all, which makes students fearful of sharing their work or their ideas:

> It's very cut-throat. Everybody's struggling to be in that top percentage. And
> everything is curve-graded. As far as people leaving the College of Engineer-
> ing, I think that might be something to fear. (Female white engineering
> switcher)

> The key was to break the curve, break the curve. People would study all
> night—and you couldn't study with your friends—you couldn't exchange
> information. It was very intensive. (Male white science switcher)

Curve-grading forces students to compete with each other, whether they want to or not, because it exaggerates very fine degrees of difference in performance. Where there is little or no difference in work standards, it encourages a struggle to create it. From a focus group of white male engineering seniors:

> I mean, some people will take their project or their homework and will put it
> on a MacIntosh laser printer, print it, bind it, and hand it in...I call that
> brown-nosing.

> And if one person starts doing it, then everyone has to follow suit.

> Because you're competing for a grade.

> You definitely compete for grades in engineering; whereas you earn grades in
> other disciplines...I have to get one point higher on the test than the next guy
> so I can get the higher grade.

> You're set a moving standard.

Right. And because everything's computerized, it's real easy for them to rank you just by telling the computer to, 'Rank in descending order.' And it will be printed up by student numbers—they barely use names. And it's all just a fraction of a point here or there. It's really tough.

Students criticized forced competition as counter-productive to getting a good basic education in science and mathematics from a number of standpoints. In the first place, competition perpetuates the high school habit of focusing on the grade, rather than on the learning experience:

They weren't really into learning the material—just memorizing it for the exams, where they could regurgitate it, and get that grade...I mean, it's nice to get an A, but, an A is worth nothing if you don't understand what you are doing. I'd rather get a C and understand what I did, than get an A and totally forget what is going on. (Female black science switcher)

It was an uncomfortable atmosphere: everyone was in a bad mood all the time—a competitive mood which emphasized success to the exclusion of anyone's ability to enjoy the learning process. And *that*, more than anything else, is one of the main things that made me rethink what I wanted to do. (Female white engineering switcher)

They also felt that curve grading encouraged students to narrow their educational objectives, and limit their intellectual and social horizons:

I almost think that some of my class-mates are pathetic. They don't know how to write an effective paper...or how to communicate. (Male Hispanic engineering non-switcher)

That's all they talked about is school. It seems like engineers have so few outside interests—to go out and do things—that drives me away. (Female white engineering non-switcher)

Competition based on curve-grading distorts normal social interaction between students. It creates isolation, mutual suspicion, and promotes a grossly protective attitude to the acquisition of knowledge and skills:

And a lot of students felt threatened—that they were in competition against the others—and they would not even associate with other members of the class. (Male black engineering switcher)

People are more comfortable with studying on their own, and feeling that nobody else is getting a ride on it...I mean, 'cause if nobody's gonna help you out, then you're, 'Well, then, I'm not gonna help anybody else out.' (Male Asian-American engineering switcher)

There's one guy who's not really in our group, and he'll come to me to check his answers. And he ends up copying some of my homework. And it really bothers me...Because I don't get anything from him...It seems like I'm just being milked. It feels that way sometimes in my study group—that my brain gets picked. And sometimes I think, 'Why am I helping all these people out?'

'Cause it's gonna hurt me 'cause it brings up the average of the class, which hurts my grade. (Male white engineering non-switcher)

Say, you went to the library, and xeroxed the previous mid-term. People normally have no problem sharing that...But in chemistry, people would not show it to someone else. They would say, 'Go to the library and get it yourself.' I don't know if they need to get As to get into med school, but it definitely took away a lot of the joy. (Male white engineering switcher)

The first two years here, all you think about is hoping you do better than everybody else—actually, you hope that everybody else fails...It's bad. It breeds competitiveness and singles out certain kinds of people to succeed, as opposed to other, more gentle types of people—*people* people. (Male Hispanic engineering switcher)

This last comment is particularly telling. It pinpoints one of the non-educational (primarily unintended) functions of the weed-out system—that of culling students with particular character attributes:

I think they do lose some able people—people who are able to do the work, but fall behind. And, if they're not as aggressive or assertive, they won't seek out the help they need—just because they feel afraid to ask in that climate: it's just so competitive. (Male white science switcher)

Rather than expressing a normal tendency of 'human nature', as is sometimes asserted, many students saw the competitive atmosphere as a 'divide and conquer' strategy, which perverts what they regarded as the more normal preference for co-operative work—a tendency which they saw realized in other classes:

I noticed a big difference when I switched to management. In every class I swear they have some sort of group work...Now, when I go from class to class, I've had all these groups so I know everyone in the class. And that makes it comfortable to ask the professor questions because you don't feel stupid like you do with a bunch of strangers. (Female white engineering switcher)

The professors didn't encourage team work. It's individual competition—whereas, in management, there's still some individual competition, but it's not so intense. And we're usually grouped together; so you compete with other people, but then you also get together as a group and compete as a group. Teamwork is always encouraged. (Female Asian-American engineering switcher)

Students also discovered for themselves that cooperation, rather than competition, is a normal, valued working style for colleagues in work organizations:

When you do an internship, you find out that engineers in the real world actually work together to get stuff done. (Female white engineering non-switcher)

When you get out there, you have to know how to co-operate...In the field, you have to have good communication skills; you have to work well with others. (Male Hispanic engineering non-switcher)

It is not accidental that so many of the speakers cited in this section are women. More women than men found the one-size-fits-all psychology that underwrites the competitive ethos of S.M.E. majors alien or offensive—although it was not necessarily one of the most important factors in their decisions to leave. Women's responses to the competitive culture are discussed in some detail in Chapter 5.

Broadly speaking, students responded to the competitive culture of introductory S.M.E. classes by finding ways to play the system, or to distance themselves from it. The most innocuous form of system-beating was, wherever possible, avoiding those classes known to be very competitive. More damaging to other students was the practice of taking introductory classes below one's performance level:

We know quite a number of people who have taken A.P. physics who are in this class, and they shouldn't be. This is a first class. And they whizzed through everything. Just people who wanted to get a good start on their transcripts. It was really discouraging, because so many people already understood, and the professor went so quickly for them, the rest of us got lost. (Female Asian-American engineering switcher)

However, the most common system-playing response was to get the grades any way you could. This, as we have already indicated, sometimes included cheating. Most people felt ambivalent about cheating, but accepted it as a regrettable, system-driven necessity—a finding which calls into question the effectiveness of the weed-out system as a way to select for strong moral character. The high degree of support for a very competitive system, shown by the next speaker, illustrates one extreme of educational instrumentalism:

Why should I waste my time going to a school which isn't competitive. I mean, if our school's slower in the employer's eyes, why should they want to hire me? Why should I waste my time when I could be preparing for something else?...It's like competing in a race...You wanna know who you're competing against...There's a system that you've got to figure out, so you can make it work for you—or it will hurt you. (Male white engineering non-switcher)

Those who disliked the competitive atmosphere either found ways to ameliorate their discomforts, or were at risk of leaving. However, not all students were prepared to deal with a competitive culture as a normal feature of their working life:

> I was surrounded by people who were trying to get entrance into the program, and we were all fighting each other. There was always a sense of distrust—of people not wanting to help other people, to share answers, or to encourage other people morally—just no support between students. And I began to rethink what I wanted to do. I felt I wasn't capable of fitting into an environment like that, or of making a difference. Who the heck would I be in a world of people I can't communicate with? (Female white engineering switcher)

For 14.8 percent of switchers, such concerns contributed to the decision to leave their S.M.E. major:

> My main reason for switching was that I did not like the people I was involved with…It was a pre-med sequence, so there were some really aggressive students. And in chemistry too, there was a lot of unsavory grubbing going on. (Male white engineering switcher)

> The competition was so intense, I didn't want to deal with it. And, I was thinking, 'There's got to be something better to do here.' (Male white science switcher)

Study groups have to deal with strong faculty prohibitions against plagiarism, and with the hostility of other students who feel that refusing to compete on one's own is a form of cheating. (We shall discuss the significance of such groups in the section on peer group learning later.) These students distanced themselves both from the competitive struggle and its supposed rewards by framing their educational objectives within an alternative set of life goals:

> I've always said that I'm happy with Bs…because I do a lot of other things. I can't just sit at home and study. I work, and I have other things that interest me. (Female native American mathematics switcher)

The Weed-Out Tradition

'Weed-out' is a long-established tradition in a number of academic disciplines, but it is dominant in all S.M.E. majors. It has a semi-legitimate, legendary status and is part of what gives S.M.E. majors their image of hardness. It is, thus, an important feature in students' informal prestige ranking systems, both for individuals, and for majors, disciplines, or sub-specialties. 'Weed-out' strategies are perceived as a test for both ability and character and are the main mechanism by which S.M.E. disciplines seek to find those students presumed to be the most able and interested. There are no references to weed-out systems in official literature, and when questioned, deans and faculty may be evasive, or deny their existence. Weed-out systems parallel the hazing practices of military academies and fraternities. These practices are also officially denied or suppressed, but flourish because they are thought to serve valued functions which are difficult to achieve by other means. Switchers who reported that they were 'weeded out' typically went on to explain which aspects of the 'weed-out' process had been critical in their decision to leave. Some of these have already been discussed in the sections on under-preparation: problems with curricular pace and load, the effects of assessment and grading practices, and the competitive atmosphere to which these practices contribute.

Students become aware of a weed-out system in their S.M.E. classes in one of three ways. It may be directly referenced by a dean or faculty member:

> When I went to the orientation with my mom, the dean actually sat there and said, 'Don't be surprised if about three-fourths of the people sitting here don't make it—particularly not in four years.' (Female white engineering non-switcher)

> They do the usual speech: 'Look to the right of you; look to the left of you. Forty percent of you won't be here next year.' I think that's the standard speech at every university. (Male black engineering non-switcher)

> The freshman advisor for the engineering school gave us a little talk about the number of incoming freshmen they expect to lose each year...They seem to keep very accurate records on this. (Male white engineering non-switcher)

> 'Only 25 percent of you are going to go on and become engineers.' He said that in the very first class. And I thought, 'This is making me feel good.' (Female white engineering switcher)

> But, of course, you hear through all your basic level classes, 'This is a weed-out class.' The professor will tell you right there in class that they're doing this deliberately—making it exceptionally hard—to scare the people out that they don't think can cut it in engineering. They try to get them to fail on purpose. (Female white engineering non-switcher)

The existence of a weed-out system is also widely discussed among students—both within, and across, years:

> The word would always be, 'So many of you are going to flunk this class, no matter what you do.' It's sort of an unwritten, unspoken thing that goes back and forth between students. (Male white science switcher)

> I got it through the grapevine at orientation, talking to the students that were our advisors. (Male white engineering switcher)

> The sophomores who were on my floor who had already taken the classes I was about to take were always saying, 'Oooh, that's a weed-out class!' And it kind of scares you. (Female Asian-American science non-switcher)

Weed-out systems also became evident to students because of the ways in which their curricula are constructed, classes are organized and taught, or assessment and grading practices are set up:

It wasn't that it was all that hard: it was just too much. I left with the feeling that, 'Okay, they are really making this hard for people.'...I think they make the classes so big so the ones they think are good—the ones who can handle the load—will keep going, and the rest will just go away. (Male Hispanic engineering switcher)

It's ridiculous that they make you learn that much in so much detail—because you never, ever need it all. You just look it up in a book if you need it. So I think they do try to weed people out that way. (Male white engineering non-switcher)

You get the impression it's intended to force you out the first time you go to check your test grade posted on the wall. You see that the median grade for Physics 1 is, like, 30 percent. And you realize, 'Wow, that's the way the professor designed the test.' (Male Asian-American engineering switcher)

When you have a class average for Chemistry 103 that gives you a B for scores of 62, I say that's because they're trying to fail you out. (Female white engineering switcher)

For the exams, they choose questions on things that don't matter just to catch people out. It's so blatant. (Female white science non-switcher)

People get discouraged when they are given such hard tests that no one passes them. Then they curve the scores. What's the point of giving a test which you know everyone is going to fail? It's an ideology I just can't understand. I guess they want to weed people out: but there are a lot of good students in there. (Female white science switcher)

Under-classmen also became aware of the weed-out purposes of their introductory classes by their appraisal of faculty attitudes toward them. They developed the strong impression that faculty who teach weed-out classes were, at best, indifferent, uncaring or unapproachable, and at worst, positively hostile toward them:

In Physics 161, it didn't seem like they were interested in what they were doing. They didn't care. They had better things to do. It was like, 'We're trying to fail you, to cut you down.' (Female white engineering switcher)

It was like, 'We're gonna make this harder on you guys, because we don't want just anybody going into engineering.' (Male white engineering switcher)

When I was a first-year student, just the general attitude among the faculty seemed to be, 'Learn this stuff and get your grade, or you won't be back.' (Male white engineering non-switcher)

If everybody failed the test, then the teacher behaved as if no one was studying or knew their stuff. Why didn't he think that maybe the class was going too fast, or that the test wasn't that good? (Male Hispanic mathematics switcher)

It was at this point I thought that the school was out to get undergraduates. (Male black engineering switcher)

> It's sort of the old attitude, 'Let's make it tough for them and get rid of the trash. We'll skim the top for the prime.' (Male white science switcher)

> I've noticed that in most of these classes the professors have a tendency to hate freshmen. (Female black engineering non-switcher)

> They just want you out—unless you are hard core. (Female white engineering switcher)

> The teacher was relatively young: I think he had just finished graduate school—and he was kind of cold and cynical—kinda like, 'I know a lot of you are going to drop out, so you might as well do it now so that the rest of us can get on with this thing.' (Female white engineering switcher)

The last observation underscores our own—that acceptance of, and support for, the weed-out process, is a matter of professional socialization. We noticed that seniors who were planning academic careers had begun to express the same morally-disapproving attitudes towards switchers, and the same rationale for the weed-out process as faculty.

Students quickly learned that, notwithstanding the official system of faculty advisors, it was difficult to get help. Some faculty did not keep their office hours; and most discourage students from seeking their help with problems of comprehension. Making academic help hard to get conveyed the message that to continue in this major students must be ready to make it on their own:

> You couldn't talk to your professor. The classes were so big that they didn't want to give any personal attention. It was almost like they were against, rather than for, the student. (Male white science non-switcher)

> The dean just said, 'Sorry. You're in it; it's too late. You're just gonna have to deal with it.' They say they're there to help you, but when the time comes that you have a real problem, they kinda turn their back on you, and tell you to do it on your own basically. I don't see why it's necessary for them to do that—when they have the power to help you, but choose not to. (Male white engineering switcher)

Students were able, without hesitation, to recount which were the "weed-out classes" in their discipline. From a focus group of science switchers:

> Interviewer: Are there any particular classes that are known as weed-out classes?

> Three voices recite simultaneously: You have Chem 103, Chem 106...

This litany varied very little from campus to campus: it always included particular calculus classes, organic chemistry, and several early physics classes. Less universally mentioned were some introductory biology classes, zoology, general chemistry, chemical calculations and circuitry. Some higher level classes were also cited as continuing the weed-out process into late sophomore or junior

year: analytic chemistry, animal cell biology, electromagnetics and some
chemical engineering classes.

Both from the direct statements of deans and faculty, and by the way the
curve-grading system operated, students had fairly clear ideas about the
proportion of any class that was expected, or required, to fail or to leave. Their
estimates of what they assumed were official departmental attrition targets
ranged from 30 percent to 75 percent, with a median of around 50 percent.
Seniors reported that, in retrospect, their estimates had proved pretty accurate.
They also had a visual impression of how the weed-out process was progressing
by shifts in the classroom seating patterns in their classes:

> You can always tell. There's what we call the 'T'—the students in the front
> two rows and down the middle—they're the A students, and everybody else,
> you're gonna lose. By the time I got to the upper division, I could walk into
> a class and tell you whose grade's gonna be what. I mean, you didn't need to
> take the class any more. I could have assigned the grades just by who was
> there. (Male white science non-switcher)

> I used to be a back-seat person, and I'm now more front-seat. Just based on
> seating, you can see whether they want to be there, whether it's a requirement
> they just have to take, where the interests of most people lie, and whether
> they're gonna make it. (Female white science non-switcher)

Seniors also assumed that these attrition rates were intended, and that their size
was a constant, regardless of variations in the calibre of particular student
cohorts:

> They're probably not surprised that they lose as many people as they do. (Male
> white engineering non-switcher)

> They have a certain number of people they would like to scare off in the
> sciences, and they are pretty proud of hitting their target pretty accurately....
> They certainly do have a figure: it's published on the bulletin board outside of
> the first physics classes...These are the figures they are shooting for. (Male
> white engineering non-switcher)

Undergraduate weed-out lore included stories about departments and individual
professors who came to be seen as over-zealous in their weed-out strategies:

> Well, if you've only got 10 majors that year, I know the deans are not going
> to be real pleased—I mean, if you start out with a big chemistry class and
> you're only left with 10...and the psychology department's got 5,000 and
> you're getting more funding, you'd better be ready to justify that in some way.
> (Male white science non-switcher)

> Some of them even tell you they're going to mess you up. Some of them have
> reputations for it—like I heard one is on probation for failing too many. (Male
> white science non-switcher)

They had to talk to this professor. You didn't take this class until your fall quarter, senior year. If you fail, you have to come back for another year. And they finally talked to him and said, 'You're failing too many students. We can't afford to do this. Will you please just pass them?' (Male white science non-switcher)

Students assumed that the weed-out system had two major objectives; it is a way to sift large intake classes for intrinsic interest, talent and fortitude, while, at the same time, drastically reducing the large entry classes to a size that departments can handle in the upper division:

You have to get rid of the extra 2,000 or 3,000 people enrolled in the course so that you can get down to the people who you really want. (Male white engineering switcher)

It's such a weed-out program because the school can't afford to keep all of the people who are really good—just a small percentage of them. (Male white engineering switcher)

I think undergraduate admissions is very keen on having science-oriented people admitted. Then that puts the burden on the chemistry and physics department to get rid of so many of them. (Female white science switcher)

I thought, 'At some point it's gotta get easier. I mean, you've cut everybody else out.' (White male science non-switcher)

Many students did not question the objective of reducing numbers, and most did not propose alternatives to this reduction process, unless prompted to do so. The weed-out process acts as a *post hoc* selection system which avoids conflict with the ideal of open entry to higher education. Having been raised with the democratic ethic of the American educational system (which includes the idea that most people should be able to go to college if they have the desire and entry qualifications), most students were uncomfortable with the idea of a more selective or competitive system of college access. With the notable exception of students at the private research university (who were chosen by competitive selection at a level above basic entry requirements), most preferred to retain the current system in which entry requirements are set at a moderate level, and a highly competitive selection of students is made after, rather than before, college entry. Although they disliked the weed-out system, and often thought it worked contrary to its aim of selecting the best students, on balance, they were prepared to tolerate it rather than to further restrict college entry or access to freshman S.M.E. classes:

Anybody that can get in, I think they should give them a chance. So in a weird way, I'd sort of defend the way engineering does it...I think you kinda let as many as possible go into it, and then you have to wean out stringently. I think that's how it has to be done. The other side to that is I know they are losing a lot of good students in the process. There's drawbacks either way. (Male white engineering switcher)

The preference for a more stringent pre-entry selection process was more infrequently voiced:

It seems like you let a lot of people in, and then you try to weed a lot of people out. I think it would be better to work the other way around and make it harder to get in, so you don't have to have the weeding out process once you get in. (Male white engineering switcher)

No one discourages you from being a pre-engineering student, although only a small number will be allowed into the major. The whole huge class might have all the requisites, but there's no way they can ever let them all in. They have to discriminate somehow...I would rather have known up front. It would have been kinder to know that only the top 10 of the huge number were actually going to be accepted. In a five-year school, this selection process adds another whole year. (Male white engineering switcher)

Students with professional aspirations understood the need to restrict entry to those professions. They took it for granted that it was part of the faculty role to keep the number of graduates at an annual level which broadly matched the number of jobs available, and thus, to protect professional salary levels. This function of the weed-out system does not serve any academic purpose. In effect, academic faculty are performing the traditional gate-keeping role of all professional bodies, from medieval guilds onwards:

The class below us is 170, and we have close to 100. So I'm sure that's gonna put some pressure on faculty, 'cause it'll be harder for us to get jobs. (Male white engineering non-switcher)

I guess a lot of people want to come into engineering because it's a prestigious job. It's a lot of money right when you start; it's a promising career, and you can make good money, so a lot of people want to do it. I guess, if you had everyone doing it—I mean, there are only so many jobs out there. So they have to weed out over half. (Male white engineering switcher)

I don't think they dare make it easier: there would be too many engineers, and people wouldn't make so much money. (Female white engineering switcher)

Oh, I think it's to maintain the prestige of the profession—only to let highly qualified people in. (Male white engineering non-switcher)

It is notable that the weed-out tradition is particularly strong in those S.M.E. majors which serve the professions (most notably, engineering and the medical professions) as well as in non-S.M.E. majors—such as accounting and law—which also lead to professional careers:

> There's an entry-level accounting class that is definitely weed-out. It's intended to discourage people from applying to business school. That's what it's for. (Female Asian-American science switcher)

The three years of this study was a period in which seniors in science and mathematics foresaw difficulties in securing well-remunerated work following graduation, especially in academic careers. Many had come to doubt whether their decision to stay in science or mathematics had been wise, given what one senior in physics called its "poor profit-to-grief ratio." Engineers, by contrast, saw themselves as still able to command jobs and salaries which were a reasonable reward for their hard work, and were more accepting of the weed-out-related discomforts of their majors.

The second major function of the weed-out system, as perceived by our informants, was to identify which students were best fitted to continue in the major. Both switchers and non-switchers seemed ready to accept that, in principle, this was a reasonable aim. Most thought it preferable to a pre-college selection process which placed more responsibility on the high school system whose reliability many of them had good reason to doubt:

> I think it's a good weeder because they're working at a really high theoretical level, and they're looking for people who can think in that theoretical way. (Male white science switcher)

> I'm not one of the more intelligent students in my classes, and I have to struggle to keep going. But those who left didn't want that. So I think the weed-out system has maybe accomplished its purpose. (Male white engineering non-switcher)

> If you fail your first two chemistry classes, you probably aren't going to get into med school...In a sense, it's a reality check. (Female white science non-switcher)

> I guess it's almost like the survival of the fittest. If you can't do it, you weren't meant to. (Female white science switcher)

> It's sort of the fire that forges the sword. If you make it through, you know you'll make it through modern physics and real analysis: there's nothing stopping you. (Male white science non-switcher)

> I know people who are on the edge—who are not quite sure if this is for them. There's organic chemistry, real analysis and modern physics, which are all tailor-made to force you to make up your mind to be, or not to be, in that major. (Male white science non-switcher)

> I'm inclined to think that they're doing a good job, and I just couldn't deal with it. I don't think it raises the calibre of the students, but at least it makes sure that all of the people in it are serious. So I guess it does serve some purpose. However, it can be a bit ugly. (Male white engineering switcher)

As the above extracts indicate, many students are willing to accept testing for ability, seriousness of interest and willingness to work hard. However, they were not always convinced that the weed-out system achieves this and often saw it as counter-productive. The emphasis on student selection over teaching explains why course material is presented at a pace which drives students away. It also explains why students learn to memorize at the expense of comprehension, why those who persist often have insufficient conceptual grasp, and why those who enter with an interest in science are apt to lose it:

> I think it's better to learn fewer things well, than to know a little about a million things which you just skimmed over—like in that calculus class. Then you go on to the next class, and they assume you know things you never did properly. (Male Hispanic mathematics switcher)

> There's a danger that you aren't giving people who are going into science or engineering the really good, solid base that they need. (Male white engineering non-switcher)

> I didn't see why it was necessary to include that in the freshman year. It wasn't necessary for the sequence. It was only necessary as a way to filter people out. (Male black engineering non-switcher)

> Designing a class to be hard, and not because it's good to teach a particular thing—I don't see the practicality there. Like memorizing organic reactions—it's neat to know you can do a fifteen-step reaction, but unless that teaches you some sort of principle that you can apply, what good does it do? (Male white science switcher)

> You lose a lot of the essence of doing chemistry. It came down to who could memorize the best. And what it did was to take the science away from it. It stopped being science, and turned into a sort of competition. You really lost that good level of learning in that class. The long-term scars are just an absolute disinterest in the field. You never understood the actual mechanisms that created the reactions. He would just say, 'These are the three reactions. One of them will be on the exam. Memorize all three.' I don't think that's learning. I was really turned off taking a future interest in it. (Male white science non-switcher)

Most students respected those who showed sufficient determination to persevere through and beyond the weed-out classes. However, they questioned whether the weed-out system was a reliable way to identify students with the potential to become good scientists and engineers, and wondered whether faculty knew how many good students were lost in the process:

> Their *intention* is to get rid of the people that would not be so good in the major—but that's not a *proof* of it. (Male Asian-American science switcher)

> They lose quality people...Some that, with just a few more years, would have made the kind of engineering students they would have liked, and would have

brought the profession more into balance. (Male white engineering non-switcher)

It's bad that they use these courses to weed students out. I knew people that didn't want to go on after that experience, but they were good students who liked learning. (Female white science non-switcher)

They do it by intimidating you. They *think* they're getting rid of all the wimpy people—the people who aren't willing to work hard. I think they really *believe* that's what they're doing. The head of the department would always make things sound much harder than they were, and would tell us we were stupid, and give us exam questions that no one could answer. I had several friends—all women—who switched out. They were capable people, but they were just so intimidated by the professors and the male students. (Female white science non-switcher)

I thought the first engineering class I had was kinda silly, and it was really easy, and I was with some other people who thought so too...But we left and went into other things. (Female Asian-American engineering switcher)

Occasionally, we met a student who not only illuminated facets of a problem through their own story, but who also offered a coherent analysis of its causes. The following (from a male, white, engineering switcher at the highly-selective private research university) summarizes the latent dysfunctions of the weed-out system in terms which are highly consistent with our data:

What it does to people is to weed them out psychologically. When people come in with inherent doubts about whether they are meant for the field—especially women, and minority students—they don't have that base of self-confidence. They are less likely to tell themselves that everyone else is having the same problem, because their confidence is more fragile...The teacher believes he is testing for ability, but in fact, he's testing for self-esteem and self-confidence. I don't think he consciously knows that, but it still has that effect...The weed-out system has side-effects that professors are not aware of. They accept that they are losing people, but may not realize that they are losing people unevenly from different categories...They're fine with the fact that people are weeded out. They want a core of dedicated people. But, what they're not realizing is that people are also being weeded out, not so much in terms of ability, but in terms of other qualities. (Male white engineering switcher)

Students also saw the weed-out system working in ways that contradicted its value as a test of character and were concerned that it encouraged some less admirable qualities. They saw it as both encouraging and providing a rationale for cheating. It also made students suspicious, grudging and ruthless in their behavior towards each other, discouraged the development of collaboration and good communication skills, and instilled the idea that failure is a normal part of learning science.

The most serious criticisms of the weed-out system, however, focused on its disproportionate impact on men of color and on all women. Even well-prepared, these two groups tend to enter basic classes feeling uncertain about whether they 'belong'. The loss of regular contact with high school teachers who encouraged them to believe in their ability to do science exposes the frailty of their self-confidence. Faculty who teach weed-out classes discourage the kind of personal contact and support which was an important part of high school learning. It is, as some students described it, a 'weaning away' process by which faculty transmit the message that it is time to grow up, cast aside dependence on personally-significant adults and take responsibility for their own learning. This attitude is perceived by students in the reluctance of teachers to answer questions, brusqueness in response to 'trivial' inquiries, failure to offer praise or encouragement, disinclination to discuss academic difficulties in a personal manner, carelessness in keeping office hours, and a 'no excuses' stance on test results. The difficulty of getting personal attention was troubling to many students, but it was especially troubling to those whose presence in S.M.E. classes was the result of considerable personal attention and encouragement by particular high school teachers. Forcing students to compete for, or learn to do without, help and attention, was an important part of the problems reported by women and by men of color (as well as some white men). This arises because the system has evolved in an exclusively white and male context. It tests for qualities of character traditionally associated with 'maleness' in Anglo-Saxon societies and is based on motivational strategies understood by young men reared in that tradition. The cues are more likely to be missed, and the messages lost on students whose education was grounded in different normative systems. The disproportionate effects on women and men of color arise as an unintended side-effect of the intention to force young, white men to become self-reliant. Among many women and young men of color it produces feelings of rejection, discouragement and lowered self-confidence. The weed-out system works as it is meant to work for young white men, who are more likely than young women to switch in response to its more overt features—especially the overwhelming pace and load, and fierce competition for grades. Women were much *less* discouraged by these aspects of the weed-out process than were young white men. We shall discuss these issues in more detail in the chapters concerning gender, and race and ethnicity.

Students wondered how much of the system was consciously designed, how much was part of an unthinking, learned tradition, and how well faculty understood its counter-productive consequences. S.M.E. faculty do not necessarily define high attrition rates as problematic: 'attrition' was discovered, and defined as a 'problem', not by science and engineering faculty, but by academics in other fields and by those concerned with labor economics or public policy. Notwithstanding S.M.E. faculty's focus on identifying the 'best' students, our data suggest that the proportion of students allowed to proceed to each new stage in these majors is pre-determined. Before faculty can actually estimate the range of ability in any particular cohort of new students, they already know what proportion they will discard. The average demonstrated performance level of students varied across the seven different institutions by the level at which entrance requirements were set, and by the degrees of selectivity and competition employed in admitting S.M.E. undergraduates. Despite this, we found no evidence of differences between institutions, departments or colleges in their expectation (or requirement) that similar proportions of students would fail or leave weed-out classes. Competitive-entry institutions did not weed out less of their highly qualified intake than did more open-entry state institutions, even though the quality of their freshmen cohorts was much higher. Many of the 40 to 50 percent of students weeded out at competitive-entry schools could have been 'stars' of S.M.E. majors in less selective institutions. This fact was not lost on students who, with hindsight, felt they would have done better had they entered their own state university. The following was offered by a male white engineering switcher at a highly-selective private research university:

> In my high school, I did *really* well, and my teachers thought I was a future engineer—that it was a given. So then I got a place here—and I saw all my friends who didn't do as well at high school as I did getting straight As at colleges back home. Those are still very good schools. But they didn't have the problems that I had here...Because, it was like you had to teach yourself. Going to lecture was completely worthless...Meanwhile, my friends back home did really well.
>
> Interviewer: Why didn't you go back?
>
> Why didn't I? Because it's (name of the university).

The Unsupportive Culture

Students identified a number of needs which they seek to meet by approaching faculty and other advisors:

* advice on academic and career alternatives and how best to pursue them

* accurate information on required courses and appropriate sequencing in order to fulfill particular degree requirements

* help in understanding the academic material presented in particular classes

* practical help or advice with problems that impinge on academic performance—especially problems with finances, employment, time conflicts, health and other personal matters

    *   someone to take a personal interest in their progress, problems and overall career direction

Failure to find adequate advice, counseling, or tutorial help was cited as contributing to one-quarter (24.0%) of all switching decisions; it was mentioned as a source of frustration by three-quarters (75.4%) of all switchers (for whom it was the third most common source of complaint); and it was an issue raised by half (52.0%) of all non-switchers, for whom it was the second most commonly cited concern.

Among all of the factors contributing to attrition, student difficulties in getting appropriate help is the factor which is most clearly derived from flaws in the institutional structure. We found that most students had experienced some problems with the support systems at all of the seven institutions. However, the perceived effectiveness of particular advice and counseling services varied as much within campuses as between them. On every campus, we found gaps, over-laps and confusion in the division of responsibility between departments (or colleges), central advising services and advising programs for under-represented groups. One of the most difficult problems for freshmen is to learn how the campus system of advising, counseling and tutorial services works quickly enough in order to prevent small problems from becoming large ones:

> Everything deterred me from going on. I was feeling like there was nobody I could go to talk to...I thought, 'Well, I'd better switch now. I don't want to end up a year down the road still in this major when it's not going to work out.' (Female white science switcher)

> If I had had a good counselor who *understood*, and who could have made some suggestions, I would probably not have dropped out of aerospace. I could have taken the classes I'm taking right now, and decided later. I felt like I'd wasted a semester, but didn't know what else to do. If I'd just had a good counselor, I know I could have got it all straight in my mind. (Male white engineering switcher)

Freshman are particularly at risk because they often need several different kinds of help simultaneously—advice about career alternatives, accurate information about choice and sequencing of classes, help to set up finance and work-study plans, tutorial help with early academic difficulties and personal encouragement. Students tend to see their problems as interrelated, and would prefer to discuss them as such. They are likely to seek some mixture of advice concerning career direction, course information, tutoring, and encouragement from a single professor or professional advisor, and become frustrated with support systems which assign each kind of problem to a different agency:[3]

> You don't get an individual faculty advisor. It rotates day-by-day. Almost all of the professors are nice guys, and they mean well, but they don't really

expect students to come in and talk about problems they are having with their classes. (Male white science non-switcher)

There's an advisor system—but that's just to choose classes. There's no help with things you find difficult to understand—unless you could get the guts to approach the professor. (Male white science non-switcher)

Students become frustrated with the splintering of support functions between different administrative units, the unreliability of the advice they sometimes receive, and the difficulty of finding the right agency for particular kinds of problems:

You really feel lost in the shuffle. Nobody really knows where to tell you to go to get advice with a problem. You can go to the dean, but he doesn't know what to do either. I mean, who can you turn to? (Female white mathematics switcher)

It's really hard to figure out 'This is what you do and this is where you go.' When I was a freshmen, it was so confusing. (Male white engineering non-switcher)

It's frustrating when you can't get help. But if it's not good help, then it's even more frustrating. (Male Hispanic science non-switcher)

Well, all I got was the little booklet that they sent us. I didn't get any kind of advice on what kind of classes to take. (Female black engineering non-switcher)

I was never assigned someone I could go and speak with—to make sure that I was taking all the right things. I just kind of floated through the system. (Female white engineering switcher)

It is, perhaps, not surprising that freshmen find it difficult to navigate the administrative complexities of large, unfamiliar campuses. However, it would be easier to dismiss their reports of difficulty in finding appropriate sources of help as a purely temporary problem were it not for the testimony of half of the non-switching seniors who reported that confusion and gaps in provision of support had continued throughout their academic careers:

There aren't any advisors. That's another problem with this department. Every semester I get all my advising by going around and harassing some of the professors that I've had. I don't know how anyone else manages it. (Male white mathematics non-switcher)

I've never seen an advisor. No—actually I did see one when I had to fill in my senior packet to graduate—well, I saw his secretary, and she did that...I wish I had someone I could go to—someone who was assigned, or that I chose—so, after a while, they'd know who you were. (Female white science non-switcher)

> I wish I would have had some better advising...I don't know if faculty don't know the system, or if they're just not interested. (Male white engineering non-switcher)

> Nobody ever said, 'Hey, there's a tutorial system available.' It was more like a 'consumer beware' type of thing. And no one ever sat down with me. (Male white science non-switcher)

> If I was the dean, I would make sure faculty knew exactly what courses their majors had to take. That would be the first thing. Because they kinda screwed me up. The head of mechanical engineering told me to take the wrong course. He put me behind a whole semester. (Male Hispanic engineering non-switcher)

Students' most basic need is reliable information about which classes to take to accomplish particular academic goals in an appropriate sequence and time-frame. The official task of giving course direction is often split between faculty and professional advisors. However, students also get information or advice from special program directors, student counselors, official literature, departmental assistants and more experienced students. Indeed, seniors often cited departmental assistants as their most reliable sources of information about course requirements and institutional rules:

> We have an award that we give to advisors every year, and, pretty consistently, the lady that wins it is the department head's secretary...I think that's pretty ironic because it's supposed to be one of the faculty's roles, but she's the one we all go to if there's a crisis. (Female white engineering non-switcher)

> She works in the department office and she really keeps an eye on students...I always double check classes with her. I've got sort of a safety net there. If it hadn't been for her, I'd be in a big mess. (Male Asian-American engineering non-switcher)

Seniors also indicated that the best information about which classes to take, or to avoid, came from students who had experienced them. Use of these unofficial sources of advice were strongly advocated as survival strategies.

One very common complaint of both switchers and non-switchers was the discovery that they had chosen a particular class sequence on the basis of information from an official source which subsequently proved to be inaccurate. Some negative consequences were: taking classes in the wrong order; missing classes which were offered infrequently; failing to take pre-requisites; being excluded from desired specialties; and delayed graduation. We collected a large sample of iatrogenic problems—that is problems students would have avoided had they not followed advice from an official source:

> And the professor said, 'Of course, I don't have to explain this theorem, because you had that two years ago in Math 400.' And I was totally thrown. For some reason, the course catalog made no mention of this prerequisite...I

started at a higher math level because my advisor bumped me up several classes on the basis of my S.A.T. scores. Big mistake. I had to drop that class, and go backwards to pick up the math. I lost two semesters over that. (Male white engineering switcher)

They don't let you know that, for some of your upper-level work, you have to take prerequisites. And they don't tell you that some courses are only offered in the fall, and others only in the spring. (Female white engineering non-switcher)

She didn't know that it didn't count for my major. It didn't count for anything in the end. (Female white engineering switcher)

For the first year, she advised me to ease into it, and gave me all these classes that had nothing to do with biology—except microbiology—and that didn't count as it turned out...I just trusted her, and signed up. (Female black science switcher)

I brought my transcript, and showed him the classes I had taken and asked if they were okay for what I wanted to do. He said, 'Yes,' when he should have said, 'No.' (Female white engineering switcher)

I never knew exactly whether or not I was playing by the correct rules, because it seemed like I talked to one person, and they'd say something; and I'd talk to someone else and they'd say something else...And they definitely need to get their T.A.s advised about how the system works. I mean, even the dean didn't know what to do. (Female white mathematics switcher)

I'm gonna end up being here a full five years, and that wouldn't have happened if I'd had some good advising along the way. Every semester the advisor told me what to take, and I ended up with all these classes which didn't count for the major. I nearly lost my scholarship, and had to write an appeal to explain what had happened. (Male Hispanic engineering switcher)

They signed his paper, and said, 'You've got all the stuff you need.' When it came time to graduate, he was missing one class, and had to come back for another semester just to take it. (Male black engineering switcher)

I was led down the garden path. I'm trying to keep myself under restraint here: any further description would probably involve foul words. They withheld information; they told me things that weren't true...The consequences were that I moved campuses when I didn't have to. I could have stayed where I was; kept my job; finished in four years; and saved myself, conservatively speaking, about $20,000. (Female white science switcher)

From a focus group of engineering non-switchers—

I asked if I was going to have any problem taking some of these upper-level classes in the summer while I was co-opping. And he said, 'Sure, no problem.' When I went to register I found out they never offer these classes in the summer. It nearly cost me my graduation date.

I've been screwed over by advisors who didn't know the policy about which classes transferred from community college, and which classes you needed to take to keep your scholarship. It's one of the reasons I'm not pursuing a master's degree here. I couldn't find out how to go about it without actually applying.

Students look for two kinds of help with their academic career paths: help in making an informed choice of career direction based on the alternatives open to them, and reliable information on how best to navigate a path they have already chosen. Faculty seem more suited to the first task, professional advisors to the second. However, the division of labor is often unclear, and students can get into difficulties by asking for the kind of help which an advisor is not qualified to give. This may reflect their confusion about whom to ask; sometimes it reflects flaws in the advisory system. Most students look for someone with whom they can periodically review their overall academic and career strategy. For this, they need an advisor with particular knowledge of their discipline, career options and institutional requirements for graduation, who is willing to spend time discussing such issues. Few students seem to find this combination of skills and availability in their advisors. Indeed, it may be unreasonable to expect them from any single source:

She's a really nice woman, but she's an advisor. She can't know about physics—she just hears things from other students. Once she told me I didn't need differential equations for thermal dynamics. (Male white science non-switcher)

He didn't know much about the university, or what courses to take. He told us what the medical field was like, so I guess he was more of a mentor—but he really didn't know much about the courses. (Female white science switcher)

I came in with a pretty specific list of things I wanted to know: Would taking these classes help with my major? I was thinking about doing nutrition, and wanted to know how these classes fit together...And he couldn't even find it in the course book. I thought, 'He should be able to find it: it's his job!' (Female Asian-American science switcher)

That whole four year experience, my advisor pretty much looked at my list of course work and signed it. There was no discussing what you wanted to do five years from now—no real planning. (Female white mathematics non-switcher)

The search for an appropriate advisor with whom to discuss their progress, problems, and options is of special importance to students thinking about switching. They need to know whether the problems they have experienced are common to others at this stage in their major, and should be tolerated as such, or whether they indicate a need to rethink their career plans. They encounter the practical difficulty that faculty who can give advice about their discipline know little about alternative careers. More seriously, those who raise the possibility of leaving an S.M.E. major are often encouraged to switch, whether or not this is the right decision:

> When I was in that flux period, thinking about business school, he didn't help me at all. His attitude was he was there to help the science majors, not people who were thinking about transferring. (Male white science switcher)

> I found the science professors very unresponsive—I mean, in terms of, 'Let's work out what route you're going to take.'...I got the sense they didn't really care if I switched majors. (Female Hispanic science switcher)

> It's either sink or swim. That's where we lost the most people—because there was no assistance when they needed to talk about whether they were doing the right thing. (Male white science non-switcher)

> Interviewer: Did anyone in the chemistry department try to persuade you to do something else in the sciences?

> No. The advisor was pretty much indifferent. When I came in to see him because I was troubled about whether or not I should switch, it was pretty much like I was an interruption in his day. (Male white science switcher)

The final decision to switch is usually taken after a prolonged struggle with an array of difficulties and is invariably painful. Those close to switching usually want to discuss their dilemma with someone knowledgeable about the major and about other options open to them. One of the most distressing aspects of the switching process is, therefore, the discovery that there is no exit interview with an advisor or dean in the major which they are leaving:

> You have to go to your own dean's office to get the transfer form, and I assumed that was so they could talk to you and see what was going on. But at no point did they suggest this. I went in and said, 'I'd like a transfer form,' and they asked, 'Where to?' and I told them, 'The business school.' And they said, 'Sure. Here you are.' (Male white engineering switcher)

> Nobody called and said they wanted to talk to me about my switching decision. I was disappointed about that. There was just no reaction. (Male white engineering switcher)

> I did honestly expect some sort of exit interview, where you could explain your reasons, and just talk about it—you know, it's a pretty big psychological step—but there's nothing. (Male white engineering switcher)

Students do not necessarily blame advisors personally for the informational errors they make. They understand that faculty get no training for their advisory role with students, and tend to be limited in their knowledge of classes which lie beyond their own disciplines or specialties. They appreciate that professional advisors are working with an overly-complex requirements' system, with too few trained staff, augmented by too many part-time student advisors:

You can go to two different advisors, and they will tell you two different things about the same requirements issue...But there are just too many schools in this university, with so many different requirements that change so often that it's impossible for them to keep up. I think there's only one qualified full-time advisor for every 8,000 students. So give 'em a break! (Male white engineering switcher)

It's a long-term commitment to their students, and it takes a lot out of them. They don't really have the time to keep up with the requirement changes, and I don't think they get any training on how to do it. (Male white engineering switcher)

Most professors are just assigned to be advisors. They have no idea what's going on. They don't know what to tell students. Some go to tremendous efforts to find out, but most are so busy, they just throw up their hands. They do the best they can. (Female white science switcher)

However, what students could not forgive in advisors was failure to spend time with them, or take an interest in them. Indeed, some of the problems they experienced with erroneous course advice arose from the cursory nature of advisory interviews:

There were decisions that were wrong that he didn't stop me from making. They cost me another semester of school. I just wish I could have seen it. But I think he should have caught it and stopped me. Instead, he just kinda sat there at his desk and said, 'That'll work. That's okay.' (Female white science switcher)

I didn't understand how people could look at my transcript and not say, 'There's something wrong here. She's doing well in classes that are non-science, and she's a science major.' They never said anything. They just wanted to hurry up and sign my paper and get me out of there. (Female Asian-American science switcher)

I was unsure about physics and chemistry. I was unsure about everything. I didn't know what I was going to do. But he just said, 'These look like good courses,' and signed it. I didn't talk to him for more than a minute. (Female white engineering switcher)

And they just kind of sit there. You have 15 minutes to get through the stamping and the signatures, and then you're out. (Female white engineering non-switcher)

What students wanted from advisors, above all else, was personal attention:

What you actually want is to spend some time with an advisor who takes the time to know you personally, understand where you're trying to go, and advise what you need to do to get there. (Female white science non-switcher)

I was thinking, 'genetic engineering,' and he was a biological statistician. But he was a nice man. I remember him saying, 'Well, tell me something about yourself.' He was the only advisor that ever really spent more than five minutes with me. (Female white science switcher)

Some students complained that faculty advisors were negligent about keeping office hours, or were otherwise unavailable:

> I kept trying to contact my advisor, but I never did find him, and finally gave up on him. I'd leave messages at his office, which he's never at. I don't know if he ever gets them. (Male white engineering non-switcher)

> When I switched majors, I couldn't go in and talk to my advisor. I was told she only had appointments for an hour and a half on Friday afternoons, and at no other times. Well, I had classes then. I don't know who she is, but she's very unaccessible. (Female white engineering switcher)

For some students, the system of assigned advisors completely broke down:

> My advisor went on sabbatical for two years. I just got to know him a bit, then he was gone. After that, I got trucked around to the advisor of the week...When I got into chemical engineering, they assigned me to a professor who was never in his office...When I started to look for recommendations, I had absolutely nobody I could turn to. (Female white engineering switcher)

> They assigned me one who wasn't here for six months. I was going to different teachers, explaining what I wanted, and they signed off on it. I just did it on my own. (Female white engineering switcher)

The difficulties of under-classmen (especially) in persuading faculty to take some personal interest in them may arise because other aspects of their work have higher professional priority. However, there is also a fundamental conflict between the faculty's role as academic advisor and their role as gatekeepers. As we have already discussed, the weed-out tradition requires faculty to adopt a formal demeanor with students in order to discourage them from over-dependence. Faculty may take an interest in questions about career direction, but are less inclined to discuss problems about class materials. This is very confusing for those students who assume faculty are supposed to take a personal interest in their progress. By far, the commonest words freshmen use to describe encounters with S.M.E. faculty are "unapproachable," "cold," "unavailable," "aloof," "indifferent" and "intimidating":

> It's a very indifferent kind of atmosphere. They seem happy to talk to you if you have no problems, but as soon as you need a little help, they are quick to tell you how busy they are, and how it's all your responsibility. (Female white engineering switcher)

> He told us his office hours, but I haven't gone yet. I feel very intimidated by him. He does not seem approachable at all. I've noticed that with a lot of the science professors. They seem almost condescending, like, they're on one level, and we're on another, and there's no way to meet. (Female white science switcher)

> My advisor really upset me one time. He didn't realize I'd had two quarters of physics, not two semesters, and he got really negative with me. I was so upset. I thought, 'I don't need my advisor—the person who is supposed to give me support—to bring me down.' (Female white engineering non-switcher)

> I was extremely distressed after one session with him. I don't think I ever saw him again after that. For a couple of years, I would just call him, and he would tape the form to the outside of his door. (Female white science switcher)

A painful experience with a professor at an academic crisis point was often the 'last straw' incident in the process leading to switching. Non-switchers also described how close they had come to switching following a discouraging encounter with their faculty advisor:

> I left his office crying...I wanted him to take the time to explain it. And he just got irate, saying, 'Well, how many hours did you put into this? You'd better reconsider what you're doing in college.' He really put me down. I left thinking, 'Well, I'm not going to listen to that. I know the reason I'm not doing well in his class *isn't* that I'm not smart enough.' (Female white science non-switcher)

> I didn't do very well the semester before, and I went to him for advice, and he told me that I should switch my career field because I'd never make it...I was a sophomore, and that broke my heart...I didn't know what to do, but my mother said, 'Don't let anybody tell you what is going to happen in your life. You're the only one who can decide.' (Female black science non-switcher)

Many of these extracts illustrate a fundamental clash of perspectives about the appropriate boundaries of the faculty advisory role. Students do not perceive the need to distinguish between advising, counseling, and tutoring functions, while faculty tend to resist all but the most formal of these functions—course advising.

With hindsight, some switchers faulted themselves for not seeking help from faculty, advisors, or tutors, and wondered if they might have survived in the major had they done so:

> I never went to tutors or anything, and maybe I should have. Now I would recommend it to anybody if you get behind in a math class—go get a tutor. I just tried to tough it out and study harder. (Male white engineering switcher)

> I was set in what I wanted to do, and wasn't looking for help until I started *not* doing it. Then I couldn't find anybody, 'cause I thought I was too far gone. (Female native American science switcher)

> The walk-in advisor was very helpful, but this was when I was switching out. She said she understood it was tough, and that I was not alone in feeling like I did, and told me the things I could go into. You know, if I had reached out before, I might not have got into a state where I felt I had to switch. (Male white engineering switcher)

Deans and faculty also ask why students do not make better use of the support systems available to them, and we found a number of reasons for this: some students are intimidated by the unapproachable demeanor faculty customarily project toward under-classmen; some fear humiliation if they ask "dumb questions"; students who work may not be able to attend scheduled office hours; and most freshmen quickly pick up the message that faculty consider it inappropriate for students to approach them—as opposed to T.A.s or tutors—for help with academic problems:

> That may be part of the reason why people don't go to office hours. You really have to go with a specific question, and if you're having trouble seeing something, and are confused, why go in and embarrass yourself? (Male white science non-switcher)

Some seniors remain wary of contact with their faculty. They prefer not to approach faculty about any academic matter, rather than trying to guess what professors may, or may not, consider an appropriate matter for consultation. From a focus group of male white engineering non-switchers:

> I don't wanna waste his time having him show me something I could probably do with a T.A. He might get a bad impression of me, and it might get reflected in my grade somehow. I've always wanted to stay clear—participate in class, but not get too involved afterwards.
>
> Interviewer: What would be a legitimate thing to go and talk to a faculty advisor about?
>
> Like, if there was a grading discrepancy which was really obvious, or if I had to leave town and couldn't be around to turn in the homework, I'd check to see if he wanted it early—things like that are okay.
>
> I would agree with that. I hardly see my advisor unless I need a letter of recommendation, or need to talk to him about some requirement.

Students who absorb the faculty ethic favoring solitary rather than collaborative endeavor are reluctant to ask for help of any kind. As already indicated, some switchers belatedly find this to be an error.

In order to get the best out of campus support systems—whether as advising, counseling, or tutoring—seniors advocated: learning to be assertive and persistent; taking risks in order to make contact with faculty; using multiple sources of information; double-checking all information about graduation requirements; soliciting first-hand knowledge from more experienced students; making full use of T.A.s, tutoring services, and programs for particular student groups; keeping on top of course materials; and refusing to be brushed off with unsatisfactory answers. In short, they advocated an active, consumer approach to the undergraduate life:

> I have to take care of myself on this campus. I'm the only one looking out for me. This is not high school. This is a business. I'm a customer, and if I don't like the service, I have to say something. I can't just sit there and keep paying. (Female black science switcher)

> I've learned a lot about how to deal with a problem. Do it yourself if you can, and if you can't, make somebody help you. Start with a couple of questions, then you go back and do it again—and keep on asking. (Female white science non-switcher)

> There's a lot of encouragement to see a T.A., but I think the professor is paid to teach us. I mean, I've paid them so much each year to do that, so they need to take time for each individual as part of their job. If they reject the contact, go ask someone else, but always start with the professor. (Female white science non-switcher)

> I'm not afraid to go and ask a professor for what I need. I mean, I'm paying good money, so why not? I think more students would find that, if they took the initiative to find a professor they could work with, they would do better. But a lot don't. (Male white engineering non-switcher)

Students preferred departmental advising whereby all students were required to meet with faculty on a regular basis. This avoids the stigma or anxiety of deciding whether or not to approach faculty. For academic discussion and consolidation of class material, these could be meetings between faculty and small groups of students. They liked situations—whether formal or informal—where faculty and students of different years could meet and discuss topics which enhanced their appreciation of syllabus material or the discipline overall. Some elements of these arrangements were in place on particular campuses, and were well-supported by our interviewees. Students also wanted an advisor with whom they shared academic or career interests, and the opportunity to change advisors to get a better match of interests or temperament. They needed reliable information about which classes they should and should not take, and about the best teachers or classes. They appreciated departments advertising research or apprenticeship opportunities and relevant summer work. They also wanted up-to-date information and advice about career options, graduate schools, scholarships and contact with field professionals. Above all, they appreciated faculty, professional advisors and departmental assistants who showed an active long-term interest in their learning, their problems and their progress.

It is sometimes proposed that some of these needs are best met by a system of mentoring, and, indeed, seniors who had developed such a relationship valued it greatly. However students have fairly predictable, cyclical needs which lie beyond the scope of mentoring relationships. Many of their problems with advising arrangements made by their department, college, or institution arise because these provisions lack the coherence of 'a system'. Structured, regular contact over time with advisors whose role boundaries are clear to the students, who will listen, encourage, and give direction to other system resources, is what can make an otherwise incoherent battery of services work for students.

Teaching and Learning

In this section, we discuss the six 'iceberg' items which reference the learning experiences of S.M.E. students, and the comparisons they make with their experiences in other majors. These include the three most commonly-cited factors contributing to switching decisions, namely:

* lack or loss of interest in the disciplines which comprise S.M.E. majors, which ranked first (43.2%) among reasons for switching, and was mentioned as a concern by 59.6 percent of all switchers, and by 35.5 percent of non-switchers

* a non-S.M.E. major is seen as offering a better education, or more interest, which ranked second (40.4%) among reasons for switching, was mentioned as a concern by 58.5 percent of all switchers, and by 31.6 percent of non-switchers

* poor teaching by S.M.E. faculty which ranked third (36.1%) among reasons for switching, was mentioned as a concern by 90.2 percent of all switchers, and by 73.7 percent of non-switchers

Four less commonly-cited factors are also discussed:

* lack of peer study support, which ranked 15th (11.5%) among reasons for switching, was mentioned as a concern by 16.9 percent of all switchers, and by 7.2 percent of non-switchers

* preference for the teaching approach experienced in non-S.M.E. classes, which ranked 17th (8.7%) among reasons for switching, was mentioned as a concern by 24.0 percent of all switchers, and by 15.1 percent of non-switchers

* poor teaching, laboratory, or recitation support by teaching assistants (never mentioned as a reason for switching) was mentioned as a concern by 19.7 percent of all switchers, and by 10.7 percent of non-switchers

* communication problems with foreign faculty of teaching assistants ranked 20th (3.3%) as a reason for switching, was mentioned as a concern by 29.5 percent of switchers, and by 20.4 percent of non-switchers

Engineering switchers and non-switchers mentioned learning issues more often than did those in science or mathematics (cf., Chapter 1). Gender differences in these items are more difficult to summarize, because, as we shall discuss in Chapter 5, men and women varied in what they considered 'good' teaching, and in what they expected from teachers. However, men were more likely than women to experience difficulty with their S.M.E. major because of failure to make use of peer study groups.

Problems with Faculty Pedagogy

Reports of poor teaching in S.M.E. classes were by far the most common complaint of all switchers and non-switchers. Poor teaching was mentioned by almost every switcher (90.2%), and by far more non-switchers (73.7%) than any other issue. Among non-switchers, concerns about faculty pedagogy ranked first or second, and were among the top five concerns of switchers on all seven campuses except in the two small private colleges which do not offer engineering majors (cf., Table 1.6, Chapter 1). Concerns relating to curricula, the structure and pacing of courses, course assessment systems and student work loads, were universally rated as far less serious than concerns about the quality of S.M.E. faculty pedagogy.

Students were very clear about what was wrong with the teaching they had experienced and had many suggestions about how to improve it. They strongly believed that the source of these problems was that S.M.E. faculty do not like to teach, do not value teaching as a professional activity, and lack, therefore, any incentive to learn to teach effectively:

> About the end of the semester he said, 'I guess by now you've all realized that the university is not for teaching students.' He put it plain, right out in the open...In effect, he was telling us, 'If you want to succeed here you're going to have to do it by yourself.' (Male white science non-switcher)

> It seemed like it was a waste of their time to talk to undergraduates. They could have just printed the lectures and handed them to us. (Male black engineering switcher)

> In the biology department, the professors treated coming to class as a big chore. I've actually had teachers say, 'Well, I don't wanna be here, and you don't wanna be here.' (Female white science non-switcher)

> They just can't understand your questions. They don't understand why you don't understand, and they can't explain what they are telling you any other way. And they just look at you with this blank stare going, 'I don't understand what your problem is.' And the department knows very well that they're not good professors, but they keep them on because they're good researchers. (Female white science non-switcher)

Students constantly referenced faculty preoccupation with research as the overt reason for their failure to pay serious attention to teaching undergraduates, and for specific inadequacies in their attitude or pedagogical technique:

> The full-professors are here for the research. They have the attitude that students are barnacles. Undergraduate students just kind of prevent professors

from doing the research they really want to do. (Female white mathematics switcher)

Thermal dynamics is the one course where all the professors say, 'No, no, not me.' They're trying to not teach the course because it's not related to their research. We got stuck with one professor—you could tell his motivation towards the class, because he always came in unprepared. But he had to give us something—so it was basically the same material we read in the text. (Male white science non-switcher)

The dominance of research-related activities over pedagogy was seen partly as a matter of faculty's interest in their discipline, but also as realism about the source of collegial and institutional prestige, and the criteria for tenure and promotion:

The basis for tenure is not whether or not you're a good teacher, it's how much money you bring in. It's well-known that they can't teach, but they bring in research money. They usually teach the toughest classes too. Or maybe they're the toughest because they're teaching them. (Female white engineering non-switcher)

We met very few students who had been given the chance to work with S.M.E. faculty in a research capacity or to observe them in a hands-on relationship with their discipline. However, students (largely non-switchers) who reported such experiences pointed to the pleasant and open way in which faculty treated undergraduates in a research relationship, compared with their apparent indifference in a teaching context:

I'm working for a professor who doesn't like to teach. He likes research, and is great to work for. He's always happy out there—always smiles and treats me with a lot of respect, and encourages me, and so forth. But in class he's a different animal. (Male white science non-switcher)

Faculty dislike of pedagogical contact with students cannot be entirely explained by their greater interest in research, or by the bias of departmental rewards systems. As some students pointed out, these aspects of their work were shared with academics in all other disciplines. They offered many examples of faculty in non-S.M.E. departments who treated teaching as an integral part of their professional role and took the trouble to do it well:

The classes in my new major seem to be about the same size, but there's so much more interaction between the professors and the students. In the math classes it seemed like the professor would just go up to the chalkboard and start doing problems. And when the bell rang, he'd set down the chalk, and he'd never turn around or say anything to the class. (Female white engineering switcher)

I found myself drawn towards the social sciences. I was having a great time studying with the teacher, talking with the teacher, talking with the T.A.s.

That's what settled it. I don't have any regrets at all. (Male Asian-American engineering switcher)

In chemistry classes their image is more, 'I'm the teacher and you're the students.' And in the social sciences, it's more like, 'I hope we both get something out of the class.' I mean, you both feel like you gain something. So I'm definitely very happy that I got into this major. (Female Hispanic science switcher)

There's a lot different style. The engineering professor is up at the blackboard, while the art teacher is walking around and talking. (Male white engineering switcher)

I think that in sociology and humanities, the quality of the teachers was better. They were more interested in teaching you. They seemed more interested in if you learned something, rather than just the grade you got. The biology teachers were just interested in telling you what they had learned, and you'd better learn it too. (Male white science switcher)

My literature professor's fantastic. They should ask her to teach the science professors how to teach. For the first time, I had a professor who asks your ideas—not just what you've read. And she respects your ideas and your thought processes. (Male white science switcher)

As the foregoing extracts indicate, important elements in what students saw as 'good teaching' were openness, respect for students, encouragement of discussion, and the sense of discovering things together. Students' comparison of the teaching styles they encountered in S.M.E. classes with those experienced in other classes are permeated with dichotomies: coldness versus warmth, elitism versus democracy, aloofness versus openness, rejection versus support:

The humanities classes are much more personable. You feel that the teachers are on your side as opposed to trying to trick you on tests. I know my entire department, and they know me by name. (Female white science switcher)

I've taken human development courses and it's so different, because it's not so cold. Whereas, in the science classes it's just like a wall between the professor and the students. (Female Asian-American science switcher)

The amount of respect is based on grades and not on the person. Whereas, in other departments, I never felt that the professor didn't respect my work. (Female black engineering switcher)

In environmental design, there's an interest from the faculty—that students are in some way valuable to them. Whereas, in the sciences, the students are seen as a distraction. I think it's more personal in the other departments. The professor seems to be a human being and not some kind of machine, and they're not as scary to go and talk to. (Female white engineering switcher)

Students described experiences which suggested to them that S.M.E. faculty disliked or avoided undergraduates, were indifferent to their academic problems, despised teaching and lacked any motivation to teach well:

> Some who just don't like to teach, they'll hold office hours like at 8:00 a.m. in the morning 'cause they don't want you to come in. (Male white science non-switcher)

> I withdrew from his class. He was just horrible...He was very unapproachable. I felt that he just didn't seem to care about what he was doing. (Female Hispanic science switcher)

> You just get this feeling that the material was so much more important than the people who were supposed to be learning it—a sense that, 'It's much more important that I get this material *out* than that you take it in.' I might be making these engineering professors out to sound like big cocky bastards, but they didn't take a very active interest in whether the students learned or not. (Male white engineering switcher)

Students reported that formal evaluations were solicited on a regular basis, but they were cynical about their purpose or utility. They believed that most faculty did not feel a sense of responsibility for students' learning:

> They introduce it to you; they show you the concepts; then you go home and teach yourself. Other instructors will teach you, and they go slower and they explain more. In engineering, half the time they don't even tell you what it's for. It's, 'This is how you do it. Let's move on to something else now.' (Male white engineering switcher)

> I was kind of mad that I wasn't taught better. I had covered all that stuff and beyond in my high school chemistry class, otherwise I probably wouldn't have passed. I mean, you had to teach yourself. Going to lecture was completely worthless. (Male white science switcher)

> Who's to say that they don't just take the evaluations and throw them in the trash. They probably don't even look at them. I just feel that they're not taking into consideration what we're saying. (Male black engineering switcher)

> Part of the problem with the math department is their attitude. I think they realize they're bad, but they really don't care. It's not their problem that their students are failing their courses. It's the students' problem. (Female white science non-switcher)

Students also interpreted the dismissive, rejecting attitude of professors towards those who approached them with questions as an indication that faculty placed all responsibility for learning either squarely on the students' shoulders, or saw it as a matter for delegation to teaching assistants:

> I had engineering teachers who seemed very indifferent; who didn't seem to be concerned with the student that was struggling. There's a couple times I

went to office hours and I was treated like an idiot just because I didn't understand something. (Male black engineering switcher)

I didn't feel comfortable talking to him. I didn't feel like he wanted the students to talk to him. It was more that this was the teaching assistant's responsibility. He just seemed real unapproachable. (Female white science switcher)

I've had professors who have said to me, 'If you don't understand it, talk to your T.A. If they don't understand it, talk to your friends. If worse comes to worst, come see me.' They just didn't want to be bothered with it. (Male white engineering switcher)

Not only was lack of student-teacher dialogue thought to reflect faculty indifference to students, it also meant that faculty received no feedback about what students were, and were not, learning. Students had no way to influence the pace or depth of the syllabus:

There's no sort of interaction back and forth. Just the professor sitting up there presenting material to you. It's sort of a one-way kind of lecture. In high school it was always, like, back and forth. (Female white engineering switcher)

The distancing of S.M.E. faculty from undergraduates was sometimes enhanced by sarcasm, degradation, or ridicule:

There are professors who will call on you and ridicule you if you don't know the answer. You're always on your guard and you're kind of jumpy, and you're not really learning 'cause you're unsure whether you're going to be called on. That's a very poor way to teach in my opinion. (Female white engineering switcher)

Indeed, part of the perceived 'coldness' of S.M.E. classes lay in the creation of an atmosphere in which students were afraid of "saying something wrong":

In a physics recitation, people would rather shut up than say something that could be wrong. That's why there was so little interaction, and strong feeling of intimidation. In my Chinese class, we had an at-ease atmosphere, and mistakes were never scorned. There was a greater acceptance of not being perfect at first. There was a lot of pressure in engineering to appear perfect all the time. (Female white engineering switcher)

Again, students made invidious comparisons between the aloof, forbidding demeanor of many S.M.E. faculty, and the openness they experienced in other classes. Not only did students feel more comfortable in talking about academic difficulties to non-S.M.E. professors, they also found the atmosphere in their classes intellectually stimulating:

I took a history course and that professor has wound up becoming a mentor towards me. He always wants to know what courses I'm taking. He said to come to him if I ever need help. I've had several mentors in the history field that really fostered my interest in it. (Female Asian-American science switcher)

The first chem class was totally *dead*. It wasn't like that when I went to psychology. That was like an alive subject—there was emotion put into the lecture. And that wakes you up. (Female white engineering switcher)

I liked science, I really did. But in the liberal arts, you would bring more of yourself into the class. I really felt like I got to know the teachers. They weren't just flinging numbers at me. And I really, *really* enjoyed that. My parents didn't go to college and it was the first time I had really had an intellectual discussion about issues with someone. And it opened this entirely new world to me that I just fell in love with. (Female white science switcher)

Again, we were made aware of the 'push-and-pull' nature of decisions to leave: poor teaching and the dullness of S.M.E. classes made it hard (even for students with a strong liking for science and mathematics) not to feel drawn towards disciplines where teachers offered the excitement of intellectual exploration and debate.

Students also made very specific criticisms of the pedagogical techniques of their S.M.E. professors. The most common of these were that lessons lacked preparation, logical sequencing or coherence, and that little attempt was made to check that students were following the arguments or ideas. Students interpreted poor preparation as reflecting faculty disinterest in how well their students were learning:

I think poor organization is the major problem with their teaching—just coming to class and trying to teach off-the-cuff without having put any preparation into what will be presented. (Female white science switcher)

There were some math classes where we would be writing frantically to keep up with the professor. He'd just sort of spew equations across the board as he was talking. He wrote really fast, and equations were being put up and wiped off, and we're like, 'What's going on here? Are we just gonna write and figure it out afterwards?' (Male white engineering switcher)

Poor preparation was also cited as evidence of a low level of pedagogical competence, knowledge, or professionalism among S.M.E. faculty:

You run across teachers who don't prepare for lectures. They just look at the section that they're covering in the book, or they have some scribbled notes and just start talking about it as if they were talking to grad students or colleagues. (Male Hispanic engineering non-switcher)

He sometimes gets lost, and then he'll have to erase everything and start over. Or he'll be at the end and realize he made an error, and have to go back to the beginning of the problem. And we have to wait for him to figure out what he did wrong. By that time, I'm lost. (Female black engineering non-switcher)

The professor is up there fumbling and going, 'Oh, no. Correction.' And going off in six different directions because he has no teaching skills. (Female white science switcher)

Students were frustrated by professors who seemed unable to explain their ideas sequentially or coherently:

I've had professors that know their subject backwards and forwards and, in fact, one of the instructors won some engineering prize for his work in physics. Great person. Great mind. But he couldn't communicate effectively. (Male white science switcher)

If you're not conceptualizing what's going on, it's hard. The professor understands everything so well that they have a hard time expressing some of the basic concepts. (Male white engineering switcher)

They had so much knowledge and they got almost none of it across. Or whatever they got across was in such pieces, so distorted, that there was no integration. So that was really frustrating, to go to a class with really intelligent people who could not communicate. (Female white science switcher)

Teachers defined as "poor" did not appear to understand the relationship between the amount of material which can be presented in a single class, and the level of comprehension and retention which they could expect from students:

He covered approximately 500 pages in the regular text book. That was too much information being shoved into too small a space at one time. (Male white science switcher)

Nor did they pitch their class materials or test questions at a level which was appropriate for students at a particular stage of conceptual development, or break down syllabus matter into sequences which promote conceptual grasp:

You feel like you almost have to know stuff when you go in because they are not trying to explain or break down these concepts, but are somewhere up here that you have to just catch up to. (Female black engineering switcher)

You're struggling to get out of the muck at the bottom of the pond and he's sailing away. (Male white science non-switcher)

Sometimes I find that exams are worded in a way that you're misled. I don't think it's intentional. I think it may have to do with them being on a level so far removed from the students, and forgetting we're just learning this. (Female Asian-American science switcher)

He could not understand how students wouldn't understand something. Everything he did was so easy and blatant to him, he didn't know how to explain it more simply. (Male white science switcher)

We went to the department head and voiced our complaints. The teacher was such a nice guy, but nobody had learned anything. I think he was used to teaching upper-division classes. He was going over our heads all the time. (Female white engineering non-switcher)

Students also looked for, and mostly did not find, illustration, application and discussion of the implications of material being taught:

They're used to just going through the equations on the board and not really illustrating it—just sorta cranking through it. (Male engineering non-switcher)

Seemed like they just said, 'Do it,' and you did. And they don't tell you why; they don't explain it very well. I kind of felt sorry for everyone—it was just going over their heads. (Female white engineering switcher)

They just spit it out at you, and they don't say, 'This is like...,' or, 'You can imagine this being....' Even when you're in a large room you can tell when someone's talking at you or speaking to you. (Female white mathematics switcher)

I did a lot better in the hands-on classes because there I could actually see an outcome from the knowledge that I was acquiring. Had I had close experience with engineering, maybe I would have seen some applicability, but I didn't see it at all. (Male white engineering switcher)

Students also found it hard to retain their interest in the subject where their professors failed to present the material in a stimulating manner:

Physics I found absolutely *useless*—mostly because the instructor had a monotone. And I tend to tune out something that has a regular, constant pitch—for example, the fan. (Male white science switcher)

You'll sit through the lecture, it'll be so boring, they'll be so monotone. (He mimics the style.) That really got to you in about two seconds. Imagine sitting through an hour and 15 minutes of it. You kind of lose track, think about different things and learn it from the book. (Male white engineering non-switcher)

S.M.E. classes were often faulted for their dullness of presentation. The most tedious classes were those in which professors over-focused on getting students to memorize material:

I didn't like chemistry because so much of it was rote memorization. You just sat and listened to the professor drone on and on. It just really wears on you after a while...I think it would help to change the way they teach it. (Male white science non-switcher)

Chemistry was the worst class I've ever taken in my life. It was very dry—just learning the numbers and the formulas and memorizing everything. It just wasn't connected to anything. In high school chemistry, you learned about the elements, and then did an experiment so you could see how it worked. (Female white engineering switcher)

However, by far the most effective technique for dissipating student interest was the widely-reported practice of reading or copying materials straight from text books. Reports of this teaching method came from every S.M.E. discipline and were reported on every campus. The following examples came from four different campuses:

> If you look in the book you can say, 'Oh, I know what he's going to do today,' and by golly, that's what goes on the board. He'll just say what he writes. All he's doing is copying the book. It's pretty sick. If someone asks a question, he goes through this robotic quoting of the book again. (Male white engineering non-switcher)

> I had one professor who would literally pick up the book and read it to the class. I mean, he would just read. We had 60 percent of the class drop the course. I counted one day, and out of maybe 180 students, 17 showed up to the lecture. I was happy with the course content, and the facilities were wonderful, but the teaching was just a *vast* disappointment to me. (Male white engineering switcher)

> Nothing really bothers me more than to have the professor just read what's in the textbook. I mean, you could have saved the $30. Actually, one semester I did that. I just relied on the notes, and did just as well as I'd been doing with buying the books. (Male white science switcher)

> I got a B+ in both math and chemistry, but I felt it was a waste of time to go to the class itself. When we went into class, they would read out of the book. And I'd think, 'I can do that. You're the teacher: I want you to explain it some way other than what I've already read.' It was just a waste of my time. It wasn't teaching. It was just reading. (Female white engineering switcher)

Another version of this method was sometimes referred to as 'silent teaching': the professor writes on the board with his or her back to the class, and addresses the students infrequently and minimally. Again, students read in this behavior the message that these professors take no responsibility for their students' learning:

> They just continually write. And they're standing in front of what they write, but they don't care. They'll look over their shoulder now and then, and say, 'Okay, you all are still there,' and just keep going. And the number of people that don't go to classes is amazing. (Female white mathematics switcher)

> You walk in, you sit down, and you get your pencil going. It's just write, write, write. And the guy's going across the board, talking as fast as he can. You have no idea what he's saying; you have no idea what the concepts are. All you're trying to do is write as fast as this professor. If he would just take the notes he's been teaching from for the last 20 years, mimeograph 'em, and hand 'em to you, we could look at them, make little notes on his notes, ask intelligent questions, and try to get hold of the concepts, rather than scribbling down the formulas. (Male white engineering non-switcher)

Unfortunately, what many S.M.E. faculty did communicate all too well to students was their own apparent disinterest in the class subject matter. This was a commonly-offered and strongly-stressed reason for the dissipation of interest in the S.M.E. discipline students originally chose:

> The professors I've had for physics and engineering bored me, although I don't ever think the material was boring. The professor has a lot to do with how students learn, and how excited they are about the material. I believe some of these professors didn't care if you stayed or not. I remember this one guy, he never even made eye contact with the class. It was just like he was staring off into space. That sort of thing is a big factor in people losing interest and switching. (Male white science switcher)

Another set of criticisms focused on faculty's limited understanding of how students learn. The absence of apparent structure in the selection of class materials, or in the order and logic of their presentation; and the lack of fit between class materials, home work and the content of tests, suggested to students, that faculty knew nothing about learning objectives, did not know how to organize their teaching around them, or were deliberately perverse:

> I had a physics professor who taught stuff that was totally unrelated to what we were being tested on and totally unrelated to what we were reading—to anything that applied to anything, in fact. (Male white engineering non-switcher)

> They tell you to read the book, and it seemed like it was talking about something completely different than the professor. They didn't fit at all. The only thing that fit were the problems in the book, but you weren't likely to see them on the board. (Male black engineering switcher)

> A lot of professors are really bad teachers. There doesn't seem like there's any pattern. They'll give you a syllabus, but they kind of go off on tangents and there's really no lesson plan. (Male Hispanic science non-switcher)

Students did not accept the argument that some S.M.E. subject matter is inherently tedious, and that learning it is just part of the hard grind of being in an S.M.E. major:

> I'm retaking quantum physics right now. With my first professor it was all deadly dull, with *this* professor some of it is very interesting. So I don't think it's the *material* that has changed, I think it's the way it's being taught. There's no way they are going to be interesting if they don't *care* about what they're teaching. (Female white science non-switcher)

Where two professors taught the same material, but only one of them structured their presentation and assessments so as to build comprehension, students reported a marked difference in how well they did in the two classes, and in how much they feel they had learned:

I failed Calculus II and had to retake it. But the class was full, so I asked if I could take the arts and science practical calc instead. And I was really surprised: it was the same material, but there was an extreme difference in the pace we took; a totally different calibre of professor also. He seemed concerned about us and taught us well, even though there were so many of us. I did very well the second time: I got a B, although I got a D the first time. (Male white engineering switcher)

The professor is *by far and away*, I think, the main determining factor in how well you do in a class, and how much you learn. I could give several examples of courses I've taken with one professor, which my room-mate had taken with another. And you'd think they were teaching two different subjects. It's definitely the teacher thing. (Male white engineering non-switcher)

A friend of mine who's taking the class that I struggled through—and I couldn't tell you one thing I learned out of it—he's loving it. He's doing hands-on, practical experiments. And I sat there learning more theories than I'd ever know what to do with.' (Male white engineering non-switcher)

Failure to build syllabus structure around learning objectives was also evident in the presentation of materials at a pace which was too fast for comprehension or mental digestion:

They'll rush though the material. And I think that's why sometimes my grades suffer because I don't get to digest what the professor puts on the board. You're moving so fast already. And three days later you're on a whole new subject. (Male white engineering non-switcher)

Finally, some faculty appeared to address their own rather than the students' intellectual needs:

It was kind of self-serving for him. He just liked to prove that he could go through this one theory and figure it out on the board. I learned more out of the book than in the lecture. (Female white science switcher)

My physics teacher would just ramble on about whatever sparked his interest. Then he'd give an exam that had nothing to do with what he talked about in lecture. *Nothing at all!* (Male white engineering non-switcher)

As we discussed earlier, curve-grading tends to shift the focus of teaching away from what students get out of classes intellectually toward what they acquire in terms of grades. As students are painfully aware, a gap then opens up between grades they receive and the level of knowledge and skills which the grades are supposed to reflect:

His system was the most screwy I've seen yet. He didn't like averages on exams to be above 50 percent. He curved them 20 to 30 points at the end of the semester, but throughout the entire semester you're getting like 40 percent on the exams. Even if you know the average is that low, it's still really demoralizing. And I didn't learn anything, 'cause I was only able to do less than half the problems on the exams. (Male white engineering switcher)

If you see yourself getting a 25, and you're getting a C, that's not like getting a 75 and getting a C. It's not at all. They value the grade on what you're getting. They don't value the learning. (Male white engineering non-switcher)

I got a C, but I didn't learn anything. You should get an F if you don't learn anything. (Female white engineering non-switcher)

In the science classes you may end up with an A or B but only get 50 on a test out of 100 points, because they had to curve it up. That always bothered me because it seems like if you're only doing 50 percent of the work or getting 50 percent of the points you're not really learning everything. Even the highest grade may have been a 60 and that means that the top person didn't even understand all the work. You can beat the average, but you still don't understand all the material. (Male white science switcher)

Although most students did not make the connection, treating learning objectives as the main focus of teaching is an aim which runs directly counter to student selection by the criteria inherent in the weed-out system. If students enjoy and understand the materials presented in class, are intellectually stimulated, learn well, and show this in their examination answers, then it may become difficult to discard enough students to match departmental resources by the start of junior year. This is not to suggest that faculty deliberately teach badly in order to meet a weed-out quota. This is, nevertheless, the inevitable consequence of learned and institutionalized pedagogical incompetence. The perceived need to use introductory classes for selection purposes encourages collegial toleration and reinforcement of poor teaching. It also makes it difficult for faculty to value good teaching, to view their teaching responsibilities as a professional priority, or to educate themselves in pedagogical techniques built upon learning theory.

One important student group whose intellectual needs are not met by the current focus on weed-out objectives are those who continue in their S.M.E. majors to graduation, and/or into graduate school. As seniors made clear, the teaching methods they experienced in introductory classes often resulted in a shaky theoretical foundation for higher level work. They described uncertainty about particular bodies of material, and described gaps in understanding which they had not been able to close. They were angry that their education had suffered in the process of discarding other students. Another large group whose needs are not met by the weed-out approach to introductory classes are non-science majors who seek a grounding in college-level science and mathematics as part of their overall college education.

As we shall discuss in more detail in the following chapter, increases in the costs of higher education and in the time needed to complete an S.M.E. degree in a period when a growing number of students are assuming the primary financial responsibility for their education, dispose S.M.E. majors to view the pedagogical inadequacies of their classes in terms of poor value for the money:

> The thing that just drove me nuts was that I was paying all this money. I'd be in a classroom with about 300 other students and I was thinking, 'Well, I'm paying about $1,000 tuition and at this rate these guys must be earning $70,000 a year.' It just didn't make sense. (Male white science non-switcher)

> I would say that 50 percent of the course work you do is poorly delivered, and is a struggle. Not only do you pay to take the course but you wind up taking the course at home. You might as well not even *show up* for class. You're not getting *any* help. And you're paying money to learn the course yourself out of a book. (Female white science switcher)

The student as disgruntled consumer is, in effect, arguing that it is inappropriate to take the fees of the many in return for a service whose quality is determined by a primary focus on selection of the few.

Experiences with Teaching Assistants

Graduate students employed in S.M.E. teaching support roles (largely in recitation, laboratory and tutorial contexts), are in a peculiarly difficult situation. On the one hand, many S.M.E. faculty are poor role models as teachers, either for the acquisition of good teaching skills, or for the development of positive attitudes toward the value of learning them. On the other hand, S.M.E. faculty often delegate a high degree of responsibility to their teaching assistants for teaching the fundamentals of their disciplines, and for responding to undergraduates' questions and problems. Because undergraduates find it so difficult to learn from S.M.E. faculty, they also depend more on T.A.s than students in non-S.M.E. majors in order to acquire basic concepts and skills. When undergraduates complain to deans and chairs about the quality of S.M.E. teaching, or give negative class evaluations, the focus of blame for undergraduate dissatisfaction is sometimes shifted onto graduate teaching assistants.

It is clear, however, from our data that most S.M.E. undergraduates do not place primary responsibility for their learning difficulties on teaching assistants. Not one of our informants cited poor teaching by T.A.s as having contributed to their decision to leave (cf., Table 1.6, Chapter 1). Indeed, undergraduates reported that graduate teaching assistants had a higher level of interest in teaching and a greater willingness to meet the intellectual needs of undergraduates than did faculty. Undergraduates were particularly appreciative of T.A.s who treated their questions seriously (and sought to answer them), reinterpreted material they found difficult in terms they could understand, offered them applications of theoretical material, showed them alternative ways to approach problems, shared their own know-how, bolstered students' confidence, and reinforced their enthusiasm for the discipline:

In my upper-division mechanical engineering classes they carry the same T.A.s for a lot of the classes so you get to know them and they usually know what they're talking about. They're usually more helpful than the professors. They know the professor's not making any sense. They'll tell you, 'Here's a better way to explain it.' (Female white engineering non-switcher)

All T.A.s I've had have been pretty enthusiastic and they're pretty good about showing short-cuts. (Male white engineering non-switcher)

They will do a full review for you before the test. That's very key. (Female white engineering switcher)

They always knew where the tough spots on the problem sets were so we could focus on those. It was just very helpful. (Female white engineering non-switcher)

I've had T.A.s that were even better than professors, I felt, just because of their enthusiasm for teaching. And that made a big difference in students wanting to learn the material. (Female white engineering non-switcher)

Students looked to T.A.s for a teacher-learner relationship which they sought, but rarely found, in faculty:

T.A.s are the closest recourse that a student would have to a real teacher. Professors are larger than life. They're a little out of reach. Yeah, T.A.s are definitely the way to go. (Male white engineering switcher)

They are the ones to go and see if you have a problem. They are easier to talk to and they don't put you down in the same way as the professors do. (Female white engineering non-switcher)

Students expected T.A.s to be more open and approachable than faculty, and more ready to explain things in plain terms. When the T.A. support system worked well, students expressed satisfaction with their classes. This was true even when faculty teaching was seen as inadequate:

The T.A.s are very important to the class because if the professor's up there lecturing, and you don't understand a word they're saying, most students want to go see the T.A.s rather than the instructor. Because if you can't understand them in lecture, you don't want to get more confused. (Female white science non-switcher)

The classes are a lot easier to handle when you have a good T.A. to explain things to you when the professors can't. (Female black science non-switcher)

My opinion is that it's the T.A.s who really teach the course. The instructors just administer it. (Male black engineering switcher)

There are classes where almost everyone's clueless, but no one will ask a question. Then you get with the T.A. in a smaller class situation and that's where the learning really goes on. Because we're not afraid to ask the T.A., and they will explain things down to every last step. (Male white mathematics non-switcher)

There were, however, some complaints about T.A.s (i.e. from 15.5 percent of all students interviewed). Many of these dissatisfactions focused on replication by T.A.s of the poor pedagogical skills and indifference towards teaching modeled for them by faculty. These inadequacies were additional to the normal shortcomings of graduate teachers, namely, insufficient familiarity with the syllabus material to teach it with confidence, or in depth:

> They seem very disorganized, and I feel like they're confused. I really like it when T.A.s prepare something to talk about, to try and incorporate the material. I don't like it when the T.A.s are there to just tell you how to do problems. I mean, that's not what we need. (Female white engineering switcher)

> This is a research school and what happens is that inevitably you're getting Ph.D.s that are doing research in really abstract areas trying to teach freshmen undergraduates. And they're just not equipped to do that. They're totally unprepared to teach low level math and calculus to engineers. And the same thing goes for the physics department. (Male white engineering non-switcher)

> He's not had any experience teaching a class. He doesn't have the organizational skills that you need to direct a class. He obviously knows the material very well, but he's having a hard time relating it to the average student who doesn't know anything about it. (Male white science switcher)

It is clear that most S.M.E. teaching assistants had not received any instruction on how to teach effectively, were teaching in the same way that they themselves had been taught, and were, perforce, repeating the pedagogical errors of their professional mentors:

> The problem is that they don't have any education classes behind them. They don't know how to get people to learn. They do not know how to give information. They can't get their ideas across. It's a self-taught class. If you don't get what he does on the board, you go to the book. If you can't teach yourself from the book, you don't make it. (Female white mathematics switcher)

> My teaching assistant was really smart and tried to help, but, actually, she didn't. She was aiming for everyone to get an A instead of everyone to understand. She would give us a lot of the answers, but she wouldn't really explain them very well. I think that was partly because she just didn't know how to explain things. She would just *tell us* the answers, so you could memorize them, but never understand them. (Female white engineering switcher)

> I want someone who can answer my questions. But, a lot of the T.A.s pretty much have a one-track type of mind. They just know it the way they learned it. (Male Hispanic science non-switcher)

Graduate T.A.s also appeared to be replicating the negative attitudes of faculty toward teaching, and a learned incapacity to communicate effectively:

> Not very many of them plan to be teachers. This is just a job. (Female white engineering switcher)

From a focus group of women science non-switchers—

> They aren't interested in teaching you. They're doing it because they have to. They're grad students and this is part of their package. They have to teach this course.

> Or even if they're interested in teaching because they're excited about what they're doing, they just can't manage to communicate it in a way that we can understand.

What was also alarming, especially to switchers who sought individual help, was that many graduate students expressed the same indifferent attitude towards undergraduate learners that they had found in faculty:

> I would say they are very similar to faculty. I think that people who have made it far enough to be T.A.s have the same sort of attitude. I had a T.A. teach me math, and it was the same old thing as the professors—not exciting at all. He was already kind of on the same path. (Male white science switcher)

> T.A.s always say, 'We're here.' But I don't think they would go really far out of their way to help you get the basics. They wouldn't be willing to spend the time. They just try to confuse you more or they say, 'Well, you should have learned that; you should be in a simpler class.' (Female white engineering switcher)

> The T.A. was really impatient. He didn't like repeating himself. I would ask him a few questions, and he became impatient. (Male Hispanic science switcher)

> The section leaders were just kind of inept, but the head T.A. was really arrogant. He seemed much more interested in his own learning and advancement than anybody else's. (Male white engineering switcher)

Graduate assistants were also seen to mirror faculty in their professional priorities and constraints:

> I had a T.A. that was in engineering and he was so wrapped up in what he was doing that it was hard for him to teach. (Male white engineering switcher)

> I had one or two helpful T.A.s. But most of them are taking their own course-load, which is very heavy, and they also have to do this to make money. So they have a bunch of pressures. (Female white engineering switcher)

As they did with faculty, undergraduates made unfavorable contrasts between the teaching they received from some S.M.E. graduate teaching assistants and that experienced in other disciplines:

> I've noticed in history or psychology, those T.A.s seem to be really good. They will talk to you and help you. They're excited about what they're doing. But around chemistry or physics, they don't plan on teaching. They just want to make money so they can get through this. (Female white engineering switcher)

The absorption by graduate teaching assistants of S.M.E. faculty norms and practices with respect to teaching appeared, happily, to be far from complete. Most undergraduates reported a mixture of good and bad experiences with T.A.s, whereas their experiences with faculty as teachers were more consistently disappointing:

> He really didn't care about the students. He was interested in doing research and he had to teach Calc 1221. You know, he put his time in and that was it. Then I had another one who was willing to see people and made special study groups, and was much more supportive. So it depends on the individual. (Male white science non-switcher)

We were surprised to find that some S.M.E. departments did not offer recitation sections in support of large lecture classes. Students complained that recitation sections were often too large for the kind of interactive, interrogative learning they sought. It was also clear that some faculty delegated responsibility for teaching original material to graduate teaching assistants rather than keeping recitations as an opportunity to clarify and consolidate material taught in class:

> Our section probably had 40 people in it. A lot of times our prof had T.A.s teaching in the section. So it's not even like we went over the old stuff. We actually did a lot of new stuff in recitations. (Female white engineering switcher)

> These recitation sections are enormous. They usually consist of just a smaller lecture where the T.A. will work problems on the board, but students don't get a chance to speak or ask questions. (Female white engineering switcher)

Students wanted small, well-organized recitations in support of their large classes. Where this was provided, class size was not, in and of itself, reported to be a problem. They also wanted graduate teaching assistants to receive training for the teaching and tutoring work that they did:

> At that school, graduate students are required to take a course in teaching, and about the way their particular school requirements work before they start T.A.-ing...They didn't believe that this university didn't have something like that—that T.A.s just came in without any training at all. (Female white engineering switcher)

They've got to make sure every T.A. is qualified, and on an equal level within any course. If the class has five T.A.s, make sure you've got five equally qualified T.A.s. (Male white engineering switcher)

Language Problems with Teaching Assistants

A theory which is sometimes offered to explain either the phenomenon of high S.M.E. switching rates, or poor student evaluations of S.M.E. pedagogy, is that the proportion of graduate teaching assistants whose first language is not English has increased in recent years. Throughout this study, we asked students to comment on the significance, either for switching decisions, or for their level of satisfaction with S.M.E. teaching, of being taught by foreign-born faculty or graduate students. As the iceberg table (Table 1.6, Chapter 1) indicates, the effect of foreign teachers on switching decisions proved to be negligible (3.3%). However, 29.5 percent of switchers and 20.4 percent of non-switchers cited language-related problems with foreign T.A.s as a concern at some level. Almost all of their observations concerned graduate students rather than faculty, and only a handful related to problems other than those of communication. Interestingly, by far the greatest number of these concerns were expressed on just two of the seven campuses, although this seemed unrelated to differences in the proportion of foreign T.A.s to non-foreign T.A.s.

Students' problems with the English spoken by non-American T.A.s were of two kinds. The least commonly-cited problem was insufficient command of the language to explain complex ideas or to understand and answer undergraduates' questions. The more commonly cited difficulty was that of adjusting to fluent English spoken with an unfamiliar accent. Students tended not to make these linguistic distinctions, but glossed them both as difficulties of "fluency":

> The problem generally with people who don't speak English is that they don't understand *your* questions. They don't understand what you mean. And that is somewhat of a minor irritation, but it doesn't bother me that much. That wasn't any influence on why I left. (Male white engineering switcher)

> Fluency in English, I would say, is a factor in physics. Several T.A.s that didn't have enough communication skills to impart pretty complex ideas. Not only that, but their confidence level is affected by their inability to communicate effectively. And they become withdrawn. (Male white engineering non-switcher)

> I would say the language problem depends on the T.A. I had one who was from China, and he was really a good T.A. Conceptually, he explained it really well. Every once in a while you couldn't catch a word—just a small irritation really. I also had T.A.s where you couldn't understand them. And then it's not an irritation, it's a wall. (Male Asian-American engineering switcher)

The perceived importance of both types of problem varied enormously. Most complaints were ancillary to other learning difficulties, or to complaints about T.A.s in general. Also, undergraduates' high level of dissatisfaction with faculty pedagogy puts more stress on teaching assistants to compensate for those perceived inadequacies. The communication skills of T.A.s, therefore, assume a higher degree of significance than they have in majors where students are satisfied with faculty teaching:

> You expect to go to the T.A. and get extra help, 'cause the professors aren't really there for you. But, if they don't understand what you're asking, and you don't understand what they're trying to tell you, it's terrible. (Male white engineering switcher)

The following speaker was one of the few who explained his switching decision partly in terms of frustration at being unable to understand his T.A.:

> Well, I don't mean to keep putting down foreign T.A.s, but because I didn't have professors who were able to explain it clearly enough, it made it that much harder—which made the next step harder. So although it was not the main reason, it's what finally caused me to switch. (Male white engineering switcher)

The primary source of this student's difficulty was the poor teaching skills of American-born faculty. Inability to understand the T.A., who was his last resort, was the final frustration.

Many students expressed doubts that accounts of linguistic difficulties with T.A.s could be taken as "the real reason" for switching:

> One of my T.A.s didn't speak English as his first language, but I mean, after a while, you kind of got used to what he was saying and then you'd pick it up. I think a lot of the times people just don't want to give 'em enough of a chance. I think the people who bail out because of that, would end up bailing out anyhow. (Female white science switcher)

> I had a Japanese math T.A. my freshman year. I didn't find any problem. My current instructor is Turkish and her accent just takes a little getting used to. That's kind of a cop-out I think. It's just making an excuse, you know, for your own inadequacies or something—just to blame it on the T.A. (Male white engineering switcher)

> I had a guy from Africa in Chemistry. A lot of students complained that he was hard to understand, but I thought he was great. I think some students were using that as an excuse as to why they weren't doing as well. (Female white science switcher)

> I think that's kind of a cop-out personally. It's kind of an inside joke with most people. It's an irritation sometimes, but I can't imagine anybody ever actually quitting because of it. I mean, if that was what they said, there would have to

be another reason that they weren't letting on to. (Male white engineering switcher)

As the last group of speakers illustrate, the predominance of this type of "excuse" for academic difficulties on only two of the seven campuses suggests an easy resort to ready-made explanations which are available in particular student sub-cultures. The inter-weaving of accounts of other learning difficulties with accounts of communication problems with foreign T.A.s also lends support to the scape-goating theory offered by undergraduate peers:

> A lot of my T.A.s did not speak English adequately to convey the material. I couldn't understand what they were talking about. I remember my first real problem was my T.A. I didn't go to section for the whole quarter and that's when my interest started falling off. And then spring quarter the same thing happened. By this time I was totally discouraged. And my grades of course, were falling off because I wasn't going to section. (Female white science switcher)

Rather than allowing their situation to deteriorate to the point where switching seemed the only option, most students who reported problems in understanding their T.A. simply dropped that class and retook it later. In disciplines with a high proportion of graduate students who were not educated in this country, it is clearly important to make sure that those who are given teaching assignments have sufficient fluency to be effective in a teaching support role. However, the communications problem with foreign T.A.s most commonly expressed is the difficulty that American students have in adjusting to different cadences in pronunciation by people who are fluent, or native, English speakers.[4] Poor teaching by faculty places undue stress on all teaching assistants, most of whom receive no training for this work. In this situation, as we have illustrated, by far the most important quality in teaching assistants, regardless of linguistic differences, is their willingness to work with undergraduates on an individual basis.

Students' Suggestions for the Improvement of S.M.E. Pedagogy

Switchers and non-switchers were virtually unanimous in their view that no set of problems in S.M.E. majors was more in need of urgent, radical improvement than faculty pedagogy. All related matters, including curriculum revision, were deemed secondary to this need. We feel that this point cannot be over-stressed because, as we have observed in visits to S.M.E. departments where reform initiatives are already underway, the first reforms that faculty undertake invariably concern curriculum structure rather than the quality of teaching. This is understandable. Faculty currently hold a wide spectrum of beliefs about the extent and causes of S.M.E. undergraduate attrition—including, at one extreme, serious doubt that a problem of any kind exists. In this situation, it is easier for reform-minded faculty to begin by proposing structural changes which can be made without threat to established modes of thought, practice and belief. However, if a serious attempt to reduce undergraduate attrition in these majors is to be made, sooner or later, faculty will be faced with the question of how to address their collective shortcomings as teachers. In their role as paying customers, our informants offered a number of suggestions about how to improve the teaching service being offered. These are summarized below.

Training and Planning for Undergraduate Teaching

Students offered two different approaches to the issue of how to guarantee a professional level of pedagogical knowledge and skills in teaching the fundamentals of each discipline. They were in general agreement that all teaching assistants should receive training for their assignments; that they should be monitored and mentored by faculty committed to good teaching; that they should not be required to teach new material in recitations or laboratory sessions; and that their role in giving individual and small group tutorial assistance should be paramount. Strong support was expressed for a system in which all faculty who regularly teach freshman and sophomore classes should receive professional pedagogical training. Faculty who devote time to undergraduate teaching and planning should be given special credit for this in the rewards system, and regular opportunities for the enhancement of teaching techniques should be offered by institutions. Some students doubted, however, that this was possible, given the faculty's paramount interest in research, the customary faculty rewards system, and the financial dependence of departments and colleges on research funding from sources outside the institution. Students in the two major research universities especially felt that the best compromise would be to augment the relatively small number of faculty interested in teaching by appointing a special group of faculty who were specifically recruited for their teaching skills:[5]

> I suggest improving the teaching by having a certain number of professors that just want to do research, and other professors that are interested in teaching. Or, maybe have them teach alternately with research, so they don't have to worry about both during the same semester. (Male white engineering non-switcher)

> Teachers need to have more of a focus on teaching, and their teaching skills need to be developed if they don't have them. Otherwise, people need to be hired who have good teaching skills, even if they're not doing the research that brings in all the money. (Female black engineering switcher)

A more sophisticated version of this idea, was to develop departmental teaching 'teams' to address curriculum planning, teaching, student learning and assessment. The regular members of these groups would be faculty skilled in teaching, T.A.s., undergraduate advisors, and where they existed, special program directors, and peer counselors:

> The faculty who should be planning the basic classes need to be a team, with the people who are involved in teaching included, as well as the people who know what's going on—like the advisors and the women's program director. There's not much point telling your advisors about your problems with a particular class if they can't pass that along where it can do some good. (Female white engineering non-switcher)

> The T.A.s and the faculty teaching big classes need to work much more closely. The T.A.s need to learn how to teach from people who really know how to do it—and how to plan out the class material and the labs in a way that makes sense. And the faculty need to keep checking in with them, and getting feedback on the questions the students are asking. And they need to give the T.A.s direction. One of these days, they're gonna be professors too. (Female white science non-switcher)

Teaching teams also need ways to coordinate their offerings to students across disciplines and with departments whose students are 'serviced' by their introductory classes. They also need to develop ways to monitor the outcome of their work—including formative and summative evaluation techniques. Above all, they need to redefine "professionalism" to include openness to collegial review and critique of their teaching, and to develop departmental systems of peer review. Unless these review mechanisms become part of normal departmental structures, teaching innovations are unlikely to gain wider collegial acceptance, or to survive.

The Structure and Content of a Well-Taught Class
The point at which good curriculum planning and good teaching converged was, in the view of students, in those classes which placed primary emphasis on helping them to understand, and to apply, theoretical concepts. They saw this as the best framework for teaching formulas and problem-solving skills. One of the more seductive aspects of students' experiences in some non-S.M.E. classes—whether or not students actually switched—was discovery and exploration of their own thinking processes:

> It's the concepts that they need to teach more than the formulas. Because if you know the concepts, you can figure out the formulas—or look them up. (Male white engineering non-switcher)

> My advice would be to teach people to think—give people a love of learning, don't just give them a love of problem-solving. That's the thing that I see that's gone wrong. They don't teach people *why* they're learning, and encourage them to read a book outside of class; I don't think I ever picked up a science book or a journal outside of class. (Male white science non-switcher)

Don't teach by example alone. Encourage them to solve the problem by thinking about it. But you gotta take the time to do it. (Male white science non-switcher)

If they would put the emphasis on this being a process of thinking rather than just a way to solve a specific type of problem, people would understand it better. (Male white science non-switcher)

I even thought about changing my major because it just seemed like all memorization. You don't have to do any critical thinking. I think that professors should always ask questions that test your understanding, and not just your ability to memorize. (Female white science non-switcher)

Dealing with 'why' as well as 'how' questions, and planning syllabuses, teaching methods and student assessments in ways which encourage students to think, read about, discuss and apply concepts were common themes. Students liked to "figure things out for themselves," but they also needed an intellectual structure within which to do this. Asking them to discover underlying principles without a conceptual framework was merely frustrating:

I've had maybe three teachers tell us how it all fits into the big picture—as opposed to just giving you topics all over the place, and you're supposed to figure out what that means in the whole scheme of things. (Male white engineering non-switcher)

A lot of them seem to have this idea that if you figure it out for yourself you'll know it so much better. Well, that is such a joke, because if we could all just figure things out for ourselves we would all be Isaac Newton. You must be shown how it works, and *then* you can recreate or extend it. There's no logic to me in the other method. It's a waste of time. It's frustrating. (Female white engineering switcher)

In mathematics and physics, they teach you the problems, how to use the formula, how to solve the problems. But they don't give you a general view of where it's all leading. It was one of the biggest problems, I think. (Male native American science non-switcher)

Students appreciated class content that was lively, stimulating and up-to-date. They liked to be mentally (rather than morally) challenged, and developed their own rationale for working hard for teachers who stimulated them and encouraged them to think creatively:

Someone who challenges the student, I think, is a good teacher, but they need to do it in a way that is encouraging and challenging, not just a hard-ass challenge. (Male white science non-switcher)

Medical microbiology was great. I loved it—got an A—but I worked harder than ever before. She motivated you, excited you, and demanded your very best. And I like that. In a class where someone is just doing a general coverage of something, it lulls me into sleep. I wonder whether this person is really teaching me, or is the book my best friend? (Male white science non-switcher)

The texts they choose are quite recent, but they don't really recognize modern technology or talk about its implementations—which is the exciting part about learning this, I think. So I'm disappointed. (Female white engineering non-switcher)

I might have stayed in engineering, but I don't think that they really teach you to be creative—where you look at something and can put it together. I see engineering as a very creative discipline. But here, it's more numbers. They're important too, but I think that if people are going to make real break-throughs, they need that creative stimulation from their teachers. (Male white engineering switcher)

Important aspects of lively classes were illustration, application and demonstration:

And if you teach something, show an experiment that goes along with it. (Female white science switcher)

The chemistry professors taught to the people who had already had it and who really comprehended it. They didn't apply it to something that the rest of us would understand. There weren't any analogies. (Female white science switcher)

A good teacher can explain it not only in generalities, but can respond when I say, 'Please give me an example of how to do that.' Examples are very important to me. (Female white mathematics switcher)

It's the lack of examples, especially complex examples. They'll give you a simple example, but when you go to do the homework there's always other factors. One important thing the professor should do in class is to supplement the book with lots of examples. But that doesn't happen. (Female white engineering non-switcher)

In contacts with faculty engaged in pedagogical renewal, we have become aware of growing support for experiential, hands-on methods of teaching theoretical material.[6] However, few of our informants had experienced learning techniques focused on doing or discovering science at the college level—although some had experienced this in high school. Because of their poor experiences with laboratory sessions, most students spoke of them as a chore rather than as the heart of their scientific education. It did not, therefore, seem to occur to most students that labs, field work and experiential classroom work could occupy a more central role in undergraduate learning.

What students wanted universally, however, were well-prepared and organized classes, based on a good understanding of what students could be expected to know and do at any particular stage, and empathy with the learner's insecurity. Students wanted to be able to follow the teacher's logic through the structure and style of their presentation. In their view, the good teacher walks students through the ideas, emphasizes his or her mental route with 'signposts' and regularly checks that students are following the flow of ideas:

> A good teacher works in a very detailed manner, in an organized top-to-bottom, beginning-to-end kind of order. They also have some sense of how it feels to be a beginner. (Female white engineering switcher)

> I had a calculus professor who approached it from the level of the student and it was just the greatest course. A lot of them don't care or they don't know how a student learns. They just throw it on the board and expect everyone to be able to see it. (Female white engineering switcher)

> I've had courses where you sit in the class for an hour and 15 minutes, just like a bullet train, and don't know what happened. And I took other courses and it was just fabulous. He would say, 'Okay, now I'm going to tell you about this. And here's what it is. Okay, this is what I just told you. Do you understand that?' And you go, 'Wow, that is so clear.' He said it three times, as opposed to, 'Oh my God, what's going on here?' (Male white engineering non-switcher)

> He'd wait and make sure that we understood everything and didn't assume that we knew it and say anything to make us feel stupid. And he went over the book in a logical order. He didn't skip around and get us all confused. (Female white engineering non-switcher)

What students mostly wanted from class assignments, tests, and examinations, was the chance to consolidate, confirm and enhance what they knew. They advocated making assignments serve the learning process such that grades became an honest reflection of their state of comprehension and skills rather than prizes in a contest where the criteria for success were obscure:

> I think they need to come into the classroom with the attitude of, 'I've got to help these people understand sections one, two, and three today. That's my goal by the end of class.' Not, 'We're gonna cover one, two, three, you're going to be tested on it next week.' (Male white engineering non-switcher)

> My physics teacher was excellent...He also held problem sessions where he'd go through problems and explain things. He was very helpful, and not critical at all. (Male white science switcher)

> It makes a big difference with me that the homework is discussed, so I learn why this or that was wrong. Sometimes you're missing a major point, but if you go back the next day and the teacher reviews it, it makes sense, and it stays with you. (Female white science switcher)

The Good Teacher

Good teachers do all of the foregoing, but were also defined as those who, through the manner of their teaching, show a primary concern with their students' learning and appreciation of the subject. In the classroom, the most important personal attribute of good teachers is their enthusiasm for the discipline in general, and for the materials being taught that day:

> A good teacher is one who makes me want to learn more about the topic—or presents the material in a way that I'll want to go and read things. You know, there's a spark there. (Female white engineering switcher)

> Most of them just act like, you know, 'Here we go again. Another semester of this.' I say come in excited about it! Show people how much this really means, and what you can really do with it, and where you can apply it in the future. (Male white science non-switcher)

> He was an older man—65 perhaps—but he was still really excited about what he was doing. He had a lot of enthusiasm, and you couldn't help catching it. (Male white science switcher)

The good teacher focuses all his or her efforts on maximizing student learning. This attitude pervades the structure and tone of their classroom presentation, and is seen in their readiness to organize effective tutorial back-up sessions, whether with T.A.s, peer learning groups, or on a personal basis:

> The computer class that I had was phenomenal. It was taught jointly by the associate dean of engineering and another professor. They did an extremely good job of teaching us, and they gave you lots of extra help when you needed it. You just knew they were there to help you out. (Female white engineering switcher)

> He covers stuff quickly, but he's very thorough with it. He covered everything in the chapter and encouraged people to ask questions over and over again, and he tries to explain them to everybody. And he's available. And we have review sessions before tests, so people can ask last-minute questions. (Female black science switcher)

> The biology professor would come to lab sessions, and you'd feel like he knew you, and would help you out. A lot of the professors give the lecture with a microphone down at the bottom of the room, leave, that was it. They provide office hours, but you know they don't want you to show up. It's not the same as the professor who says, 'Well, let's hold a review session.' (Female white science non-switcher)

> A good teacher encourages you to seek help from your friends, from your T.A.s, from them. (Female white engineering switcher)

> There's two ways to teach. There's, 'I want everyone to do well, and I'm gonna' try to make everyone do well,' or, 'Well, this is the way I'm gonna do these tests, and if you don't like it, tough. If you can't handle it, that's too bad. You haven't learned the material and that's your fault.' I've had teachers both ways, and it's so much better to have the first kind. You learn more. (Male white science switcher)

Finally, good teachers use all the resources available to them, including the learners themselves. Students recognized that the dominant culture in S.M.E. disciplines defines collaborative learning as cheating, plagiarism, or circumvention of the competitive imperative. Though not all students liked collaborative learning, there was overwhelming support for a shift from faculty insistence on solitary endeavor:

> There's no logic to me in figuring out how to do it by yourself. It's a waste of time, it's frustrating, and it gives you the false idea that it's wrong to share information. There's an intensely individualistic feeling that they use to try to push students out. Students are afraid to talk to each other about the most general of ideas. (Female white engineering switcher)

> In the liberal arts classes there is group interaction, sometimes they'll actually force you to interact with fellow students. And I think that helps people to develop socially, and provides a better overall learning experience. If you're working with someone you get different ideas rather than trying to get everything from a text and from a really dry lecture. So more group work in hard science would help. (Male white science non-switcher)

Collaborative Learning

Failure to make effective use of peer study groups was cited as contributing to 11.5 percent of switching decisions, and was reported by 16.9 percent of switchers overall. However, it was a stronger contributor to attrition among engineering (14.3%) than among science and mathematics (8.7%) switchers, and (for reasons we will discuss in Chapter 5) was more common among male (15.7%) than among female (7.5%) switchers. The explanation for this disciplinary difference appears to be that curriculum overload, promotion of the competitive ethic, and proscriptions against collaboration, are all strongest in engineering majors:

> We were expected to know so much, that if you didn't know it and someone else wasn't willing to explain it to you, then you didn't get the information. You couldn't do the programs. A lot of the students felt threatened—that they were competing against the other students—and would not associate with other members in the class as far as getting the homework done. I failed that class. (Male black engineering switcher)

> I still have a horrible time getting people to work with me. It forces you to do a lot more on your own. And I think that's detrimental. Because here you are, racking yourself over a problem that could be explained very simply in a group. (Female white engineering non-switcher)

Ironically, as engineering seniors made clear, the significance of collaborative study for persistence is even greater in engineering precisely because the weed-out system (including competitive grading) is most strongly established there:

The only way you can survive in an engineering program is if you can share information and work problems together. If you try and do it by yourself, you're not going to make it. (Male white engineering non-switcher)

Female students were generally more accustomed to seeking out peer working groups, and were less inhibited by the competitive ethos than were male students. However, both women and students of color were hampered by isolation within their classes:

I was very shy, so I wouldn't go up to someone and say, 'Want to have a study group?' I would just go home and be confused. It's very different from high school where you talk with other students and with the teachers. I had to change my major. (Female black science switcher)

In describing why they failed to establish study partnerships or groups, switchers most commonly reported either that they had tried to set up a group, but had met resistance to the idea, or that they felt an inner resistance to working with others:

I was looking forward to having study groups but no one seems to suggest it, or when I do, no one ever follows through. That bothers me a lot because it helps to be in a group to explain things. (Female white science switcher)

It's hard for me to get into a group and start working on a project or assignment. To me, it's akin to cheating. I want to do the whole thing. I stretch myself a bit thinner because I have to do that much more work than the next person. (Male white engineering switcher)

Though they acknowledged the cultural obstacles to working collaboratively, switchers commonly felt they might have resolved them had they appreciated how vital to their survival group study would be:

I figured it was just a matter of buckling down, and I studied on my own pretty much. I didn't study with groups. I think it's probably better to do that, but I just didn't take advantage of it. (Male white engineering switcher)

The significance for survival of working together to understand materials presented at speed, for a firmer grasp of concepts, and for emotional support through difficulties, was strongly emphasized by non-switchers:

I've finally learned to form study groups. At first the impression was that I *had* to work alone. I didn't realize other people had the same problems and all I had to do was talk it out a little bit. (Male Hispanic science non-switcher)

If it weren't for other students, I'd be a lost dog. I would be hurtin'. (Male white engineering non-switcher)

That was just essential for me. Otherwise, I would have felt really alone. It made me feel a lot less scared in physics. (Female white engineering non-switcher)

I probably would have dropped out if I was all alone. But with so much support and all of the people around, you're like, 'Yeah! I love this!' (Female white engineering non-switcher)

The classes where I did study with people were the best. That is absolutely the best way to do it. Working together you get different insight on how to solve problems. (Female white engineering switcher)

The predominance of observations in support of group learning by women and students of color is not accidental. Though study partners and groups were almost unanimously cited as a valuable—even essential—element in persistence, they were more sought-after, used, appreciated, and missed when unavailable, by students from under-represented groups.

Study relationships also have a number of indirect, long-lasting effects. Among these are development of a sense of bonding to, or belonging within, the discipline:

It's kind of a bond, a sense of belonging, being a part of the group. I think that helps people do well, too. It helped me to stay interested. (Female white engineering non-switcher)

I have a group who get together and have dinners, and we call ourselves, 'The Geologists from Hell.' We study together and we help each other out. We check each others' answers and encourage each other along. (Female white science non-switcher)

My group was so small that when one person got down on something everybody just sort of helped out. If one person was having a problem on a problem set and was frustrated with it, it was not a problem for someone to sit down and say, 'You're not thinking about it right.' (Female white engineering non-switcher)

It's great. We study together all the time. I mean, these are friends that I'm sure I'll keep for the rest of my life. (Female Asian-American science non-switcher)

It's nice to know that someone else knows what you are going through, someone that can share the joys and pains of going to class. (Female black science non-switcher)

It gives you people to identify with and feel special on campus. It shrinks the campus down. (Male white science non-switcher)

Both switchers and non-switchers described the unique educational benefits of collaborative learning which took them far beyond what was possible in class work alone. These included: reinforcement of understanding and skills; learning at a deeper level; learning by teaching; generation of new ideas and applications; personal intellectual challenge and growth; willingness to share mistakes and learn from them; pleasure in debating intellectual issues; and discovering the enjoyment of learning:

Even the smartest ones still need that other perspective to make them say, 'Oh, I never thought in that way.' So we became almost a class in ourselves, you know, teaching back and forth. (Male black engineering switcher)

There's a constant rehearsal of the process of thinking and using the strategies. (Male black engineering switcher)

You try and teach somebody and you strengthen your own knowledge—so that is really beneficial. That helps you keep the information long after you've taken the course, so you're just not down-loading it on the test. (Male white science switcher)

If you help someone out in something you understand well, they'll help you out in their area in return. 'Cause most students do have areas where they're really good and areas where they're bad. (Male white engineering non-switcher)

I learn more from going over the homework with my friends because they pick up on my mistakes and on their mistakes, too. And we all benefit more than just someone showing me how to do it. (Male white science non-switcher)

I think it helps most to go to your group first, to the T.A.s next, and to the professor last. But working together is the very best thing. (Male white engineering non-switcher)

Some other valued forms of help which peers or more senior students in the major can offer include advice on classes and sequencing, and support and encouragement at times of difficulty:

I had an upper-classman help me through a lot of times. He was just a year ahead of me. You need someone like that, sort of a mentor. (Male white science non-switcher)

I just gave up going to my advisor and figuring out which teachers I should take. You go talk with other students to find out what classes they had good experiences in. (Female white science switcher)

Help of this kind is sometimes formally organized by the institution, but is more often part of a fraternity/sorority network, or a service offered by women's and minorities' societies or programs.

Not all students liked working with others, and in the hostile and mutually-suspicious environment encouraged by strong weed-out systems, had observed students who used the work of others to gain a competitive advantage. Those who appreciated the value of group study, nevertheless highlighted the need to choose partners of a similar intellectual and commitment level, and to establish a working focus from the outset:

I've always studied alone. I find it a lot easier just to concentrate on my own...And if some people aren't prepared, you just waste time. (Male Asian-American engineering non-switcher)

> There's a risk. They might talk about other stuff—talk about girls, or whatever, and you can waste hours like that. (Male white science non-switcher)

> I just work so many hours on top of school, I don't have time to waste while someone else gabs about everything under the sun except what needs to be done. I find it very annoying, and I get more done when I do it myself. (Female white science non-switcher)

> It's important to find the right people. I have a lot of friends in those classes, but we didn't study together very well. We just had different study habits. It's true that much of what I learned came from studying together, but with some others, it was not a good idea. (Male white engineering non-switcher)

> You really need to be selective about your study partners. (Male white engineering non-switcher)

> I study much better in groups of two, three and four—where everyone is sort of on the same level and can help each other out. (Male white science non-switcher)

These observations again alerted us to the difficulty of establishing effective collaborative learning arrangements in learning cultures focused on individual competition. They suggest that group study may be more effective where faculty take an active role in setting up the system and offer guidance about the choice of study partners and the most effective ways to conduct study sessions. Students' observations on the circumstances in which they had formed study relationships also offer pointers to the kinds of institutional arrangements which encourage their formation. On all seven campuses, we found that communal living arrangements (whether dormitories, houses, or fraternities/sororities) based on academic interests or majors were an important natural inducement to the formation of study partnerships:

> Living in the dorm and having older engineering students there, I learned how to study with other people. (Female white engineering non-switcher)

> Seven people in my dorm are in the same classes and we just get together and try and work it out. That's helped me a lot when it gets hard and the teacher leaves you hanging. (Male white science non-switcher)

Less commonly, we found faculty or the directors of programs for under-represented groups actively supporting or organizing activities-based group work. However, most students made their own informal arrangements, and found mutually useful study groups largely by chance:

> I didn't purposely seek out someone, but was just lucky to find someone who had been in some of his classes. But it should be something that people know about. (Female white science non-switcher)

On every campus, we were struck by the enormous informal contribution made to persistence by collaborative study arrangements which students had initiated themselves. On three campuses, communal living arrangements were offered to some S.M.E. freshmen, and some S.M.E. departments at the two large research universities had introduced peer learning or regular student-faculty small group tutorials. Elsewhere, we found few formal attempts to incorporate collaborative learning into freshmen or sophomore classes. Departmental initiatives tended to begin only after the weed-out process was complete. However, non-switchers stressed the importance of introducing students to group learning at a much earlier stage:

> When you're in a lecture hall of 100, you're very lucky if you create bonds with people in your own major. In the lower level classes you don't see so much of that. But I think it's important. (Male Hispanic engineering non-switcher)

> If you make it through your first two years, engineers tend to come together because you paid with blood, sweat and tears. I stayed friends with people who stayed in engineering. (Female black engineering non-switcher)

> You have to draw these new kids in, and give them a sense of community, 'Look, we're all engineers: we're gonna stick through this thing together'—like the few of us who are left from the freshman year, I mean, we're tight. (Male Hispanic engineering non-switcher)

What is so striking about peer group learning is that it is relatively simple to organize, costs very little, and, in the almost unanimous opinion of students, is so clearly and immediately effective in increasing persistence. If the cultural impediments to collaborative learning in the first two years of S.M.E. majors can be overcome, its formal incorporation into the curriculum and pedagogy of basic classes clearly offers one of the most immediately-available, cost-effective ways to increase persistence.

Loss of Interest and the Appeal of Other Majors

Lack or loss of interest was the most common (43.2%) of all reasons offered for leaving the sciences, and was mentioned as a concern by 59.6 percent of all switchers, and 35.5 percent of non-switchers. Taken as a group, criticisms of S.M.E. pedagogy (36.1%), development of greater interest or perceptions of better education in non-S.M.E. majors (40.4%), and (a related but less often mentioned) preference for the teaching approach experienced in non-S.M.E. courses (8.7%), these four factors contributed more to switching decisions than any other group of issues.

We have often been told by S.M.E. faculty that, for the most part, the loss of bright students to other majors is not cause for alarm; that it is largely a benign phenomenon and represents students' realization that other majors are more appropriate given their (presumed) greater intrinsic interest in and talent for them. We found some support for their position among students who discovered disciplines not offered in high school, and among those who had been pushed into science and mathematics to the neglect of other talents:

> I just made myself believe that I wanted to go on to engineering, because math and science were the classes that I liked in high school. But when I got to college, I really hated the work, and found the liberal arts classes much more challenging for me. Philosophy was so much more interesting, more enjoyable. (Female white engineering switcher)

> The kids who are really bright in high school and junior high are pushed into math and science. This is what happened to me. I was pushed into those fields, and when I got here I found things that were outside the science fields that were really interesting. (Male white engineering switcher)

> I think it's realizing that these choices are really there, because you don't see all that's open to you in high school. (Female white engineering switcher)

Where the theory of the 'appropriate switcher' appears to have most validity, however, is not among the white male majority to whom it is most often applied, but among those students of color who are recruited in pursuit of increased minority participation in S.M.E. majors, but with insufficient regard for their interests or level of preparation. (This issue is discussed in some detail in Chapter 6.) Contrary to popular faculty belief, we found switching in recognition of a stronger interest in a non-S.M.E. discipline to be much rarer than switching in response to a pedagogy which engendered loss of enthusiasm for an S.M.E. discipline in which the student *was* interested:

> I enjoyed the lab work—that was really enjoyable. But I guess the physics and the calculus classes really turned me off. (Female white science switcher)

> I had enough of the sciences, largely because the classes were so boring. I found there was a lot more to learn, to expand your mind, within the social sciences. With strict science, it's just textbook, textbook, textbook. (Male white engineering switcher)

> I was passing okay, but I wasn't doin' as well as I knew I could because it had started to become a real chore—memorizing dull, old formulas. So I kind of gave up on the idea, and began to think, 'Well, maybe business.' (Male white engineering switcher)

As we, and others, have stressed, to have a good chance of completing an S.M.E. major requires, primarily, a combination of intrinsic interest, ability and adequate preparation. Students strongly endorsed the critical role of interest in their motivation:

> I think that if you really enjoy the subject, I don't see a need for any reason to switch out. (Female white science non-switcher)

> You have to have the interest and the desire. I don't think the problem is preparation. I think it's more interest. (Male white engineering switcher)

> I spent more time actually doing homework than I've done in any other courses, but I couldn't have cared less what happened—I mean, what the answer was. I was finished. I was just trying to get through it. Once I had the answer done, I didn't remember what it was. (Male white engineering switcher)

> The main switch for me was I got to the point where I felt, 'I just can't do this because I don't want to.' I think I had to get to that point before I could leave engineering. (Female white engineering switcher)

As we discussed in Chapter 2, not knowing enough about the nature of the major being selected was an important reason for loss of interest. The further some students went in the discipline, the more they realized their dislike or disinterest:

> It's very practical and some of the application stuff is really fascinating. Unfortunately, when it comes down to the hard core stuff a lot of what you're doing isn't all that appealing to me. (Female white engineering switcher)

> I realized that although I like programming, I really had almost no interest in anything more complex than that. I'm really not into compilers or operating systems or such. (Male white science switcher)

> There were some classes I really wasn't enjoying. And as I got into some of the more technical and more theoretical classes, I found I had absolutely no interest in making the time to study. (Male white engineering switcher)

As both switchers and non-switchers strongly asserted, students who were prepared, adequate to the task and entered with a well-founded initial interest in science and mathematics, often found their interest dissipated by the educational experience itself:

> A lot of them were very, very capable. It's just that they didn't want to spend the rest of their lives doing chemistry or math...It was just too boring for them. (Male Asian-American science non-switcher)

> Most of my friends did really well. And I think a lot of people in engineering can do it. I think it's just a matter of whether they want to or not. (Male white engineering switcher)

> I like math theoretically, but just day after day after day, it just wore me down. And it's not that I couldn't do it. I just didn't want to. (Male white engineering switcher)

> I think a lot of people could have gotten through it. I know that by the end of my sophomore year I was ready to quit too, and that's just because you have so few courses that are creative, or that are really into your major. (Female white engineering non-switcher)

I just like taking things apart and putting things together. I think there's other people who have a natural inclination for that, and if you wanna keep them in there, you have to teach it better to keep them from getting sidetracked along the way. (Male white engineering non-switcher)

One serious cause of loss of interest was disappointment with the perceived narrowness of their S.M.E. majors as an educational experience, compared, in some cases, with experiences in non-science classes:

I think my four years would have been terrible if I only focused on science classes, because everything would have been facts, and regurgitation of facts—no real conversation, no studies of civilization or culture. (Male white science non-switcher)

I think the engineers that come out of here...I mean, they're totally one-track minded, tunnel-vision people and it's really sad. (Male Asian-American engineering switcher)

It's hard to be creative in an atmosphere like this. (Male white engineering non-switcher)

I've found that there's very little tolerance for anything that has any kind of subjective quality. It got to the point where it was very boring. (Male Hispanic science switcher)

You think, 'Well, all I have to do is make it through the weed-out courses and then it'll start getting interesting,' but you're completely wrong. There's no room in the sequence for humanities, and you find out you'll be taking six aerospace courses a semester. And that's just inconceivable. You'd have to be some kind of drug addict. (Male Asian-American engineering switcher)

I think staying in gets you more and more narrow. In order to stay there you have to have a certain mentality not to look any further. (Female black engineering non-switcher)

You need to read more than one source; you need to accumulate different opinions. I think the biggest shock to me is that sciences is nothing more than a paradigm; it's a way of solving problems. It's no different than the philosopher's way of solving problems. But they don't look at it as a paradigm. It is a religion. I mean, these people are devout to it. I mean, 'This is the way you do things. If you want to do it another way, get out of here.' (Male white science non-switcher)

I think, having shifted into history, I enjoy it because it allows me in on intellectual kinds of pursuit. In engineering, I always felt I was struggling to find out what the big point was. With history, it's expected that's what you are doing. (Male white engineering switcher)

To me, it's sanity to take other courses because if I had only engineering courses, I would feel like my mind was in a box and that I couldn't relate to the real world. (Female black engineering non-switcher)

> It's just a place to get certified to get a job, not really an education. (Male white engineering switcher)

As we shall discuss in Chapter 4, students looking for a more unusual blend of disciplines which include mathematics or science, in pursuit of a particular career or interest, sometimes encountered an unimaginative or inflexible attitude toward their aspirations:

> I was trying to double major in personal relations. I couldn't find any professor that was even thinking that had anything to do with engineering. There's a certain way that the two intertwine, and they just can't see it. (Male white engineering non-switcher)

Students who lost interest (as opposed to those who were misguided or mistaken in their choice, or who had insufficient interest at the outset), typically reported a gradual shift out of the major which we have described throughout this account of our findings as a 'push and pull' process. Because of their initial interest, and because they were doing well enough to continue, these students became involved in a prolonged dialogue with themselves, and with those close to them, in which they debated the pros and cons of switching. For these students especially, the experience of good teaching, encounters with faculty who took a personal interest in them, and good internships, were often important in rekindling a flagging interest. This group was an important sub-set of those whose persistence might have been secured by timely faculty intervention, or by a more lively educational experience:

> I came in here dead set on becoming a chemist. But there's not too much creativity at the lower levels. And that concerned me. I took some German, then some linguistics classes, and the next thing I know I'm graduating in linguistics. I came in very techie, and ended up very fuzzy. (Male white science switcher)

> It didn't have anything to do with grades—just the class was pretty boring. Perhaps it's tough to make calc tremendously interesting. There's a ton of math in economics, and I've really come to view math as much more of a tool than as an inherently interesting subject. (Male white mathematics switcher)

> I was still doing just fine, but I wasn't so excited about the day to day grind stuff that we did. I knew I was looking for something more. (Male white science switcher)

> I had begun to be bored in aerospace, and I knew that I didn't want to stay. I took a few Spanish classes, at first because you need to for your core requirements. But I loved those classes. I thought about changing from engineering, but I wasn't sure. I was still doing well, so I stayed with it for another semester. But after that, I stopped doing so well, because it's not what I wanted. (Male black engineering switcher)

I always liked math, and I was still good at it, so I was thinking maybe I'd integrate it with business. Then, after looking at it some more, I had to confess that I'd lost much of my interest in it, and I changed to geography. (Female white mathematics switcher)

It was also this group who, having debated the personal relevance of their S.M.E. major for some time—not uncommonly the whole of their first two years of college—were apt to take a rather sudden final decision to leave. Knowing precisely what incidents finally triggered their decision to switch was rarely helpful in understanding its causes:

I got out of my last final and I went home and I said to my room-mate, 'I hate this, I don't want to do this. I want to be a sociology major.' (Female white engineering switcher)

I was struggling for a couple years, trying to decide what I wanted to do. Somewhere in the middle of the summer I'd made up my mind that engineering was what I was gonna do—I was just gonna stick it out. Then a week before classes started, I had this divine inspiration that I wanted to change it all. (Female white engineering switcher)

Several lines of practical action in support of greater persistence are suggested by our findings. The strongest, by far, involves a radical revival of the quality of teaching, and more attention to the liveliness, educational breadth and intellectual challenge of syllabus offerings. Such initiatives need to include: organized departmental support for the training (or recruitment) of faculty and teaching assistants as teachers; rewards for good teaching and teaching innovation; developing the habit of collegial discussion, review, and evaluation of teaching and student assessment practices; greater emphasis on student learning, especially discussion, application and hands-on discovery; and creative, systematic use of peer group learning strategies. Greater personal interaction between faculty and undergraduates, not solely in time of academic difficulty, also helps to bond students to the discipline, reinforces academic interest, and improves the chance that students whose interest is flagging will be noticed, supported, and counseled towards an appropriate decision.

There will always be some proportion of students who enter S.M.E. majors with insufficient interest, preparation, or knowledge of what will be involved, and some who discover that their greater talents lie in non-S.M.E. majors. However, evidence from our text data leads us to conclude that the proportion of 'appropriate switchers' is far smaller than is popularly believed: we propose that a significant proportion of able, interested students could be retained, and the educational experience of those who stay considerably enhanced, by paying greater attention to the teaching and learning concerns which have been highlighted by students in this study.

Notes

1.   We do not, of course, assume that these experiences are unique to undergraduates in S.M.E. majors.

2.   The widespread acceptance of Advanced Placement curricula and performance scores as a measure of high school achievement is an interesting exception to the popular nation-wide distrust of educational standards.

3.   The exceptions to this are advisory services provided for women and students of color. Where these have a good reputation among students, they are envied by white males precisely because they offer a one-stop personal service, and deal with problems in an interrelated way.

4.   One of the co-authors of this report, who was born in Britain, experiences this difficulty—from the other side of the communications exchange—on an almost daily basis.

5.   The appointment of teaching specialists had already begun at one of the two research universities, but the numbers involved were still small, and none of the students whom we interviewed had, as yet, encountered these faculty.

6.   This philosophy and these methods are, for example, promoted in the pedagogical workshops offered by Project Kaleidoscope; the "modular" approach to undergraduate chemistry being developed and tested in the N.S.F.-sponsored multi-institution consortia such as ChemLinks and MC^2; the "New Traditions" innovations of chemistry faculty at the University of Wisconsin, Madison; and "Workshop Chemistry" at the University of Rochester, New York.

4

Career and Lifestyle, Time and Money

In this chapter, we consider six factors contributing to attrition which reflect student perspectives on their university education as a preparation for life and work. They comprise: rejection of careers based on S.M.E. majors, and of the lifestyles they are presumed to imply; the choice of non-S.M.E. careers which seem more appealing; doubting whether the rewards of an undergraduate S.M.E. degree will adequately compensate for the effort required to complete it; switching as 'system-playing'; concerns about the financial problems of completing an S.M.E. major, and about the length of time required to finish them. These considerations illustrate the 'push and pull' nature of the processes leading to switching decisions. They also reflect the traditional role of undergraduate education in the exploration of major life issues and the making of major life choices.

Considerations of Career and Lifestyle

Like all other undergraduates, S.M.E. students seek to imagine the nature of their future work and lifestyles. About one-third (29.0%) of switching decisions and 43.1 percent of all switchers' concerns reflect reservations about the kinds of work that will be available, and the lifestyles that these careers may imply. About one-fifth (21.1%) of S.M.E. seniors also expressed anxieties about these issues.

What Students are Rejecting

A dominant (and growing) concern among S.M.E. undergraduates was that the work available to graduates—particularly for those without a higher degree—would not be fulfilling, enjoyable, or have a worthwhile purpose. They worried that the only work available to them would be at low levels of responsibility and autonomy, or would demand time and commitment at the expense of other valued life interests:

I knew people who were graduating, and the kinds of jobs they were getting seemed to be quite dead-end to me. (Male white engineering switcher)

My father had all these plans that I could come to I.B.M. and get a stable job. I mean, stability is fine, but if I'm not enjoying what I'm doing, then I don't care how much money it pays. (Female black science switcher)

For the first few years, you're under someone else doing back-up work...It seems as though business will give me more fulfillment. (Male white engineering switcher)

If I'd ended up in civil engineering, I was picturing myself taking these concrete blocks and putting them in compressors and finding out when they exploded, and why. It didn't seem like a thrilling prospect. (Female white engineering switcher)

Oh, the tedious calculations, and the desk work. And not being able to relate to people in a way I want to. (Male Asian-American engineering switcher)

For switchers, these thoughts often came late in the process of discovering the actual nature of the major and the careers to which it seemed to be leading. Their projections were not necessarily well-founded, but they were often powerful enough to prompt or reinforce the discussion to leave:

I had no doubts that I would be able to make it through engineering school. I just don't know if I would have enjoyed it when I got out there. (Female white engineering switcher)

People really need to figure out what it's really all about. I think that happens when they start to say, 'Well, maybe this isn't what I want to do. It's not what I thought it was when I got here.' (Male white engineering non-switcher)

Just finding out that I wasn't very interested in the career, even though I did well. I started to worry about that. I didn't want to do this all my life, and I was frustrated that I would have to. (Female Asian-American engineering switcher)

Once I found out what an engineer actually did, I was kind of bored with it. I found that I didn't actually want to be an engineer. But I didn't discover that until I actually got here. (Male black engineering switcher)

I had romanticized engineering—I did not have a grip on what it really was. I mean, what you do every day—how you work, and how you relate to people. (Male white engineering switcher)

All the time it's in the back of your mind that you'll have to get a job in four years, but you don't want to toil at something you're not enjoying. (Male white engineering switcher)

I heard that engineers made more money than chemists, and that sounded good to me. And it was a big mistake. As soon as I started the real engineering classes, I realized I hated what engineers did. (Female white engineering switcher)

I would try to see the end product, but teachers were always very unwilling to talk about that, especially the pure science teachers in your elementary classes...I went on several informational interviews with women engineers to get a feel for what kind of future I might be setting myself up for. But that only led me further away. Their jobs looked boring to me. They were nice people, but they didn't seem excited. They weren't lively; they weren't talking about what they were doing with interest. They didn't seem to be on the cutting-edge either. I wondered if there was a trend to tuck women away in some little cubicle. (Female white engineering switcher)

Some of these conclusions were reached as a consequence of student work experiences, including internships; some were influenced by contacts with working professionals; and some were derived from observation of the work of academics:

I enjoyed the puzzle of genetics, but I didn't have a lot of knowledge about the actual work until now. When I got my first field experience, that was what finally turned me off—realizing that I'd be working in a white lab coat with test tubes in some dry lab didn't excite me at all. I wanted something where I was working with people. (Male white science switcher)

My first class after coming back from that camp experience where I'd been outdoors, and surrounded with people, I realized I didn't want to work in an office building dealing strictly with numbers. (Female white mathematics switcher)

I mean, look in industry at the younger engineers—thirty years old. They wanna solve a problem at all costs, even at the cost of involvement in anything else in life. It's the engineering disease (sighs), you know, compulsive behavior. It's often characterized by no girlfriends, because they are too wrapped up in the work. (Male white engineering non-switcher)

I don't recall coming across anyone who was excited about what they were doing, or who actually enjoyed it. I would sometimes find the project they were working on interesting, but not what they were actually doing to achieve it. They seemed very removed intellectually. It was like there was part of you that you were going to have to ignore every day. (Female Asian-American engineering switcher)

I had kind of an idealistic view of being able to work on a project that I felt might be important. But, since 3M is a big employer here, most of the chemical engineering women that I met were working on glue and tape. I can't see getting excited about perfecting the process of putting adhesive on webbing. (Female white engineering switcher)

I began to wonder what I was supposed to do. And they took us on a tour of this place working for the defense department—building weapons. And I began to feel this was definitely something I wouldn't want to do. And then there was also the hostility towards us from the men who worked there. I thought, 'I can't deal with that every day.' (Female white science switcher)

It was clear that many engineering freshmen entered with little idea of what engineers actually do. As they developed a picture of engineering—accurate or not—some students began to question whether they would really like the work. Their first engineering experiences, usually as interns or 'co-op's in their junior year, often settled the matter. Conversely, some non-switchers, who had worried whether they were in the right major, reported that their first professional experience had been critical in their decision to remain.

As we shall later discuss, some science and mathematics switchers left, in part, because they rejected the prospect of graduate school and the academic life. However, science and mathematics switchers generally had much less clear ideas about the nature of the work they might do—other than academic work—than did engineering majors. This was particularly true of switchers from mathematics, whom we consistently found to have least sense of direction about their careers. Both current and former mathematics majors complained that, from high school onwards, their advisors promoted mathematics as a flexible major which would open doors to a variety of careers. However, they had found difficulty in getting concrete information about career options, either from career counselors, or from mathematics faculty. On every campus, we encountered a number of mathematics switchers (predominantly female) who were high achievers, both in high school and in college, but had been unable to find satisfactory career goals in mathematics:

I always loved math, but, coming into the sophomore year I started thinking more about what I was going to do with my life...And people kept telling us there were all sorts of things you could do with math, but they never told us what these were. (Female white mathematics switcher)

I talk to some of my friends that are math majors right now, and they're saying, 'What am I gonna do?' I mean, they look to grad school because they don't know what else to do...People say you can do so much with a math major—the problem is *finding* it. (Female native American mathematics switcher)

You start broad, and now you're just narrowing down your life to this straight path going somewhere. But no one ever gives you a clue about what kinds of things you're supposed to be doing out there. (Female white mathematics switcher)

In our earlier discussion of the C.I.R.P. data, we noted the high proportion of mathematics switchers who were undeclared in their senior year. This finding is consistent with our informal observation of mathematics switchers as more uncertain about their career direction than any other group of science or engineering switchers.

Science and mathematics switchers, whose reasons for rejecting their majors included career and lifestyle concerns, gave more complex, diffuse reasons for their decisions than did engineering switchers. They described their search for a balanced lifestyle, in which work was an important (but not the dominant) factor. They valued work for it's intrinsic satisfactions and the social purposes it served, rather than for its material rewards. Some rejected the lifestyle that careers in corporate science (including those in the defense industry) connoted for them:

> You hear of the competition, and you think about what the world of science has become. I think my generation doesn't want to do the conventional thing anymore. We don't want to dedicate ourselves to one career—to have a job with one company and work our way up. (Female white science switcher)

> I don't need to be pushing myself in this math major just to make money—to keep this lifestyle I've been brought up with going. (Female white mathematics switcher)

> I kinda looked at a couple of jobs, but I realized, no matter what I did with math, it's pretty much going to be a nine-to-five job in an office. Right away, that was my biggest turn-off. It's not so much math; I still love math. (Female white mathematics switcher)

> It's an ethical kind of thing—a large proportion of the jobs are defense department. (Male white mathematics switcher)

> The top scientists are employed by the government. So many of them end up building weapon systems. You're left wondering if that's what you should do. (Female white science switcher)

> I was concerned about staying in physics and ending up like my father— making parts for nuclear weapons—which we have had a lot of family arguments over. A lot of it was a matter of personal ethics for me. (Male white science switcher)

In describing the nature of the work available to graduates, switchers in all S.M.E. majors drew upon a set of myths and stereotypes. We found the same set of beliefs strongly represented on every campus and across all S.M.E. disciplines. The mythology included images of scientific workers as automata doing solitary work in confined, sterile, prison-like surroundings. Work was imagined to be intellectually dull, repetitive ("brain-numbing") and defined by unknown others in a remote organizational hierarchy. Working conditions were conceived in terms of long hours under stressful conditions with little job security. Metaphors of entrapment, life sentences and solitary confinement permeate the descriptions:

> I see myself in some room surrounded by a bunch of machinery, punching in little things, and making connections. (Female white science switcher)

I think my perception of what someone who went into the sciences did was fairly narrow. I assumed that most people went on to work in computer labs, worked for cities as civil engineers, or in design companies. And I perceived a life spent in kind of a white room. (Male white science switchers)

It seems like it could be narrowing—like it could block you in...If I didn't get into medicine, I'd have been stuck with microbiology. It's the narrowing, or the locking in, that's part of it for me. (Female white science switcher)

I'll be more comfortable in an office that's a little more laid back and sociable, and discusses a little more of what's going on in the world rather than what the latest computer developments are. (Female white engineering switcher)

One reason I dropped out is because I like to be around people. I didn't wanna be designing something at a desk by myself. I think that guys are more apt to like working by themselves as opposed to working with groups of people. (Female white engineering switcher)

I had this nightmare vision of being locked into this sterile white lab, punching a computer, and it seemed really cold—like a cog in a bigger wheel. (Male white engineering switcher)

Students also imagined that, in order to pursue S.M.E. careers, they would have to embrace a persona which was alien to their own personality. They portrayed engineers, especially, as dull, unsociable (often materialistic) people who lacked a personal or social life and were unable to relate comfortably to non-engineers. They were also portrayed as uncreative people, who avoided or decried the idea of a broader education. Some thought the sciences tended to attract people who already had these personality traits. They also saw themselves and their peers beginning to develop these undesirable characteristics as a consequence of the lifestyle they were constrained to adopt in order to survive in the major:

I guess I'm too creative of a person. Everyone seemed so one-track. I didn't find a single engineer that would go with me to a good film—they wouldn't focus on anything except math and science. I couldn't relate to them at all. I was doing all right, but I got extremely frustrated with the life. (Female white engineering switcher)

People who stay in physics are pretty introverted socially. The more outgoing people go into something else. (Male white science switcher)

When I started out as a freshmen, I thought, 'Well, at least I'll always have a date.' Damn, was I ever wrong! You don't date those guys (laughing). (Female white engineering non-switcher)

You have to be very tedious and a perfectionist—so, yeah, it does take a certain kind of person to do it. (Female white engineering switcher)

I got so tired of people talking about school—that's all they talk about. It seems like engineers have so few interests. It kinda drives me away. (Female white engineering non-switcher)

I'm glad I didn't go into physics: I'm too much of a thinking, sensitive person. (Male white science switcher)

The science professors, probably more than the other professors, tend to be a little more narrow-minded. I never saw myself like that. (Male white science switcher)

You have to believe there's only one way to do anything. There's no room for movement. It doesn't allow you to formulate your own opinions, or to grow. (Male white engineering switcher)

You find a lot of money-grubbers in engineering. (Male Hispanic engineering non-switcher)

I guess that's why it's hard to stay in the major. You look around, and you see all the other people have become like the professor. And you think to yourself, 'Maybe I'm in the wrong place, I'm not like these people with pocket protractors. And I don't want to be that professor. I don't want to sit in front of a chalk board. And I don't want to wear clothes like that.' (Female white science switcher)

The truth, or otherwise, of these perceptions and projections is not the issue. However distorted they may seem to S.M.E. faculty or field professionals, they matter in so far as they contribute to the loss of students whom S.M.E. departments might prefer to retain. However, any effort to correct the imagery has to take into account what generates and perpetuates it. Direct personal knowledge of the work of a family member or friend may lend it credence, as may student work experience:

My dad spends all his time at a desk without any interaction with people at all. For people who are introverted, it might be great, but for those who like contacting people, it would be kind of a nightmare to do that for the rest of your life. (Male white science switcher)

Like my dad's an engineer, and he sat in the office all day. I'm not that type of person—I'm not a pencil pusher. (Female white engineering switcher)

The imagery also suggests that students make projections about the personal and working lives of scientists and engineers based on their current life of confinement, restriction and drudgery as undergraduates. Some have already begun to feel changed by the experience; they observe changes in others; and they note that some of the most successful students have personality traits which they dislike:

It's probably a very skewed picture—to envision myself working in a lab by myself, with no interaction with people—but that's just the way you are when you're a student...and you see it going on forever. (Female white engineering switcher)

When I first thought of being a doctor, it wasn't like a lot of people brown-nosing and scrambling to get As. It's hard to keep that vision and then see the kind of people we're becoming. (Female white science non-switcher)

I think they are made compulsive by their education. I got married to a wonderful girl, and that gave me a bit of focus and more motivation. Suddenly, I couldn't see myself doing that work for the rest of my life—stuck in a room with a florescent light, no windows, and laboring over a microscope. (Male white engineering switcher)

If you compare my social skills to my room-mate's—I mean, he acts like an idiot when we go out. We were at a bar, and he was even embarrassed to order a drink. And I said, 'It's okay to do this. It's okay to go out now and then.' It was right at that moment that I realized how bad it really was. It seems all right when we're all together, but not when we're with other people. (Male white engineering non-switcher)

With little opportunity in the first two years to 'do science', to observe the faculty (with whom they have little other than formal contacts) at work, or to discuss what they, and other field practitioners, actually do, the mythology goes uncorrected, and is continually renewed.

Shift to a More Appealing Non-S.M.E. Career Option

Almost one-third (26.8%) of switching decisions were made with an alternative (i.e., non-S.M.E.) career direction in mind. Feeling drawn toward a non-S.M.E. career was not, however, confined to switchers. On every campus, we found a group of seniors who were, in effect, switchers, in that, although they intended to graduate in their S.M.E. major, they had either decided upon or were seriously considering working in a field which was not S.M.E.-based. Overall, these 'graduating switchers' accounted for 16.5 percent of our sample of S.M.E. seniors.

What Students are Looking For

Most students had clear ideas, at least in broad terms, about the kinds of work, or work contexts, which were appealing to them. Feeling drawn towards a particular arena of work was seen as an important reason either for staying in a major, or for leaving it. A few strong themes dominated switchers' descriptions of the kinds of work and/or lifestyles they were seeking. First, they sought work which was intrinsically interesting, and were often prepared to settle for lower material rewards in order to do it:

They didn't seem to love it: it wasn't a passion. It was more, 'Well, it's a stable job.'...My goal is to find something I like, and I guess I don't care so much about the money. (Male white science switcher)

I look at my friends who graduated last year, and who are making a whole lot of money working 80 hours a week. It's just not the kind of life I want. I'd be willing to take less pay to find something more suited to the way I want to go. (Female white engineering switcher)

It's a very stable job, and you're gonna make a lot of money. But I decided I didn't really care about the money because I felt it was kinda limiting my choices. In the end, I chose the International Relations field. (Male white science switcher)

Second, they looked for work that served a social purpose of which they approved. This included a desire to teach. Teaching was consistently portrayed as an 'alternative' or 'deviant' career, which a handful of switchers and non-switchers pursued despite the disapproval of faculty, family and peers. The desire to work in support of environmental protection was also a recurrent theme, which on some campuses was supported by a number of relatively new, cross-disciplinary majors:[1]

The main reason I changed my major was that I wanted to teach. I'd an internship with Honeywell for both of my first two years. I actually had a deal for the last two years, and employment guaranteed afterwards. But it wouldn't have fulfilled me because of my interest in the community, really engaged with people. Not that I didn't like math and science—I love them to this day. But other more important things were pulling me away. (Male black engineering switcher)

I liked going to classes—I liked the material—I still do. But I wondered if I wanted to be still doing this 40 years from now, when what I actually want to do is something I believe in. I could see myself doing a lot of things—from writing, to teaching, to being a campaign manager. (Male white science switcher)

Bottom line—I didn't care about engineering. I could care less about making the next dishwasher. I think we are in a fine state of technology right now. I'd rather improve something socially, because there are so many social problems in this country. That's where I feel I'm needed more. (Female white engineering switcher)

I'm thinking of going into journalism and using my biology and environmental science that way. My career won't be in pure science: it has to deal with social organization. For me, work has to serve a good cause. (Female white science switcher)

I have a great deal of respect for all the people that I worked with at the prosecutor's office. I don't know how big a difference I could make, but I would like to work at that larger level. (Male black mathematics switcher)

I really didn't want to be a researcher because you'd be off by yourself a lot of the time, and I wanted to do something interactive. But I also decided that my values weren't matched enough to the values in the kinds of jobs the major was leading me towards. (Female white science switcher)

To go into management and make a lot of money is not necessarily something I need for success. I think I would be more fulfilled doing something different. It's really a decision from the heart. Environmental studies appeals because I feel I might be helping the world more than hurting it. It was a difficult decision, because I've been offered a full-time job by Ford with whom I did a co-op. It was a hard thing to turn down. (Female white engineering switcher)

But I felt, in engineering, I just wasn't going to be contributing much. Maybe in environmental engineering, I'd be contributing a little more, because at least you're trying to solve problems for future generations. Maybe you'd never get into a position where you could have much influence, but simply to be designing more cars seemed kind of dead to me. (Female white engineering switcher)

What is striking about this set of observations is the willingness of students to reject job opportunities they had already been offered in favor of work which incorporated preferred lifestyles, values and social goals.

Switchers often stressed their desire to work with people in some kind of work which served community needs. As indicated in our discussion on the choice of S.M.E. majors, both male students of color and all women tend, more often than white males, to enter S.M.E. majors with altruistic career motivations. This difference persists in their reasons for switching:

I knew what I wanted to do with myself. I wanted to do something where I'm around a lot of people, and I'm helping—something human-oriented. (Female Asian-American science switcher)

I was interested in exploring ways I could help the black community...I didn't just want to go and work in industry...I was more interested in how to educate the community—to use my technological skills for that somehow. (Female black engineering switcher)

I'm thinking of teaching, writing and bi-lingual education. I plan to bring a native American curriculum back into the school system on the reservations. (Male native American mathematics switcher)

I think I'd like to translate. But I'd also like to do social work with immigrants from Mexico. I'd like to help people. (Male Hispanic science switcher)

I can't honestly say I've closed myself off to math, it's more that math is cutting me off from the things I love—like just really understanding people, and being around them—like this summer in camp. I'm taking off next semester, and I'm going down to Guatemala to work in an orphanage. (Female white mathematics switcher)

We have consistently observed that women find it easier to give themselves permission to reject a conventional, materially-focused career path in favor of an 'alternative' career based on intrinsic interest, self-development, altruism, or the need for social interaction. We discuss why this may be so in Chapter 5. However, here it is important to reflect that one reason why S.M.E. majors seem to be less attractive to women and to many students of color, is that they are seen as offering an insufficiently congenial (or worthwhile) career or lifestyle. Again, the validity of students' perceptions about the work of science and engineering is less important than their consequences.

As we intimated in the previous section, switchers are also looking for what seems to them to be a healthy balance between their work and the rest of their lives:

This rush just came to me. I knew I was not going to be happy doing this for my life's work. I think the tedium was the major part. I just couldn't see myself doing this for the rest of my life. But it was also the feeling that engineering just churns out people that know nothing about anything else—just no contact with society—who don't know what's going on. It's just plug ahead, do what you have to do, and never understand the ramifications of what you're involved in. (Male white engineering switcher)

I didn't enjoy the people I was working with. Everything seemed to revolve around money and prestige. I guess I'm more concerned with enjoying what I do. They were pretty one-track in their thinking, and I had a hard time relating to them—just no views about politics or art—I guess they had never had time to develop them. I just don't want to work with people like that my whole life. (Male white science switcher)

Not feeling comfortable with either my superiors or my peers made it hard to feel part of the program—even though I was getting through my classes. They were a very single-minded group—which I admire and respect—but I couldn't relate to them. They were very intense; and spent all their time on their engineering studies, because that's all they seemed to care about. I thought of it as an interest, but it had to be your life pursuit. (Female white engineering switcher)

Just the importance of going to a museum, or a gallery, or the theater, or something—I mean, if I mentioned this to the typical engineering major, they'd say something like, 'Oh, why do that? There's a programming contest.' They wouldn't see the appeal. (Female black engineering non-switcher)

I like to have conversations about stuff that's happening in the world, and discuss what we are doing in the light of its implications...But interpersonal dynamics isn't something a lot of engineers are prepared to deal with. (Female white engineering switcher)

I wanted to study physics, but I didn't want to become a physicist. I don't have anything against the discipline. In fact, I may well go back into it later, but I just couldn't confine myself. People who don't have an education beyond math and science aren't really whole people...They didn't really push me out: I sorta decided to leave them. (Female white science switcher)

For some men, concern to find a balanced working lifestyle also included a preference for a work context in which the gender distribution more closely reflects that of the normal population.

We noted on every campus that a sub-set of our informants (some switchers, some non-switchers) were looking for 'a good compromise' major. These students wanted a career in which they could combine the knowledge and skills gained in S.M.E. disciplines with those of other disciplines and/or with areas of personal interest:

> I still wanted the math because I liked it, but I'm pretty idealistic, and I wanted to do something useful with my math—not just a straight major. (Female white mathematics switcher)

> Well, I do like computers, so I took some extra courses to build that up. And I like working with numbers, so, eventually, I thought I would bring everything together in a business degree. (Female white mathematics switcher)

> The ethics and economics of health care interest me so much more than straight biology. If I can pursue them without losing my schedule, I can stay with biology. (Male white science non-switcher)

> I still have the sense that I'm still in science—and I still have a math minor—but my concentration now is computer cartography. I still do a lot with computer algorithms. But after working in a lab my freshman and sophomore years, I just didn't enjoy it or find the motivation...I guess I always felt there would be a relevance for it down the road, but I didn't always see the application. (Male white engineering switcher)

> As I worked more with the analysis part off my internship, I found that I liked working as a liaison between the end-users and the programmers. That's when I started looking at the School of Management. (Male black engineering switcher)

> I wanted to stick to numbers, but deal with people as well. So I thought that accounting would be the best area for me. (Female Asian-American engineering switcher)

> It was simultaneous: I was being pushed out of science while I was being pulled into psychology. It was interesting to do the experiments and to deal with people one-on-one. I thought, 'Wow, I'm really using my math in a skilled way'—as opposed to just number-crunching. (Female white engineering switcher)

Alternatively, while retaining their interest in science and mathematics, these students sought careers that met the kinds of personal and social goals described earlier:

> I definitely see a need for people with my background to go out there and change things—clean things up...There's a great need for people to meet the

> sustainable needs of their forests...I'm going for a master's in forestry. (Male white engineering switcher)

> Math and science are still important to me. I mean, I still enjoy doing physics, calculus, and chemistry, and I have no problem doing mathematical equations. So I'm not really escaping science. I'm using it for a purpose that I see as practical, and that I can see benefitting others. I have begun to consider myself a climatologist—I've taken all the available classes any way I could. (Male white engineering switcher)

> I was taking math courses because I thought they were interesting, and that kept me going for a long time. Now I'm in education, and it's like the light at the end of the tunnel. I decided teaching would be something interesting and constructive to do with my life. That's what made me switch. (Female white engineering switcher)

> The career I'm looking at is systems analysis, in which companies come and tell me what they need; I develop a system for them; then I implement it and train people how to work with it. It's getting away from the terminal and getting out and dealing with people more. (Male white science switcher)

> I'm a history major now, but I'd like to work with water and land education. There's a need for that. (Male Hispanic engineering switcher)

> I wanted to open my eyes to a more people-oriented way to use math. (Female white mathematics switcher)

Some departments had developed cross-disciplinary majors which blended aspects of traditional science or engineering with environmental applications and engineering specialties with a strong design component. Where these were offered, they were popular with students seeking multi-disciplinary options which included science:

> I think the environmental classes in civil (engineering) will eventually become a major—because a lot of people are drawn that way. I think this brings the humanities and the sciences together, and that's what a lot of people want now. (Female white engineering non-switcher)

Some students went to considerable trouble in pursuit of their educational and career goals—undertaking double majors, or successfully arguing with their institution that they be allowed to major in a non-traditional blend of disciplines. Students did not necessarily feel they had to switch in order to find their own good compromise, but some did—often with regrets—in order to pursue a personal goal.

Many of these accounts, again, illustrate our assertion that switching decisions are predominantly the result of a multi-factored push-pull process. Some of the 'graduating switchers' described earlier were also looking for a career in which they could use their scientific knowledge and skills without entering in a traditional science-based career:

I had a job lined up before I graduated, working as an electrical engineer with a *Fortune 500* company. I worked in three different areas—design, testing and then in a business area. And I was always interested in economics—I had taken some classes while doing my Double E degree...And that was when I knew I wasn't going to take that job—that I really wanted to make the change to business. (Male white engineering non-switcher)

Some of this group of switchers reported that they intended to return to science or mathematics at a later stage—perhaps at graduate level. We were struck by the inventiveness of the career plans which students developed in order to incorporate their interest in the sciences with other interests and priorities. We were also struck by the part played by serendipity in setting the direction of their 'good compromise' career paths they were seeking—often a chance conversation or work experience. We also found a number of angry and disillusioned former S.M.E. students who had sought, but failed to find, the right cross-disciplinary path, and who had settled for what they described as a bad compromise. Where departments and colleges are particularly concerned not to lose their multi-talented students, we feel it would be fruitful to support their search for a congenial disciplinary blend, and to consider a broader offering of cross-disciplinary majors tailored to emergent student interests and new market needs.

The appeal of alternative non-S.M.E. majors did not always lie in their intrinsic characteristics. Some switchers found non-S.M.E. careers appealing because of extrinsic factors, such as attractive salaries or good job availability. Switching in response to instrumental considerations is discussed in the following section. It is also touched upon in the sections on teaching and graduate school as career choices, and on switching as a form of 'system-playing'.

Wanting to Become a Teacher

Approximately one-fifth (19.7%) of our total sample (20.8 percent of the switchers, and 18.4 percent of the non-switchers) told us that they had considered teaching science or mathematics as a career. Of this group, approximately two-thirds had, at the time of their interview, decided not to follow through on this option. Those who had decided that they would teach, or were still considering it, were 8.7 percent of all switchers, and 6.6 percent of non-switchers (7.8 percent, overall). The reasons offered for considering a teaching career were a mixture of altruism and pragmatism. They reflect the search for a fulfilling, people-oriented job with a worthwhile purpose, combined with an acceptable level of material rewards. Some students who felt tempera-mentally suited to teaching and who could picture themselves in the role, drew inspiration from good teachers they had known, liked working with children, or had enjoyed an informal teaching experience of some kind. More pragmatically, students also mentioned that there were job opportunities in teaching, at a time when the work options for graduates with a science or mathematics baccalaure-ate seemed limited. Some students saw themselves teaching at a later stage in their careers, perhaps at professional or college level, or after spending time in industry or research. Among the more idealistic motivations for teaching, we heard the following:

> That one math teacher made classes a lot of fun. I've always liked math, but I can see that some people find it difficult. He kind of inspired me to want to teach math—to pass it on, and make kids really enjoy it. (Female white mathematics non-switcher)

> There's a big shortage of teachers in math, and that's another reason I want to do it...I was so impressed with my high school teachers. They were just incredible. (Female white mathematics switcher)

> I taught basic algebra to kids who were having trouble with it. And I discovered it's not their intelligence—it's how the material is presented. (Male white science non-switcher)

> I've done some tutoring and I like it a lot. It's very satisfying—helping people to understand something. That's the kind of person I think I am...I seem to be pretty good at it. (Male Hispanic engineering non-switcher)

> I had a math course this semester which I just loved. I loved everything about it, and it made me want to go into pure math. But I also want to do math education, because I love little kids. (Female white engineering switcher)

> I'll be working with computers in the sciences with students in junior high...Hopefully, I'll be able to provide some motivation for them. (Female white science switcher)

> I'd like to be a teacher, or even a professor. I like tutoring people, and I seem to be able to show them how to enjoy the classes people often don't like. (Female white engineering switcher)

We commonly heard that more people would follow their inclination to teach were the pay or prestige of the profession better, or were it less time-consuming and expensive to undertake an education qualification on top of a baccalaureate degree:

> I would love to be a high school teacher, but it doesn't pay. Teachers just don't get enough money or prestige. (Male white engineering switcher)

> If there were any prestige or money attached to it, there's a good chance that I would become a math teacher—but there's neither. (Male white science non-switcher)

> It's awful to think that money is such an incentive, because you think if you're dedicated to what you're doing, you shouldn't care. But we have to be able to make a living. (Male white science switcher)

> I've busted my rear for four years—I'll be damned if I'll take $18,000 a year when I could earn $42,000. You can't even live off that. I can volunteer to

youth organizations, but earn a good living as well. (Male white science non-switcher)

Going to teach in a public high school is something I admire, and in some ways I wish I could do it. But, honestly, I never could live on the pay. (Male white science switcher)

You don't make money being a mathematician. It's not a glamour job, and it's not necessarily a well-paying job. About the most common use for it I can think of would be teaching—which unfortunately, is not a high-paying position either. The United States places such a premium on success, and that usually means monetary success. So unless you're *really* dedicated, you're not even going to *consider* teaching as an alternative. (Male white mathematics switcher)

Many students looked back with respect and admiration to particular high school teachers. They gave credit to former teachers for the inspiration, motivation and skills that had helped them decide on an S.M.E. major, or sought their advice and encouragement on visits home. Students frequently made invidious comparisons between the enthusiasm and good pedagogy of their former high school teachers, and what they viewed as the poor skills of many college faculty and their failure to inspire student interest. They quickly learned that teaching was viewed as an inferior form of professional activity by S.M.E. faculty, though not necessarily by faculty in other disciplines. Though they did not necessarily agree with this assessment and wished their faculty would pay more attention to this aspect of their professional role, they found it hard to maintain an interest in a teaching career for themselves in the face of so much discouragement:

You're pretty much looked down on as a high school teacher in chemistry—I mean, there's still that stigma. The first response would be that you couldn't cut it in graduate school. (Male white science non-switcher)

I want to put my major directly to use, and I think teaching will be very satisfying for me. But it's a difficult transition, telling people that I wasn't going to grad school or medical school. (Female white science non-switcher)

Speaking ideally, everybody says it's a great thing. But it still doesn't seem respected. My friend who wants to be a college professor will probably get a lot more respect than me wanting to go play science with elementary kids. (Female white science switcher)

Teaching science? That's really like a whole separate thing for us from really being in science. (Male white science non-switcher)

Students also saw teaching as a form of professional activity that was under-valued by the wider community. It seemed to pay poorly compared with other options, and family and peers tried to dissuade them from choosing to teach:

I want to teach biology, but most people I talk to are kind of negative about it—especially friends. (Female white science non-switcher)

> I came with the intention of being a math major with an education minor, and people kept asking me why I wanted to teach math. (Female white mathematics non-switcher)

> Because of my dad, I had it so much in my head that I wanted to be an engineer. But I wanted it for him. It was hard to tell him that what I really wanted was to teach math—in high school. (Female white engineering switcher)

The prospect of two more years of study, a greater student loan burden and limited material rewards at the end, was also daunting:

> Teaching in high school? No way. The education qualification is another two years on top of the five years you've already gone through. (Male white science non-switcher)

> I thought I'd want to go into education, but it's a post-baccalaureate 18-month program. And once you've graduated with a math degree, why in the world would you want to go through all that—unless you were really drawn to teaching? If they made it easier, there would be a lot more people with science and math degrees willing to become teachers. (Female white mathematics non-switcher)

Worst of all, the professors—whose support and approval they sought in formulating a career path—effectively defined their ambition as deviant. S.M.E. faculty were also commonly believed to withdraw from students who openly expressed an interest in teaching:

> I think that's ultimately the problem with math and science in this country—we don't value teachers enough. Professors are valued, but the high school teachers are not. If you wanna teach science in high school, that's taboo: you're treated as an outcast by the faculty here. (Male white science switcher)

> I've never expressed it to any of my professors. They don't know. I don't think they'd support it. I get the impression they don't particularly like teaching, and, although they're a great bunch of guys, they're actually not very effective teachers. (Male Hispanic engineering non-switcher)

> I've never discussed it with any of my chemistry professors. For the most part, I get a feeling of disdain for teaching from them. This is something they feel they have to do, but they don't really support anyone who wants to do it. Fortunately, I had an incredible chemistry teacher at high school, and I go back and chat with him still. He tells me, 'You're going to be a good teacher.' I get more encouragement from him than from anyone on campus. (Male white science non-switcher)

Those who wanted to teach, despite all these discouragements tended to become covert about their intentions.

Traditionally, women who studied mathematics were the strongest national source of high school mathematics teachers. However, as the C.I.R.P studies record, as the range of opportunities open to female graduates increases, fewer female mathematics majors choose teaching as a career:

> Maybe another reason why people aren't going into teaching any more is they realize they now have access to a whole array of careers with the math degree, including computer science. At one time, I probably would have taught. (Female white mathematics non-switcher)

Students of color were the only S.M.E. seniors who reported any encouragement to consider a career in teaching from faculty or professional advisors:

> Actually my advisor recommended teaching: there's a shortage of science teachers, especially of minorities. (Female native American science non-switcher)

In some of the institutions in which we conducted our interviews, and at many of those at which we have been invited to discuss our findings, we have been made aware of programs intended to enhance the quality of high school mathematics and science teaching or to promote S.M.E. enrollment. Ironically, at only one institution to date have we found S.M.E. faculty engaged in the promotion of mathematics and science teaching as a career option for their own baccalaureate students. Nor (with this single exception) have we found S.M.E. departments engaged in dialogue with College of Education specialists in science and mathematics teaching, with S.M.E. career advisors, or with the relevant state licensing boards, to develop a coherent career path for S.M.E. baccalaureates wishing to teach. Indeed, we have found very little dialogue of any kind between the faculty in S.M.E. disciplines and those in science and mathematics education. There was no doubt in the minds of that fifth of our overall sample who had considered teaching as a career that their ambition was regarded as deviant by most of the significant people in their lives. In the face of such discouragements, that almost 8.0 percent of current and former S.M.E. majors still intended to teach—or had not ruled it out—seems quite remarkable.

The Profit-to-Grief Ratio

In rejecting the drawbacks of the careers and lifestyles which one-third of switchers felt were implied by graduation in their original S.M.E. major, it is clear that some students were prepared to accept a modest level of material rewards in order to pursue a career path which was more congenial to them. By contrast, one-third of all switchers (31.1%) had rejected their S.M.E. major partly because it did not lead to a level of extrinsic career rewards commensurate with the effort required to complete the degree. Poor material rewards and rejection of S.M.E. careers or lifestyles were mentioned by identical numbers of switchers (43.1%) as having contributed to their switching decisions, or as additional issues of concern. One-fifth of all non-switchers also raised each of these two issues.

With respect to the perception of insufficient rewards, switchers commonly argued that had the educational experience in S.M.E. majors been more fulfilling, they could have tolerated its discomforts. However, where their academic work had not been intrinsically interesting, or had ceased to be so, they expected some extrinsic post-graduate rewards to compensate for their effort. Where these seemed uncertain or unlikely, they were ready to consider other majors and career options. A group of seniors in an early focus group described this as weighing the "profit-to-grief" ratio. Some strong statements on the "grief" side of the equation include the following:

It's been unadulterated hell. Major overloads, no rest, stress—and it's getting worse. That's why I'm looking elsewhere. (Female white science switcher)

I would have liked to get a double major in math, but it's not worth the agony. I'd really have to put it to the grindstone, and it just isn't worth it to me. (Male white mathematics switcher)

It wasn't a pleasure any more. It became pure torture. (Female white science switcher)

Life's too short, and I don't want to waste any more time. (Female white science switcher)

I consider myself someone who works really hard for my classes...but I really began to wonder if the trade-offs would be worth it. (Male white science switcher)

I knew I could have done it if I wanted to. But I just said, 'Do you really want to do this? Is it really worth killing yourself for?' (Female white science switcher)

I think I'm an intelligent person, and I came to think this wasn't a noble lifestyle. I felt like a slave to something that no longer seemed worthy of all the effort. (Female white engineering switcher)

I mean, why stay there? You know, there's no reason. And the rewards are—there's no rewards. I mean, I can see no logical reason why you'd stay. (Male white science switcher)

For these students, the "profits" of remaining in science and mathematics were thought not to be worth the "grief":

$16,000 to $18,000 starting salary is about what you can expect around here—in fact, a couple of our post-docs are only getting $19,000...Some people who leave expect more—particularly if their parents are professionals. (Female white science switcher)

Not only did these students suspect they would be offered low salaries, they also suspected there would be few job opportunities; that the available work would be at a low level of interest or responsibility, and offer poor fringe benefits or job security:

I was concerned just how many people are getting laid-off instead of being hired. (Female white science switcher)

There aren't really any jobs out there for bachelor's degrees. And, as soon as you graduate, no more health insurance, no more anything. (Male white science non-switcher)

I would say, Why would you wanna go into M.C.D.B.? Because now I know that majoring in biology is not to have much of a job opportunity. (Female Asian-American science non-switcher)

Well, I kinda ran into a problem. What am I gonna do with a biology degree?...Do I want to be in a lab somewhere? Really, I didn't want to do that...And, actually, there weren't any jobs out there. (Female native American science switcher)

Working with only a bachelor's degree, I figured there wouldn't be as much real intellectual work to do. It would be mostly working in a lab and doing the same things over and over. I felt I was spending an awful lot of time struggling through classes for an end result I really didn't want. (Female white engineering switcher)

You go through hell in the sciences without any guarantee that you will be able to work. Why do it? Why not be an English major? (Male white science non-switcher)

Science and mathematics majors who were anxious about limited job prospects tended to think that engineering majors had more options, and could expect better salaries, even in their first jobs:

After you graduate, if you just have a bachelor's degree, it's hard to find a job. I think that's one of the turn-offs. It's why people would rather go into engineering instead of physics...You don't have much future in this major. (Male Asian-American science non-switcher)

Nobody wants anyone with a bachelor's degree in physics. There's nothing you can do. Whereas, if you graduate with a bachelor's degree in engineering, you can go out and get a job right away. (Male white science non-switcher)

When we first began interviewing students in the spring of 1990, engineers were indeed much more confident about their prospects than were science and mathematics majors. At that stage, we heard more about poor material rewards from non-engineers. However, three years later, engineering seniors were expressing doubts about the certainty of work, and we heard less and less about the expectation of high starting salaries:

Well, I don't know if anybody's marketable. It's hard to get engineering jobs right now. (Male white engineering non-switcher)

I can't find a job, so, anybody who'll hire me, I'll probably do it...I've got resumes out, but, with the recession and everything, there's not a lot of people hiring right now...A lot of my friends don't have jobs. (Male Asian-American engineering non-switcher)

A lot of my friends were interviewed last year and, right now, I don't know if any one of them got a job. I had one friend who went to 35 interviews, and he didn't get a single offer. (Female white engineering non-switcher)

I'm in an internship with U.S. West, and it's really not my area of interest. But I'll stick with it, because I've been applying to General Motors and Ford for something in mechanical engineering, and they just don't have any openings. It's hard to get in right now. (Male white engineering non-switcher)

It's very devastating. The market is very bad. Overall, the push for new technology is slow...I've a friend working in J.C. Penny's shoe department with his degree in engineering... I think a lot of people are more nervous than they were just a few years ago—with the recession. I know at least three people who have dropped out of aerospace. They all stayed in the technical fields, but got out of the ones with no jobs. It's a big concern. (Male white engineering non-switcher)

Right now there's a surplus of engineers. And that's because they were saying five years ago there was a shortage. A lot of us are scrambling for work now. (Male white engineering non-switcher)

When I was a sophomore everyone was telling me, 'We need more engineers in this country.'...But with seniors in aerospace right now, the job market sucks...The engineers we need are civil, electrical and computer—although the electrical people will also tell you competition is tough, because there's so many of them. So you ask yourself—it's almost like this big lie. (Male Hispanic engineering non-switcher)

Engineers who entered their major with expectations of good material rewards with a baccalaureate (only), and who also spoke of their undergraduate education in return-on-investment and risk terms, offered growing uncertainty about jobs and income levels as an important reason to switch to a major which seemed to offer better prospects of employment and material rewards. Their concerns were often founded on direct evidence of unemployment (either generally within engineering, or within particular specialties), or of the difficulties of friends who recently graduated in securing work appropriate to their qualifications:

If you can get through five years of that, you deserve a decent job...My cousin spent a winter as a waiter trying to find a job until he finally got a break over at N.A.S.A. (Male white engineering switcher)

Some of my best friends that graduated in engineering are now in business—including some who graduated with very decent G.P.A.s. One's selling yogurt; another works in a clothing store; and one guy's a bar-tender. There's no jobs for engineers right now. None whatsoever. And aeronautical—forget it—that's a useless piece of sheepskin. (Male white engineering switcher)

> When you're a freshman, I don't think you should go for what's hot, because it probably won't be hot by the time you get out. (Male white engineering switcher)

> Technology changes so quickly in each of these areas, that they suddenly have a demand because they have a break-through, and everybody goes for that. And by the time they get there, it's over. So you are left trying to chase down the few jobs that are out there. (Male white engineering switcher)

Those students who stayed, whether in engineering, science, or mathematics, tried to increase chances of success in a number of ways: they worked to raise their G.P.A.s in the hope of becoming more competitive; sought inside tracks with prospective employers through internships; developed flexible career plans with alternative goals and looked for new market niches:

> Some of the engineering specialties still have openings. I think fire protection is one that is supposed to be a less over-subscribed specialty. (Female white engineering switcher)

> I've declared a minor in education, so I could teach for a few years, or come back for a master's to be a school counselor. If I don't like teaching, I can still apply to med school or nursing. So long as I keep my G.P.A. up, having the biology degree with education gives me more chances. (Female white science non-switcher)

Some non-switchers were delaying their baccalaureate graduation, or considering application to graduate school, largely as ways to delay their job search. This response is discussed in the final section of this chapter. They also considered professional graduate degrees in less popular fields:

> I'm thinking of going on to dentistry. There should be a lot of work, that's for sure. (Male white science non-switcher)

Concern about the limited availability of jobs without an advanced degree was another reason for the phenomenon of 'graduating switchers':

> There's not much reward once you get out of school, and it seems like you're much more marketable with a degree in business than in science. And it's so tempting just to say, 'Well, I've put in all this work, and I'm probably gonna have to put in even more schooling,' and just to go out and find a job in another field, and to avoid struggling quite so much. (Female white science non-switcher)

> Even before I finish my physics major, I'm thinking about going into something else. (Male Asian-American science non-switcher)

The perception that the career opportunities and material rewards of completing S.M.E. majors were not worth the considerable effort required to succeed in them were mentioned as a factor in the switching decisions of 40.2 percent of science and mathematics switchers (for whom these factors ranked second among all factors contributing to switching), and by 30.8 percent of engineering switchers (for whom they ranked fifth). The main difference between the two groups of majors is that, from the outset, engineers were expecting more in terms of material rewards than were non-engineers. They were willing to put up with the discomforts of engineering majors in large part because they seemed to promise that all the hard work would pay off in the end.

Current and former science and mathematics majors (with the notable exception of those hoping to enter medical schools) had much less clear expectations of a high level of material rewards. In the early stages of their college education, they tended to focus on their discipline, rather than their career options. However, concerns about the job market, and about the difficulty of finding employment without an advanced degree, grew the longer students remained in the major, and were a major topic of discussion among non-switching seniors. Generally, science and mathematics majors expected much less in material terms than engineers, but felt entitled to some choice of work commensurate with the considerable effort which their science and mathematics majors had demanded.

Financial Problems and their Consequences

Our study was undertaken in a period when workers needed to acquire increasing levels of knowledge and skills to compete in the rapidly changing labor market. However, as Mortensen (1995) points out, between 1979 and 1992, the federal government reduced its contribution to higher education by $4.5 billion, and 49 state legislatures reduced their collective contribution by $7 billion. State financial resources were largely diverted from higher education to fund Medicaid and to expand and operate state prisons. Universities and colleges have sought to cover this loss by increasing tuition and fees, and a much larger share of their operating revenues is now derived directly from students. Since 1980, the average annual increase in these charges has averaged two to three times the annual rate of inflation. Students have experienced this shift as fewer grants, more loans, and more time spent working. It is experienced by institutions as falling enrollment. Mortensen argues that the opportunity for higher education has become increasingly unequal: "In 1979, a student from the top quartile of family income was about four times more likely than a student from the bottom quartile to earn a baccalaureate degree by age 24. In 1993, the difference was 13 times" (1995, p.4).

Our findings reflect this trend, and illustrate its direct, personal consequences for many of our informants. Over one-quarter (26.6%) of all the students in our sample reported financial problems which were serious enough to influence their academic progress and/or career direction. Financial difficulties were a factor in 16.9 percent of all switching decisions, and were of concern to 29.5 percent of all switchers and to 23.0 percent of non-switchers. Engineering seniors reported more financial difficulties than science and mathematics seniors (28.8 percent compared with 18.6 percent), as did current and former engineering majors overall (30.6 percent compared with 23.0 percent for all science and mathematics participants). As we shall further discuss, engineering freshman and their families were more likely than freshmen in science and mathematics to have expected that their degrees would take four years, and to have made financial plans in accordance with this expectation.

Only two of the seven institutions (the most selective, prestigious and expensive university, and the small, private liberal arts college) worked out financial aid packages for all freshmen, including a mixture of scholarships, loans and work study. Despite this, financial difficulties ranked second among switchers' concerns at the private research university. With the exception of students in special recruitment programs, students at the other five institutions, had to discover for themselves which on-campus and off-campus agencies offered what kind of financial help. Less than one-third of our participants were funded (to any extent) by scholarships, sponsors, or by private resources. Approximately two-thirds (63.3%) had taken out loans at some point during their undergraduate career; and about half (56.2%) were currently meeting some proportion of their educational and/or personal expenses. Those who were employed spent an average of 18 hours per week in paid work. However, in a discussion of attrition risks, this average is misleading. At the four public institutions, students worked longer hours—commonly 20 hours per week or more—than students at the three private institutions. We met many students—both switchers and non-switchers—who worked between 30 and 45 hours a week. Financial aid was universally reported to be difficult to get. The application system was seen as overly complex, often illogical, and with too many possibilities for limitation or exclusion:

I gave up on financial aid a long time ago. I kept trying to plead my case, but eventually, I gave up...It's just too much of a hassle to fight them. (Female Asian-American science switcher)

When they count financial aid, they count loans—which is not at all the same thing as grants and scholarships. It makes no sense. I've paid my own way through. Even though I worked 15 or 20 hours right through, I'm still graduating with huge debts. (Male white engineering non-switcher)

You get financial aid from wherever you can. And its verging on fraud sometimes, but you have to get it if you are going to finish school. It's all in how you present the information. You have to get a bit creative to survive. (Male white science non-switcher)

It's the most bizarre thing: if you're not on financial aid, your work-study is unlimited. The school is giving you a grant that is not audited by the government. Whereas, if you're getting financial aid—as a guaranteed student loan, a Pell grant, or even a school grant that comes from government funds—your work study is treated as part of your aid package. The people on

work-study have to pay their bill at the end of the year, but they can't because
they're not allowed to make enough. So they have to take on another
job—which you can't if you're a science major. (Female white mathematics
non-switcher)

More seriously, in the opinion of seniors, getting any kind of financial
assistance, including loans, had become increasingly difficult at a time when
tuition, fees, books, other class materials, and the cost of living were all
increasing:

I got a little bit of financial assistance this year—it's only the second year I've
gotten anything. Otherwise, I pay everything on my own. It's not easy. And
they keep raising the tuition. (Male white mathematics switcher)

The longer I'm at this university, the more I see it; the more I hear about
people struggling against the financial-aid system, and I see more of my friends
working to put themselves through school. It's got pretty tough. (Male white
mathematics non-switcher)

Across the board, since I've been here, tuition has been raised 50 percent.
(Male white science switcher)

Nobody's got work study. We're begging for jobs. I was hired as a T.A. and
three days later they cut the budget for T.A.s, so I was the first one out—not
even one day of work. (Female white science switcher)

There was some kind of computer fee of $100 each semester...And books are
more expensive...I'll have four books, and it's $240...When you're a junior,
you can't find used books, because everybody's keeping them. (Male Hispanic
engineering switcher)

I'm a mature student, working 30 hours a week and going to school full-time.
And, when I write out that check for $1,200, I remember it cost that for a
whole year here 10 years ago. It's made me more of a consumer than when I
went to school the first time (Male white science switcher)

It's getting worse...There used not to be the limitations on the availability of
loans that there are now...Some time during the '80s, I felt the consequences
of it—Graham-Rudman brought in a lot of changes. I was getting a loan right
when that was going through, and suddenly there were limitations. (Female
black engineering switcher)

I'd say to the vice-provost, come down to the coffee room and talk to us. A
lot of people are really financially strapped. I fell a week behind in my classes
because I couldn't afford the books. (Male white engineering switcher)

Some students who were excluded from financial aid programs, or limited in
what they could get, because of their family's high income bracket, reported
little or no help from their families. This was sometimes a consequence of
family attitudes or priorities. However, it also reflected the competing demands
on family budgets made by multiple marriages which pit the needs of younger

children in a new family against those of college-aged children from a previous marriage:

> You're considered dependent on your parents, even though you haven't lived at home for two years, and they haven't claimed you in their income tax. They're paying child support on three kids to my step-dad's ex-wife, and they can't pay for my education on top of that...I suppose you must find that everywhere now. (Male white engineering switcher)

> I think a lot of people come here [to the state school] because they can't afford to go anywhere else. The financial-aid system is terrible. Whether your parents are helping you or not, that's what determines how much help you get. (Male white engineering switcher)

> In my family, once you leave the house, that's it. You're on your own. So both my brother and I had to come here [former land-grant institution]. It's not so bad for me because I'm not the Harvard type, but my brother is. He finally got out because he won a National Science Foundation Fellowship, and now he's in graduate school for math at Berkeley. But the financial side of it really held him back. (Male Asian-American science non-switcher)

> There's a lot with no financial help at all, because they come from upper middle-class backgrounds. They just have no money at all—like this friend of mine that changed from a science major, she worked 20 hours a week through all four years of school. I don't know how she did it. (Female white science non-switcher)

Students were aware of, and broadly supported, the national effort to recruit more students of color into S.M.E. majors. Unfortunately, this has been undertaken in a period of sharp increase in the proportion of higher education costs that students must meet from their own earnings. Focus group discussions at the state institutions especially revealed covert, but very strong, feelings of resentment toward students of color who were believed to be receiving public funds to which white students in financial need had no access:

> As it takes people longer and longer to graduate, you start to see it in more resentment, like, 'That damn black kid sitting next to me must be getting more money than I can.' And I think that's real unfortunate. (Male white science switcher)

Such feelings were exacerbated where the declared ethnicity of grant recipients was thought to have been fudged in order to get access to funds ear-marked for particular racial or ethnic groups. This issue, and its consequences, are discussed in more detail in Chapter 6.

The need to undertake employment—especially off-campus—in order to complete an undergraduate degree had a number of adverse effects on academic progress. Being employed while undertaking an S.M.E. major commonly lengthened the time taken to graduate. This was, ironically, further compounded where financial aid was refused in the final year(s) on the grounds that the student was taking too long to finish the degree:

> All my friends who came when they were younger graduated in four years. But it's gotten so tight with the budget cuts around here, and the fact that tuition is *so* much higher than it was then, no one gets out in four years any more. You just have to work your way through, and it all takes so much longer. (Male white science switcher)

> Most people at this university work at least 20 hours a week. So the average graduation time here is at least five years—if not more. (Male white science switcher)

> Most of my friends are working 15 to 30 hours a week. That's why people take longer to graduate here. (Male Asian-American engineering non-switcher)

> I know there are a lot of people taking less classes, because they can't afford to go full-time. (Female white mathematics switcher)

> I'm working 26 hours a week, but I'm only taking two classes. I planned it this way because I need the money. It's been a long grind. (Female white engineering non-switcher)

> There's a problem when people get close to finishing, they get in trouble because they don't have the money to finish. And they are forced to leave for a while, or go part-time—take one class a quarter—that kind of thing. And, all of a sudden, a four-year degree becomes a seven- or eight-year degree…And if you're not done when they say you have to be done, you're severely punished—because you're not eligible for financial aid—just when you need it most. When you get close to the end is when your resources start to run out, and that's when you can't get any others. (Male white science non-switcher)

The time spent at work was often at the expense of academic study, and the consequences were sometimes reflected in lower grades:

> It was the money. It was hard for me to organize myself to work and to go to school at the same time. Eventually, my grades were falling off, and I had to stop, because I couldn't keep them both up together. I've had good grades recently. But I've taken out a lot of loans. (Male white science switcher)

> I've put myself through school. I work about 30 hours a week. Sometimes I get a C in class instead of a B because I have to work. (Male white engineering non-switcher)

Meeting the needs of their employers could also make it hard to meet important academic commitments such as studying for examinations, or keeping advising appointments:

> I work a lot since I'm paying out-of-state tuition. And it's hard for me to take off from work to go and see a professor. They don't like it at work, but I do it sometimes to go to the lab. (Male white engineering non-switcher)

It's difficult if you have an exam, and you have to work the day before. Some employers will let you off. (Male Asian-American engineering non-switcher)

The time spent in travelling to and from work could also reduce the time available for study:

You're tired after you already went to school, and then you've gotta work—you gotta drive out to work, and then you gotta drive back, and, and then the next day, you've got an exam—it's difficult. (Male Asian-American engineering non-switcher)

Students who had to work saw themselves at a great disadvantage, particularly in classes where there was intense competition:

You get caught in the trap: how are you supposed to be an A student if you're having to work your way through school?...I couldn't get enough financial aid, so I was working 40 hours a week, and I took my physics classes one at a time. There's a few really intelligent people in the classes. But there's also a lot of people who get As and Bs mainly because they are hard workers. But they don't have to work. Those are the ones I'm competing against. It angers me no end that I am being measured by the same criteria as them. It was a hurdle I was constantly battling. And I didn't overcome it until this last semester when I took out enough loans so I didn't have to work at all...It's like swallowing a very bitter pill to understand that you just *have* to put yourself in that amount of debt to be able to compete. (Female black engineering switcher)

Some students wondered if faculty realized that the weed-out system was, in effect, a means test biased in favor of students with independent funding. Among those with inadequate funds, weeding out helped to select only those who had the stamina to meet both heavy economic and academic demands:

A good friend of mine in this major pays for college on her own. Sometimes she gets discouraged. She feels like, 'Should I really be putting myself through this misery when it's me that's putting out the bucks?' If I was in that position, I probably wouldn't be that strong-willed. If I don't make it in a class, I'll take it again. But she can't afford it...In the freshman classes, they think they're weeding out the weak students. But it's some of the students who are paying for college on their own they're weeding out—people who say, 'No way am I going to go on doing this.' (Female white science non-switcher)

S.M.E. degrees were thought particularly hard to reconcile with student employment because they made greater formal time demands than other degrees: they had a more intense curriculum structure, a high commitment to laboratory time and often required a higher number of credits than other majors. Students who had to work were constantly forced to choose between academic commitments and the need for financial survival:

I have to work every afternoon and I can't take a lab class. It's difficult when I have a math class that has a problem session every afternoon from one to five. I just can't do it. If you want to be a science major, and if you need a job, it had better be an on-campus job. If you work as a waitress, there's no way. (Female white mathematics non-switcher)

Because I lost a year of financial aid, I had to work more hours to keep going. I got no help from my family, so I was trying to work 30, 40 hours a week and stay in school full-time. But, with that, I just couldn't keep up with my courses.... (Male white science switcher)

By the time I graduate, I'll have to pay back $15,000. I daren't borrow any more, so I have to work. But, on the other hand, you're here to study. If you go to work, you don't get your problem set done. You are always having to figure out priorities. (Female white engineering non-switcher)

It's the intensity of engineering classes that is almost impossible when you're trying to work. I would say that's probably the reason a lot of people leave. I even thought about it two weeks ago—if I could get out any quicker by going into computer science—I was actually thinking about getting a master's. Because the way the master's is set up, you actually have to satisfy less requirements than if you had come through the engineering ranks. Maybe I'd be better off. (Female black engineering non-switcher)

That was my downfall. If you have to work and do engineering, it's really tough. I worked 25 to 30 hours a week. At times, I worked 40 hours. (Male white engineering switcher)

It was very hard with the labs, working full-time...I think that would be pretty much it, just time—it required so much time, so much problem-solving—calculations, doing computer work, and not having access to a computer system other than on campus; having to run back and forth...And I sat there and asked myself, 'Did I really want to put myself through this?' Because I had to work. If I wasn't working, I couldn't be in school. (Male black engineering switcher)

Students who paid most of their own way through school had less margin for error than did those with scholarships or family assistance. Those who worked more hours than was consistent with good scholarship were at constant risk of failing classes or earning poor grades. Mistakes in the choice of classes, or class failures, had a disproportionately negative effect upon them because they could not easily afford to repeat classes. The risk of subsequent failures was exacerbated by the need to work harder to pay for repeat classes:

It's the financial aspect...Sometimes you have to take classes over because you got a bad grade. But you don't have any money to continue, so you drop out for financial reasons for a while...All my room-mates are out of school because of financial difficulties. (Male black engineering switcher)

> You miss one course, and you have to go to summer session. A lot of people can't do summers. I always had to work in the summers. (Female white engineering switcher)

For some students, the constant strain of juggling time and energy between the demands of work and school was a major factor in their abandonment of S.M.E. majors. A few came close to dropping out of school altogether:

> The thing that really got me to switch was financial—every year, tuition goes up at least eight percent, and I was spending all this money I didn't have. Finally, it pushed me out of science, because I could graduate with another degree faster. It wasn't the department that pushed me out, it was the system. (Male white science switcher)

> It came down to this. I had to have the money in order to go to school, but I couldn't have the money *and* go to school...Well, I needed the money so time for school had to be cut back...My grades had been suffering so long—not entirely because of the money, but it was a very big factor...I worked full-time, and I would occasionally take a night class and register through extension school, and just tried to keep going. I felt if I stopped completely, I'd never start up again. (Male white science switcher)

> It's impossible. And, it's an unfortunate truth that an awful lot of people must do it...I was pushing myself at 45 hours a week, working at several little part-time jobs, and still had to get the studying in....I changed my major when I had become sick with mononucleosis. I also developed a kidney tumor, and had to have surgery. But a lot of it was stress-induced. (Female black engineering switcher)

> Most of the people I know who had financial problems couldn't afford to come to the university full-time. So they had to pick up an extra job, cut down on the number of classes, and study engineering part-time. It takes a long time. So they switched to other majors that were not as intense as engineering, but maybe they had a better chance of graduating. (Male Hispanic engineering switcher)

> I've paid my way through everything...I work 20 to 30 hours a week. And if I don't get out in May, I'm not coming back. (Female white engineering switcher)

Notwithstanding the belief of some white students—particularly those who had to work long hours to sustain their education—that students of color were at an unfair advantage in getting scholarships, or other forms of financial aid, it was clear that students of color (especially black and Hispanic students) were actually over-represented among those whose decision to switch was directly related to their financial difficulties. It became clear that students of color from poorer communities were not only more at risk of switching majors, they were, as both Porter (1990) and Rotberg (1990) have reported, also at greater risk than white students of dropping out of university altogether.

Most students coped with the financial difficulties they encountered in completing their education by some mixture of work and borrowing. Loans were universally disliked because of the long-term limitations they placed on future work and lifestyle, including the chance to marry and have children. Unwillingness to live with the consequences of debt also affected persistence:

> My room-mate works to keep him from debt. I work too, but I've also collected some loans. And the thought of all that didn't help me stay. (Male white engineering switcher)

> I mean, I'm gonna be paying for school forever. I mean, emotionally, I'm definitely ready to get out. (Female white engineering switcher)

> Some are thinking they're gonna have to leave without a degree. That happens a lot. By the time I get out of law school, I'll probably be $50,000 in debt. (Female white engineering switcher)

> I'm just backing up student loan after student loan. They're all going to hit when I get out of school. (Male white engineering non-switcher)

> I have to push it out of my head: 'Another loan. Don't think about it. Just sign it. That's it. Just sign it.' (Female white mathematics non-switcher)

Financial problems had other consequences for student decisions. Some students chose a particular major or institution because they were offered financial help. Some stayed in majors in which they had lost interest rather than lose a scholarship (for example, from a corporation or R.O.T.C.). The debt burden accumulated by those who chose borrowing over employment could also have profound consequences for career choices:

> If you're borrowing less, you have more options about the fields you can go into. If you have a $150,000 debt, you can't go into primary care in a rural area...There's a correlation between the price tag for your education and your degree of freedom. (Female white science non-switcher)

> I'm putting myself through school—entirely with work and student loans. I've got five brothers and sisters, so it wasn't possible for my parents to help...So switching to business really made sense to me. I can go straight to work...I'm looking for a job with security 'cause I've got large student loans. I want to get on my feet—make some money. When I've paid my loans off, I'd like to come back to grad school for an M.B.A. (Male white science switcher)

As we shall discuss in more detail later, delaying graduate school entry was often a function of the need to pay off undergraduate loans, and to build up financial reserves:

> I have to put myself through school. So I'll probably not be going to grad school right after I graduate. I'll have to take some years to work and pay off some of these debts. (Female white mathematics switcher)

You build up this loan, and so you have to go out and get a job. Grad school just isn't possible. And you think, 'I'll build up some money; get out from under some of this debt.' But you want to get married and have a family some time. And it's hard to go have a family while attending grad school. (Male Asian-American science non-switcher)

To a very marked degree, students accepted the responsibility of contributing to their own education by working. What they found hard to accept were the inadequacy, inequity and unnecessary complexity of the financial aid system. They also expressed anger at what they saw as political and institutional insensitivity to recent increases in the proportion of higher education costs which students have to meet by working and borrowing, and to the academic and career consequences of this:

What the faculty don't take into consideration is that financial aid is going down, so we get less help, and we have to work more hours to pay for the rising tuition. They are still thinking about how people graduated in four years, 10 or 20 years ago. (Male white engineering non-switcher)

A lot of my professors are older white males who were in industry back in the 1960s when Kennedy said, 'Let's go to the moon.'...They don't come from where I come from, and they don't see the world the way I do...You know, I'm not sitting here crying for anything special, but they don't know what it's like. (Male Hispanic engineering non-switcher)

Making it through and paying the bills is very tough...What a senior administrator said last week really caught our attention—that students ought to stop watching soap operas, get off their butts and go out and get jobs—even though 80 percent of the students at this school already have jobs outside school. I can tell you, that got a lot of peoples' backs up. (Male white engineering non-switcher)

I think, if they want more math and science and technical students, they should be more willing to offer funds to them, and allow them to go through without having to hear stories of, 'Well, when I was in college, I walked through the snow to my second job to make it.'...It's just not a possibility these days...I haven't seen any administration do anything to help students. (Female black engineering switcher)

Problems with the Length of S.M.E. Majors

Problems with undergraduate majors which took more than four years to complete figured in only 7.6 percent of switching decisions, and were mentioned by 12.0 percent of switchers overall. The problems of trying to finish majors which were taking longer than planned were, understandably, of more concern to seniors, 19.8 percent of whom mentioned difficulties in this regard. However, this was a factor which affected students in some majors, and in some institutions, more than others. Problems with the more-than-expected length of the degree were reported by more current and former engineering majors than by those in science and mathematics. Although this difference is insignificant as a factor in overall switching decisions, it was mentioned as a concern by 37.9 percent of engineering seniors (compared with 27.6 percent of seniors in science or mathematics), and by 28.6 percent of all engineering switchers (compared with 20.2 percent of switchers in science and mathematics). Seniors at two of the four public institutions had particular difficulties in completing their majors within a four-year time-frame. In the largest public institution in our sample, this problem was closely connected with a high level of financial difficulties, both among switchers and S.M.E. seniors (where financial problems ranked second in importance). On this large, mainly non-residential campus, where many students attended on a part-time basis, faculty and administrators expressed concern that students in all majors took five or six years to graduate. Both the switchers and non-switchers at this institution were agreed that the primary reason for this slow pace was insufficient funds to attend college in a more concentrated manner.

The expectation that a baccalaureate should, and could, be completed in four years was an institutional expectation in colleges of engineering. However, engineering majors quickly learned (by their own experiences, and from those of peers) that this was unrealistic:

> Well, the engineering school passes out the course handout which lays out what you have to take, and in what sequence, and they've got everything planned except your electives. And the only hand-out they've got is a four-year program with 17 or 18 units a semester. But I know of very few people who take that many—12 is closer to what you can actually do. It's a five-year degree for almost everybody—four and a half if you were extremely well-prepared. (Male white engineering non-switcher)

> Unless you can take 18 or 19 credits a semester, you can't do it. They structure it for four years, but it's a joke. There's no way you can take five engineering classes in one semester. Impossible. (Male white engineering non-switcher)

Finishing in four years also depended on success in completing classes in the right sequence. The four-year time-table left no room for error in the selection of classes, and no possibility of re-taking any class:

> What they didn't tell me was that if you delay in taking one class, you have to wait a whole year to take it again...That can really mess you up. They assume you're going to take this class, followed by that class—all in logical order—when, sometimes, no matter how much you try, you can't do that. (Male Hispanic engineering switcher)

> And you can't mess up a single class because, if you do, you're a semester behind, and if it's not an upper-level course it may not be offered in summer school...What they don't tell you is that sometimes a course is only offered in

the fall, and you don't find out until it's too late and you're already a semester behind. (Male white engineering switcher)

Another consequence of the tight schedule was that it severely reduced the possibility of a broader educational experience:

It was frustrating to look at how they'd set out your whole curriculum, and you'd maybe 10 hours of liberal arts for the whole time—and that was to be able to graduate in four years. I didn't think that was giving people a good education. (Female white engineering switcher)

They are trying to introduce humanities requirements to broaden engineering, and it's a good idea in some ways. But if you mention it to most engineers, they'll laugh at you...The curriculum can't be completed in four years as it is. (Male Asian-American engineering switcher)

Both current and former engineering students expressed anger at what they saw as deliberate misrepresentation of the time it would actually take for most of them to complete their major. Most engineering seniors had accepted the necessity of a five-year program, but wished they had been advised at the out-set to plan the pace and sequence of their classes in accordance with this longer, more realistic time-frame. They could, thus, have avoided both the academic problems created by trying to follow official guidelines that proved unworkable and the financial crises provoked by needing money for an extra year. Had they known in advance that engineering would be a five-year degree, some students reported they would have considered another major:

I think the administration talks out of both sides of its mouth. It says, 'Oh, we have this program you can take in four years,' but your freshman engineering advisor warns you, 'Only take 14 or 15 credits because this is your first year, and you won't manage more.' It's good advice—but it immediately puts you one class behind the official schedule and messes up the sequence of all your pre-requisites. I think they need to make up their minds. It's officially on paper as a four-year degree, but only about eight percent of us make it in that time. (Female white engineering non-switcher)

I knew it was going to be five years because I'd talked to a lot of people before I committed myself. But most freshmen come in with the wrong impression. They ought to put it in bold print somewhere that, unless you're taking 18 to 19 credits a semester, you're going to be here for five years. (Female white engineering non-switcher)

Of course, they lose some people in the first year because of stretching it to a five-year curriculum. It's mainly because of money—people can't afford to stay in school for five years. (Male white engineering switcher)

I elected to change my major because of funding. My financial situation was getting to the point where I was not going to have the time to finish. (Female black engineering switcher)

> If I'd known at the beginning it was going to take five years, I'd have considered something else. (Male black engineering switcher)

Students understood the source of the covert five-year engineering degree but felt the profession should find a way to resolve this problem, rather than leaving students and their parents to deal with the consequences of avoiding it:

> In order for the school to be accredited, it has to be a four-year program. So they try to cram everything into the four years. And, on paper, it looks possible—if everyone takes this real rigorous schedule with 18 hours a semester, and almost no electives. Once they have the accreditation on the basis of a schedule that looks do-able on paper, they can unofficially encourage you take it a little slower. That way they look good. But what about the chaos it makes for us? And what about our folks who were led to expect they were paying for a four-year degree? (Male white engineering switcher)

Students who did make it in four years acquired legendary status:

> We were just talking about one person who made it in four years, without even going to summer school—that's remarkable. (Male white engineering non-switcher)

From a focus group of women engineering seniors—

> I know some people who like to punish themselves: they get done in four years after taking 21 unit quarters just of engineering classes.

> Yeah—I know someone who did it. From junior year, she took four Double E classes every quarter until she graduated.

> God!

> She probably didn't see the sun rise 'til she was done.

We asked students what were the conditions under which a student could be one of those who did complete an engineering major in four years. Their answers were, it could be done if: you were exceptionally bright; you were very well-prepared by your high school, and had all your pre-requisites on entry; your parents were paying all, or most, of the costs, and you did not have to work; you managed to take the required 18 to 20 credit hours each semester; you did everything in sequence, and did not have to re-take a single class; you lived either on, or very close, to campus.

In science and mathematics majors, some students also had problems in completing their majors in four years, but the reasons for their difficulties varied and were not so clearly and universally associated with the formal structure of their majors. Some science and mathematics seniors took longer than they had expected because: their majors demanded a larger number of credits; they experienced difficulties with weed-out classes, and had to retake some of them; they sought a broader education than was allowed for in their discipline, and took classes in the humanities or social sciences not allowed for in the official program.

Those students whose problems with the extra time required to graduate were predominantly financial, faced a set of related difficulties. First, the idea that students who work hard are supposed to be able to finish any undergraduate degree in four years is a strongly-rooted norm among parents:

> My father's paying for college, but he said, 'Four years is all I'm paying for.' (Male white engineering switcher)

> My dad's only paying for four years, and if I can't get done in that time, that's it. So that was a major consideration in switching majors. How could I pay for an extra year? I needed to get out. (Female white science switcher)

Those with fathers (sic) in engineering faced the special difficulty of getting their parent to accept that the modern engineering curriculum demands mastery of more academic content than was demanded of former engineering majors:

> Do I think an engineering degree's feasible in four years? God, no! You would just kill yourself trying to do the 18 credits—unless you were exceptionally talented. The problem is my dad thinks it's feasible, because he did it in four. But he got a lot of credits dropped because he was in the services. We figured out the credits he took, and the ones I needed to get out—128—and his were a whole lot less. And then there's just more to know for this generation of engineers. But don't ever tell him that! (Female white engineering non-switcher)

The norms, both of peers and of the wider community, also placed pressure on those who realized that completing their S.M.E. major would require more than four years:

> They leave because they can't afford another year, but also because they think other people will feel that they're deficient because they took five years instead of four. (Female black engineering non-switcher)

> They don't acknowledge that it actually takes five years. I don't know why. But there's definitely a stigma to admitting it. (Male white engineering switcher)

The four-year tradition is also reflected in the financial-aid system, which students found made no allowances for the extra time which many S.M.E. majors need to graduate. Thus, the period just prior to graduation, when students need to focus exclusively on their academic work, was the time when they were most likely to face an economic crisis which was unacknowledged and unrelieved by the financial-aid system:

> After four, four and a half, years, you're not eligible for financial aid any more, and there's a lot of problems that come just from that. (Male white engineering non-switcher)

This is the very first semester I've been eligible for financial aid, and it's also my last, because I'm gonna go over the credit limit. (Male white science non-switcher)

They will only give you work study for four years. (Male Hispanic engineering switcher)

I thought it would take four years, until I got into it and realized it wasn't possible. I have to pay out-of-state tuition, so to do the extra year is especially hard. (Male white engineering non-switcher)

We asked seniors how they had coped with the problem of lengthy majors, and what they thought would mitigate the problems they had encountered. Establishing a system of financial support for S.M.E. seniors was considered paramount:

There should be more scholarships for seniors who need two years to do their senior-level specializations. As it is, I'm missing a number of special courses that I know I'm going to need once I get out there. I didn't have analogs, or any power courses above the junior level. And that's two whole branches of engineering I know I'll need. And one of the biggest problems right now is finding engineers to build power supplies for computers. I wish I could stay another semester, but I daren't take the time, and I don't have the money. (Male white engineering non-switcher)

Engineering seniors expressed their preference for an official four- to five-year degree, often in strong terms:

I would have preferred an official five-year program that I could have stuck to rather than this stumbling on the truth by failing courses I didn't need to fail, and having to re-take things, which lengthens it even more. (Female white engineering non-switcher)

It would just be a better education if it were five years. I mean, why can't they just say, 'This is our curriculum, and it takes five years'—or even four and a half? I know a lot of people who take four and a half, and they come out happier, and with better grades. (Male white science non-switcher)

Make engineering a five year program—officially—right off the bat. It's what it's turned into anyway. There are a few very impressive people who make it in four—there are always the exceptions—but it's more sensible to plan on five. (Male Asian-American engineering non-switcher)

They called for the ending of what they saw as misrepresentation of the nature of the major to students and their parents, and of 'victim-blaming' in faculty explanations of why students have difficulty in keeping up with the official time-table:

The catalog is fraudulent. Once you get here, they let you in on the secret. I guess nowadays more colleges are starting to tell you it's five years; some have started two-plus-three year programs—or even six years with a master's at the end. The rest need to get with it and stop fooling themselves—and us. (Female white engineering non-switcher)

They should get honest about it. Nationwide, more than half the engineers stay more than four years. They know that. So why don't they advertise it the way it is? They need to face up to it, and not make us take the heat. (Male white engineering non-switcher)

The really miserable thing about not telling you the truth up-front, is that you start off thinking that it's your fault—that you're to blame for not studying hard enough—that engineers have to do everything at the double—and that everybody can do it but you. Bullshit! But they've lost a ton of people before those of us that are left get smart. You have to learn to ignore that stuff; pace yourself; and don't let anyone tell you there's anything wimpy in taking a bit longer. (Male white engineering non-switcher)

Both engineering and science seniors described how, after trying to keep up with a pace and load to the detriment of a solid understanding of the work, and always feeling too stressed to appreciate the implications of what they were doing, they had shifted into a more measured time-frame. As a matter of survival, and in order to get the most out of their education, they advised younger students to give themselves 'permission' to see their major as more than a four-year commitment, and to work at a less intense pace:

Now, if I was coming in fresh, and know what I know now about school...I'd stay around 14 or 15 credits...You learn so much more by taking 15 hours than 18. (Male Hispanic engineering non-switcher)

Five years is a much better plan. I've met a lot of engineers at work, and very few of them did it in four. It's better to be realistic and make the most of your time here. (Male white engineering non-switcher)

It's a matter of maintaining your sanity—slowing down a bit, going an extra semester if you need to, and getting out with a decent G.P.A. (Male white science non-switcher)

This is my fifth year. I did some extra things which I enjoyed. And I watched my friends who were struggling all through their last semester doing interviews, and taking 17 hours, and not doing well, and hating life. I decided it was more sensible to slow down and take it all in. I'm glad that I did it that way. (Male white mathematics non-switcher)

I used to think only a flake or a goof-off took five years—that somehow I'd failed. But I've learned a lot of other things—like when I've been to conferences, or doing co-ops out there in the working situation. I mean, you have to be able to understand the structural system, be able to apply what you know, understand the economics of the project, and be able to work with the people around you. You need to take the time to think about these things. (Female white engineering non-switcher)

Playing the System

The question of switching majors in order to gain some career advantage was an issue for a small number of students. It was most commonly mentioned by science and mathematics switchers (12.0 percent of whom raised it as a consideration, and 9.8 percent as a factor in their decision to switch). We think it is of interest, nevertheless, because it reflects one extreme of a highly instrumental, 'commodity' view of education which may be growing among students and their parents. By this approach, graduating with good grades and a high G.P.A. is the student's main objective. If the structure or demands of a particular major make it difficult to achieve that goal, it makes sense to switch to a major with better prospects. This is, in large part, economic realism. Students and their parents understand that prospective employers rely heavily on academic scores:

> I am looking to get a good job with computer firm. My goal was to graduate with at least a 3.25 G.P.A., and I was concerned about taking any more classes which threatened that. (Male white science switcher)

> The job market's very rough, and there's no point in taking the major unless you're getting at least a 3.3. (Male white engineering switcher)

> My room-mate was doing okay in civil engineering. She was getting Bs and Cs like the rest of us. But she decided to switch into liberal arts because of the grades. She was looking for a *cum laude*. (Female white engineering non-switcher)

> I have a 3.44, and I really need a 3.5. And with math that wouldn't have been possible. I've gotten an A in every economics class so far. (Male white mathematics switcher)

Some students whose baccalaureate degree was only the first stage in an education which included a post-graduate professional degree such as law, medicine or business, left their S.M.E. major because getting into one of the 'better' schools required a more competitive G.P.A. than seemed possible if they remained:

> I went into public policy...I was frustrated because it had been a long time since I'd gotten an A—I kept getting these B+s—and I thought, 'I'm not gonna get into law school with these grades.' I even have a C on my transcript from physics. (Female Asian-American engineering switcher)

> I was thinking, 'This isn't gonna work with my original plan. I'm never gonna get into a business school if I'm gonna do so poorly.' I mean, it's okay if I just wanted to be an engineer, but that was never my original intention. So it didn't make sense to me to keep going. (Female Asian-American engineering switcher)

I'm glad I'm not majoring in biology any more, especially as I want to go to med school...Anyway, there's so many biology majors applying to med school, it means you have to really distinguish yourself in that field to stand out from the pile. If you are an American Studies or English major, it gives a different focus, and makes you look twice as good. (Female white science switcher)

The perceived necessity of switching majors as a way to cope with a system which encourages an over-focus on grades was widely accepted by other students who were not facing this dilemma:

A lot of pre-meds leave because things are just too hard, and they have to keep their G.P.A. high. A lot of them go into business or history. They have to get through organic, but once they've done that, they can get out. But see, they've gotta boost their G.P.A. to get in. They've gotta do something they can ace. (Male white science non-switcher)

If you wanna go to an Ivy League med school, you can't be a chemistry major. Your chances of keeping a 4.0 are just not good enough. (Male white science non-switcher)

I mean, if I wanted to get into the big-boy network, I would definitely move real quick to get my G.P.A. up—if I had to try to get into graduate school, or do anything that had a little bit more status or prestige attached to it. (Female white mathematics switcher)

However, some seniors who had witnessed the move into non-S.M.E. majors of former class-mates concerned about getting into medical school also expressed disquiet about the implications this might have for the quality of future doctors:

I mean, there's as many pre-meds in sociology and English as there are in biology. They take the bare minimum—maybe three biology, three chemistry, two physics, and two math, and that's it—they move...My room-mate's one of them. He's got accepted into a few places. And I know he just doesn't want to deal with the biology—you know, the lab work every day...I know it's a good idea for doctors to have a broader base, but I just wonder whether they know enough of the science they are going to need. (Male white science non-switcher)

We have commented throughout our account of findings on indications that students have come to view their education as a commodity, an investment, or a business risk and have discussed the role of pragmatism and materialism in the choice of a major. In describing faculty teaching and assessment practices, we noted student criticisms often include a value-for-money component:

They're apparently not here to teach. They're here to do research. And I'm paying a $1000 a year to come here, and I've got teachers who are incompetent—I got *six* percent on one physics exam. And *that* was a B. It's outrageous. (Male white engineering switcher)

In our discussion of the competitive culture, we described the strategies which students advocated in order to survive in the major, or get the best out of their institution. Thus, switching in furtherance of career goals is but one manifestation of an instrumental orientation which we found to be widespread among students.

The Choice of Graduate School

In the course of discussions about career plans, we learned something about the considerations which prompt seniors either to choose, or to reject, graduate school. Given current concerns about declining graduate school enrollment by non-foreign S.M.E. students, we thought it useful to include a summary of students' perceptions about the costs and benefits of graduate school.

Among S.M.E. seniors, 12.5 percent had decided to go to graduate school, or to undertake a post-graduate professional degree; a further 3.3 percent thought they might do so after a break; and 17.1 percent who thought they were sufficiently qualified to be accepted at graduate school, had decided against application. Among S.M.E. switchers, a very similar proportion (12.0%) intended to enter graduate school or undertake a professional degree, despite the disruption caused by their shift of majors. This underscores our hypothesis that multi-talented, high quality students leave S.M.E. majors in sufficient numbers to be a cause of concern.

The simplest case was that of engineering seniors, whose strong practical orientation made it less likely that they would follow a research and teaching career track. Engineering students showed a more materialist orientation than most science and mathematics majors and tended to view academic careers as offering a poor return on their educational investment:

> I think my idea of engineering is getting the hands-on work. You design at a drafting table, on a C.A.D., or watch a building go up, rather than teaching classes and stuff. (Male white engineering non-switcher)

> I think most people see it as a lot more work going to grad school, when you can go out and get a job with a company right away, and probably make as much as a new professor right from the start. And there isn't as much prestige in being a university engineer as there is in working for a big corporation. (Male white engineering non-switcher)

Some of the engineering seniors who had decided to pursue a master's or doctoral program in engineering did so to further their chances of a job at a higher level, or in a specialized area of industry rather than a career in research or teaching:

> I guess my experiences in work have led me to go on to grad school. I want to move into materials. I have a good idea of what I want to do, and I'm willing to put in the extra effort to get into that field. I've recently been talking to a woman professor, and she's been encouraging me to go on for a Ph.D.,

but I'm pretty set on a master's. You can be over-qualified with a Ph.D. No one will hire you if you get too specialized. (Female white engineering non-switcher)

Very few of the grad students I work with want to teach. They are looking to go out into private industry at a more specialized level. (Male white engineering non-switcher)

I feel there's not the reward. State institutions cannot provide the financial funding to pay competitively like the private market. They have to really want to do the research to stay because the financial rewards with a higher degree in industry are so much greater. (Female white engineering non-switcher)

However, some engineering seniors were considering a higher degree for a more basic reason. They had come to suspect that the traditional promise of engineering as a four-year major with a well-paying job at the end of it was an out-dated notion:

You can't get a real engineering job any more without a master's degree and a lot of experience. That's something they don't tell you until senior seminar. All of a sudden, they pop it on you that, sooner or later, you're gonna have to come back for a master's degree. Without it, you don't ever get to be a project manager. You end up acting as a technician. You can make a living, but anyone who's gonna excel, they have to go on. (Male white engineering non-switcher)

I don't want to get shut out of a career, because, right now, jobs in chemical engineering are available. And some of the things they are doing are really interesting, innovative, and exciting, and I sort of want to participate in that. But, then you think, 'God, I'd better go to grad school now, 'cause then I might never get a job.' Everybody's going to have a bachelor's one of these days. (Female white engineering non-switcher)

In a depressed economy, they wondered whether there would be sufficient jobs for all those graduating with a baccalaureate in engineering:

I think there's a lot of people who are beginning to get interested because it's not a good market right now. I mean, they might as well try a graduate school, and delay their entrance into the market. (Male white engineering non-switcher)

These concerns were not, however, widely discussed and only four of the S.M.E. seniors who had decided to go to graduate school (or who were considering it as a future option) were engineers.

For science and mathematics majors, the issues were more complex. On the one hand, seniors commonly expressed feeling 'burned-out' after completing the baccalaureate. As indicated earlier, the career decisions of many S.M.E. seniors were also shaped by their accumulated debt burden:

It's got a lot to do with feeling burned out when you finally finish what is often now a five-year undergraduate degree—struggling through an over-loaded curriculum, and paying your own way through at the same time, with no proper social life, and always short of sleep. And then, there's all of the loans you have to repay. Grad school is just too much to ask of us. (Male white mathematics non-switcher)

Why don't I want to go to grad school? Money! Either money to do it, or the lack of money at the end. In your upper-division classes, you get to meet a lot of grad students, and you see how hard they've worked, and the pittance that they get. I need to work for a company and make a reasonable living after all the costs of this degree. I've got loans to pay off. I've got to make some money now. (Female white science non-switcher)

Seniors also expressed doubts of the kind discussed at the beginning of this chapter about the context and nature of research work, and the lifestyle which an academic career connoted for them:

I know I can cut it in grad school. I could beat the grad students they've got here—I know, because I take classes with them. But you look at those professors who come in and work 70 hours a week. And then your working conditions are horrible. In a chem lab, you're exposed to toxins every day. Or you're stuck with a computer. So if you're a people person at all, forget grad school. (Male white science non-switcher)

Even if they get their graduate degree, there's years and years to be spent working as an understudy to somebody else before they can get to do their own research. (Male white science switcher)

Their rejection of aspects of the academic life were also rooted in their own research experience:

Maybe it's a bad thing having so much research experience, because I realize how cut-throat it all is—particularly in fly genetics, which is what I work on. I just felt it wasn't appealing any more. And there's no funding for academic positions. (Female white science non-switcher)

I've been working in physics since I was a senior in high school, including every summer. And I'm sick of the politics—you know, you only present theories if your boss likes them. You write papers and your boss gets credit for them. And you have to justify your research to some government official and tell him why it's valuable, even though you haven't done it yet. It doesn't square with my ideas of what research should be. I'll go back eventually, but I need a break right now. (Female white science non-switcher)

Despite encouragement by their faculty to apply to graduate school, some seniors had decided to seek work in a non-academic context:

I've gotten a sales job. I'm all locked up at the lab, and I'm gonna leave and do that and get on my own ground for a while, and try to get away from the science élitism. Although I didn't initially think of a career with a company like this, the opportunity has really turned my thinking around, and I'm very excited to think about working for a big international. So I stopped the research, started volunteering and doing things that way instead of staying in science. (Male white science non-switcher)

A few seniors thought they might postpone graduate entry until they had saved some money or tested out the job market:

I'm going to graduate in December, but I'll wait until next fall to go—unless I find a good job meanwhile. Otherwise, I need to make some money for grad school. (Female white science non-switcher)

I used to be under the impression that everyone wanted to go to grad school—now, I'm not sure. I'm practically the only person in my group of friends that's intending to go next year. Most of them are going to apply the year after next. (Male white science non-switcher)

I've spent a lot of money coming here, and a lot of it has been my own personal money—I mean, I've had to work a lot. And, if I'm not getting a return on my investment in the job I get, say, after a year or two at most, well, I would probably consider grad school. (Male white science non-switcher)

On the other hand, many science and mathematics seniors expressed the concern that some form of qualification beyond the baccalaureate level was increasingly necessary in order to secure relevant, interesting or reasonably well-paid work:

Oh, I never questioned that I was going to get an advanced degree. I mean, a bachelor's degree doesn't get you very far in the world these days. (Female Asian-American science non-switcher)

A biologist isn't going to make any money, even when you finally get the Ph.D. I mean, you have to laugh, or you'd cry, it's so ironic. But what's the choice? If you come out as an undergraduate biologist or chemist, you can't do anything. You can be a technician. (Female white science non-switcher)

In physics, the only prospect of employment is after grad school...The people with bachelor's in physics aren't going to starve, but if you want a good job, you need a Ph.D. There's no two ways about it. (Male white science non-switcher)

Unlike engineers, some of whom saw practical merit in a master's degree, most science and mathematics seniors who chose a graduate degree saw it as the only viable, non-professional, higher degree option available to them:

There really aren't any jobs for physicists without a Ph.D., unless you want to teach in high school, which is really looked down on. So teaching undergraduates is the price that you have to pay for being in science. (Male white science non-switcher)

> With a master's degree in mathematics and 60 cents of change, you can get a
> Coke out of most machines. There's not much you can do unless you go all the
> way. (Male white science non-switcher)

In the later interviews, we noted seniors across all S.M.E. majors were
beginning to consider graduate school as a way of delaying entrance into a
depressed job market:

> I know a lot of people who are thinking of going on to grad school who
> wouldn't necessarily have gone otherwise—to make themselves more hire-able.
> Also postponement is a big thing. I mean, hopefully the economy will turn
> around in however many years it takes you to get your next degree. (Female
> white science non-switcher)

> I've been thinking about it—depending on how the job market is—'cause I
> don't want to find myself doing nothing. At least, if I'm going to school, I can
> do something. (Male white mathematics non-switcher)

Some concern has been expressed in recent years that the proportion of
foreign graduate students in S.M.E. disciplines has increased to about 25
percent, while the proportion of American-born graduate students in these
majors has fallen. Such concern should, perhaps, be tempered by the observation
that foreign students also constitute a large proportion of non-S.M.E. graduate
school entrants (for example, 31 percent in sociology),[2] and their presence in
graduate and professional schools is a traditional feature of university life in all
western countries. However, in so far as this issue is perceived as a problem,
our data suggest that, the desire to enter graduate schools among graduating
S.M.E. seniors is likely to increase, rather than to diminish, during a period of
restricted job opportunities for S.M.E. baccalaureates. The main obstacles to
graduate school entry are clearly economic. The best chance of increasing the
proportion of S.M.E. seniors who apply to graduate school would be to address
the issue of financial aid for undergraduates, whose burden of work and debt is
the strongest deterrent to their graduate school ambitions.

Conclusions

Throughout this chapter, we have documented a tension for S.M.E.
undergraduates between their widely-expressed desire for interesting work that
is in balance with other important aspects of their lives, and the difficulties they
experience in achieving these goals. Careers within engineering and the sciences
are rejected because they are thought likely to be unfulfilling, to lack worthwhile
purpose, and to limit the possibility of full participation in family and social life.
Some, though by no means all, students' reasons for believing it hard to achieve
a satisfying career and lifestyle within the sciences were based on a pervasive
set of stereotypes about the work contexts one could expect in professional
science and engineering jobs, and about the kind of person one must become to
do them. These beliefs are important in their consequences, especially as little

is done to replace them with a more accurate representation. From their limited contact with S.M.E. faculty and with field professionals, under-classmen draw enough data in support of the popular mythology to ensure its continuing power to discourage persistence.

The broad career aims described by most students (whether they switched or stayed) appear realistic and laudable. They want interesting work with valued end-products in collegial settings, and in the main, valued these attributes as much, or more, than materials rewards. Many of those who switched wanted to incorporate their knowledge of science into careers in other fields. They saw social as well as personal value in this. Approximately one-fifth of both switchers and non-switchers expressed the desire to teach (whether at two-year or four-year institutions, or in pre-college education). The dissipation of these aspirations to 6.6 percent among non-switchers was caused by the financial difficulties involved in further training, and by direct discouragement from S.M.E. faculty, family and friends. We count this loss of graduate science and mathematics teachers as one of the most serious negative findings of this study.

By contrast, the proportion of students who leave S.M.E. majors for instrumental or materialist reasons is low (less than 10 percent). A much higher proportion (one-fifth of all non-switchers, and 43.1 percent of all switchers) struggled with expectations of limited job prospects and low extrinsic rewards following graduation. These concerns were exacerbated for one-quarter of all students by financial difficulties and for one-fifth of all seniors by related problems with the length of their majors. In a situation where less than one-third of all students received any scholarship funds, two-thirds had student loans, half paid some of their own school and living expenses, and the average number of employed hours was 18 per week (rising to 20 to 45 hours among students in state institutions), we observed growing financial dis-incentives to enroll or continue in the sciences. Although the desire to go on to graduate (or profes-sional) school was still well-supported (approximately 12.5 percent for S.M.E. seniors, and 12.0 percent for switchers), the "burn-out" of completing lengthy majors reported by seniors and their large debt burdens were strong dis-incentives. An increase noted in the appeal of master's degrees was rooted in concerns about job availability and shrinking opportunities for career advance-ment in a troubled economy. The stresses of paying one's way through school in a period of escalating tuition and living costs (especially housing) and declining public and family financial support for undergraduate education, contribute both to growing student consumerism and (as we shall discuss in Chapter 6) to increased racial tensions on campuses.

Notes

1.   We found the preference for an alternative or service career (including teaching) most commonly mentioned at the most prestigious, highly-selective institution, where it appeared to be promoted by faculty and by the campus culture.

2.   Stevenson, Robert J. 1994. Where do all the sociologists come from? *Footnotes, 21 (9):* 11-12.

5

Issues of Gender

Tables 5.1 and 5.2 portray differences between the male and female students in our sample in terms of student concerns represented in Table 1.6 (cf., Chapter 1). This pair of tables should be read with the caveat that more is involved in the ways that young men and women interpret their experiences in S.M.E. classes—and the consequences of those differences—than is represented in these numeric summaries. The main purpose of this chapter will be to explore what these differences mean, what else is involved, how these differences may be explained, and what students find useful in overcoming gender-related problems. We begin with a summary of what is known about girls' and women's participation in science and mathematics, and of attempts to explain why the vulnerability of women to leaving S.M.E. majors greatly exceeds that of men.

Explaining Women's Under-Participation in the Sciences: Puzzles and Clues

It is reasonable to expect that girls' pre-college experiences in science and mathematics will have consequences for their subsequent experiences as undergraduate or graduate women (Baker, 1990). From work which explores the processes which encourage or inhibit the development of interest and career aspirations in these fields, and of students' confidence in their ability to undertake them, we have gained some insight into the subtle deterrents to active participation in mathematics and science among pre-college girls.

Much of this work has focused on observed disparities in classroom interaction. Boys consistently receive more attention, praise, critical feedback and support for assertive behavior. The learning experiences of girls are more passive, less demanding and less experiential—even in all-girls' schools (Jones & Wheatley, 1990; Kahle, 1990; Tobin & Garnett, 1987; Morse & Handley, 1985). Differential expectations for boys and girls which are exhibited by mathematics and science teachers have also been documented (Kahle, 1990). The overall effect is a generalized lowering of girls' confidence in their mathematical

TABLE 5.1 "The Problem Iceberg: Female Students." Factors Contributing to
Switching Decisions of Female Students, All Concerns of Female Switchers, of Non-
Switchers and of All Female Students.

Issue	Factor in switching decisions (%)	All switchers' concerns (%)	All non-switchers' concerns (%)	All students' concerns (%)
Non-S.M.E. major offers better education/more interest	46	60	38	50
Lack of/loss of interest in S.M.E.: "turned off science"	43	58	32	46
Rejection of S.M.E. careers and associated lifestyles	38	50	24	38
Poor teaching by S.M.E. faculty	33	89	80	85
Inadequate advising or help with academic problems	29	84	43	66
Curriculum overload, fast pace overwhelming	29	38	42	40
S.M.E. career options/rewards felt not worth effort to get degree	27	39	17	29
Shift to more appealing non-S.M.E. career option	27	30	18*	25
Discouraged/lost confidence due to low grades in early years	19	37	12	25
Conceptual difficulties with one or more S.M.E. subject(s)	16	33	21	28
Inadequate high school preparation in subjects/study skills	15	40	41	40
Reasons for choice of S.M.E. major prove inappropriate	14	91	36	66
Financial problems of completing S.M.E. majors	11	24	22	23
Prefer teaching approach in non-S.M.E. courses	10	22	7	15
Discovery of aptitude for non-S.M.E. subject	10	12	5	9
Lack of peer study group support	8	10	5	8
Unexpected length of S.M.E. degree: more than four years	7	17	29	22
Morale undermined by competitive S.M.E. culture	4	23	10	17
Switching as means to career goal: system playing	4	6	1	4
Language difficulties with foreign faculty or T.A.s	3	34	10	56
Poor teaching, lab, or recitation support by T.A.s	0	19	9	15
Problems related to class size	0	17	13	15
Poor lab/computer lab facilities	0	5	7	6

*Issue raised by non-switchers intending to move into non-S.M.E. field following graduation.

TABLE 5.2 "The Problem Iceberg: Male Students." Factors Contributing to Switching Decisions of Male Students, All Concerns of Male Switchers, of Non-Switchers and of All Male Students.

Issue	Factor in switching decisions (%)	All switchers' concerns (%)	All non-switchers' concerns (%)	All students' concerns (%)
Lack of/loss of interest in S.M.E.: "turned off science"	44	62	39	51
Curriculum overload, fast pace overwhelming	42	54	40	48
Poor teaching by S.M.E. faculty	39	92	66	80
S.M.E. career options/rewards felt not worth effort to get degree	36	48	23	37
Non-S.M.E. major offers better education/more interest.	35	57	25	42
Shift to more appealing non-S.M.E. career option	27	36	14*	26
Discouraged/lost confidence due to low grades in early years	27	32	13	23
Morale undermined by competitive S.M.E. culture	26	35	8	22
Financial problems of completing S.M.E. majors	24	36	23	30
Inadequate advising or help with academic problems	20	68	42	56
Rejection of S.M.E. careers and associated lifestyles	20	37	18	28
Lack of peer study group support	16	25	9	18
Inadequate high school preparation in subjects/study skills	15	42	34	38
Reasons for choice of S.M.E. major prove inappropriate	15	74	43	60
Unexpected length of S.M.E. degree: more than four years	10	24	26	25
Switching as means to career goal: system playing	10	11	4	8
Discovery of aptitude for non-S.M.E. subject	10	11	4	8
Conceptual difficulties with one or more S.M.E. subject(s)	9	20	29	24
Prefer teaching approach in non-S.M.E. courses	8	27	10	19
Language difficulties with foreign faculty or T.A.s	3	25	20	44
Poor teaching, lab, or recitation support by T.A.s	0	20	12	16
Problems related to class size	0	22	9	16
Poor lab/computer lab facilities	0	3	1	2

*Issue raised by non-switchers intending to move into non-S.M.E. field following graduation.

abilities (Eccles et al., 1982; Brophy, 1985; Sadker & Sadker, 1985). Elements of gender-based socialization which originate in the social milieu beyond school also tend to set girls up for failure in the competitive ethos of science. They include: a preference among girls for cooperative learning strategies (Kahle, 1990; Koehler, 1990; Eccles, 1989; Johnson & Johnson, 1987; Peterson & Fennema, 1985; Smail, 1985); and a tendency for girls (and their teachers) to attribute success in mathematics to effort, but failure to lack of ability, while the reverse is true among boys (Fennema, 1990);[1] and serious doubts about the value of girls' achievements in math-based subjects—doubts engendered by sex-role stereotyping which is carried into school and reinforced there (Kahle & Rennie, 1993; Mayer & Koehler, 1990; Whyte, 1986).

The consequences of these processes are discernable by ninth grade, though prior to this, girls and boys are almost identical in mathematics and science achievement. Thereafter, girls and boys increasingly diverge, both in the number of science and mathematics classes they take (especially in advanced mathematics and physics) and in their academic performance in these subjects. (For a review of this literature, see White, 1992.) The consequences are also clear in the low ratios of women-to-men among college freshmen indicating an intention to major in science and engineering—five or six men to one woman in engineering, and two or three men to one woman in the sciences (College Board, 1988; Dey, Astin & Korn, 1991). Despite women's generalized and culturally-reinforced low level of confidence in their ability to 'do math' (Tobias, 1993a), the proportions of women and men who declare an intention to enter mathematics majors are similar. Women are in a slight majority among entrants to the life sciences—where the cultural deterrents are fewer.

We know far less about the undergraduate (or graduate) experiences of the relatively small number of young women who actually choose S.M.E. majors than about their pre-college experiences. What we do know is that their persistence rates are significantly lower than those of their male peers. In a review of recent studies, Strenta and his colleagues (1993) found that the persistence rates of men in S.M.E. majors varied between 61 percent for highly selective institutions to 39 percent for national samples, and between 46 percent and 30 percent for women. As Astin & Astin (1993) additionally observe, because the proportionate loss of women from S.M.E. majors is greater than that of men, the under-representation of women increases during the undergraduate years. This picture is especially puzzling because there is some evidence that women entering S.M.E. majors have higher average performance scores than their male counterparts. For example, at the University of Colorado, for freshmen entering between 1980 and 1988, women who chose S.M.E. majors had higher average Predicted G.P.A. (P.G.P.A.) scores than their male peers (i.e., 3.05, compared with 2.99 in engineering, and 2.84, compared with 2.72 in science and mathematics). Both women who persisted, and those who switched, had higher average P.G.P.A. scores than men who either persisted or switched to non-S.M.E. majors (McLelland, 1993).

Sources of explanation for these phenomena are limited. Tobias (1990) was among the first researchers to document the role of faculty pedagogy in dissipating interest in science among both women and men. Rosser (1990) argues that some aspects of traditional science pedagogy are inherently more disadvantageous to women—a view which is supported both by the Higher Education Research Institute studies of college freshmen (Astin, 1993), and by the University of Michigan study of enrollment and completion of science degrees (Manis, Sloat, Thomas, & Davis, 1989). By the end of freshman year, 61 percent of the Michigan sample of high ability women had experienced science and mathematics classes which had seriously dampened their interest. A matched group of men were much less troubled than the women by "poor teaching," the dullness and poor organization of the syllabus material, or the fiercely competitive atmosphere. They did not experience, as did the freshmen women, diminished self-confidence in their ability to do science. Other work specifically targeting the negative impact on women of the "climate" of S.M.E. classrooms (most notably, that of Hall and Sandler, [1982]) is discussed later in this article in the context of our findings.

One approach to the question of how well-prepared, able women come to be lost from undergraduate science is suggested by two studies of gender differences in S.M.E. persistence (Strenta, Elliott, Adair, Scott, and Matier, 1993; and Ginorio, Brown, Henderson, and Cook, 1993), both of which were based on large institutional data sets. Their authors reached the same conclusion: where the performance scores of men and women in S.M.E. majors are the same, there is no difference in their persistence rates. Strenta drew upon survey data from 5,320 well-prepared, talented students who entered four highly selective institutions. Despite the high calibre of these students, the loss of women from S.M.E. majors was predicted by low science course grades during the first two years of study. These findings raise the further question: what would cause a large number of well-prepared, well-qualified young women, particularly those at highly selective institutions, to perform more poorly than their male counterparts in freshman and sophomore science and mathematics classes?

Another clue comes from the consistent finding that women at both graduate and undergraduate levels report that feelings of psychological alienation or depression played a critical role in their decisions to leave S.M.E. disciplines, and that despite good academic performances, they experience diminished self-esteem, self-confidence and career ambitions. Arnold's (1987) study of high-ability high school seniors found these effects to be marked among women in S.M.E. majors by sophomore year. Over the same period, the self-esteem and career aspirations of their male peers rose. Strenta also reports less confidence among women than among men in their ability to do science and more feelings of depression about their academic progress. These self-reports are independent of actual performance levels. This apparent misfit between actual and perceived competence in science-related majors has been noted in a number of other studies, including that of Ware and Dill (1986), who found the most marked difference between male and female science students lay in their levels of self-confidence. (For a review of this literature, see Kimball [1989]; and Oakes [1990b].)

These findings leave us to ponder the connections between high demonstrated ability among a consistently smaller number of women entering S.M.E. disciplines, a tendency to lose confidence after entry, and a vulnerability to switching which exceeds that of the male majority. How are we to interpret the finding of Strenta, Ginorio, and their colleagues, that similar performances produce similar persistence rates, regardless of gender? Can we, given the apparently depressing effects of some (as yet unidentified) factors in S.M.E. undergraduate (and graduate) experiences, assume that women who perform at the same level as men share the same level of ability? We began this study with the hope that our findings would throw some light on these issues.

Gender, Student Concerns and Switching Decisions

Tables 5.1 and 5.2 show the relative importance that women and men assigned to each of the 23 concerns about their S.M.E. undergraduate experience collectively raised by our informants. The tables reflect some broad differences in approach to college education taken by male and female S.M.E. students. A number of issues cluster around the question of what students see as the primary goal of their education. Many students of each group choose an S.M.E. major largely because they are intrinsically interested in its subject material, and almost identical proportions of male and female switchers report that a diminished interest in their discipline contributed to their decision to switch (i.e., 43.0% by women vs. 43.8% by men). Among seniors, the proportion of men who lost interest was slightly higher (39.0%) than that of women (31.6%). Beyond this parity in terms of lack or loss of intrinsic interest, the educational focus of young men is more instrumental than that of their female counterparts in that they are more willing to place career goals above considerations of personal satisfaction. By contrast, young women show a greater concern to make their education, their career goals and their personal priorities fit coherently together. Men appear more willing than women to shift majors as a means to improve their career prospects (10.1% vs. 4.0%). Similarly, more male than female switchers (36.0% vs. 26.9%) cited the poor expected material return on their investment of time, money and effort as a factor in their switching decisions. Both more male switchers overall (48.3% vs. 38.7%) and more male than female seniors (23.4% vs. 17.1%) expressed dissatisfaction with "the poor profit-to-grief ratio" of S.M.E. majors.

It might have been predicted, on the basis of traditional assumptions that young women might be more prone than young men to leave S.M.E. majors because they had less 'natural aptitude' for them, and had, in their early college years, discovered a stronger aptitude for a non-S.M.E. major. We found no support in these data for such a hypothesis. Indeed, relatively few switchers left (9.8%) or considered leaving (11.5%) because they had discovered that a non-science discipline was more suited to their abilities and/or temperament, and there was no gender difference in this regard.

However, more women than men (46.2% vs. 34.8%) switched, in part, because another major seemed to offer greater intrinsic interest, a better overall educational experience, or because the career options and/or lifestyle which their S.M.E. majors appeared to offer were less appealing to them (i.e., 37.6% women vs. 20.2% men). These differences are also echoed by seniors, among whom more women than men felt that other majors might have given them a better education (38.2% vs. 24.7%), or expressed doubts about the personal and job satisfactions they expected from S.M.E. careers (23.7% vs.18.2%).

This comparison of reasons for dissatisfaction with S.M.E. majors and for switching decisions, independently considered, offers a picture of women in S.M.E. majors as students with lower instrumentality than their male peers, and with greater expressed concern about the quality of their education and their working lives beyond college. However, it offers no explanation for the disproportionate loss of women, nor for women's greater loss of confidence early in S.M.E. majors. Indeed, returning to our discussion in Chapter 2, the strongest difference between male and female students was found to lie not in their reasons for leaving S.M.E. majors, but in their reasons for entering them. As already recounted, women differed very sharply from men in that the personal influence of family, high school teachers and other significant adults was a much more important factor in their choice of an S.M.E. major than was the case with men.[2] Also, on entry, women had less well-developed views of what they wanted out of college than did male freshmen, less clear ideas about what drew them to a particular major intellectually, or what they wanted from it in career terms. Women were also more often altruistic than men in their career goals and were more likely than men to switch in order to pursue careers which offered a greater prospect of more humanitarian or more personally-satisfying work.

Differential Impact of the Weed-Out System

A second set of three items in the tables, namely, curriculum pace and workload, the impact of lower-than-expected grades in basic S.M.E. classes and the effects of the competitive S.M.E. culture, reflect the differential impact of the weed-out system on men and women. For each of these factors, the effect on the switching decisions of men was greater than that on women. Feeling overwhelmed by the fast pace and heavy workload of early S.M.E. classes figured in the switching rational of 41.6 percent of male switchers, compared with 29.0 percent of female switchers. Considerations based on low grades were reported by 27.0 percent of male, compared with 19.4 percent of female switchers. The most pronounced gender distinction in this set of factors occurs with students' difficulties in tolerating the high degree of competition they encountered in S.M.E. classes. This problem contributed to 25.8 percent of the switching decisions of men, but to only 4.3 percent of the switching decisions of women. These distinctions are similarly reflected in the concerns of switchers overall, but do not appear among seniors because concerns about competition and grades dwindle, or change their character, after the weed-out period is over. Problems with the pace of their work and with excessive curriculum demands remain at a high level (41.4%) among seniors, but there are no appreciable differences among men and women in complaints about them.

Tables 5.1 and 5.2 offer some explanations for the greater impact of the weed-out system on male rather than female switchers. Failure to establish peer groups for collective study and mutual support is more marked among male switchers: 24.7 percent of men (compared with 9.7 percent of women) described themselves as working in a solitary, unsupported way, and 15.7 percent of men (compared with 7.5 percent of women) ascribed at least some part of their switching decisions to failure to seek out appropriate peer help. Female switchers also complained more (83.9%) than did male switchers (68.5%) about difficulty in getting help with academic problems or advice about other concerns—though the level of these complaints was high among all students. Although they often reported being unable to get the help they sought, women were more willing than were many young men to admit to the need for help, and to seek it at an early stage. Both this, and the tendency to work collaboratively, offer women a buffer against the negative impact of the weed-out experience.

Among students of this calibre, what cannot be used to explain the differential gender effects of the weed-out process are students assessments of the adequacy, or otherwise, of their high school science and mathematics as a preparation for college work: very similar proportions of male and female switchers referred to the inadequacy of their high school preparation in explaining either their problems in the major, or their switching decisions.

It is clear that we cannot adequately understand the dimensions of gender differences in student responses to the pressures of the weed-out system by reference to the numeric data alone. Later, we will argue—on the basis of evidence in the text data—that the weed-out process has a greater impact on young men because it carries messages which are intended to have meaning for them, and to which they respond. Its encoded meanings are obscure to young women, and they are thus less directly affected by them, at least in terms of switching decisions.

Differences in Evaluation of the Learning Experience

In a third group of issues—those concerned with the learning experience—we also need to turn to the text data for an understanding of differences in the ways in which students respond to S.M.E. pedagogy. There is little difference between male and female switchers, either in the high level of criticism of faculty pedagogy which they express (i.e., 92.1% among men, and 89.2% among women), or in the contribution made by poor teaching to the switching decisions of men (39.3%) and of women (33.3%). What the text data reveal is that male and female students diverge not in the perception that pedagogical problems exist, but in their definitions of 'good teaching', in what they expect of the faculty-student relationship and in the consequences of their unmet expectations. Among seniors, dissatisfaction with faculty as teachers remains high among women (80.3%), while among men, although it is still high (66.2%), it is much lower than it is either for male switchers or for either group of women.

Loss of, or failure to develop, interest in the discipline is closely associated with disappointment with faculty as teachers. Disinterest, which is reported by approximately two-thirds of all switchers, contributes to about 40.0 percent of all switching decisions, and (as already mentioned) is undifferentiated by sex. A low level of interest in their discipline remains a problem for seniors, and is reported by 31.6 percent of women and 39.0 percent of men.

Female switchers generally report more conceptual difficulties than do male switchers (33.3% vs. 20.2%), and more academic problems which they view as serious enough to be a factor in their switching decisions (16.1% vs. 9.0%). Because the men and women in our sample were undifferentiated either in their (high) demonstrated ability in mathematics or in the frequency with which they reported inadequacies in their high school preparation, we again turned to the transcripts for explanations. The key issue is whether female switchers actually encounter a higher degree of difficulty with the material than their male counterparts, or whether they experience more doubts than do young men about the adequacy of their abilities. This question is addressed later in this chapter.

Gender Differences in Other Student Concerns

Among the remaining factors contributing either to switching or to student concerns, male switchers report financial problems more often than do female switchers, both as a reason for switching (23.6% vs. 10.8%) and as a general concern (35.9% vs. 23.7%). Male switchers also report slightly more difficulties than do women with the unexpected length of S.M.E. majors. Overall, men are more concerned to weigh the costs (including the financial costs) against the tangible benefits of their persistence in a major.

Although very few male or female switchers felt that the inadequacies of foreign-born T.A.s or faculty had much to do with their decisions to leave, approximately one-third (34.4%) of female (vs. 24.7% of male) switchers complained about the teaching or tutoring they had received from foreign faculty or graduate students. (Curiously, this difference reverses among seniors.) On the basis of the text data, we find that the greater difficulty reported by female switchers in adjusting to the teaching or tutoring of non-native English speakers has rarely anything to do with cultural differences in attitudes to women.[3] Indeed, where women encounter direct hostility, or the minor irritations of prejudicial attitudes towards them, it is much more likely to be expressed by white, American males. Where their concerns are focused on difficulty in understanding material presented with a foreign accent, there are no discernable differences in the complaints of male and female switchers. The greatest apparent difficulty for women in the early years of their S.M.E. majors with foreign T.A.s or faculty is that difficulties with language place yet another obstacle in the way of establishing a personal teacher-learner relationship. Where young women manage to overcome difficulties with their teacher's accent and are able to bond with him or her, the problem is dissipated. Male switchers concerns' with foreign T.A.s and faculty are (again) more instrumental: they focus on the threat that difficulties with language pose to their comprehension of material they need in order to do well.

In the balance of this chapter, we draw exclusively upon the text data to explore what the differences evident in Tables 5.1 and 5.2 mean, how they may be explained and what else is involved. In developing an explanatory framework for the findings from this and other studies, we drew upon students' observations about the nature of their difficulties, issues which were embedded in their accounts and upon the responses of women to the observations and perspectives of men, and vice versa. The latter either arose spontaneously in discussion, or were offered in response to our summary of points which had been raised in other focus groups or interviews. All of the features of the experiences described below were found, to a greater or lesser extent, on all campuses.

The Experiences of Women in S.M.E. Majors

The Legacy of Pre-College Socialization

Although it was not a primary intention of this project to explore the pre-college experiences of young women who chose S.M.E. majors, our informants often drew on these influences in explaining why persistence was difficult, or how it had been achieved. Most women reported they had experienced good teaching, individual attention and encouragement from their elementary and high school teachers. This had fostered and legitimated their interest in mathematics and science, and built confidence in their ability to continue in these fields at college level. However, among both switchers and non-switchers, some women had pursued their interest in science or mathematics despite the gender prejudices of particular teachers and counselors. The negative consequences of these experiences persisted into college:

There were six of us in the high school physics classes, and I was the only girl. The teacher walked in the first day and said, 'So guys, what do you think about *it* here?' And they called me 'it' for the rest of the year. I'm serious. And I came here with zero self-esteem—it's been a big issue for me here too—all four years. (Female white science switcher)

I was put in the dumb group. I never thought I was dumb, but it still had an effect on me. I thought other people were better at science and math than I was. And yet, I got As and Bs in math all the way through high school, including pre-calculus. (Female white mathematics non-switcher)

The gate-keeping role of teachers and high school counselors is clearly critical, but it was not a major source of discouragement for most of our informants. However, despite their teachers' support, many women described difficulties in 'giving themselves permission' to choose S.M.E. majors and found it hard to explain precisely what had discouraged them. Their explanations referenced the dampening effect of cultural messages which suggested that women either couldn't, or shouldn't, do science. Some had felt the social stigma of being a girl who was good at mathematics, or were intimidated by the prospect of entering majors which were reported to be competitive and hard:

So many women just kind of say, 'Well, if there's going to be so much competition out there, and men are obviously better than we are at this, then why go into the field?' (Female white mathematics switcher)

For some reason it just clicked, and I always loved math from then on. I'd been pretty much ahead since first grade, and one of my girl friends and I would always be two grades ahead. It was fun up to about sixth grade, but suddenly I didn't want to be this Einstein who was always ahead. In the next two grades, I never felt behind, and always got As, but I was more caught up in the social thing and never wanted it to be known that I excelled in math. (Female white mathematics switcher)

On entry to college, and while in the process of considering possible majors, some women reported overt discouragement by faculty advisors against their attempting particular S.M.E. classes. For women with limited self-confidence in their abilities, this could tip the balance of their decision:

In Calculus III and advanced calculus, there were only two women in the class. There just have to be more capable women out there than that. One was a friend of mine. She just didn't think she could handle it—and that comes with your self-image. I was advised not to take it by my physics advisor, but I was confident enough to know I could do it. And the women with me in the earlier class were very smart—they knew how to handle it. But, like me, they were advised not to try it. (Female white science non-switcher)

Although they often could not point to so direct a source of discouragement, women acknowledged the consequences of a process of discouragement during which they had learned to set their aspirations at a level lower than their abilities, and had developed attitudes which reduced their chance of survival. Prominent among these were concerns about whether they 'belonged'—which was not an issue for their male peers. Their doubts were manifested as: less assertiveness in asking for what they needed; less inner-strength to cope with set-backs; and more dependence on others for reassurance:

> There's a certain kind of self-questioning that's a big part of it. I saw much less self-questioning from the men. (Female white engineering switcher)

> You don't know you're good. You feel you just maybe made it by accident—you know, the imposter syndrome...'And, gee, I didn't do well on this test, so that proves I should drop out.' Those thoughts really bind women from the very start. You don't have that drive that the guys do...A lot of the guys don't know the jargon either, but, if necessary, they'll fake it...Whereas, you 'fess up when you don't know, and don't expect them to value your opinion if you do know. You don't have that confidence that you can do this...and that's what you need. (Female white engineering non-switcher)

> I'm far enough along now that I'm strong enough in myself to stick with engineering. But, if I was a freshman struggling with these inner-uncertainties, I might be gone by now. (Female white engineering non-switcher)

Male students noticed uncertain, self-doubting behavior among the women in their early classes, and were not necessarily unsympathetic. However, they explained it as critical for survival to overcome—or to hide—a lack of confidence.

Another common deficit in the pre-college education of many women was hands-on technical or laboratory experience. This deficiency was more than a practical handicap. It meant that women approached technical tasks with more temerity than they subsequently found was warranted. This gave their male peers a psychological advantage and was another source of fears about incompetence and doubts about 'belonging':

> A lot of the Double E professors come with the assumption that we've been tinkering with electronics all our lives, and that we knew how to put together circuits and knew about resistors and transistors and everything—'cause we've been brought up with it, right? Wrong! I'd never seen a booster, and when the T.A. said, 'Just wire this up,' I didn't know what to do. It was pretty intimidating. I had a good lab partner who helped me get started, but I felt such an idiot. I wish they would offer an intro lab. (Female white engineering non-switcher)

> The guys definitely have all the advantages: there's more of them in the class; there's mostly male professors; and they're brought up with it. Their fathers teach them useful stuff when they're little. I have a much better grip on technical things than some of my guy friends doing English, and it's not because I have this natural gift to do engineering: it's because I've spent time looking under the hood of a car. (Female white engineering non-switcher)

Women were also concerned that male acceptance of their academic worth would have negative consequences for their sense of who they are as women. The problems of belonging and identity are linked, because the qualities that women feel they must demonstrate in order to win recognition for their 'right' to belong (especially "smartness," assertiveness and competitiveness), raise the anxiety that such recognition can only be won at the expense of 'femininity':

> Looking back, I see that maybe I was afraid to be too good at it...that if I showed how good I was, I would lose my femininity—that men wouldn't find me attractive. I think I've always been encouraged to mess up, then guys come and help you out (laughs)—even though I didn't really need the help. But they have to think that you do...Subconsciously, I really felt that if I succeeded, then they wouldn't see how attractive I was. (Female white engineering switcher)

> It's set up that women have to be more male in engineering to get along. I notice that women in other majors don't seem like they have to change themselves like I did in order to fit in. To make it in engineering, I had to learn to be more male...Eventually, you've learned to take more stuff—maybe are stronger than when you first came in. But it always bothered me that I had to change. (Female white engineering non-switcher)

These speakers touch on a number of issues which have significance for attempts to change the S.M.E. culture in ways that will improve women's persistence. They highlight the double-bind situation of women who feel they can only win male acceptance, in academic terms, by losing it in personal terms. They point to the extrinsic nature of traditional female identity, which is both male-defined and male-confirmed (see, for example, Eccles, 1994; Unger & Crawford, 1992; Gilligan, 1982, 1979; Miller, 1991; Surrey, 1991). They also clarify that women can be set up to fail unless they are helped to see how the existing male-dominant power structure can play upon their anxieties about their image, and are offered some strategies to protect themselves from it (Belenky, Clinchy, Goldberger, & Tarule, 1986; Komarovsky, 1985; Roychoudhury, Tippins, & Nichols, 1993; Rosser, 1990). We will return to the significance of women's problems with self-perception and self-presentation later in this chapter.

Negative Experiences with S.M.E. Faculty

We considered it important to establish from the outset whether or not switching behavior, or the problems of those who remained in S.M.E. majors, were in any way related to discriminatory behavior or expressions of prejudice against women by S.M.E. faculty, T.A.s or fellow students. We, therefore, asked all our female switchers to give accounts of any negative incidents which they had either experienced or observed and to estimate whether these had influenced their decision to switch. We asked all women students to discuss their level of comfort within S.M.E. majors, and all male informants to comment on any unpleasant behavior they had noted towards their female peers.

Out of the 173 women interviewed, only eight (four switchers and four non-switchers) reported a direct experience of what they considered unacceptable behavior by S.M.E. faculty. These accounts included discriminatory behavior to individual women, rudeness to all the women in a class, and two accounts of behavior perceived as sexually inappropriate. When we introduced the topic of gender, both men and women tended to assume that we were asking primarily about sexual harassment by faculty. However, women were overwhelmingly at pains to make it clear that this was not "the real issue."

More common than direct negative experiences with faculty were 'war stories' and a whole array of more subtle experiences by which some faculty were seen to convey the message that women were not welcome in their major. 'War stories' described the experiences of room-mates, friends, or class-mates and included the speaker's interpretation of what faculty intended to convey by their behavior:

> My old room-mate—who graduated in engineering last semester—on her first day at the university, her engineering advisor said, 'You won't make it: you look like a partier.' I had this man for a few courses and he was very chauvinistic. (Female white engineering switcher)

> These women were complaining the other day about a physics professor who gave a B+ to a woman who had got 89.5 percent as a total for all her tests and homework, while he gave an A- to a man with the same score. (Female white mathematics non-switcher)

> A friend in engineering—who's really, really bright—got the same grade as another girl on a quiz. They were sitting rows apart, but he said, 'Well, you two must be communicating telepathically.' Then he accused them of being too cute to be doing so well. (Female white science non-switcher)

> My room-mates have experienced some discrimination—both subtle and blatant. The tone is, 'You're a woman in engineering, so you're a failure as a women,' or, 'You're just a pretty girl; you didn't do this right,' or, 'You must have copied this from someone else.' (Female white engineering non-switcher)

 These stories matter because, as they circulate, they reinforce any negative feelings about being in the major that women have already developed. In focus groups, a story told by one woman would often evoke a series of stories from the others in the group.

Negative experiences with faculty (whether personal or those of women that they knew) were mostly subtle rather than blatant. They often occurred in stories of how women had felt excluded by faculty from some of the activities of their class:

It's hard. Because a lot of the connotations that professors use are male. They'll refer to us all the time as 'You guys,' and everything is kind of male, and I didn't feel that I was included. I'd tell myself, 'Come on; you're not being yelled at because you're a girl.' But it was so hard not to be included in the conversation...I don't know if professors *see* women. (Female white engineering switcher)

He wouldn't let any of us three women use the machines. I had a friend who took me round the lab after class to make sure I got the hands-on experience I should have got in class. But he was real blatant about not letting women think it was okay to run the machines. (Female white engineering non-switcher)

I never want to take a class from A---. He's so chauvinistic. One of my good friends was one of three girls in his class last year, and he invited all the guys over for breakfast one morning at the end of class, but he didn't invite any of the girls. (Female white mathematics non-switcher)

Although the source of the feeling was illusive, women also sensed that some male faculty disapproved of their presence through the constant air of tension in the atmosphere of particular classes:

There's just a lot of tension—you can feel it when you take classes where there's only three women. It's not based on really discriminating things being done—just a feeling that's always there. (Female white mathematics non-switcher)

They just don't know how to act with women students. They don't know *what* to do with you. Their whole attitude, and facial expressions and body language says, 'You belong in the kitchen. What are you doing here?' They're not allowed to say it, but you overhear it in conversations. (Female white science switcher)

Some faculty set a misogynist tone by encouraging, ignoring, or failing to check the rudeness of young men towards the much smaller number of women in their classes:

I was the only woman in a graduate-level physics class with seven men. They would tell jokes in bad taste, and watch to see how I handled it. Sometimes they would do really lewd things. They just did it to bother me. And, if I reacted, they would laugh at me until I would just want to kill them. But the professor would just ignore it. He wouldn't intervene to stop it, or to help me. He'd just say, 'Okay; let's get a move on,'—trying to make it as if nothing had happened. (Female white science switcher)

The degree to which faculty did (or did not) tolerate rude classroom behavior toward women was reported to be transmitted to their teaching and laboratory assistants, who then repeated the pattern:

The experiment involved a bolt that I had done up too tight, so I asked the T.A. for a wrench. The lab coordinator walked over and managed to untwist it without the wrench, and he looked at the T.A. and rolled his eyes, and laughed at my asking for a wrench. I was perfectly capable of doing it myself; I didn't need them to do that. (Female white science non-switcher)

There are these guys in physics labs who supply all the electrical things. This one wouldn't talk to the girls at all. But it shows you how all the men that are involved in physics have this camaraderie about them—and you're not included. (Female white science switcher)

The physics department is horrid. The only other woman and I in my lab were treated like we were stupid no matter what we did. If I got a wrong answer, it would be that I was stupid. If a guy got a wrong answer, it was just that he just hadn't explained it right. (Female white science non-switcher)

I kept feeling stupid asking questions in the lab. The T.A. was like, 'God! You don't know anything.' He made me feel like just some stupid girl who didn't know what I was doing. (Female white science switcher)

The women who recounted these experiences often proffered explanations for the behavior of their male professors: some faculty were seen as covertly attempting to drive women from the major by making them feel uncomfortable and unwelcome; others were seen as ignorant of how to behave toward women in an academic or collegial context. Most women assumed that their negative experiences with faculty reflected insensitivity, clumsiness, or out-dated modes of thought rather than intentional discrimination. An apparent inability to treat women as serious students was seen as reflecting a generalized male prejudice about the mental capabilities of women which they had also experienced in other contexts:

You get the whole range, you know, from actual sexist remarks and jokes, to saying things that are just childish. And I think mostly they don't even realize it. You can't believe the preconceptions these people have about women. I've had professors tell me that they just don't take some of the women in the class as seriously. And it's clear they don't respond to you in the same way as the men. And it's not any one science department—it's very widespread. (Female white science switcher)

They tend to be tougher on the women. They'll say in a new class, 'Wow, we've got girls in here again!' I don't think it's intentional: it's the way they were raised...I've had a couple of instructors who are never gonna help you, and they make it very plain. And you ask, 'What am I doing wrong?' And the guys will say, 'Well, he doesn't really like women—at least not in his particular field. He's just an old-timer kind of guy.' (Female white science non-switcher)

It's not so much that the professors act badly towards you. It's more the sense that you're not seen as capable of the same kind of thinking. You know, I can think just as abstractly or intensely as a man. But that's part of the way that most men out there think too. You tell them your major, and they look at you as though there's no way you could be doing that. (Female white science non-switcher)

We asked women whether, and how, negative experiences with faculty had affected them. Most had little direct contact with faculty in their first two years, which limited their opportunity to cause direct distress during women's highest risk period for switching. Indeed, the behavior of male T.A.s and peers was reported as having a more direct impact on women's level of discomfort in this period than the behavior of male faculty. As we shall argue later, for most women, it was not so much what the faculty did that caused them to consider leaving these majors as what they failed to do. Women responded to negative experiences with S.M.E. faculty (either their own, or those of peers') by avoiding particular faculty and leaving classes where they were made to feel uncomfortable. Overwhelmingly, women wished to impress upon us that negative experiences with faculty had not influenced their decisions about persistence in the major. They did not believe that either the covert or overt attempts of faculty to discourage them from continuing were successful, whether for themselves or for other women they knew. If anything, this kind of behavior appeared to make women more determined not to be driven away:

> I've gotten the feeling from several of my male professors that I shouldn't be able to do this because I'm a woman—the, 'Here let me show you,' attitude. And my response is, 'Oh, I've already finished; help this guy over here. He doesn't know what's going on. Leave me alone.' (Female white engineering non-switcher)

> I don't really get too discouraged by it. If anything, it makes me want to do it even more. (Female white science non-switcher)

> Most of us have never felt that really overt discrimination stuff. And I don't think that's the problem. People who think that are missing the point. (Female white science switcher)

This finding supports earlier studies which found little overt "gender discrimination" against female students by male faculty (for example, Strenta et al., 1993; Constantinople, Cornelius, & Gray, 1988; Krupnick, 1984; Sternglanz & Lyberger-Ficek, 1977). It also supports the findings of Manis, Sloat, Thomas, & Davis (1989) that women gave low ranking to the discriminatory attitudes of faculty as a deterrent to persistence. By contrast, Hall and Sandler (1982, 1984) describe the role played by rudeness, disattention, lower faculty expectations and overt discrimination by undergraduate instructors in maintaining a range of classroom inequalities. They propose that these directly lead women of high ability to feel that their academic and career ambitions are less important than those of their male peers and to under-achieve in the longer-term. This group of findings is not necessarily contradictory if the effects of these daily stressors are seen as undermining and gradually wearing down women's desire to persist, rather than as a direct cause of switching.

Negative Attitudes and Behavior of Male Peers

An apparent difficulty in seeing physical attractiveness and intellectual capacity as other than mutually exclusive qualities in women who choose certain S.M.E. majors was a marked feature of the behavior and attitudes of their male peers. The overtly-expressed belief that all women in their discipline were, by virtue of their having chosen it, inherently unattractive was held by young men in engineering, and to a slightly lesser degree, by male physics, chemistry and applied science majors. Curiously, it was little found among male students in mathematics and the other sciences:

> What it just comes down to is the pretty girls do something else, and the brainy girls stay in engineering—and I think that goes beyond engineering...that's just a general cultural thing. (Male white engineering switcher)

As a consequence, young men in these majors avoided social contact with female class-mates and sought dates with women in non-S.M.E. classes, whom they believed were inherently more attractive.

In individual interviews, male students rarely offered an opinion about the way that the women in their S.M.E. majors appeared to them. However, the topic produced lively debates among young men in focus group discussions which centered, not on whether the belief that most women in S.M.E. classes were unattractive was valid, but on why it was true. Because they tended to view any woman's interest and ability in science or mathematics as "unnatural," they were apt to portray those women who chose S.M.E. majors in one of four ways: as inherently ugly; as having been too busy with academic work to learn the arts of attractive self-presentation; as having lost their attractiveness after they entered the sciences; or subtly inferred they might be lesbian:

> I would say they lose their feminism. They stop wearing make-up; they dress more like a man. (Male white science non-switcher)

> I remember seeing some beautiful girls in the engineering department whom I felt were the exception rather than the norm...I mean, if you're someone who's going to spend that much time and effort to become a good engineer, you'd probably spend a lot of your childhood studying. And maybe that means you forsake the fashion awareness, the make-up, and the social kinds of things. Maybe they don't value those things. (Male white engineering switcher)

> I just don't like the women in engineering school to be honest with you (laughs). There were these three girls in my last class, and they all had Heavy Metal shirts—not my types...I was trying to think of a nicer way to say it

(laughs). I never went out with anybody out of the engineering classes. (Male white engineering switcher)

Most young men reported, however, that they enjoyed the presence of attractive, intelligent young women in non-S.M.E. classes. Interestingly, men who had switched into non-S.M.E. majors, such as finance, in which women were also a small minority, noticed that women who had also switched from S.M.E. majors had, in doing so, changed their status from 'unattractive' to 'attractive':

> I think a lot of the guys carry this assumption that women in techy fields are just unattractive...I think if they had known them in any other major, all of them would have been considered attractive. It's some sort of conceptual shift. And it's not open for discussion. (Male white science switcher)

As with the last speaker, some men acknowledged that many of their male peers behaved badly towards the women in S.M.E. classes and expressed sympathy for the dilemma of self-presentation this posed for women.

Women in engineering, physics, chemistry and the applied sciences saw their male class-mates as over-focused on the issue of female attractiveness and reported that some male peers refused to respond to women in terms other than the sexual interest that they did (or did not) hold for men in their major. In all academic contacts, but especially in situations calling for collaborative effort, women noted that male peers commonly did not know how to relate to them as colleagues, work-mates, study partners, or friends. We learned both from women, and from more sympathetic men, that women were subjected on a daily basis to unkind and sexually-suggestive remarks and jokes intended to make women feel uncomfortable and unwelcome:

> They are always making jokes and stuff. I haven't really confronted any of them—I just kinda keep walking. I try not to stay around them. (Female Hispanic engineering switcher)

One common way by which women tried to reduce the strain of dealing with constant attacks on their self-esteem was to make their appearance as plain and 'neutral' as possible—often by wearing a version of male student dress—in the hopes of avoiding notice. This response was commented on by the many women who adopted it, by those women who did not, and by sympathetic male peers:

> There's no way I'd wear panty hose, or mascara, or throw my hair up—like when I go to my art class. (Female white engineering non-switcher)

> I went out with Colorado's Junior Miss as a freshman, and she found it really hard to deal with. We studied physics together, and we'd talk about it a lot. I mean, just all the engineers would hit on her, and it made her feel uncomfortable. They made her feel that, because she was so attractive, she couldn't be smart enough to be in there with them—so it was okay to hit on her. (Male white mathematics switcher)

> They try to play down their femininity—not to show it as much—so they won't
> get picked on. The attitude against them, it's so overt. (Male white science
> non-switcher)

Those women who attempted 'invisibility' hoped both to draw less attention of
unwanted kinds, and to be taken more seriously as scientists or engineers than
those women whom the men considered attractive. This kind of response also
had a psychological counterpart, in that some women adopted a 'one of the
boys' persona that, again, served to minimize their sexual differentness. This
form of self-presentation was often criticized by other women, and, perversely,
by male peers. It was also, in retrospect, a source of self-reproach among those
women who had used it as a coping strategy. Most young men were unaware of
the role played by their own behavior in distorting the ways in which their
female class-mates presented themselves.

One of the rewards of persistence in an S.M.E. major is the admiration
offered by people outside the majors—especially to women. Indeed, many
women who switched admitted they found it hard to give up being treated as
someone rather special. Part of this respect comes from the assumption that
those who succeed are an intellectual élite in majors which demand more in
terms of stamina and resolve than any other group of majors. Men in these
majors seem reluctant to share their élite status with women. As they could not
ignore the high grades earned by some female class-mates, male students sought
to explain these good performances in ways that did not concede intellectual
merit: women were acknowledged to work very hard—perhaps harder—than
many of the men. If there were some women who were good at mathematics,
it was perhaps a freak occurrence, or women might do well in aspects of the
discipline which men considered easier:

> I don't know why they drop out. The top rank in terms of G.P.A. would be
> mostly women. But they would work harder: I don't necessarily think they are
> smarter than us. Well, some of them may be. But a lot of them are just more
> dedicated. (Male white science non-switcher)

> Everybody's looking at her because she's good at math. But her being that
> good isn't like a trend. She's kinda like a circus performer—a freak. (Male
> white engineering switcher)

> There's just two women in my sophomore mechanical engineering classes, and
> a few more in civil and architecture. But the word has it that civil and
> architectural are the two easier options. (Male white engineering non-switcher)

Among young men, doing well by working hard 'counted' for less than
doing well because you were inherently 'smart'. Being considered very smart
placed a student at the top of the male peer prestige system. The less apparent
effort a student put into achievement of good grades, the smarter his peers
assumed him (sic) to be, and the more respect they accorded him. Not asking

questions in class, and avoiding peer study situations, were two methods by which male students sought to preserve their 'smartness rating'. Women could unwittingly break the rules of the male status system by openly discussing their problems, or by asking questions in class. They were largely unaware that this reduced their claim to 'smartness' among the men:

> I can't see myself actually telling someone else, 'I'm killing myself in this class.' It's just forbidden. If you're having a horrible time, you can't acknowledge it...The women in my class are all smarter than me—but they seem to want to say things like, 'Man, this is hard; I've been working like crazy.' But there's no one here that wants to hear that. (Male white engineering non-switcher)

As 'smartness' in mathematics especially was believed by many male engineering and science majors (though, curiously, not by male mathematics majors) to be an exclusive male attribute, it reinforced the need to explain the good performances of some women by means other than their ability. As already indicated, good grades did not count as evidence of 'smartness' if they were seen largely as the product of hard work. They could also be discounted if they were held to be the result of flirting with faculty or T.A.s. Notwithstanding the theory that most of the women in their classes were unattractive, there was a widespread belief that some female students did well because they used feminine wiles to gain an unfair advantage. Interestingly, this belief was expressed by both men and women. Though women might acknowledge flirting as a way to survive in a hostile atmosphere, most women frowned upon it as counterproductive to acceptance and respect for women overall:

> I hate it when women flirt with professors. It's really annoying—they're ditzy too. I guess I feel it's insulting to other women. They make an image for the whole group of us. (Female white science non-switcher)

> When they flirt their way to the grade, it's more like fighting each other than supporting each other...In an area like engineering, women fight each other more than in other places, because they are more oppressed than in other places: the more oppressed the group, the more the individuals in it fight for the crumbs. (Female white engineering non-switcher)

> There's people like me who don't want any favors, and who work very, very hard—harder than the men. And we get irritated with women who think they're gonna get by because they flirt with the faculty. It makes me mad. And I know it makes the guys mad too. (Female white engineering non-switcher)

Women reported that some male students got angry, and behaved unpleasantly when they did well on tests and assignments. They tended to cope with this by keeping quiet about a good grade. From a focus group of women science seniors:

I think you tend not to want to tell them that you did well on a test.

Right. When they give back the tests, if you get a good grade, you slip it into your folder, because heaven forbid you should do well.

They're jealous if you do well—'cause we shouldn't be smarter than they are.

Right.

Women were generally very aware of the threat that their good performances posed to the male prestige distribution system. They understood that this was an important source of the unpleasantness of their male peers, and of the distorted, self-limiting responses of women:

> There's a perceived threat that feeds male anger about bright women. People tell jokes that are negative to women, which just fuels it. And it encourages the women to pull back into safer ground—to choose more traditional majors, or to adopt a more neutral style—as a way of protecting themselves from that anger. (Female white science non-switcher)

Many women described and commented upon the behavior of the young men with considerable anger. They deeply resented the accusation that they could not do mathematics:

> Math was always one of my favorite subjects. And I always helped everyone else out...I've heard that stuff before about women and math, and it always made me mad. (Female white engineering switcher)

Nor did they devalue hard work as a means to achievement: women who had worked hard and earned good grades often expressed anger at male peers who suggested that faculty might have "given them a break":

> If I took the time to write up the lab properly and got a higher grade, they got mad—'Oh, it's just because you're a girl. Girls get all the breaks—that's why they get the better grades.' That's irritating. I work harder than they do and they tell me I get the breaks because I smile. Very frustrating. (Female Hispanic engineering switcher)

> We were at a party recently and another engineer in her class asked my friend, 'So are you sleeping with the professor? Is that how you do it?' (Female white engineering switcher)

> This guy wrote me a note telling me it was because of him I scored five points higher on the homework—he was telling me I was riding on his coat-tails...So I called him up and chewed him out...But they really have to push me before I'll say something. (Female Hispanic engineering switcher)

Women were also angry when men made inappropriate remarks and jokes, which they assumed were intended to make them feel unwelcome and to devalue them, both as women and as intellectual competitors:

> They are always making jokes and stuff. I haven't really confronted any of them—I just kinda keep walking. I try not to stay around them, 'cause, I mean, it's too negative. (Female Hispanic engineering switcher)

> They were making these wise jokes. I don't think a lot of that stuff is intended. They don't know that you can be really offended by that. But it makes you feel like an outsider. (Female white engineering switcher)

If they responded by showing their anger, this only seemed to make the situation worse. Men appeared to enjoy provoking a reaction, or defined their behavior as "aggressive," and thus, as further proof that women who chose S.M.E. majors were (by their definition) inherently unfeminine:

> It's like there's two ways of dealing with it—passive angry or active angry. Passive usually works a lot better. You kind of say, 'Yes, yes, yes,' and then you do whatever you damn well please. (Female white science non-switcher)

Another set of male behaviors which made women angry arose from the assumption that they were incompetent in practical matters, such as laboratory work. Women complained that in lab and other practical situations, their male peers often took charge, ordered them about, gave them help they did not ask for or need and sometimes took credit for work that they had done:

> I would like to strangle half the students at times. When I first came here, they wouldn't let me touch anything in the lab. They let me take down the data—that's all. The last day of class, they let me weigh something. (Female Hispanic engineering switcher)

> I had a lab partner who ordered me to pick things up when he dropped them. After a day of that, I asked for another partner. (Female white science non-switcher)

> When we made a presentation, the guys would suggest that we hold up the signs, while they did the talking. (Female white engineering switcher)

Here, again, we were aware that both women and men found it hard to relinquish traditional ways of relating to each other in spheres of activity which have a long history of gender separation. Those women who had worked to establish their competence in technical areas of activity were frustrated by female peers who feigned helplessness rather than learning how to undertake technical tasks for themselves:

> Because the male thinks he has to take care of the female, this flirtatious interaction seems to benefit them both—kind of feeds some male egos, and at the same time, the woman obtains what she wants...I don't know if those women are really capable of doing the work—the problem is, they've never been tested. (Female white mathematics non-switcher)

> The faculty and the T.A.s are colluding in making them more helpless. My friend gets by that way. But she never learns how to do it, and she's never

going to like lab if she really doesn't know how to do anything in it. (Female white science non-switcher)

Women who are new to the labs get intimidated by the machinery, so they'll ask their T.A. or their male partner to do things for them. Even though it's well-meaning, it hurts both the men and the women. It discourages women, because they don't get a sense of accomplishment, of knowing what they are doing. The women are perfectly capable of doing this: they just need to be pushed a little. (Female white science non-switcher)

Policies which have attempted to encourage more participation by hitherto under-represented groups sometimes have counter-productive side-effects. Particularly in engineering, the assumption among undergraduates that women graduates might receive preference in a very competitive job market was an additional source of strain:

More women than men are getting hired in our particular field—chemical engineering—so there's a lot of bitterness between men and women. They see it as reverse discrimination, and they have a point. But it makes it difficult. (Female white engineering non-switcher)

My grades are probably better than theirs, but they have jobs right now. I think companies are looking for women engineers, especially if they have high G.P.A.s. And a lot of girls are pretty smart, so they usually try to hire them every chance they get. (Male Asian-American engineering switcher)

I'm gonna have a lot of opportunities, which is nice...I'm sure a lot of people would view that as a bad way to get where you're going, but, right now, in this world, it's the only way to get there. If, when you've gotten there, you can prove you were worth going through a quota, that's all that matters to me really. (Female black science non-switcher)

Some women felt that preferential hiring policies, scholarships which promote women's participation in science, and special programs to support women through S.M.E. majors, added to the difficulties which they already faced in establishing male respect for their abilities. Such women avoided any kind of special treatment, did not use women's advisors or programs, or join women's professional societies. They preferred to cope with the discomforts of their major by distancing themselves from all sources of official help based on gender:

I haven't had anything to do with the women's program. I don't know much about it...I don't want to be treated special because I'm a woman. (Female white engineering switcher)

I got a scholarship once because I was a woman, and I took it. I mean, why wouldn't I take it? But I felt kind of diminished by the fact I had gotten it. (Female white science non-switcher)

As with their experiences of hostility from male faculty, women switchers impressed upon us that, although the behavior of their male peers was a source of anger or irritation, it did not directly lead to their decisions to switch. As indicated, the rudeness of male toward female students was much more pronounced in some S.M.E. majors than others—notably engineering, physics, chemistry and the applied sciences. However, the propensity of women to switch is not greater in those majors than it is from mathematics and other science majors. Nevertheless, the rude behavior of male peers was a constant, daily source of stress for many women. In those classes where it was prevalent, it was clearly a background factor making women's decisions to leave easier when other, more significant, factors came into play.

Explaining What Women Experience in S.M.E. Majors

Understanding why men in some S.M.E. majors behave badly toward the women who enter them, and the relationship between these more overt forms of unpleasantness and other factors which bear directly and indirectly on women's self-image and career decisions, requires that all of these factors be set in a conceptual framework which can account for them. One way to do this is to regard the behavior and counter-behavior of men and women in S.M.E. majors as reflecting the collision of two very different social systems, one of which is infinitely more powerful than the other. A salient difference in these two systems lies in the content and methods by which socialization proceeds, and group membership is defined.

When women first enter S.M.E. classes, they encounter two kinds of experiences, both of which are new and uncomfortable. They share one of these—the weed-out system—with their male peers. They do not, however, assign the same meaning to the weed-out experience as the men and, therefore, do not respond to it in the same ways. We have described the consequences of the weed-out system in some detail in Chapter 3. The questions raised here are: why the weed-out process affects men and women differently; how women interpret it; and how they respond to it. The other new kind of experience for women arises as a consequence of entering a social system which has been traditionally all-male. This creates problems for women which men do not have to face. By exploring each of these kinds of experience as our informants saw them, we sought to clarify their contribution to attrition and to other difficulties commonly experienced by women in S.M.E. majors.

A common theme that distinguishes the accounts of women and men in S.M.E. majors is that of rupture with past educational and social experience. Notwithstanding the discriminatory pre-college experiences of some women, or the doubts generated by a generalized cultural discouragement from the pursuit of non-traditional disciplines, most women we encountered had entered college at a peak of self-confidence, based on good high school performances, good or adequate S.A.T. scores and a great deal of encouragement and praise from high school teachers, family and friends. Within a relatively short time of their entry to college, women who felt intelligent, confident in their abilities and prior performance level, and who took their sense of identity for granted, began to feel isolated, insecure, intimidated, to question whether they 'belonged' in the sciences at all and whether they were good enough to continue:[4]

> It's not because they're rude to the women—though they are sometimes—it's more that they never consider that you, as a woman, can have the same ability—and that's how they treat you. And maybe I was insecure about that. (Female white science switcher)

> Because I was a woman, immediately, I had a lot of things going against me that I didn't, at the time, understand. But I felt a lot of fear and intimidation—that was really why I switched. (Female white engineering switcher)

In comparing their own experiences with that of women freshmen, the more sympathetic of their male peers observed that women faced a loneliness which they did not have to experience:

> For 12 years of your life you've been going to school, and you've had both women and men peers, so it's totally depressing just one girl to take a class with 400 men. I'm sure it's disheartening for the women. (Male Asian-American engineering switcher)

> If you're one of 30 in a history seminar, and you're exchanging ideas and people are asking each other about their thoughts and opinions, it's a warm exchange of ideas. That's one thing. But if you're one of two women in a thirty-person math lecture, where you sit there listening to what the professor has to say, hardly ask any questions, go home, open the book and do the problem sets on your own, it's very different. (Male white science non-switcher)

For the first time in their lives, white women suddenly experience what it is like to be in a minority which is negatively viewed by the majority:

> It's intimidating to be in a class with 97 men and just three women—at least it used to be: I think I've finally gotten used to it. (Female white science non-switcher)

From the outset, they are excluded from conversations and activities solely on the grounds of characteristics which they cannot hide, and over which they have no control. Many men are well-aware that they or their peers often exclude the women in their classes from their working or social groups simply because they are women:

> Women just can't break into those solid ranks of men. It may just be as simple as that. It's always been male, and they're gonna keep it that way. (Male white science non-switcher)

There are more women than when I first started. At that time, women didn't even come into the physics lounge...They'd have conversations, and just not even listen to what the women would say...It's obvious; when you're excluded from things—like, if you can't hang out, and talk about your field with equals, then you're going to feel left out—and you're gonna want to just leave. (Male white science non-switcher)

Because of the unfamiliarity of this experience, and because they lack contact with senior women who understand the nature and source of their problems, first-year women find it difficult to make sense of their discomfort:

I need to feel like there's someone there sharing it with me. I don't want to feel so alone. I live far from home and I've felt very isolated...Your phone bills get outrageous, calling your friends once a week...I think the major thing is, it gets you down...And if you get down about something, it snowballs because you've no one to talk to. That's when you get to the point of, 'What am I doing here?' (Female white science switcher)

I grew up with four sisters and a strong mother, and I'm used to having someone show some understanding, listen and take an interest in me. And I had friends back home whom I'd talk to. Here, I've almost nobody. (Female white science non-switcher)

I think perhaps the worst thing is, it's lonely. Because you don't have the support that you get from talking to women...You have to get your friends somewhere else because there are so few women. But we are all too busy either to get together, or to find women friends from other majors. (Female white engineering non-switcher)

Few had received any guidance about what to expect, and how to survive. They lacked a female folklore offering ready-made explanations or remedies for their difficulties, and most had little knowledge or acceptance of the analytical framework offered by feminist theory. In short, they were inexperienced 18 year-olds who tended to blame themselves when people behaved disapprovingly towards them. Receiving what are normatively viewed as adequate, or even good, grades for their classes was not, in and of itself, sufficient to prevent what women commonly referred to as feeling "intimidated" and "discouraged":

I was very intimidated. In my study group for the dorm, they were mostly guys. They were actually very helpful to me, but I always felt they were teaching or tutoring me. And that was discouraging. (Female Asian-American engineering switcher)

Half of the women dropped out of the physics sequence after the first class. I mean, half of them. I went on to the second semester, and most of the remaining women left. I was the only woman who finished the sequence. I think they were just discouraged. (Female Asian-American engineering switcher)

One reason why it is so difficult to take accounts either of academic problems or institutional records indicating lower grades at face value is precisely because what may seem like an adequate, or even good, performance to an objective observer, is not necessarily seen as 'good enough' by the woman herself. Without knowing why women (and others) may be unable to define their work as 'good enough', it is hard to make meaningful connections between 'objective' data about student performances and subsequent student actions, such as switching. One important source of the difficulty women experience in defining their performance as adequate to the task is their isolation. Without a support network of people with more experience, it is easy for each of them to assume that they alone are struggling:

> In the first three days of the class, I was really discouraged because the teacher was hard to follow. And I felt all the other students in the class understood what was going on better than I did. I finally got a B in that class. But I felt I was working as hard as I could, and not doing as well as I should. I felt overwhelmed that there were so many other people who seemed so much better prepared than I was. Why was I even trying to be an engineer? (Female white engineering switcher)

With hindsight, senior women had a clearer understanding of what they had encountered, and why they responded as they did:

> I wish we could find a way for women who are coming in to make them feel more secure, or to bolster that feeling of independence and self-worth that so few of us have. (Female white engineering non-switcher)

> Most girls take it to heart, and guys are like, 'Oh, *yeah*! I don't need to listen to you.' Girls say, 'Maybe they're right.' They are more apt to make something into a criticism. A guy would just blow it off. I'm not good at blowing things off. I take it personally. I'm hurt. (Female white engineering non-switcher)

> What scares me is getting in 18 year-old girls who have no idea how to defend themselves. I've had to learn the hard way. If you're going to be a good student, you've got to be sound; you've got to be stable; and you've got to be secure. To get more good women students graduating, we've got to help prepare them emotionally, as well as mentally, for what they are going to have to face. (Female white engineering non-switcher)

To understand just why women do not develop sufficient independence to discount hostility and deflect attacks upon their feelings of self-worth, requires some examination of differences in gender socialization. We posit that entry to freshman science, mathematics or engineering suddenly makes explicit, and then heightens, what is actually a long-standing divergence in the socialization experiences of young men and women. The divergence in self-perceptions, attitudes, life and career goals, customary ways of learning, and of responding to problems that have been built up along gender lines throughout childhood and adolescence, is suddenly brought into focus, and into practical significance. This occurs because young men and women of all ethnicities are entering an educational system which has evolved to support the ongoing socialization process of only one group—namely, white males.

The essential opposition between two categories embedded in the traditional gender-role system has consequences for all students and faculty. It occurs when a relatively small number of inexperienced young women are encouraged (with little prior preparation in the cultural and personal dimensions of their undertaking) to venture into an institutionalized national (possibly international) teaching and learning system which has evolved over a long time period as an approved way to induct young men into the adult fraternities of science, mathematics and engineering. Most young white men seem able to recognize and respond to the unwritten rules of this adult male social system. The rules are familiar because they are consistent with, and are an extension of, traditional male norms that were established by parents, and which have been reinforced by male adults and peers throughout their formal education, sports, and social life. Broadly, the same set of norms are to be found in the education and training systems used by many occupations and professions, including the military. The ease with which young men adjust is variable; however, the nature of the undertaking is at least familiar. Indeed, the learned ability of male students to recognize and respond appropriately to these gender-role norms seems to transcend national boundaries. For example, at one institution which regularly attracts students from Norway, a Norwegian woman in our sample commented on the ease with which her male Norwegian peers seemed to adjust to their engineering and science majors. She contrasted this with her own difficulties in developing a sense of belonging in her major—a difficulty which she shared with American women:

> I'm the third Norwegian girl they've had in the department. The first one there had to go and see a shrink. She couldn't take it any more. The second one moved to applied math. And I went through something like that—but so did the American girls—we just didn't fit in...And yet, talking to the Norwegian guys, it seemed just nothing—it was all totally natural for them. None of them could see the problems. They thought it was us women making up funny ideas. (Female white engineering non-switcher)

An important element which is redolent in the rhetoric of traditional male education is the idea that young men should be 'challenged'. Rising to meet the faculty's challenge is an important facet of the weed-out tradition. Moral challenges are also found in other academic disciplines: in military training, sports coaching and in the educational systems of traditionally male-dominated professions such as law and medicine. The metaphor of challenge is a central theme in many rites of passage into manhood: the boy is challenged to test his mettle against that of the established adult males who set hurdles for him to surmount before he is allowed to join them—initially as an apprentice, ultimately, as an equal. The nature of the challenge is as much moral as it is intellectual, in that it is intended to test the ability of young men to tolerate stress, pain, or humiliation with fortitude and self-control. By a deliberate denial of nurturing, young males are forced to look inward for intrinsic sources of strength, and outward to bond with their brothers in adversity—their peer group. Young men must demonstrate by their demeanor that they have left behind their dependence on nurturing adults in order that the dominant males may acknowledge their worthiness to belong to the adult male community. We posit that these processes are an important latent function of the weed-out system in the first two years of S.M.E. majors. In the junior year, when those who have proved unequal to the challenge have been weeded out, faculty can begin mentoring their apprentices and making a place for them within their fraternity. Some women notice that a peculiar feature of the pedagogy of some S.M.E. faculty is the tendency to make the material being presented seem more difficult than it actually is. This does not constitute any particular problem for women, but they interpret such mystification (probably correctly) as part of the way that faculty build up the mystique of a discipline which can be revealed only to an initiated élite:

> The élitist male attitude comes up in the way the subject matter is presented. They make it seem like what they're teaching is very, very esoteric—even if it's only Math 110. There's no reason to complicate things, but they act like what they're teaching is very secret, and you're gonna have to be a genius to understand it. And the T.A.s copy their style. And anyone who is easily intimidated will be thrown, even if they're quite capable of learning it. (Female white engineering switcher)

None of this is essentially or exclusively an intellectual process, although it may, with honesty, be perceived as such. Those who operate within any social system are not necessarily aware of its functional or dysfunctional consequences. People may be honorably engaged with one set of declared objectives, while perpetuating another, less overt, agenda. The process may be partly or wholly obscure to those who perpetuate it, because they too have been socialized in this manner, and therefore, assume it is the most logical way to ensure that only the very best survive.[5]

If women are going to survive and bond independently to science and science careers, they must adjust to a system of which they have little prior knowledge. Lacking prior experience of the educational norms and attitudes they encounter on entry to S.M.E. majors, women do not know what to make of them, or how to respond appropriately. The system is actually not intended for them. It does not relate to the (different) way in which they were taught to learn, nor to the models of adult womanhood which their socialization has encouraged them to emulate. The women sense (quite realistically) that it is very 'male'; that it does not apply to them; that they are not welcome to participate in it; that men would prefer to exclude them from its agenda and its rituals; and that their presence is considered intrusive, and is resented:

> Science is a wonderful example of how men just have their own little world—just men, and men's ways, and men's concerns, and men's thinking. (Female white science switcher)

> A young man has a much easier time—just by virtue of being seen as more capable, and because he's gonna have an entirely different social and personal experience than he would if he was one a few of his own sex in a world created entirely for the other sex. (Female white engineering switcher)

> No one could tell me where the bathroom was. I'd never been in the building before. There were no women in my lab. There were no women on the floor where I was. I walked for probably 20 minutes, and it turned out it was two floors down. (Female white science non-switcher)

> We were both real math and science-oriented. We always loved it. But it wasn't enough. A large part of the decision to just get out was just feeling that guys are socially prepared for this, and that girls just don't know enough about this world to survive in it. (Female white engineering switcher)

Most of the unpleasantness with which some faculty and many male peers treat women in 'their' majors can be explained in these terms. For them, the presence of women is as inappropriate as it would be at any other male initiation rite.[6]

Notwithstanding the hostile behavior of some faculty, most young women did not feel that the majority of S.M.E. faculty treated women in a manner which was very different from that in which they treated young men. However, in treating male and female students alike, faculty are, in effect, treating women in ways that are understood by the men, but not by the women. For example, by 'challenging' everyone in the class to 'prove' their manliness by standing up to the harshness of their teaching methods, curriculum pace and student assessment system in introductory classes, faculty are sending out a meaningless message to the female minority. Faculty are unwittingly discouraging women more than men by behavior which is actually the same for both men and women. However, women do not know why they are being treated in this way and do not know how to respond appropriately. From a focus group of female engineering seniors:

> Male professors are—I don't know what the right word to use is—rude? You know, they're attacking and aggressive.

> Yeah. They don't encourage you. They attack you. However, it's not just the women: they attack everyone.

That's true—they are just as awful to men. But I'd say most women respond poorly to it—so do some men—but I think most men find it easier to just blow it off.

When I was a freshman, I felt they were trying to get everybody out—especially the women. They don't want women in there. And when you look around and see how well they're succeeding, you start to think maybe you shouldn't be there either.

But it seemed like the men saw that as more of a challenge—that they're gonna be one of the people that sticks it out—while I saw it just as a threat.

Those young women who rise to meet the challenge intended for young men by showing ability, competence, or moral strength under pressure, risk (as illustrated) a negative response from their peers. We posit that much of the hostility of male peers, and of some faculty, which female students experience, arises when women unknowingly contradict stereotypes about the female-other, whose function is to help men define themselves as 'masculine'. Female S.M.E. students who are conspicuously successful literally 'cannot win without losing'.

Not only is the meaning of the metaphor of 'challenge' totally obscure to female students, so too are other elements in the traditional male educational process. The idea of 'proving yourself' by standing up to the weed-out system is important in establishing the claim to adult masculine status in these disciplines. It has no meaning for women, but they find themselves constantly reproached, either for attempting (inappropriately) to 'prove' themselves, or for being unable to meet a challenge which is relevant only to men. From a focus group of women science seniors:

> You just feel so overwhelmed that you have to prove yourself to the men. The women who walk up and get the awards, they earn it as far as I'm concerned—just for proving they can make it in a male-dominated world. The proving process goes on and on. It takes years. I still feel like I'm battling the whole male ego.

> I think it gets easier after you've had a few classes from the same professors and they get to know you, and see you around, and know what you're willing to put in. It's an uphill battle to start with. But it seemed you didn't have to fight as much the further you got on, because you've proven you're not going to quit now.

> It's more intense. They have more of a focus which includes not letting anyone get in their way. I'm not going to waste any more of my time proving myself. I know who I am, and what I can do.

The last speaker's comment is particularly insightful. She has come to understand that 'proving yourself', while an appropriate form of gender-defining activity for men, is risky and inappropriate for women. To be drawn into it is to court anxiety, insecurity, and confusion about the basis of one's own sense of self as a woman.

Competing for grades is another aspect of the male testing process. It has negative consequences for both women and men, though not necessarily for the same reasons. Competition is about 'winning', which is the most traditional way of placing individual men within male prestige and ranking systems. It is a central feature of all military, political and economic activity and is metaphorically represented in sports and games originally developed by men. As women increasingly involve themselves in these areas of activity, some women adopt the competitive imperative and learn how to compete in male terms. Men are often not comfortable with this. It is their game, and there is no place in their prestige system for a woman who competes successfully with them. Some women seek to change competitive social systems by interjecting elements of women's traditional ways of working which are more collaborative and supportive of others. How easily the women who enter S.M.E. majors adapt to the competitive way in which their curriculum is presented, and their comprehension is assessed, will depend on the degree to which they have already accepted competition as a way of relating to others in high school, or in sports and games:

> One of the female physics majors in our graduating class is fiercely competitive. She is at the top of the class. She's incredibly smart, and she is extremely stand-offish. She won't share her information with anyone else. (Male white science non-switcher)

The fact that this woman is seen as exceptional by her senior male peers, underscores our observation that most women dislike and avoid the competitive forms of learning they encounter in S.M.E. majors. As the above extract also illustrates, women who compete well are not accorded the same respect that a similarly competitive man would receive. Neither are they respected by women, who tend to see competitive women as being "just as bad as the men":

> I refuse to participate in competitive activities. It makes me very uncomfortable. I've stopped doing homework with her recently because she started making it into a competition. She got angry one time because I did better than her on the homework, so I broke off working with her. It makes me very angry to have someone wanting to compete with me. (Female white science non-switcher)

Generally, women do not find competition a meaningful way to receive feedback on their level of understanding. Those who remain in S.M.E. majors continue to find the competitive approach to learning offensive and resist it:

The females were interested, and they certainly got good grades and every-thing, but I didn't see any interest in competition. (Female white science switcher)

I see a lot more of the men in my class being competitive than the women. The women worked hard, but they weren't interested in beating anyone on the curve. (Male white science non-switcher)

From a focus group of women science seniors—

Men are always competing, and wanting to be better than all the rest. Like when they play basketball, and there's a disagreement, they do a play-over or a do-again. It's like they have to re-do the whole thing to establish who won, or who was right, or first. Whereas, if there's a disagreement among women, they will kind of drop it and forget about it. It's, 'Let's move on, but stay together.' There's more of a connection and a unity between women.

That's right. Women will say to each other, 'Well, don't worry about the grade; it's just a quiz.'

And you don't see that between men, and you don't get it from men either.

My lab partner is a man, and he's always telling me I should work harder to get rid of those stupid mistakes so I can get straight As—instead of just accepting my Bs. I think he's genuinely trying to help me.

As these comments indicate, most women prefer not to see learning turned into a competitive activity—indeed, they tend to view competition as getting in the way, both of good learning and of good collegial relationships:

There are study groups, but when it comes down to the test, everybody breaks up. It's hush, hush—if you find out this short-cut on a problem, you're careful who you share it with—maybe no one. And it's all on speed, and the problems are kind of devious to trap you. And it's on a killer curve, so you're pitted against the others. It's made it hard to work together. Even in study groups there's competition and sneakiness. I always used to try to bridge that gap. But sometimes I felt from the way the men reacted that I was being too help-ful—giving away answers. I dunno. In my humanities classes, we drill each other and try to help each other out. I think that's a very big difference between how women and men feel about competition. (Female white engineering non-switcher)

While they value the attempts of some departments to encourage study group learning, women seniors see the dominant competitive ethos which pits individual against individual as a structural impediment to moving toward a more collaborative or discursive pedagogy:

The competition makes it impossible to have class discussions. There can't be that give-and-take which helps you clarify things, and improves your understanding. It's either, 'You get it, or you don't.' (Female white science non-switcher)

It's so different in my art class. There's people talking out in class—just feeling like they can talk to the teacher. In engineering, it's all cut and dried, and you just sit at the back, and you're on your own, and take notes. And you don't talk to people—there's this 'don't work together' attitude. It's just silly. (Female white engineering switcher)

Many male students also disliked competitive learning situations, felt that they did not do their best work in a competitive ethos, or saw the counter-productive effects of competition on performance and level of confidence.

Although both men and women cited competition in their major as a factor in their switching decisions, it is our contention that they did so for different, gender-related reasons. By their long socialization into the meaning of winning and losing, men—even those men who disapprove of competition as an educational tool—cannot escape the imputation of 'failure' reserved for men who do poorly in a competitive system. Competition is a problem for men because if they do not compete successfully, they risk being defined (and worse, of defining themselves) as 'failures' (that is, as 'boys', rather than as 'men'). Competition is, therefore a very powerful way to motivate young men to work hard, because they cannot avoid application of the failure label. It may or may not be a good way to motivate young women, depending on the degree to which they have absorbed the win-lose dichotomy as a way to define themselves.

However, what motivates most young women is neither the desire to win, nor the fear of failure in a competition with men, but the desire to receive praise:

It seems like a lot of times when women want to do something, it's like for praise. I can recall as far back as sixth grade when we had math contests...The girls enjoyed the praise they got from being first, but the boys liked the competition—just between each other—just wanting to better the others. So they worked on their own more. The girls seemed kinda more inclined to work together to complete the job more...And it's still that way among engineers. (Female white engineering non-switcher)

To understand the source and consequences of this and other motivational factors which bear exclusively on women, and to understand why the self-confidence of S.M.E. fresh(wo)men is so fragile, we must compare and contrast some salient features of women's and men's socialization experiences.

What Women Seek and May Not Find in S.M.E. Majors

What young women bring to their experience of S.M.E. disciplines is a pattern of socialization that is entirely different from that of young men. Many aspects of S.M.E. majors, which have evolved largely to meet the educational needs of young men, force women into conflict with their own socialization experiences. The resolution of these conflicts is sometimes accomplished by leaving the major and sometimes by making personal adjustments to the dominant male social system. These adjustments tend to be psychologically uncomfortable and some coping strategies provoke disapproval from other women, male peers, or both.

Broadly speaking, men experience a life-long pressure to develop and express an intrinsic sense of self-worth, to respond to challenge with displays of self-sufficiency and stoicism, and to show independence from the need for nurturing. By contrast, the socialization of most young women (including their formal education) encourages the development of a more extrinsic sense of identity. From early childhood, throughout the years of formal education, girls are encouraged to perform for the approval of others, and to attach feelings of confidence and self-worth to signs (such as praise) that others are pleased by what they do. The degree to which any woman depends on significant others for her sense of achievement varies (as illustrated in many women's accounts) according to the mix of cultural influences which have been part of her socialization experience. The tendency to perform for others is not gender-exclusive: depending on the circumstances of their upbringing and education, young men may (as we found) also exhibit this trait.

The consequences of these patterns of socialization were clearly embedded in most women's accounts, with one important exception—that of black women. This group reflected a pattern of socialization which encourages the development of independence in self-image and career-choice, and of self-reliance and assertiveness in getting educational needs met. This group was distinctively inner-directed and determined, compared both with most other women, and with most black men. Black women's drive to succeed and their independence—even isolation—from common sources of advice and support was reflected both in their own narratives, and in the observations of other students.

Evidence of a pattern of performing for others, and of the consequences of this behavior for attrition, appear in several aspects of our data on women. As already discussed in Chapter 2, many more women than men chose S.M.E. majors because they were promoted by family, teachers, or other mentors, rather than from personal interest in a particular discipline or career.[7] Choosing an academic direction primarily to please someone else is an accommodation which, we found, did not hold up through the rigors of an S.M.E. major, and made students more vulnerable to the attractions of other fields of study.

In Chapter 3, we contrasted the more instrumental approach to education among young men in these majors with an affective orientation among many young women. The dichotomy appears in our data in a number of forms. It arises in men's and women's (different) reasons for disliking large classes. Generally, class size was seen as a problem only indirectly in that it created or exacerbated other problems. Men disliked large classes because they "have negative effects on grades," they encourage "more competition for grades," and because "introductory courses are usually taught by less qualified faculty."

Women found the size of classes problematic when "you don't get to know the professor," "it's too impersonal," "the professor doesn't care if you learn or attend class,"—if, in short, "the professor doesn't care about you." From this, we deduced that more women than men arrived in college with the expectation of establishing a personal relationship with faculty. We also found this expectation embedded in the different definitions of 'good' and 'bad' teachers offered by male and female students. Women more often than men stressed the importance of a teacher's personal behavior toward them, and defined the 'bad' teacher as "unapproachable," "impersonal" and "intimidating." 'Good' teachers were "approachable," "nice," "friendly," "patient," "interested in how you respond," "present the subject in a friendly manner," are "around all the time, so you can ask them to explain the material" and "won't take your head off." They liked professors who "wanted to get to know you as a person," "treated you nicely," "understood you're a human being who's working at getting good grades," "calm you down and say, 'Don't worry if you don't get it, I can show you how'" and who "really care about you, and want you to learn."

Men were less concerned with a teacher's openness to contact with students than with their effectiveness in presentation of the material. The 'good' professor is "enthusiastic," "interesting," "fun to listen to," can "explain well," "be entertaining," "gives good advice," "uses good analogies," "stresses application of the material by relating it to real life situations," "provides in-class demonstrations," "allows questions," "knows whether the students comprehend," "doesn't just copy the book onto the board," "puts it in layman's language and goes over it in other terms," "challenges and motivates me" and "forces students to work hard."

We argue that it is because they are raised to work more for the approval of others than for intrinsic satisfactions and goals, that so many women fail to develop a clear personal view of what they want out of college before they arrive. This also explains why the openness of teachers to the personal approaches of their students is so central to women's definitions of the 'good' teacher. For many women entering college, engaging the teacher in a personal dialogue appears to be critical to the ease with which they can learn and to their level of confidence in the adequacy of their performance. We posit that the thwarting of students' attempts to draw S.M.E. faculty into a more personal pedagogical relationship than faculty are prepared to offer (whether as teachers or advisors), makes a major contribution to women's decisions to leave these majors. We base this assertion on strong textual evidence that failure to establish a personal relationship with faculty represents a major loss to women, and indeed, to all students whose high school teachers gave them considerable personal attention and who fostered their potential. The abrupt withdrawal of a special teacher-learner relationship, and it's replacement with the "impersonality" of college classes was reported to be extremely disorienting:[8]

I don't think he looked favorably towards women in his calculus class. I went in several times for help. I guess I expect people to be kind, warm, thoughtful and helpful, and you know, they're not. So I had to wake up. (Female white science switcher)

If a woman gets into one of these majors, there's no one there for them to relate to. There's no one there for you. (Female white science switcher)

It's harder for women than for men to handle the situation where the teacher doesn't know you—especially after being special and getting lots of attention in high school. How people get over that varies. I think I had begun to adjust before I came here, and the impersonality didn't bother me. If you can't adjust, then chances are you'll get out and look for that attention elsewhere. (Female white engineering non-switcher)

You know that not everyone has a one-on-one relationship with the teacher...so just because he doesn't know you personally, doesn't mean he actually thinks less of you. (Female white engineering non-switcher)

In one class, I was the only woman, and the professor said, 'Oh, I'll remember your name.' And he did. And in a class of 300, it was comforting for me to have someone know who I was and maybe feel that he cared a little. I don't hear that from any of the men I have classes with. I don't know if they could care less about things like that. (Female white engineering non-switcher)

Three of these women survived: two of them had learned to need the teacher-pupil relationship less, and/or had actively sought alternative sources of support; the third continued to need a sense of connection with her teachers, but was able to persist by drawing comfort from very small amounts of personal attention. Whether or not women at risk of switching can evoke sufficient personal support from faculty to keep going seems highly serendipitous. The following two women were unable to get the attention they needed and left:

They're not open to anyone. They always have office hours, but if they answer your questions, they just sort of shove you aside and don't really want to talk to you. You feel thrust away...it's just like they're not very open to students at all. (Female white engineering switcher)

When I went in to get advising, it seemed he didn't see me as a person. There was no interaction between us, period. When you get to that point where you're panicking, then you don't feel like you have anyone to turn to. (Female white science switcher)

These observations throw light on the recurrent finding of lowered confidence and self-esteem noted in other studies. A female student whose confidence in her ability is over-dependent on the judgments of others finds it difficult to judge the adequacy of her performance. Her self-confidence may already be shaken by her abrupt reduction in status: in high school, she was treated as special; now, she is part of an unwelcome minority which is treated with a hostility that she cannot explain. Her new college teachers, to whom she looks for guidance, abandon her to compete with the uncouth male mass in a contest where no one seems to know what is a good, bad, or average performance. The consequence is confusion, anxiety and a strong sense of abandonment:

> The average of all our exams are in the 40s, so if the men in the class get a C, they're happy. If women get a C, they're upset. They think the teacher doesn't think they're any good. And they line up outside his door trying to get him to explain it, or tell them that's it's really okay. I think that's a very difficult thing for women to get over at first. (Female white engineering non-switcher)

> Some of my girlfriends and I used to take it really hard when we didn't seem to do so well, you know, hiring tutors and just struggling and crying over grades—getting out old tests and working extra problems, and making flash cards, and just working extra, extra hard. And it was all because, as hard as we tried, we just could not seem to please the professors. We were just looking for some encouragement...I used to get nauseated before exams. It took me a long time to get over that. I'd go to therapy sessions and take anxiety classes...Eventually, I learned not to take it to heart. It's not *you* they're grading: it's just your work—and not always that. Men just blow it off. (Female white mathematics non-switcher)

> You'd look round the room before the exam, and the girls would be all silent and sweating. And the guys—well, some would be affected too—but most of them would be talking about football, or where they were going that night. They understood these were just weed-out classes, and they weren't looking for a pat on the back. (Female white mathematics non-switcher)

Even when their performance is adequate or good, women who have an underdeveloped sense of their abilities in mathematics or science have difficulty in knowing that they are "doing okay" without the teacher's reassurance. Teacher-dependent students (whether women or men) draw upon the feeling that the teacher cares about them as a way to motivate themselves. They work hard in order to please their teacher and use the teacher's praise and encouragement as the basis for their self-esteem. Deprived of that exchange, certainty about self-in-science is lost until the relationship is reconstructed with another supportive teacher, or a more independent self-concept is developed. Non-switching seniors also described how difficult it had been for them to forego the high level of interaction and support to which they had been accustomed throughout their earlier school years. Learning to develop an independent sense of their own ability and progress had been vital to their survival:

> One reason I did well in high school is because I cared about what the teachers thought about me. I knew I was doing well when people were pleased with me. I was always looking for that praise just so I knew I was doing okay. It took

me a long time to get over that when I came to college. I used to get very
upset because, here, the teacher doesn't know who you are...Now I love just
knowing that I am doing well—but that's not how I started out. (Female white
engineering switcher)

We noted that women consistently chose the word 'discouragement' to describe
their reaction to the experience of weed-out classes, and especially to faculty's
refusal to interact with them as individual learners:

It's terrible. It's discouraging. It sure doesn't help your confidence any. It's
bad enough going into this huge freshman physics class with just two other
women and a whole roomful of men who are looking you over with a hostile
stare. You think, 'Maybe I shouldn't be here.' And then the teacher tells you
that he's gonna fail half of you. So you think, 'Why should I try if it's that
stacked against me?' (Female white engineering switcher)

It discourages people who may not have faith in themselves, but who may be
very good. It came very close to discouraging me. But they do so much to tell
you that, 'You don't have the background. You're not working hard enough.
And if you're not gonna join in this crazy cut-throat pre-med frenzy, then
you're not gonna make it.' They don't do anything to encourage you. Maybe
they're testing you to see how committed you are. But it really doesn't make
any sense to me. (Female white science non-switcher)

They try to scare you. Maybe they think that's how reverse psychology works,
and that it will make you work harder. But you're too fragile; there's already
too much pressure from mom and dad. I don't do my best in harsh environments: I can push myself. I don't need stern teachers beating up on me.
(Female white engineering non-switcher)

A lot of people were so discouraged after that class that they left. I got a C-
and kept going for a while. I ended up getting mostly Bs and As in my other
math classes. I think they could figure out a different way. It discourages a lot
of people who could still go on. I think a lot of those people have the ability,
but they just feel so bad about themselves. (Female white engineering switcher)

Their attitude is that they don't expect you to make it through. It's very
discouraging. You know they don't encourage you to do your best. I felt they
were telling me, 'No, you can't do it. You're not going to make it.' (Female
mathematics non-switcher)

I guess a lot of it would be needing more personal contact. It's so discouraging
and frustrating. I wish they acted more like they really wanted you there—to
come and learn something from them. (Female white engineering non-
switcher)

Young women who are looking for 'en'-couragement to bolster their self-
confidence, but who cannot evoke it from faculty tend to feel 'dis'-couraged
even though faculty may have said nothing negative to them. There is no neutral
ground: failure to encourage is taken as discouragement:

> After the positive influences and positive reinforcements in high school, you feel on top of the world and that you can do anything. Then you get into an entirely new system. I noticed a marked difference in my attitude. And I believe it was because of the fact I was a number and nothing else to anyone...I had no one to perform for—and probably many other women are so used to being performers for others—that you take that away and you're left with a void. And at the time, I didn't really know it was that. The classes I do best in are the ones where the professor cares about me, and its always been that simple for me. I cannot separate my feelings for the professor from my performance. (Female white science switcher)

Depending on teachers for performance evaluation, reassurance about progress and as the basis for motivation, constitutes a serious handicap for the many women who enter college having learned how to learn in this manner. We posit that persistence initiatives that do not take this into account simply will not be effective. As some of these speakers indicate, looking to a teacher for interpretation and validation of their academic performance is a learned dependence, which people can change or out-grow, but not without first experiencing anxiety and frustration which, for some, ends in switching. To a much higher degree than is the case for young men, preserving the self-confidence which young women bring into college depends on periodic reinforcement by teachers. To be faced with the prospect of four years of isolation and male hostility on the one hand, and the abrupt withdrawal of familiar sources of praise, encouragement, and reassurance by faculty on the other is, in our view, the most common reason for the loss of self-confidence that makes women peculiarly vulnerable to switching:

> It was hard for them to understand my feelings because most boys that go into engineering, if they have problems, they don't say. They just struggle through it. I've seen that girls worry a lot more, and go to their professors right away. And for my girlfriend and myself, it was mostly that lack of confidence thing—not sure we would be able to make it. The third year, when I hit the real chemical engineering classes, they really frightened me. And I didn't know how I would make it through. Looking back, I could have done it. I think it was mostly lack of confidence. (Female white engineering switcher)

The women speculated why it was that their professors (including, to their disappointment, some female professors) were so resistant to their efforts to engage them in a personal pedagogical relationship. From a focus group of women engineering switchers:

> The teachers I liked were the ones who spoke clearly and in an organized manner, but who also treated me with respect when I went to talk to them personally, who acknowledged my question, or even my presence. That was a big one.

> Getting them to look up from their desk.

Interviewer: What's going on there do you think?

Oh, they're reinforcing the hostile message that I'm not welcome. I've felt that quite often.

Interviewer: Toward women, or all students?

Women—well, to some degree all students—but more toward women.

Interviewer: Perhaps they're just not used to women.

They're used to them. But they don't like them. So it's a kind of cautious discouragement. They want to encourage us by discouragement, to go back to our place in the home, or in the helping professions. That was definitely one of the *push* factors that took me out of engineering. I felt so much discouragement from so many members of the faculty. If they did bother to talk to me, they would counsel me to teach grade school math—nothing with any authority. And the joke is, I wasn't failing out. They knew I had more than a 3.0. I wasn't looking for a way out. That's not what I went to talk to them about. It was just their idea of where I'd be better suited.

That's right. There's a lot of active discouragement—just by denying you support. And they know what they're doing. They've had plenty of women in the department. They just know this works real well in making women think about leaving.

Faculty may or may not realize the critical role which they play in the persistence of women, both as a source of ongoing support and at times of crisis. Many women offered 'fork-in-the-road' stories in which, having plummeted into depression, confusion and uncertainty, they sought the counsel of faculty about whether they should or should not continue. They were prepared to accept their professor's assessment of their ability and performance, so long as this was conveyed in a manner that suggested he or she cared one way or another about their well-being. Describing a critical time when they felt unable to trust their own judgment about their ability to continue, seniors recounted the vital difference made to their decision to stay by expressions of support from faculty whom they consulted:

> I got lucky: I had an advisor who said, 'Don't worry about it. It will get better in the higher classes.' He says he's been telling them for years that this doesn't work with girls like it does with boys. You don't have much self-confidence to begin with, and it just blows what's left away. But they don't want to hear it. (Female white mathematics non-switcher)

The personal style of some faculty, and their active, open encouragement of women in their classes or in advisory sessions, made an enormous difference to the confidence with which women tackled their work, and therefore, to their likelihood of persistence:

If women survive, it's partly because someone noticed they had the talent and encouraged them in the first place. But it's also because they've received support along the way. It's not any one characteristic in women that stands out as making them likely to succeed—like having lots of will-power or something. It's more that their talent has been supported. They've been helped to keep going, and not let the discouraging things get them down. (Female white engineering switcher)

For those who were less fortunate, it is the "care-less" response of faculty in handling their crises of confidence which is a very common 'last straw' factor in switching decisions:

At high school, I got a lot of encouragement from both my math and my chemistry professors. When I came to college, I didn't expect anything like that much support, because I knew there were big classes and they'd be busy with their research too. But it was a huge let-down. It was either, 'You perform, and you do well, or shove off.' I think the thing that hurt most was I had some female professors who weren't supportive at all. (Female white engineering switcher)

The second semester of my sophomore year, I was having problems in chemistry. I went to the professors, but I felt like they weren't helping me at all and I got very frustrated. My faculty advisor gave me a pretty bad time, and told me not to bother going on: 'if I couldn't do it, I should just switch out.' So I did. (Female white science switcher)

The withholding of faculty support leaves women at risk in a way which seems less true of young men who have, by their prior socialization, come to understand that the denial of nurturing by adult, male faculty is a temporary hardship:

The classes are pretty cold—pretty lonely. It's you, your textbook and a bunch of numbers. I don't go to profs much for help. I try to figure things out on my own. I read that book over and over. I can see how women would be turned off by that and want to go to classes which are more human—more personal. (Male white science non-switcher)

If male undergraduates can rise to meet the challenges presented to them in the early years, they are assured of mentoring by the adult fraternity once the weed-out process is complete. As studies of graduate and professional women in science have indicated, women who successfully decode the meaning of the undergraduate testing process do not automatically receive this reward (e.g., Manis, Frazier-Kouassi, Hollenshead, & Burkham, 1993; Stage & Maple, 1993). They are not accepted into the fraternity, except as tokens, and they are not mentored by it.

The Role of the Traditional S.M.E. System
in the Loss of Able Women: A Summary

In the first part of this chapter, we have argued that the hostility women encounter from some S.M.E. faculty, and from many of their male peers, is a direct consequence of their intrusion upon a traditional process whereby young men are selected and prepared to enter an élite fraternity. The more the faculty treat the demonstration of particular 'masculine' characteristics as an essential part of 'becoming a scientist', the more resistance to their participation women will experience. Many senior women suggested that some S.M.E. faculty deliberately denied the kinds of pedagogical support which they sought to evoke. Whether this withholding is actually deliberate is an open question. However, withholding personal counsel or encouragement from under-classmen until they have surmounted the weed-out hurdles appears to be a moral imperative bearing upon all S.M.E. faculty. Young men are more likely to understand that to be accepted as serious candidates for upper-division work, they must pass tests of endurance and tenacity without faculty help. Although the nature of these tests is obscure to women, their role in the student selection process explains why many faculty resist students' efforts to engage them in a personal pedagogical relationship. Unfortunately, this is the precise opposite of what many young women—and some young men—feel they require in order to give of their best, that is, teachers who care about them, advise them on the adequacy of their work, praise or chide them (as appropriate) and who give support through periods of difficulty. Unable to evoke such responses from the largely male faculty (or from those female faculty who have adopted the agenda and style of their male colleagues), women in S.M.E. classes tend to feel they must be performing badly and doubt that they should continue in the major. Male peers advocate not taking faculty 'rejection' to heart. Many women have little experience of taking it any other way.

Young women tend to lose confidence in their ability to 'do science' (regardless of how well they are actually doing) when they have insufficient independence—in their learning styles, decision-making and assessment of their abilities—to survive denial of faculty support or performance interpretation, and refusal of male peer acceptance. Women who persist, enter with sufficient independence to adjust quickly to the more impersonal pedagogy, bond to the major through interest and career direction, and develop attitudes and strategies (including alternative avenues of support) that neutralize the effects of male peer hostility. We propose that it is these elements of college and pre-college pedagogy and culture which most directly account for the poor survival rates of able female undergraduates in S.M.E, majors. Though, as we shall argue in the balance of this chapter, other factors make an important indirect contribution to female attrition, the loss of able women cannot be reduced without changing traditional faculty norms and practices (as well as those of some high school teachers and advisors).

While this process of change is underway, some primary needs that programs for S.M.E. freshman and sophomore women need to meet are: the means to understand the source and typicality of the discomforts and self-doubts they experience; strategies to deal with them; and support to off-set tendencies to self-criticism, sinking confidence and emotional confusion. Because the difficulties we have described are part of the structure and culture of women's normal S.M.E. educational experiences, they are entirely predictable. Thus, programs for women in unremediated situations cannot be effective when they are set up on a one-on-one, crisis-based, "women's advisor" system, or when they lack the public commitment of senior administrators and departmental chairs. Successful programs draw on the knowledge of senior women students and female faculty who know how the culture of S.M.E. departments works. They also employ the help of sympathetic male faculty and a network of mentors from professional work settings. In some departments, we found cross-cohort informational and support networks developed through chapters of national societies for women in the sciences and engineering. Those most frequently encountered were the Society for Women in Engineering (S.W.E.) and the Association for Women In Science (A.W.I.S.). Other strategies include: field-based residential options; pre-college orientation programs; mentoring systems (including pairing senior with more junior women); and augmentation of classes with all-women tutorials, seminars and study groups. Some departmental and institution-wide programs which exemplify these strategies are: the residential program for women of color at Stanford; the Women In Science and Engineering (W.I.S.E.) programs at Brown University; and at the University of Washington the Women In Engineering (W.I.E.P.) and the Women In Science (W.I.S.) programs, as well as the Freshman Interest Groups for women in chemistry. The number of such initiatives is growing, and accounts of their evaluated efficacy in increasing persistence are beginning to be available. The time period over which the need for such programs will continue is determined by the speed and profundity with which changes in traditional S.M.E. attitudes and practices are addressed.

As we have learned in our discussions with the directors of programs for women on some of the campuses included in this study, and with many we have visited since its conclusion, some women's programs have been instituted in a half-hearted, window-dressing spirit. Their directors are constrained to focus on supporting women on a one-on-one advisory basis with insufficient staff and funding, without the means to track student progress, or to evaluate the efficacy of their own efforts and without the power to influence practices and attitudes of faculty. Such initiatives do not constitute a serious attempt to address the loss of able women from the sciences and engineering, and are unable to reduce attrition among women S.M.E. undergraduates. Indeed, their existence in this form may largely reflect a desire to postpone consideration of fundamental change in the ways in which undergraduate science and engineering is taught.

The foregoing discussion does not include all of the factors which we found to bear upon the quality and outcome of women's experiences in college science. In the balance of this chapter, we discuss factors which have more indirect consequences for switching and persistence. These include: traditional gender-based justifications for switching; lack of structural explanations for personal difficulties in their majors; the significance of intimate relationships; concerns about balancing family and work roles; the importance of peer and mentoring bonds with other women in science; the efficacy of some individual coping strategies; the role of women science faculty; and the importance of "critical mass" in changing the climate in which science is taught.

Feeling That "It's Okay to Leave"

If women in S.M.E. majors reach a stage where they have begun to seriously consider switching, then another set of factors comes into play, that distinguish them from men who are also tempted to leave. As Tables 5.1 and 5.2 indicate, women were much more likely than men to offer two particular reasons for switching, namely, rejection of the career and/or life-style associated with their original S.M.E. major (37.6% for women vs. 20.2% for men), and switching to a non-S.M.E. major that seems more interesting or promises a better overall education (46.2% for women vs. 34.8% for men). These concerns are also evident in the overall complaints of switchers and non-switchers of both sexes. However, their use as justifications for actually leaving the sciences was much more pronounced among women.

An explanation for this gender difference was embedded in the text data. Men felt more tied to their original choice of major and/or career as a matter of duty to parents, personal responsibility and fulfillment of future family obligations. Notwithstanding the generalized acceptance of women as workers and as contributors to family income, the accounts of both young men and women indicated that men still expect, and are still expected, to provide the larger share of their future family's income:

> The real key question is, What is it in societal pressures that would allow my sister to quit college, while my brother continues in grad school, and I continue with this math degree? I mean, I've often felt a lot of stress, and I've thought about changing majors, but never quitting altogether. (Male white mathematics non-switcher)

> Probably women aren't encouraged to challenge themselves to the same extent. When they are having trouble with something, parents would say, 'Oh, this probably isn't for you; maybe you should try something else.' If we're not doing well, parents get all over us and tell us we're not trying hard enough. (Male white science non-switcher)

Just the fact that it's usually the father that's the provider—even though that's changed somewhat in the last 20 years to two pay-check households, it's still the father who brings in the larger pay-check. So males still grow up with that role model. Even if it's subconscious, you still assume that you're going to have a family to provide for. So if it's a job you don't like doing, but it pays enough to provide, you've gotta take it. You can't take something just because it's fun. (Male white engineering non-switcher)

My husband is pre-med and he's thinking about dropping out, but he wants to support us as a family. And I'm going to be in journalism, so I won't earn as much money. So he's really reluctant to drop out because he feels he should earn most of the money in the family, whereas, I don't see it as much of a problem for myself. I have the luxury of earning less. (Female Asian-American science switcher)

Women expressed a greater sense of freedom to release themselves from commitments which had ceased to have as much interest or relevance for them as they had appeared to have at the outset. Women were more likely than men to feel that changing objectives was something they could give themselves permission to do and were more likely than men to be supported in their decisions by family and friends. Switching because they had become unhappy with their major, and believed that an alternative major would give them greater satisfaction, was regarded by women (more than by men) as a socially-acceptable switching rationale:

I don't feel a pressing need to support myself or a family, which is something that puts a lot of pressure on men to stay with even a bad decision. Not having that pressure was one of the things that allowed me to choose not to continue with something that seemed to have lost its point. (Female white engineering switcher)

I don't think women are socialized to think as much of the personal gains as men do. We think of the pleasure of doing certain jobs—like a social worker or a counselor—which are paid substantially less than a doctor or an engineer. But I would be much happier earning a lower wage and doing something I liked than to be in a lab coat all day earning triple figures. I just couldn't live with myself even though I was making a lot of money. (Female Asian-American science switcher)

I think a lot of women are interested in doing things because they are interesting, as opposed to because they are useful. And you can probably get a job on the basis of the degree, but you just accept that it won't be a $60,000 job. I think we're becoming less materialistic—which is interesting, because jobs are actually getting tighter—and you'd think it would be the other way around...Oh, there are still a lot of men that want money, but there's a whole lot of women who don't feel that way. And it's not necessarily that they think their husbands are going to provide. It's just that having a Ferrari and a house on the Potomac isn't very important. I want enough money to keep myself alive, so I'm going to do what I really want to do after this—which is horse management. (Female white science non-switcher)

In comparing the last two sets of extracts, it is interesting that men couch the pressures they feel in terms of traditional gender role responsibilities, especially the expectation that they will be the main provider of family income. By contrast, women explain their claim to greater freedom of choice in terms of being less concerned with money and prestige than their male peers. Because other people are also expecting less of them, this increases their feeling of freedom to choose a major or a career path largely because it interests them. Though women's statements may be based on unspoken presumptions that they will not be required to be the main providers for themselves or their children, we found little evidence that women assume that the main source of future family income will come from husbands rather than themselves. However, the traditional assumption that men will continue to be the main family providers is a constant theme in the way that young men see the pressures which restrict their freedom of career choice.

The gender difference in perceived degrees of freedom to choose and to change direction was especially noticeable on campuses with higher concentrations of women from socially and economically-advantaged backgrounds. On campuses where a high proportion of the female students whom we interviewed did not have to depend largely on their own economic resources, we noted the greater ease with which daughters, rather than sons, were given family and peer 'permission' to switch out of S.M.E. majors into "doing whatever made them happy":

> I can see that a man would feel they would stick to something—even for the prestige, whereas, we're going to do what we like...My brother switched out of engineering too, just about the same time as me, but he got a whole lot more flak from my parents—well, not from my mother—from my father. (Female white engineering switcher)

> I had not been enjoying physics since my sophomore year, and last fall I became very depressed and stopped going to class for about a month. Eventually, I talked to my parents, but at this stage, I was in my first semester as a senior. And they said, 'Well, you can switch and get a degree in something else.' But in the end I didn't, because it would have taken me another three years. (Female white science non-switcher)

As the first of these extracts indicates, the tradition of indulgent attitudes towards women may be passed from mother to daughter, but it is reinforced by fathers who expect more of their sons than they do of their daughters. In the second example, it is the young woman herself who makes a prudent decision, despite the failure of her parents to encourage her to finish a major she has come to dislike, but which she is close to completing.

Where undertaking an S.M.E. major is seen as unusual by members of a woman's family or social circle, and her chance of success more dubious than that of young men, her decision to switch—especially to a more traditional major—represents a comfortable return to more socially-approved behavior. The idea that a man must choose a major that will prove economically valuable continues to be strongly taught and reinforced by the families and reference groups of young men. Women, by contrast, are still 'allowed' to choose disciplines largely by the degree of personal satisfaction they offer, and to pay less regard to their economic viability. If they fail, or choose to walk away from an S.M.E. major, it is perceived as less of a loss to the discipline, to women, and to their families. Reversion to a less exacting career also resolves the doubts of primary and reference group members that women can, or should, manage the strains of a dual career—work plus a family. These traditional gender-role expectations were strongest on campuses with a high proportion of women from well-to-do families. However, on only one of these campuses were women's statements couched in terms of their own aspirations for marriage and family:

> I plan on having a family later, and I wanted something that wouldn't restrict me from spending time with my family. If I went on to be a doctor, I knew that it would be impossible. And I've never found research that interesting. So I decided if I wasn't excited about the career, I should just switch my major. (Female white science switcher)

> Even with women contributing to family income, they still think that the man should be the main support...Even though my dad is quite liberal, if I'd been a boy, he might have been different about it, and would have wanted me to stay in engineering...Actually, it doesn't hurt that my family knows that I have had a boy friend for the last five years, and he's in engineering, and they're pretty sure that he's going to make money when he gets out. (Female white engineering switcher)

In this last extract, both the woman and her parents appear to have displaced their expectations for their daughter's material success onto her fiancé. The replacement of career goals with traditional marital goals as part of the rationale for switching was found only among one group of women on one campus. These were women at the East Coast public institution who had attended private parochial girls' schools. An alternative, newer version of indulgence toward daughters was strongly represented at the highly selective, West Coast private research university. Here, thoughts of marriage or family were not mentioned by women as a factor in their thinking about switching. Reference to a different tradition—that of giving women greater latitude than men—was almost exclusively focused on choosing majors and careers which were personally fulfilling, and/or altruistic in purpose, regardless of the lower incomes they expected to receive. If their feelings of freedom to make these choices were based on the presumption that someone would provide for them, it was never mentioned:

> I hate to say this, but I'm going to say it anyway. I think women at this age tend to be thinking more about what's going to make them happy—and how they feel about things. And then a lot of men get to 40 and wake up and say, 'God, I *hate* what I'm doing. This doesn't make me happy.'...I think women are just more allowed to think about being happy at this stage in their lives. And men of our age are just concentrating on the money. (Female white science switcher)

> It's not necessarily running away. It's seeing that I have other options that are more enjoyable. It's not that I'm escaping. It's, 'Wow! Look what else is available.' It's a willingness to be more flexible. (Female white science switcher)

We do not have enough data to establish whether the tradition of giving women greater freedom to choose an academic path, regardless of its material consequences, is differentially located in particular socio-economic, ethnic, or regional traditions. However, we noted no evidence of such unfettered choices among women whose expectation of being the main providers for their families was as strong as that of their male peers:

> I know several single mothers who are sticking with their majors, even though it's much harder on their time schedule than it is for the rest of us. I think that gives them an added incentive. They need the education because they need the money. It all seems a little more immediate and more real to them. (Female white engineering switcher)

> I have friends who really pushed themselves hard to perform for their families. Like some of my African-American friends. They feel really pressured, because lots of their families didn't graduate. So they feel like they really have to perform. They push themselves very hard. (Female white engineering switcher)

The extra social pressure on young men to persevere appears to help them through periods of doubt or crisis in their major, while many young women lack the external constraints which might stiffen their resolve to see it through, and experience pressures which favor their giving up:[9]

> I'm one of three girls, and my father doesn't have expectations of us that I think he would have if we were boys. And it's fine for him that I'm gonna major in American Studies, or whatever. But it would bother him if I were a man and weren't career-focused. A lot of women, when they get into the science field and it's hard, and it's a lot of work, and they don't have anyone telling them it's important to do this—that, 'You have the capacity, and you can make it,' and that, 'A career is gonna be important to you,'—all you get are the negatives: 'How are you gonna manage a career and having kids?' And, unless you have a dream that's really pushing you, you don't get a lot of

positive reinforcement. All they ever say is that working mothers are the scourge of society, and you're never gonna be able to balance things. But for men, it's expected that they'll go on and have a career, so they can be a success. There are a lot of very talented women in the science field here, and they're very focused. But I don't know many women who are very relaxed about it, and have any kind of social and personal life. The women who succeed are the ones who make it their first priority and who really go after it...It takes so much more for a women to do science than it does a man, because everything's against her, and no one is rooting for her—in fact they undermine her at every point, and if she switches to something else, they can say it was just what they expected—and that it's probably all for the best. (Female white science switcher)

Both men and women understood the dynamics of this particular set of social pressures very well. They were clear about the constraints, degrees of freedom and sources of social support or opposition which shaped the decisions of both men and women:

I don't feel that men and women leave for the same reason. The women, I found, were leaving their second semester sophomore year saying that they didn't like this, and they needed to get into something new. The men I've known haven't left until they've had to. They've been sick, or had to miss some school, or they can't finish the major in the time they need to. (Female white science switcher)

One of my best male friends went through the aeronautical program and he hated every second of it. But with the pressure of being male and knowing he had to support a family, he didn't switch to the liberal arts where he would have been much happier. I think that's the dilemma facing a lot of guys in engineering. It's one reason why more of them stay than us. They hate a lot of the same things as us, but they are forced to stay in that track, while women have a little more freedom—although it also comes with a kick in the rear to get out...I think they might resent our greater freedom, but they can cover it by saying that we're wimps or just couldn't stick it out. But I've talked a lot to my friend about how much I loved my classes and how amazingly interesting they are. And he said he wished he could say that of any one of his classes. It was more of needing that skill than wanting to learn the material that kept him in. (Female white science switcher)

A guy in my dorm last year who was doing Calc 43 was saying one night, 'I really hate this and I don't have any desire to go on doing this for the rest of my life.' And I was asking why he stayed. And he said, 'You know, I want to have a family, and I need to be able to support one.' And I pointed out there were other ways to do that than becoming an engineer. But he was stuck on the idea that there were more good-paying jobs in engineering, and he felt he had to stick it out for that. I know it's changing and that there are women who bring in more than the men, but it's still not a very strong tradition. For myself, I'm not interested in money all that much, and I'm not worried about supporting a family...I think men get caught in the money. (Female white engineering switcher)

I mean, women have always had to reach for this interest, whereas I've never had to. It's always been pushed on me. If I start thinking that I'm not interested and that I'd like to switch, it's totally unacceptable. But it's seen as okay for women to do that. And perhaps there's more for them to switch to. I mean, it's okay for them to go into jobs that are interesting, but may not earn very much—like fashion design, or education. (Male white engineering non-switcher)

Much has changed in parents' expectations and hopes for their daughters over recent decades, and in women's own aspirations and the demands which they are ready to place on themselves. Women from families in which the pressure to persist and to do well was as strong for daughters as for sons, were less likely to give themselves permission to leave if their interests changed:

I have a few guy friends who are going though the pre-medical track. And it seems mainly because of parental influence and to make big bucks at the end. But they don't seem to enjoy the classes that much. They struggle. But there are women like that too—not so much because of the money, but because they are trying to please their parents. I've never had to deal with that. (Female white science switcher)

I got a lot of support from my family to be an engineer from ever since I can remember. It's turned into a different type of pressure now—where, if I don't fulfill that promise, there's gonna be repercussions that I'm gonna feel from the family. (Female white engineering non-switcher)

Women who had grown up in such families appreciated the extra strength that being expected to persevere had given them, and the encouragement to keep going through times of self-doubt. However, traditional patterns are still strong enough for their effects to be clearly reflected in our data as an important gender difference in persistence. When S.M.E. majors who, for a number of reasons, were at the point of weighing arguments for and against switching, women were much more likely than men, to give themselves permission to follow their personal preference, and to have this legitimated by others.

Although non-S.M.E. friends of both genders generally supported a woman's decision to switch, this was not the case with female peers in the S.M.E. major they were leaving, nor with those faculty who supported the idea of getting more women into their major. These people withheld 'permission' to leave (particularly if the switcher was performing well), and they did not allow the switcher to escape without feelings of guilt:

My advisor was very disappointed. He told me that he really hated to see a woman leave engineering. And he made me feel like a loser. (Female Asian-American engineering switcher)

When I left, she said, 'You can't leave me.' She was the only one left. I told her I didn't feel like I wanted to deal with it any more. (Female white engineering switcher)

I told all my friends in engineering I was leaving, and they didn't believe me because I had good grades. When it finally came down to it, they just kidded around, and called me a traitor and a drop-out. And a lot of them said they had expected it to happen. It really doesn't bother me any more, but it does seem a little unfair. (Female white engineering switcher)

Young women who had been inspired by high school teachers or special recruitment programs to bring more women into S.M.E. majors felt especially guilty about leaving:

When I hear about how few women there are in the field, and I know I could probably have done better if I had really wanted to stay in it, I feel like I should probably have done more. (Female Asian-American science switcher)

Women switchers were also at pains not to be mistaken for people who "couldn't make it." They had sufficiently absorbed male S.M.E. norms to worry about being defined by their peers as "failures":

I think it was definitely easier for me to quit because I was a woman. But, actually it was hard at the same time, because a lot of people just assume that a lot of girls are gonna drop out because they can't make it. And that kinda makes me mad, because I know I could have done it. And in order to do what I really wanted to do, I was left with this feeling that I let the other women down. (Female white engineering switcher)

And a lot of my other women friends *are* going to be doctors and lawyers, so I feel in some ways that I did fail—because I'm not going to be seen as successful, or prestigious. But I am going to do what I really want to do, which is to teach. But it does feel like I'm letting women down. (Female white science switcher)

However, it is hard to be a 'standard-bearer' for women in science unless that commitment is underpinned by a strong intrinsic interest in the major:

At school, I was really annoyed with the fact that women taught English and the men taught science...I didn't see why women couldn't do it, and I felt I didn't want to be part of a national norm. But it turns out that I'm following it. I found I was fighting about an idea, as opposed to being where I should be. Being a torch-bearer isn't enough—not at this level—there are enough women for whom it's right without me...At this level, it's very difficult to bear that torch against people who have such a strong aptitude. But I kept sticking with it because I wanted to help change things. (Female white science switcher)

Women who gave themselves permission to switch were not necessarily planning to change the way that the gender role expectations were presented to them for their future sons or daughters:

If I had a daughter, I don't know that I would push her. I was never pushed into it. If she wanted to do science, that would be fine. But I guess if I had a son that wanted to go into education, I think it wouldn't be so easy to say, 'Switch into education if you want to.' Even though it's necessary nowadays for women to work to also support the family, they still think that the man is going to be able to do most of it. (Female white engineering switcher—to education)

Because the learned tendency to wish to please is stronger for women than men, family pressures may be even more effective when applied to women than to men—although fewer families chose to exercise that leverage on daughters than on sons. The pressure on men comes initially from parents, but it is reinforced from a wider array of sources and is less focused on pleasing people than on demonstrating success.

The Ghost of Darwin Versus the Feminist Critique

On every campus, we found evidence of a covert debate about the source and nature of women's difficulties in S.M.E. majors. Elements of the argument surfaced in behavior or were reflected in attitudes, but the arguments themselves were not openly debated. The core of the argument was the traditional issue of whether women's poorer representation in S.M.E. majors and careers reflected innate mental limitations, or whether it was largely a product of socialization, and the unfavorable conditions for women in the sciences. The research literature germane to this debate (which would have been available to students through humanities and social science classes) was only slightly drawn upon in their representations of the issues.

The response of some female students to interviewer's questions about any difficulties they might have encountered as women in these majors might best be characterized as avoidance, or denial. They discounted classroom experiences which other women labelled "rude" or "sexist" by explaining them in terms which avoided these labels. Some women were uncomfortable about discussing whether they had experienced academic difficulties in S.M.E. classes, and whether their difficulties were of a different order than those experienced by male peers, lest the issue of inherent gender differences be raised:

I don't think being a woman makes it more difficult, or offers advantages either. Sex shouldn't matter in education, so I don't think that. I wasn't made uncomfortable in classes if that's what you're asking...I didn't feel—I wasn't directly competing with them—well, just in the math classes, not in the careers. (Female white mathematics switcher)

I don't know why women leave. I don't think the atmosphere's been a problem for me. I mean, to some people it is, but then they have a problem in every aspect of their lives. Some women must think they're inferior...One professor was sexist, but I didn't respect him, so it didn't faze me at all. I mean, I didn't care what his opinion was. And, as far as learning styles go, I don't see how

there could be different styles for men and women—that's ridiculous. (Female
white engineering switcher)

Some women were uncomfortable about admitting that gender might be an issue
at all. They felt that it should not be an issue, and therefore, it could not be an
issue:

I tend to think I'm being a sexist thinking this—and I hate to think that I'm a
sexist—but it's so competitive and it sometimes doesn't feel very comfortable
being a woman in the class. (Female white engineering non-switcher)

Once in a while I get that feeling that they think I'm inferior. But I think they
know me enough to respect what I can do. If it's there, I just ignore it. I don't
see faculty treating women differently, but I try not to look for it. I'm focusing
on other things...Oh, I do feel pressured by male students and the male
faculty, but I've never had any problems with it. (Female white engineering
non-switcher)

I had one female professor who wanted all the women to come and meet with
her in the first couple of weeks at school. And she said, 'You're in a different
kind of situation here than you're used to, so if you have a problem come and
see me.' I thought that was really kind of condescending, and I didn't go.
(Female white engineering non-switcher)

Those who took this view might express anger at women who described
difficulties related to gender, or at the implication they might have had problems
themselves. The following speaker dismisses her colleagues' experiences by
blaming the victim:

The senior who was acting as the tour guide said, 'I personally don't put my
first name on papers to avoid being discriminated against.' And I couldn't
believe it. I just stood up and said, 'I've been here for four years, and I've
never even thought about it.' But I think a lot of that is your upbringing. I
said, 'If you bring your daughter up to make her feel like she's equal to men,
then there's no reason she's ever gonna see any discrimination.' (Female white
engineering non-switcher)

Some women were also unwilling to admit to the possibility that the academic
or career 'playing fields' might be other than level. They preferred to assume
that the battles fought by an older generation of women for equality in domestic
and public spheres had been won. To suggest otherwise was irritating to them:

I really don't think any of that discrimination against women is as big a deal
as it was in the past. So to go on making a big issue out of it probably isn't the
greatest idea. Because that's what keeps the gap open, instead of closing it.
(Female white science non-switcher)

That some women denied the survival of structured inequalities in educational,
occupational and social spheres was noted by some of the older female students
who had wider life experiences:

We want to end up at a place where women and men are the same—except for whatever is inherently different. And so a lot of people sort of assume that we're already there. They ignore whatever factors have happened in the first 20 years of your life and say, 'Well, we all ought to be equal, so we'll just assume that we are.' But it doesn't work like that. (Female white non-traditional engineering switcher)

The younger women would rather forget that we really had to go through all that to be treated half-decently in education, jobs, or the family. They've grown up with what their mothers fought for, and they don't realize that those women had to work very hard to get them to the point where they are now. They've kinda forgotten. And they don't want to think that there might still be work to do. They would rather believe that all the problems had been fixed. (Female white non-traditional science non-switcher)

The culture on some campuses also seemed to make it difficult to employ sociological or social-psychological explanations for the problems experienced by S.M.E. women. Theories of this order were sometimes dismissed as admissions of weakness, as an unwelcome justification for special treatment, or as 'feminist' thinking. Women would sometimes interrupt their accounts of negative experiences to explain that, talking in this manner did not, of course, make them a 'feminist':

I don't feel like I wanna come off as a feminist or anything. But I do have the feeling that some of the faculty don't take me seriously. (Female white engineering non-switcher)

There's not a lot of help on this campus—like a women's center where women can go and talk to someone about the difficulties they are having. There are a lot of faculty here who are just oblivious...But you can't say anything too loud. People might label you as a feminist. And that's about the worst thing they can say. (Female white science non-switcher)

They have some good ways of explaining how things get to be the way they are, but you feel you don't want to get too close to them because they're too alarming. I was talking to a pre-med this week about some problems she's having, and she suddenly said, 'Of course, I'm not a feminist. I'm not that weird.' It probably shouldn't be associated with lesbianism, but on this campus it is. So people don't hear what they have to say, because that thought gets into your mind. (Female white science non-switcher)

There were four working women in science on the panel who were there to be role models and answer questions about what it was like to be a woman in their job. Someone asked them if they considered themselves to be feminists, and they all said, 'No, but....' And they went on to talk about some of the unequal things in their work situation that troubled them. I think that's sad. It's scary. To use the label is to frighten yourself with the idea you're not feminine. And you can't admit to having problems, or looking for what causes them, without getting afraid you'll somehow lose your social acceptance. I think if a woman's doing it, it's got to be feminine. (Female white science non-switcher)

The tacit debate was particularly strong among S.M.E. students at the private research university, which, arguably, contained the highest proportion of talented and highly-achieving students that we encountered. A strong, pro-active university policy in favor of campus-wide 'diversity' was reflected in aggressive recruitment and scholarship support of women and students of color, such that the campus 'over-represented' minority students compared with the national population. University personnel responsible for the orientation and teaching of freshmen and sophomores strongly endorsed the university's commitment to the principle of diversity. However, students reported that they and most others had reacted against this message because it seemed to be imposed on them at every opportunity. Indeed, we initially experienced some difficulty in getting any of our informants to discuss their thoughts about gender issues:

> Gender lines are so frustrating. It comes up in freshman orientation: they start talking about it right away. I mean, it is something that you always think about...But everyone gets sick of hearing it, and there's a sort of backlash effect. (Female white science switcher)

The aggressiveness with which this university had pursued its policy in favor of traditionally under-represented groups, had, we found, back-fired in a rather disturbing manner. Young women on this campus were uncomfortable with the thought that they might have been admitted, to some degree, on a gender basis, rather than solely on merit. Furthermore, if everyone at the university was being given an equal chance, why would there be any gender difference in persistence rates? They tended to dismiss socio-psychological explanations for gender discrepancies in S.M.E. persistence because they gave rise to special treatment for women, which they saw as unnecessary for people who were bright enough to hold their own:

> I mean, my mother makes double what my father does. But it didn't occur to me that this was an issue until I got here...And I've wondered, if I stick to my point, are people here going to think I'm a strong-willed feminist, as opposed to just being a strong woman—or a strong person...But it's just that difference, whether they're going to label me as a feminist. It bothers me because I'm not...So when it comes down—there being a problem for women in science departments—it frustrates me that there's any problem to be explained—because I don't want to have to explain it the feminist way. But you still have to wonder how the problem arises. (Female white science switcher)

Those women who rejected sociological, or 'feminist', explanations for the under-representation of women in S.M.E. fields, or for their own (unexplained) difficulties in those disciplines, were forced back upon explanations based on the presumption of inherent differences in the capacity of men and women to do math and science above certain levels of abstraction. Such explanatory theories were, indeed, mooted by some of their male peers:

> I do know a couple of science majors who think that men are actually better at math in general. That's when you get to the upper echelons of who's best at math—then the men are actually better. And it's true that there are more top math students who are men than are women, and that it's a genetic, inherent thing. In my mind, there's a fine line between cultural and genetic factors. I mean, it's true that men are better at math than women. It's that simple. Of course, it's hard to talk about this—it's such a P.C. issue. (Male white science non-switcher)

> There's a math learning plateau, and everything I've read about it says that women reach it much earlier than men—three to four years earlier. I think that most of the math we need at college should be taught at a much earlier age. I think the math learning curve for girls flattens out around 12 or 13 years old, and for boys, it's more constant until a later stage. I don't know what causes it, but I think it should be responded to, especially with very bright children. (Male white engineering switcher)

> I think that the guys just thought that girls weren't as smart. I mean, no one ever said anything to me; it's just a feeling I always got. (Female white engineering switcher)

Acceptance of the theory of inherent gender differences were also reflected in the reasons given by some female S.M.E. majors for distancing themselves from female peers and aligning themselves with the more 'intelligent' and 'serious' men in their classes:

> I tend to gravitate more toward the male students. They have more I can relate to. They're more intelligent and more serious, whereas the women are more gossipy and chatty. (Female white engineering switcher)

Even among women who had begun to understand the cultural and psychological processes which had shaped their thinking and behavior, the tendency to look for biological explanations for observed gender differences was strong:

> To be honest, sometimes I think it's in their genes. I mean, the girls in the classes, when I look around I see they're intense and they're studying all the time. And the guys are like—it almost comes naturally to them. It's like it's inherent. I have no idea how and why, but it's true, and it makes you sick. (Female white science switcher)

> That inner-confidence that you get because you know of people in the past who have been able to do certain things, it all helps to make it seem just normal for you to do it too. But if you flip through the history books, where are the women? No wonder we don't think we can do things the boys get to do when we are kids...And I never thought of myself as one of a minority until I came into engineering. But I am. I had—what's it called?—false conscious-

ness—about it...But then you start to wonder if it isn't testosterone that confers the edge in math! I have asthma and someone told me that girls with asthma have high testosterone. And I thought, 'Good! That should help my math!' We seem to grab at biological explanations rather than social ones to explain anything that is really very complicated...And it's all so subtle. I sometimes find myself accepting rude or unequal treatment as if it was just okay. But at least I'm starting to notice. But as a senior, I should be way beyond this, and at a stage where I'm trying to help other women deal with it. (Female white engineering non-switcher)

It is ironic that it was only at this institution, which had competitively selected some of the very best students in the country, that we should find women entertaining the idea that there might be genetic limitations to their intellectual abilities. These women preferred to discard socio-cultural explanations for the problems of S.M.E. women (which they saw reflected in their university's 'diversity' policy) because they justified special treatment which only women who were intellectually poorer would need, and because they smacked of 'feminism'. More women on this campus than on any other campus preferred to believe that men and women were, nowadays, treated on an equal footing in most social and economic spheres. This belief left women without an explanation for their own difficulties, other than the even more unacceptable argument that their problems must arise from some inherent intellectual inferiority. They, therefore, tended to avoid discussion of any academic difficulties they were experiencing lest they be suspected of being less able than the men.

This was the only campus where we met evasive behavior among women informants around the issue of why women leave S.M.E. majors. Initially, it was very difficult to persuade them to talk about gender differences in the experience of S.M.E. majors at all. They seemed to suspect that we were 'feminists' seeking to evoke what, to them, were a highly stigmatized set of ideas. Alternatively, they acted as if we wanted them to confess to intellectual weaknesses which would expose the fear of being thought less able than their male peers. We subsequently discovered that they did not talk to each other about their difficulties either, and so denied themselves the kind of mutual aid which, at other institutions, we had found to be a vital source of support for S.M.E. women (and men) at times of difficulty.

This extraordinary experience among the women on this campus further underscores our general observation that the degree to which women find the culture of their major, and of their campus, uncomfortable, is highly variable. It also points to the tendency of even the most benign of social engineering efforts to produce negative latent consequences which can only be known by soliciting feedback from those who are targeted by the initiative.

The Prospect of a Dual Career: Work and Family

In *Educated in Romance*, Holland and Eisenhart (1990) trace the powerful effects of the romantic imperative on college women (particularly white women) in two southern universities. We also found evidence of women over-riding their original career aspirations in favor of the traditional goal of marriage, but only among one group of women on one campus. This was a group of young women who had attended private parochial schools for girls:

> Some people joke about the M.R.S. [Mrs.] degree, and we do have a tremendous lot of very social sororities and fraternities. And there's a lot of pressure towards marriage. On this campus, it's important to have a boy-friend—to be seen as someone who's boyfriend-able. (Female white science non-switcher)

Among other women on this campus, and on all of the other campuses, we found no evidence to support the theory that women left S.M.E. majors because they were diverted into this more traditional 'career' path. We surmise that the difference between our observation, and the findings of Holland and Eisenhart may have much to do with regional variations in the norms of and about women. The following account lends support to our presumption:

> I didn't like the social atmosphere down there. I was born and raised in the West. I'm used to riding my bike to campus, doing my hair in five minutes, wearing just a little make-up, and not thinking too hard about what I wear to class. And I was so used to being active, and doing whatever I liked, without worrying about what the boys were doing. All of that was really weird to the students in the South. I began to understand what it would feel like to be in a minority. I felt I couldn't fit in. I wasn't going to buy into this looking cute stuff. I felt sort of degraded because the men looked at you as a girly girl with nothing in her head. That's why I decided to come back up here to school. (Female white mathematics non-switcher)[10]

As we shall discuss in this section, concerns about the projected difficulties of managing both a career and/or graduate school, alongside a family were important to senior S.M.E. women. However, the issue of baccalaureate versus marriage (or romance) simply did not arise for most women in the first two years of their majors when most switching occurs. This observation is consistent with the general upward shift in the preferred age of marriage and first pregnancy for middle- and upper-middle class women.

However, the issue of how to handle a 'dual career' began to be raised in conversations with senior women who were thinking about graduate school and making other career plans:

> One of the women in chemical engineering and I talk about that a *lot*—about how we could manage a family and a career. We went to a career fair last week and I only looked at companies in areas where I would consider starting

a family—even though I'm not married, or even thinking about it yet—you have to think about the school system. (Female white engineering non-switcher)

More companies are coming out with benefits and vacation plans where you can accumulate enough vacation time to plan a baby in so many years, and take good maternity leave. (Female white engineering non-switcher)

From a focus group of women science non-switchers—

My friend—who's in biology—and I were having this discussion. And we were saying, 'Well, maybe we'll have kids when we're 30. Okay—we'll finish graduate school, then we'll work for a few years, and *then* we'll have kids.' (All laughing.)

Me, too. I'm 22, and I'm already thinking about my next 10 years because studies say, having kids before 30 greatly reduces your chance of breast cancer. I mean, I'm 22 and I'm talking to myself about this! (More laughter.) It's bad.

Some male faculty had begun to offer warnings to their female students about the limitations on both career and on family life which they thought were brought about by attempting to do undertake both simultaneously:

Dr. M— said that he wasn't trying to be sexist, but that he didn't think that women could have a job and raise a family at the same time—that they just didn't have time to devote to any one thing, so everything turned out mediocre. And it's her mental state too, balancing two humongously-opposite worlds...That was his opinion from having observed women trying it...His advice to us was to seriously evaluate which was more important to you. It seems like so many people are trying it, and he's saying it can't be done. (Female white engineering non-switcher)

For most of our informants, their senior year as undergraduates was the first time they had seriously grappled with dual-career arguments:

My friends and I are having a really hard time deciding whether they want to go to medical school. We're thinking, 'Do I want to spend the next eight years of my life in med school? Am I ever going to get married or have children?' (Female white science non-switcher)

Choosing between a career and a family has gone through my mind a lot since I've thought more about going into medicine. I know how rigorous it is, and how time-consuming. And I honestly have to think to myself whether I can have a family. I think it can be done, but it takes a lot of management and a lot of commitment—for both the man and the woman—so I do worry. I'd like a family, but I don't think I could have one at the time that I want to have one. (Female black science non-switcher)

If I had children, I'd like to stay home with them for the first year. But that's virtually impossible now. And how am I going to make enough to cover my

own medical insurance, let alone a family's? I'd like to be the one who
influences my children and molds them like my mother did me. But nowadays
someone else is raising your child. It's really hard. Tough choices. (Female
black science non-switcher)

If you have the time, you don't have the money. If I have kids, it won't be for
a while. I don't want to have them when I'm 40. I dunno. Maybe I'll skip the
kids and have grand-kids. I haven't found a way to do that though! (Female
white engineering non-switcher)

In these discussions, which were common among senior S.M.E. women in
all institutions, we noted that having children and being financially independent,
rather than getting married, *per se*, were the central issues. Unlike the young
men who felt obliged to stay in S.M.E. majors they did not like because they
expected to be the main providers in future families, their female peers assumed
they were moving into a world where women were likely to be the main, or
sole, source of support for their children:

All of my friends and I are asking, 'Should we raise children first, or start a
career first? Should you bear children when your career's already begun, or
would that slow it down? Or stop it?' These are big questions. Because we all
want to get on our feet. We don't want to be dependent on anyone. We want
to be our own provider. (Female Hispanic science switcher)

I know that I'm graduating next year and I'll have to get a job. And maybe
five years down the road I will get married and have children. Meanwhile, I
have to make sure that I am financially independent—even if I'm married and
have a family. It's very important to be self-sufficient, in case something
would happen. (Female white engineering switcher)

For all my friends and me, the trend is to become self-sufficient and
financially independent before you make any kind of marital commitment.
Because we've seen our mothers, our aunts and our mother's friends getting
a divorce and losing most of their income because they've been too dependent
on a husband. And then they have to find a job in the open market. It's a scary
thought. Most of the girls of my age, the biggest priority is finding a career
rather than finding a man and settling down. The same's true for me. I intend
to get married some time, but I don't ever want to be dependent on a man *per
se*. I always want to be able to afford to pay for everything I want, and if I
have to leave the relationship, I don't want to have to change my status.
(Female Asian-American science switcher)

Most senior women (whether switchers or non-switchers) appeared to spend little
time or energy wondering whether they would get married. They simply
assumed that, at some point in the future, this would happen. Peer discussions
focused on whether and when to have children rather than when and whom they
might marry. There appeared to be little discussion of what type of marital
relationship would fit with their plans for a career and a family. There was, for

instance, very little mention of the domestic division of labor, or the question of whose career would take priority in a job relocation:

> Well, I'm thinking of moving—well, just if my boyfriend gets relocated. He's a civil engineer. (Female white engineering non-switcher)

> My fiancé and I have talked about having kids some day. But we haven't really talked about how we're going to work it out in practice—not in the detail that we should. (Female white science non-switcher)

One response to the difficulties looming ahead was to avoid or delay discussing them:

> I think I'm the only person my age who wants to have kids. I'm serious. No one else wants to talk about it. I know a few of them are engaged and getting married relatively quickly, so I don't know what they're thinking. A lot of them are very much set on going to medical school, and I guess they'll put off having children until after that. But it isn't discussed much because I guess people want to forget about it. (Female white science non-switcher)

Most seniors appeared to have recognized the practical difficulties faced by professional women with demanding careers. Until quite late in their undergraduate careers, women in S.M.E. majors had been able to discount or ignore issues of gender inequities beyond the university. However, the prospect of long professional training, the consequences of interrupted career patterns, and the pressures on working professional mothers were now becoming an uncomfortable reality. Some seniors who had switched at an earlier point, re-evaluated their decision as fortuitous in that they now had career options which were easier to combine with family life:

> It's hard for women to have a family and practice medicine. She may be in a good position in a hospital, but if you start to go part-time or take sabbaticals, you're never going to get ahead. My friend was saying, 'Well, sooner or later, women physicians will get into the top roles, and they'll start to change things.' And I said, 'The women in these fields right now are either not married, or they're not going to have kids. So I don't see how you could believe that it's going to change anytime soon.' I don't think that my female class-mates have thought it through. (Female white science non-switcher)

> If someone asks me why I don't want to be a doctor, I say, 'Well, my best friend's mom is a doctor. And she's gone all the time, and when she's home, she's panicky, because she hasn't time to deal with anything properly.' She works way too hard. (Female white engineering switcher)

Senior women also began to hear discrimination stories, especially from those who had been interviewed for medical school:

> I know it's illegal to ask these kinds of questions, but people come back from medical school interviews and they've been asked if they intend to have kids and how they will manage that. In essence, they're making it clear that it's not

worth accepting you if you're going to stop out. I think about how I'm going to answer that question a lot, but I haven't come up with a realistic answer yet. I'm a qualified candidate, but if I was really honest, I probably wouldn't get in anywhere. (Female white science non-switcher)

The importance of these conversations for the purposes of this research is that women approaching graduation represent an important source of potential loss to their field unless they can, formally or informally, get the help they need to resolve a dilemma which men still see as largely 'their problem':

My husband's an electrical engineer. He says there was one female engineer in his department, but she left. They say you can expect to work 60 or 70 hours a week. And if I have children, I want to be around them more than that. It makes you start to think of other ways you could use your degree—not in engineering. I'm sure that happens to a lot of women. Because they aren't going to be very accommodating out there. They're not pro-family. I'm sure that's a reason a lot of science graduates back out of science. (Female white engineering non-switcher)

These women had survived the risk of switching earlier in their undergraduate careers, only to face another predictable set of attrition risks a few years later.

What Helps Women Persist in S.M.E. Majors

In this final section, we consider the strategies used by individual women, and groups of women, in order to survive S.M.E. majors, and what other factors in their lives buffer them against leaving. We also consider what institutions and support organizations can do to increase women's level of persistence.

Individual Coping Skills

With respect to individual responses to the difficulties of S.M.E. majors, a number of themes recur in both men's and women's accounts of what, beyond hard work and ability, is needed to succeed. Some of these attitudes and behaviors are helpful regardless of gender, but for reasons we have discussed, they are more difficult for women to develop. These include a strong interest in the discipline and/or in the career(s) to which it leads, and an independent sense of confidence in one's own ability:

It's unfair competition and most of the women don't last long. You have to have the inner-strength and desire to do what it is we're doing here. (Female white science non-switcher)

I think it's intimidating, but the women who have made it through seem pretty solid in what they want to do—solid in the sense of direction and solid in that they're not emotionally hurt by this stuff. (Male white science non-switcher)

She was really talented. She came here as pre-pharmacy and switched into pre-med. She got a B on an exam, which was very unusual for her, and Dr. F---

told her she knew no math. He told her all sorts of stuff. But she told me about it, you know, smiling. She said, 'He told me I was stupid!' But she was confident enough in her abilities to do well, and she could discount what he was saying. She could let it go. (Male white science non-switcher)

Don't take 'No' for an answer. Stand up for yourself, because no one else is going to. And if someone tells you that women can't do science, or aren't as good as the men, that's not true. Women are different, and science needs a different perspective, and women can provide a valuable, different perspective to science. (Female white science non-switcher)

Women also have to develop assertiveness and persistence in asking faculty for what they need. Assertiveness has traditionally been encouraged in young men, but not in young women, in whom it can be negatively sanctioned as 'aggressive' or 'unfeminine' behavior. Women who are encouraged to be assertive while growing up have less difficulty in approaching male faculty and in asking questions, than women who have learned to be retiring and self-effacing:

You have to learn to be pretty assertive early on if you're going to get comfortable in this major. It's sad to think of your shyness as a handicap in your degree, but I think it's true. (Female white engineering non-switcher)

Engineering is almost forbidding. Maybe some of the guys are just more aggressive and more willing to stick their foot in the door, and say, 'Hey, here I am. Accept me.' (Female white engineering switcher)

I know that was a scary thing for me. At first, I would tag along with guy friends to office hours until I kind of got used to it, and started doing it for myself. (Female white engineering switcher)

I learned that you need to take advantage of the professors—even though they do stand off...You just have to keep going to them and letting them know your concerns. They act like they don't care and don't listen, but I've seen changes in some of them. (Female white mathematics non-switcher)

Assertiveness can be, and is, taught in some campus groups for women.

Women cite adapting to male styles of communication as helpful. This includes learning to be open and direct, and learning not to take criticism personally:

I have learned just not to take offense. I mean, sometimes they're funny, and sometimes they're really bad. But you don't take it personally. (Female white engineering non-switcher)

Rather than a direct approach, I've seen where women will attract the male professors by being a little cutesy—just I guess to try to shield against the intimidation. Because it is intimidating as a younger woman to go up to a male professor and ask questions. And you don't want to appear stupid, so you have to try to bluff it out a little. I've sometimes been real intimidated, and I've got a little dizzy—which is funny, because you're trying so hard not to appear

stupid, but that's exactly how you come across. And it's all about not having
the confidence to go up and say, 'This is what I want to know.' I guess some
of the guys feel intimidated too—but they deal with it differently. (Female
white science non-switcher)

You wanna be one-on-one with 'em, but it took me a long time before I felt
comfortable bridging that gap, and being able to say, 'Oh, how are ya' doing
Professor?' Just feeling like they're another person. If the teacher were a
woman I'd *know* how to communicate with her—I'd know where she was
coming from. I've had to learn a lot of stuff about men. (Female white
engineering non-switcher)

Women who were used to being around boys and men in a family, friendship,
or sports context, knew more about how to relate comfortably to men, and were
much less intimidated by the faculty or by the size of their male peer group:

If I hadn't felt comfortable in big groups of men, I probably wouldn't have
done physics to start with. (Female white science non-switcher)

I was always competitive with men in sports and in school. And with my
father, I got a positive, not a negative, feeling from being challenged...I think
that most of us who are still here wouldn't be if we felt intimidated. Maybe
those are some of the women who got weeded out. (Female white engineering
non-switcher)

I raised four sons, and we are more like friends. So I interact with young male
students like I would with my own children. Some of them have difficulty with
me...others seem to find me interesting...a few seem to enjoy the relationship—they bounce things off me that don't relate to school. (Female white non-
traditional science non-switcher)

It was easier for me because I took the honors physics and electronics classes
in high school, and I was usually the only girl. In my first year at college, if
I had male lab partners, they wouldn't listen to my input, even though I knew
this stuff from high school and sometimes they didn't. But I knew you just
have to blow them off. They grow out of it. (Female white engineering non-
switcher)

Women also describe the need to let go of the tendency to be self-critical, and
the fear of being wrong[11]—both of which women develop in the process of
monitoring their performance by the internalized standards of others:

I saw less self-questioning from the men. They didn't sit there saying, 'Am I
stupid? Am I stupid?' like my women friends and I did. So they seem to
internalize it less. And they can talk back for some reason. (Female white
engineering switcher)

She always looks for her male lab partner to tell her what to do. It really
irritates me, because she's capable and knows as much as he does, but she's
afraid of being wrong. (Female white science non-switcher)

Being ready to tackle all the work of the major, including its technical aspects, and not depending on male peers and T.A.s for help in practical work is critical to developing feelings of competence, and to gaining respect. As discussed in an earlier section, women lamented their lack of exposure to hands-on technical experience at an earlier period in their lives, and highlighted their need to acquire it:

> I was a T.A. and I showed the freshmen how to palpate a cow. And once the guys saw I could get my arm in a cow and get dirty and everything, they thought that was pretty cool. But that doesn't mean that the other girls are accepted. (Female white science non-switcher)

> This one female biology T.A. was trying to fix some electronic device in the class, and one of the guys in the class just took over and made it work. Very embarrassing—but, often, we lack that hands-on background. (Female white science non-switcher)

> The way you're brought up is a big draw-back in mechanical engineering. I mean, you're not shown cars and things like that. So there's a period of catching up. It can be done, but it makes it a little more difficult. (Female white engineering non-switcher)

Finally, women felt it was important to develop a balanced view of the difficulties both men and women in these majors experienced in dealing comfortably with each other. In their friendship groups, women helped each other to 'make sense' of the nature of the gender-related problems they experienced, and to gain some detachment from them. They developed theories which helped them to discount unpleasant male behavior, and to see that it was not directed at them personally. They understood that both adult and young males had difficulty in changing the ways in which they had learned to relate to women:

> I don't think it's that they consciously don't want us there, but it's just been a male way of thinking so long that women just get married and have kids and that their lives are kept separate from the man's working life. It's hard for them because it's been built up that way for so long, so it's very hard for the women of the '90s to try to cross the line into that separated world. (Female white science switcher)

> I feel we tend to be more vulnerable coming in. If we could find a way to teach these 18 year-old women when they come in how to deal more effectively with the male environment—to take what's bad and leave it to the side. It's not so much learning how to be more focused: most women can do that anyway. But women need some stability, and that comes with knowing how to deal with the men. It's developing a more effective coping strategy. That's what I feel we need help with. (Female white engineering non-switcher)

From a focus group of women science seniors—

I've known a lot of men who thought the ability to do math was gender-linked.

Gotta be freshmen—freshmen males! (All laughing.)

Yep.

They are really obnoxious at that age. They're horrible. I don't know how they get dates!

But they grow out of it.

And I think the more women they meet...You can't get it into their heads by telling—they actually have to meet women who can hold their own.

Yeah—we're part of their education!

Women also clarified the female coping styles they felt were counter-productive, either to women themselves, or to improving the situation for women as a whole. Most of these have already been raised. They include: behaving toward men in ways that are appropriate for a sexual encounter, but not for a working relationship; discarding or denying female identity by appearance or manner; adopting the behavioral style of male peers, including competitiveness and aggression; adopting male views about the inherent intellectual inferiority of women; disdaining female company; and distrusting other women. As some women seniors understood, the greatest personal challenge of succeeding in an S.M.E. major was to graduate with an intact identity:

If you have that security, you'll do alright. I've got a year and I should get through now. If you get through as a woman, you know you've been tested—put up against the men, and you've succeeded. And you've kept your identity and still succeeded. (Female white engineering non-switcher)

I had a boss who once told me, 'Do whatever you want to do, but don't try to out-man the men.' And that has stayed with me. Because men don't respect women who try to out-man them. And I have no desire to. I like being a women. (Female white science non-switcher)

As a number of the extracts in this section indicate, non-switching women seniors felt that they had received little formal help in developing either an understanding of what they were getting into as fresh(wo)men, or the personal resources, attitudes, practical and inter-personal skills which they needed to persist. What they had learned, they had either brought to college as a legacy of their upbringing and education, or had taught themselves or each other along the way. They felt it should be possible for agencies within their institutions to address some of these learning needs in an organized and direct manner.

Bonding to Other Women in S.M.E. Majors

Female S.M.E. students realized sooner than did many of their male peers how important it was to support each other emotionally and intellectually. They were helped in this by a marked preference for collaboration over competition in their approach to learning and the accomplishment of tasks, and less commonly felt it was preferable to work alone. As we reported earlier, more men than women described failure to establish useful working peer groups as a factor in their vulnerability to switching.[12] With only a sprinkling of women in early classes, it was initially more difficult for them than for men to find each other, but the impetus to set up mutual help groups was strong and was seen as a valuable aid to persistence:

> You miss someone to have camaraderie with. The guys would all be laughing and talking, and I'd sit in the corner with my math book on my own. It wasn't until the 400-level classes that there were other girls in the class. And it was much nicer after that. Two or three of us would sit together and have someone to talk to. Actually, it was out of class too—I mean we'd laugh and joke and entertain each other during class, and help each other with small things we'd missed. And if we didn't understand something the professor said, we'd huddle and check it out with each other. (Female white science non-switcher)

> We both came from small schools and we were the only two women in mechanical and we didn't like it here. So we just stuck in together. It's very important to have somebody. (Female white engineering non-switcher)

> I lasted three years, you know. And once you get that high up in the engineering program, girls really start to bond with each other and hold onto each other. (Female white engineering switcher)

Organized common living arrangements (dormitories, houses, sororities, or room-mates) for women of the same or related S.M.E. majors were agreed to be an effective way to encourage the natural development of mutual support systems, and to off-set feelings of isolation among women:

> I didn't feel like I was a minority really, because I had a lot of friends around me who were in science or engineering—especially my room-mate. So I didn't feel out of place. (Female white engineering non-switcher)

One of the difficulties encountered by all students who liked to work in a collaborative manner was that the philosophy and structure of traditional S.M.E. pedagogy is built around individual competitive activities, and is not conducive to group learning:

> The structure of the courses are very geared in a very male way—with individual problem sets. You rarely have team projects or group things. It's all kind of directed towards doing it by yourself. I think that's a flaw because nobody in real life works in isolation—you work with other people. That's a big complaint we've all had with the department...Still, the women work together a lot. We always worked the problem sets together in small groups. (Female white engineering non-switcher)

The competitive culture also tends to undermine trust and the development of friendship in study groups:

> You don't help each other. You have a feeling that everyone in the class is against you. That describes it...I just wanna cry...One of my goals was not to become one of those cliquey girls...You don't want a study group that has people who have always been flakes, but you also don't want people who have never done anything except engineering, because you can't develop a friendship with them if you've little in common. It's so nice to be able to find a study group sometime where people aren't so competitive. (Female white engineering non-switcher)

For study groups (or any other form of collaborative learning) to work effectively and consistently, faculty must rethink the competitive basis of traditional assessment practices.

The importance of women's professional societies in providing mutual support and other services to women varied greatly from one campus to another. The Society of Women Engineers (S.W.E.) was by far the most active professional society on the seven campuses which we visited, and more women were aware of its activities than they were of any other similar group.[13] Indeed, women in engineering were commonly more aware of S.W.E.'s existence than they were of any women's program offered on their campus.

Many women had mixed feelings about the value of women-only educational and professional societies. Some women avoided them because they were felt to reinforce women's marginality, and to encourage cliquishness, or fruitless preoccupation with their problems. Those women who supported women's societies found them helpful in finding mentors, building professional networks and preparing for transition into work or graduate school. Some activities cited as useful were finding relevant work experiences, career-search preparation and job networking. Meeting women from their intended career field was a valued source of employment contacts, information about different work roles, insights into working women's ways of managing the demands of family and work and coping with gender problems at work:

> I have a mentor who is getting a Ph.D. in civil engineering. And she has a two-year old daughter. She's introduced me to a lot of the women working at Apple, and some other companies, who have children or who want children. We talk about what we're going to do, and which companies are helpful. (Female white engineering non-switcher)

> I've had many male doctors say, 'Are you sure you want to go into medicine, given the time constraints?' They *say* they tell young men also that they won't have much time to spend with their families. But I had one woman doctor who told me, 'Go ahead and do what I've done. I've had kids and I made it.' That was really the best encouragement. (Female white science non-switcher)

Some women also found companionship, and a way to put their difficulties into perspective, through these societies. As in the following instance, this kind of support worked best when it was coherently organized:

> We do pairing with incoming freshmen—someone they can ask questions of if they're having trouble with the classes or are confused about anything. It's good to realize that other people run into the same difficulties and have the same anxieties. They just need someone who's been here to let them know that they're not stupid just because they got a C on a test. (Female white engineering non-switcher)

Some societies drew women into science promotion and recruitment programs at local elementary and high schools, and offered inter-campus networks of women in their discipline. The most well-supported societies used their meetings, social gatherings and outings as an opportunity to break down social barriers between S.M.E. men and women. The most active S.W.E. chapter that we encountered included in its membership one quarter of all enrolled women engineers and a 12 percent male membership.

Women seemed to know little about any support and advisory programs available to S.M.E. women on their campus, although some of the engineering schools which we visited did have a women's program (including a women's advisor). There seemed to be no departmental programs for women in science or mathematics. Where they were aware of a women's advisory program, women tended to be wary of using it and/or skeptical of its value:

> I wouldn't be surprised if these programs were just set up for the name of it—just so the dean can claim our school is better...And you are liable to get money from the government for them, because it looks as though your department is concerned about women, minorities and equality issues. I think it's probably just a façade. (Female white engineering non-switcher)

> I haven't ever been to the women's advisor. What could she do for me? Because the problems we are facing are so hard to pin-point that it's impossible for her to do anything to help us. They wouldn't listen to her anyway. She's out there on her own too. She can't make faculty give us some attention. (Female white engineering non-switcher)

As problems which women encounter go right to the heart of the character and customary practices of S.M.E. majors, we too are doubtful that they can be ameliorated by the efforts of a lone female advisor in departments which are insufficiently addressing the cultural and structural roots of their problems. To paraphrase Albert Einstein, you cannot expect to solve a problem under the conditions which produced it.

Faculty Women and Other Role Models and Mentors

Senior women saw moving toward a more equal number of male and female faculty, T.A.s, graduate and undergraduate students in S.M.E. majors as the most important factor in making the participation of women a taken-for-granted aspect of their disciplines:

> I didn't even realize it until now—until I got to this age really—that having other women around makes a definite difference. If there were more female T.A.s and women professors and students, you would feel a lot more confident about being a woman in this degree. (Female white engineering non-switcher)

Those women who had attended all-girls' high schools where science and mathematics teachers were female, knew that it was possible to create an atmosphere in which it felt natural for girls to be competent in science and mathematics. Experiencing more women as teachers was thought to give students of both genders the opportunity to respect, admire and become comfortable with women as role models:

> It's a woman who teaches quantum mechanics, which is neat because that's cutting edge physics right now. She's also teaching the highest two courses you can take in the major. That shows some of the chauvinists in my classes that women don't necessarily go into mushy things, like astrophysics. (Female white science non-switcher)

> Having a female T.A. helps because she knows what she's doing; she's helping to teach this class. And it makes me feel like, if she can do it, so can I. I hope the men look at her and see that she's doing a great job, and that women can be as good at this as men. (Female black science non-switcher)

Women in departments with no female faculty at all experienced more difficulty than other women in believing that their own presence in the major was 'normal':

> The problem with this university is there aren't any women profs in aerospace. There's not even a female T.A.—just female secretaries. I just feel the need for a link, you know, some assurance that I'm making a wise decision by staying in this field. (Female white engineering non-switcher)

> I never had one female professor, not even a female T.A. The only time I ran into a woman was in the office. It was hard being one of so few. (Female white engineering switcher)

> I have yet to have one female professor. There aren't any here. I've had one or two female T.A.s—that's it. (Female white engineering non-switcher)

> Unless for some reason you *know* that you belong in science, and you just know that yourself, I think most women need a model. I think there would be a lot fewer women in science if you just waited for them to motivate themselves. (Female white science non-switcher)

The idea of a role model is complex and references a number of different but overlapping functions. In choosing a major, women sometimes looked to established or famous women in the field for inspiration. These were women who were "out there" and "up there," and whom they desired to emulate:

Someone that you're reading about—someone you would aspire to be like. (Female white engineering switcher)

Showing you that this woman made it—that she accomplished what she wanted—that's powerful. And knowing there's a lot of capable women out here doing what they want to do—that they are not just exceptions. (Female white science switcher)

However, the remote inspirational role model was insufficient to sustain a female S.M.E. student under stress, particularly those who found themselves in the burdensome position of having to define what it means to be a woman in their field without any blueprint to follow in their department:

I think we may be a generation too early. I certainly haven't had any role models as teachers. (Female white science non-switcher)

I kinda feel like we're pioneers. It's hard to pick out women in my specific field as role models. I feel I have to make it so others can follow in my footsteps. But it would be helpful to just know that somebody else had done it. (Female white science non-switcher)

Being taught by women faculty was important in helping undergraduate women feel more confident that they belonged in their major and that they could succeed:

It would have been good to have women you could look at and say, 'They've done this too. So can I.' (Female white science switcher)

I would have liked the experience of having a woman professor earlier—a very successful one. Like the one we have now. Because it took a lot of encouragement to put myself into the role. Seeing another woman doing it so well was, like, 'Wow!' (Female white engineering switcher)

Women students also needed to see a range of women faculty, not just the exceptionally gifted (and often sole) representative of their gender in their discipline, before they could feel that there was room for women like themselves:

We only have one women in the mechanical engineering department. But she's so flawless, I don't know if she's such a good role model because I can't achieve that! It's not possible. (Female white engineering non-switcher)

Having more women faculty also helped female students learn that there was more than one way to be a woman in science, and to observe a range of personal styles and coping techniques.

Those who had been taught by women faculty and T.A.s in college noticed that female professors used a wider range of teaching techniques than male professors, and that they broadened their curriculum to include the female experience:

> In a class on nutrition, she mentioned that to get an accurate weight women should weigh themselves at the same time every month. The guy in front of me asked, 'Why do you have to do that?' I don't think a male professor would have even raised it. In a different class, the woman professor went through the hormonal and physiological changes in human pregnancy. Amazing. It's valuable to have these issues brought into the discussion. (Female white science non-switcher)

> They bring a change of pace—they're more apt to discuss the material. The men don't diverge from their script much. And they often forget to give applications. The female professors do that more. (Female white science non-switcher)

> Well, I did have one female professor. I liked her a lot: she was interesting and funny. (Female Asian-American engineering switcher)

> Right now I have a woman teacher, who uses 'she' for 'scientists'—which is shocking, you know. We should have had her when we were freshmen, not when we're seniors. (Female white science non-switcher)

Women faculty were thought to be more open to students who approached them with requests for clarification of the class material. Whether or not this expectation was met, female students were more comfortable about approaching female teachers:

> I found that the male professors were the ones who can't teach; they are the ones who aren't open to students' questions. The teachers I've had who were female were more encouraging, and more willing to step down a little and explain things in basic terms, rather than fearing they're babying the students—which I think a lot of male professors do. (Female white science non-switcher)

> It would be better if there were more female professors. You know, I find it really tough to talk to some of these tough male professors. God, they have iron faces! (Laughs.) When I finally got a female professor, it was the first time I felt I could ask a question in class. (Female white engineering non-switcher)

> They need more women—faculty and T.A.s—in the engineering school—people that we can go to and say, 'I don't understand the way this man teaches. He's not explaining how he got from A to Z. Can you show it to me?' Because I can't ever talk to the guys about it. When I talk to men, I always find they play little games. They won't give you a direct answer. (Female white engineering switcher)

> I just felt very put off by the whole classroom experience. I was often intimidated to go and talk to them in person. There were no women faculty I

could talk to about these experiences, and no black faculty...We get a backlash from bringing up these issues, and it discourages us from even talking about them. If the university won't recognize them, it's a hard thing to have to deal with, without that supportive network. So it's a big thing to have faculty there who can relate to those experiences, and who are willing to talk about them. (Female black engineering switcher)

For the same reasons, women wished there were more female T.A.s.:

I had female T.A.s in zoology, and few anywhere else. It made a difference to how I did, because I never felt I was bothering them, and I would always ask right away when I wasn't clear about something—to keep on top of the material. The men all behaved as if you were a nuisance, and I was slow to ask. (Female white science non-switcher)

I had two female T.A.s in chemistry, and they were both down-to-earth, normal people. One was a black girl who had been in a sorority and I learned many things from her. I did by far the best in that class. Maybe women need a teacher they can relate to more. It's important to have someone to help you think, 'It's maybe okay that I'm here.' (Female white science switcher)

Women faculty were also felt to create a more egalitarian atmosphere in their class-rooms, both between students, and between teacher and learners:

Some guys try to act like they know more than you do. But they're not taken seriously when the professor's a woman. (Female white science non-switcher)

Women faculty don't show any bias toward female students, but they're certainly not gonna make you feel any less than the male students. (Female white science switcher)

However, the strongest, single need expressed by women S.M.E. majors throughout this study was the need for a personal, supportive relationship with their faculty. The gender of the teacher who met this need was less important than getting the need met:

I don't think it mattered what sex they were; it just mattered that there was someone. (Female white engineering switcher)

I've had both male and female advisors who have been really helpful and who encouraged me. (Female white science non-switcher)

I talked to my advisor a lot, and he would encourage me when I faltered. He'd say, 'Look at your good grades. You can do this!' He was backing me up right from my own performance. I saw he had the same kind of relationship with some of the guys too—just that kind of mutual respect and support. (Female white mathematics non-switcher)

One of the attributes which female students expected to find in women faculty, and believed would be easier to find if there were more women faculty was a nurturing attitude towards male and female students:

You know you're the minority, and a lot of times it didn't bother me. But there's times when you would just like to talk to someone—another woman. It makes such a difference. (Female white engineering switcher)

We wished there had been a female professor we could relate to—but there was no one. (Female white engineering switcher)

By contrast with these two switchers, the following three non-switchers were fortunate in finding the rapport and encouragement which they sought with women faculty. They cited these relationships as important in sustaining their morale:

She made it known that any female physicist who's having trouble can go to her any time. There are so few people like her—who care. (Female white science non-switcher)

She's been my support this semester without even realizing it. Even if I went to talk to her about general things, sooner or later she'd say, 'Don't worry about it. You can do it.' She's always cheering you on. Willing to do anything for you. (Female white science non-switcher)

We've developed a rapport—just with me going in and talking to her about grad school. More than with any of the other professors. If we see each other in the hall, we'll stop for a while and chat. It's made it more difficult than it need have been, not to have that until so late in the day. (Female white engineering non-switcher)

Because women expected female faculty to be more approachable and supportive than their male colleagues, they felt angry and abandoned when women faculty did not live up to this expectation:

In the middle of my sophomore year, I got my first C and it really hurt. I got it from a female professor that I had gone to asking for help. And she had tried to help me, but she was very busy, and pregnant, at the time. But it still hurt, not getting a lot of support from her. I suppose it's terrible—expecting you would get more than the boys did from a woman, but I tried. She always talked about how she was the only women in her entire field, so I guess she must be tough. But women teachers in high school had been so supportive, so it came kinda hard to me. (Female white engineering switcher)

As Etzkowitz (1994) and his colleagues (Kemelgor, 1989; Etzkowitz et al., 1992, 1995) have documented, the perspectives and actions of female science faculty tend to cluster around two very different models. The first is a "traditional male" model in which women focus competitively and instrumentally on research and career, to the exclusion of family and personal life, and which discounts 'women's issues' in science and science education. The second is a "female relational" model in which women invent alternative working styles by which they seek to accommodate or resolve the strains on identity, work roles, and the work-family balance created by wholesale adoption of traditional male definitions of the scientist's role. The female undergraduates in our sample encountered female faculty who exemplified both models. Some of the seniors discussed the historical necessity which had constrained the beleaguered minority of pioneering women scientists to embrace a traditional male style, including the belief that women have to work harder and achieve more than their male colleagues, without any guarantee of acceptance or recognition. These seniors understood that female faculty advisors who embraced this role felt they were acting in their students' best interests by refusing to nurture them, and forcing them to deal with the uncompromising male climate. They did not, however, see this as the best way forward for women in science. Rather, they looked to women faculty and working professionals to model new work role patterns which addressed both career and personal needs:

> The two women professors in biology—if it weren't for them I would never have gotten here...They told me where to go, who to call, what to do. And the advice they gave me was as right as it could be. They helped me find people doing the research I'm into, finding the right grad schools. There's such slim information and little solid advice. (Female white science non-switcher)

> Practical role models are great. To see how a person has got from A to B and has enjoyed it...It's very reassuring to see there are different opportunities, and that women have done things in different ways. And to see that women can have a good time and enjoy their families at the same time. What a relief. Not this grind of having to fit only one pattern, and never have time for yourself, or a family, or enjoying your life. (Female white science non-switcher)

Other sources of practical role models and mentors for female S.M.E. majors were professional women in their family and friendship circle, women they encountered at work and in internships, and senior women in their own major, including female graduate students. Whatever the source, the needs which mentors and role models met were consistent. The most important of these needs was to make the attainment of a professional or academic career based on an S.M.E. major, and its combination with a satisfying family, social and personal life, seem normal and achievable:

> There's one woman at work that's just completely dynamic. She's totally changed my views of what I thought a woman's role in an engineering job could be. Because she's so comfortable interacting with people. She does such a good job. She's only two years older than me. So it's very inspiring. (Female white engineering non-switcher)

> It's so much better to see something in front of you—women in the field who are raising children at the same time. You know it can be done, and seeing it makes it easier to do it. (Female white engineering switcher)

> All through high school, my boyfriend's older sister was a Double E at S---. She was telling me about her experiences, and it helped me feel, 'I can do that.' I just saw myself in the role, and that helped me make the transition. If

you can't imagine yourself in the role, it's really hard to even start on it. (Female white engineering non-switcher)

I guess I had a practical role model in my mother, who got a Ph.D. in math, married afterwards, had her kids, then started work at the university. So I've seen her do it, and know it can be done. (Female white science non-switcher)

Showing you that this woman made it. She accomplished what she wanted. And knowing that there's a lot of capable women out there doing what they want to do—that they are not just exceptions—that's powerful. (Female white science non-switcher)

We are aware that the importance of mentors and role models for women and minority students in S.M.E. majors has been the subject of considerable recent discussion, and is the basis for a number of initiatives aimed at improving the persistence of women in S.M.E. majors and graduate school. The evidence in our text data underscores the value of initiatives which increase the availability of mentors and role models for S.M.E. women. It also points to the need to help fresh(wo)men understand, and to cope with, the difficulties they are likely to encounter in S.M.E. majors. However, we would also offer the following caveat. Without honest attempts by S.M.E. departments to confront and address the norms and practices which make it difficult for women to persist—including increasing the willingness of faculty to be the main source of mentoring for all students, and the appointment of more female faculty and teaching assistants—the addition of mentoring services is unlikely to make other than marginal improvements in the attrition rates for women.

Creating a Comfortable Climate
for Women in S.M.E. Majors

The most obvious statement that can be made about the contribution which institutions and departments make to the persistence of women in S.M.E. majors is that numbers matter. The more women S.M.E. departments already have as faculty, graduate students, and current and former baccalaureate students, the more female freshmen they can expect to retain as graduating seniors or as graduate students.

In S.M.E. majors where the gender balance is either at par, or where women are a larger minority (notably, the life sciences and some mathematics departments), female S.M.E majors report the atmosphere to be more comfortable, and the problems fewer:

Well, in biology it's 50-50, so I just never felt that much of a difference. (Female white science non-switcher)

I always felt quite welcome—pretty comfortable—there were at least as many women as men in biology. (Female Asian-American science non-switcher)

All the classes I've had here have been basically 50-50, men and women. So it's not possible to think that women aren't as capable of doing math. The more it's encouraged, the better it will get for us. (Female white mathematics non-switcher)

Similarly, at the two research universities and at the small liberal arts college (which were known by their students to be actively recruiting male and female students into S.M.E. majors in more equal proportions), we found the discomforts caused by male peers and faculty to be considerably less than they were in the same disciplines on the other four campuses. However, on all campuses, in engineering, physics, chemistry and in some of the applied and earth sciences where (compared with the life sciences and mathematics) fewer women were attracted to, or survived, the introductory classes, women were more apt to wonder whether they belonged:

I was nervous already, because the men were the big majority in the class. And it wasn't that they were any better in class than me, but they were more confident. I had one girl friend who was nervous all the time, although she did incredibly well. And I worried about myself too...There were a few women in my dorm that were in other engineering classes. We'd try to stick together, but it wasn't really very easy. (Female white engineering switcher)

From a focus group of three women engineering non-switchers—

Sometimes I really doubted myself in classes...At first, I thought there were a lot of women in class; after a while, I looked around and there were only three or four. And I started wondering, 'Why aren't there any women here?' and thinking, 'Do I really belong here?' It's real....

I had that problem too.

You really start feeling that—especially in Double E classes, where there are hardly any women. You look around and see the few women and think, 'Oh, people like me!'

The more women who complete S.M.E. majors, the more they collectively teach faculty and peers how to behave towards women, and the easier it becomes for the women who follow them:

Well, it's hard. But it will get easier as the years go by just because there's more women breaking into the field. They have to start questioning the stereotypes about it having to be a man's field—a man's science. (Female white mathematics non-switcher)

I'd like to think that perhaps my going through has helped make the faculty be not quite so against women—to be more open-minded or accepting...The more women that are successful makes it easier for everybody else. (Female white mathematics non-switcher)

> I think everyone here's pretty much used to having bright women around doing math and science. It seems pretty normal. (Female white mathematics non-switcher)

Where the faculty and student body are predominantly male, the male culture is stronger, and it is more difficult for women to question, tolerate, or change the atmosphere:

> There just aren't that many girls. It keeps it very clubby. (Female white science switcher)

> The fact that so many of them are men is a negative in the end, even if they don't directly say anything to you are about being a woman. Being all-men kind of ruins something for you. It takes something away from your education, compared with other majors. It could have been so much better. (Female white science non-switcher)

It would seem unreasonable to expect the existing white male hegemony in the S.M.E. academy and in its associated professions to be transformed by feeding into its student body increasing numbers of talented 18 year-old women who are totally unprepared for the difficulties they are likely to face. Encouraging more girls to develop their science and mathematics abilities and more young women to enter S.M.E. majors is important. However, it is also important to greet their entrance to college with a faculty which is more welcoming and supportive of their talents than is currently the case, and which looks more like the rest of the population. As some of our graduating seniors clearly understood, the numbers issue is essentially a power issue:

> I had no women teachers here. When I went to interview at medical schools, out of 10 schools with five people on each panel, I only had three women interview me—and one of those was a student. That's scary—all those men deciding who gets into medical school. (Female white science non-switcher)

We understand that both we, and our student informants, may be adopting an over-simple view of gender climate change. We entirely accept the caveat offered by Etzkowitz (1994) and others that while the presence of larger numbers of female faculty and students can promote a climate change which is beneficial to women in some situations, in other institutions, it provokes male hostility, resistance, conflict and power-struggles in which women are the losers, and "critical mass" is not achieved. This is not, of course, an argument against further attempts to bring the sex ratio in academic and occupational science and engineering closer to parity.

In departments where the chairs and senior administrators were actively working to change practices and attitudes which make it harder for women to bond to their major, the women's level of satisfaction was markedly higher. Setting the tone from the top clearly matters. In one department of physics and one College of Engineering where faculty had made strong commitments to increased academic and personal support for all students, and to a more interactive teaching style, both male and female seniors reported good experiences with faculty:

> You hear stories about engineering professors who don't want women in their classes. I've never encountered anybody like that. Every professor I've ever met here was delighted to have more women in his class. (Female white engineering non-switcher)

> I must say, I'm really pleased with the policy they show here. I've experienced problems in jobs, but not here. (Female white engineering non-switcher)

> I think the professors are encouraged to encourage women, and they do anything they can to help you. I went to talk to a couple of my professors before I left mechanical engineering and they said, 'We think you should stay in the program, and this is why....' There are still some men here who have very backward views of women. But there are a lot of men here who are very grown-up, and think that women have the right to be in these classes and treat them as absolute equals. I would say most are like that now. (Female white engineering switcher)

> For the most part, we feel they're happy with the fact that women have come into the field. I've never gotten the feeling other than that I'm doing well, and even that I'm a bit more original than the men. I think most of the girls have that feeling, if not consciously, unconsciously. (Female white engineering non-switcher)

> The professors went out of their way to be friendly and smile, and to make me feel comfortable about asking questions. Starting out like that, I had no problems as I moved into the upper levels—and I met girls who had also had good experiences. (Female white science non-switcher)

As the last speaker indicates, once the commitment to change is made, and women begin to feel the benefits of it, the effects are cumulative. Encouraging faculty to be more pro-active in their support of young women, also allows a more nurturing attitude toward young men.

An important task for departmental leaders is the development of a student culture that is intolerant of rude or discriminatory behavior, and in which the social and working relationships of young men and women settle into more comfortable patterns:

> The women in the physics class I took last spring seemed very, very confident in the labs, and in their ability to speak out. I'm sure it has a lot to do with some of the changes that have gone on in the department. I really noticed the change in the way women behaved—and how men spoke about them. (Male white science switcher)

> If a professor says something stupid about women in class, you will hear students making noises in the audience. It's a sensitive issue. It's taken very seriously here. (Female white science switcher)

> In my early classes, the guys treated me as an equal. I was better in physics than them, for the most part, but didn't experience any problems because of that...In this department, it's normal for the girls to date physics majors. In fact, they're inundated with offers. My boyfriend right now is the first person I've gone out with that wasn't in physics—he's in math. (Female white science non-switcher)

> My friends and I would love to see more women in their classes. There are so few of them, they're almost targets—the competition here is for access to them—for dates, I mean. In class, they always attract a crowd. (Male white science switcher)

In departments and colleges where many of the women reported difficulties, they also reported that individual faculty could make a difference to their determination to continue, despite the attitude of colleagues or the prevailing climate of their department:

> I think one person can make a difference. We've got a professor that really goes out of his way to make women welcome. Just that one smiling face—that one person who goes out of their way—makes a heck of a difference in everybody's overall attitude. (Male white engineering non-switcher)

> With Dr. M— it's almost a plus sometimes to be a woman—that you are more of an achiever because you've made it in a man's field—therefore you are bright enough to be here. That's the attitude I've always got from him. (Female white engineering non-switcher)

> He's one of the best—a good teacher. He was fair to me. He busted my chops, but he was fair. I worked hard, and he knew it. And he helped me. He knew when I was doing things wrong. (Female white engineering non-switcher)

> There's an aerospace professor who uses feminine pronouns in his lectures—'she' instead of 'he.' He's a real exception, but he creates a great atmosphere for everyone. He tells you about all kinds of meetings in his class, and encourages the women and the men to join S.W.E. or go to their activities. He really makes a difference. (Female white engineering non-switcher)

In comparing the range of faculty and peer attitudes and behaviors reported by current and former female S.M.E. majors on all seven campuses, we noted considerable variation between departments on the same campuses. However, across all S.M.E. majors, one campus stood out from the rest as the most comfortable for women—the large public midwestern research university. At the opposite end of the spectrum, two campuses, namely, the two public western universities, contained the highest proportion of reports of discomfort by women in all S.M.E. disciplines. In discussing the reasons for these campus-wide variations with our informants, women felt that the prevailing local culture also exerts strong influence on the level of acceptance, civility and support experienced by both women and students of color in S.M.E. majors:

> Yes, the atmosphere here is very inviting for women. I think, basically, this state is pretty much a liberal state, and the heart of that thinking is right here at the university. (Female white engineering non-switcher)

From a focus group of male engineering switchers—

> Oh, maybe it's the whole area. There are more opportunities for women, and people here are more open to women in non-traditional roles, and there's a trickle-down effect to the university.

> And a lot of the most powerful people in the state are women—for example, the president of the city council is a black woman; the next Speaker of the State House is a woman. All five men who ran for governor last fall had women running-mates—they all had 'prom dates' was the running joke.

> People just aren't as rude as in some other areas. There's something nicer about people here.

We should make it clear that all of the problems which we have described and illustrated in this chapter were experienced to a greater or lesser degree by women on all of the campuses, and in all of the departments which we visited.

Larger Issues and Unanswered Questions

Throughout this discussion, we have emphasized the relationship between academic and non-academic factors as a way to account for the disproportionate loss of young women from S.M.E. majors. Explanatory theories based on individual attributes of female students (such as their performance record), or upon single elements in their social situation (such as the level of gender discrimination they do, or do not, experience), are inadequate to the task. It is the translation of such factors by the people to whom they apply into a particular view of their situation which determines the nature of their response to them. What we have sought to understand here is: what shapes the nature of the experience which young women encounter on entry to S.M.E. majors; what they bring to it from their socialization experiences; what sense they make of their situation; how (and with whom) they achieve this; and which elements in the process of interaction between female and male students, their faculty, friends and parents, contribute to the actions taken by women in S.M.E. majors? There are still aspects of these processes which are puzzling, but we offer what we have found in the expectation that others will investigate further.

It is important to bear in mind that the processes which we have traced in the accounts of these students are part of a broader debate about male and female roles and identity which is ongoing in most other social spheres. We have a scant thirty-year experience during which a large proportion of the female population has moved into non-traditional roles where neither they, nor their male colleagues, have any ready-made rules by which to explain the new situation to themselves, or to guide them in relating to each other. We must expect that something more subtle and complex than the level of ability of women, and the level of courtesy expressed toward them by men, is needed to explain their mutual difficulties. These difficulties are all the greater because, within the broad male hegemony of academe, S.M.E. majors have evolved a highly refined social system for the moral and intellectual education of young men which, in many critical aspects, stands in contradiction to the socialized expectations of young women. Bright young women with an interest in science and mathematics cannot simply be recruited into the existing S.M.E. structure without willingness on the part of the disciplines they enter to tolerate a high wastage rate. Programs for women which seek to address attrition solely by reconciling the relatively few women who use them to a learning environment which is inherently opposed to the needs of female S.M.E. students as a whole, are doomed from their inception. Those S.M.E. faculty who are serious about making the education they offer as available to their daughters as to their sons are, we posit, facing the prospect of dismantling a large part of its traditional pedagogical structure, along with the assumptions and practices which support it.

Our observations about the ways in which women have learned to learn also raise the difficult issue of whether, and how, to change the traditional ways in which girls are socialized and educated. Even if we knew how to teach girls to be more independent in their learning style, we must first consider whether it is desirable to change the collective identity of one gender group so they can more easily be fitted into educational settings which reflect the socialized learning styles of the other gender. Furthermore, some aspects of the learning environment in which women feel most comfortable—particularly cooperative, interactive and experiential learning contexts—are also congenial to many young men, and encourage the development of skills and attitudes which have increasing value in occupational and social contexts beyond academe. For those faculty who question the need for institutional change, the 'problem of women' may need to be reframed. Moving pedagogy from a focus on teaching to a focus on learning, and from selecting for talent to nurturing it, will dis-proportionately increase the persistence rate of able women in S.M.E. majors. It also promises to reduce the loss of able male students.

These are necessarily slow and difficult tasks. In the interim, it is clearly irresponsible not to assist the inexperienced and outnumbered young women who enter S.M.E. majors to understand the nature of the difficulties they encounter, nor to support their search for ways to cope with them. Helping women to understand what holds them back is the first step in moving beyond those barriers. It is clear from our informants' accounts that some of the constraints come from within. However, we cannot simply blame the victims. Women's confusion and loss of confidence arise from their attempt to apply learned ways of responding in a situation where these do not apply. While the process of structural change is underway, women will continue to need help to gain insights into the inner- and the outer-dimensions of their impediments, and strategies and support to confront them.

One of the more puzzling pieces of our data is women's resistance to the theory that the rudeness, hostility, taunting, discounting, or other inappropriate behavior experienced from their male peers (or more rarely from faculty) is an important element in women's alienation, isolation, and loss of confidence, and indirectly, in their decisions to leave. It is, we suspect, women's own discounting of the significance of unpleasant male behavior which makes its actual significance so difficult for researchers to interpret. On the one hand, it would be hard not to imagine that the regular experience of unpleasant behavior from one's peers would have some sort of negative impact on motivation. On the other hand, the women themselves wanted us to understand that this had lower significance for persistence than their difficulties in getting personal attention from faculty.

We have two kinds of tentative explanation for women's down-playing of inappropriate male behavior as a factor in their diminished self-confidence. The first refers back to our general observation that the problems of women in S.M.E. majors need to be seen in the broader context of the highly transitional state of gender relationships in society overall. As part of our slow self-education, we have only recently come to understand the role played by the normalization of abuse in preserving the stability of patriarchal systems. In order for one half of the population to accept dominance by the other, many of the techniques by which that dominance is reinforced have to be treated as 'normal'. Part of the traditional socialization of women has, therefore, been the development of a high degree of tolerance for behavior which is increasingly being redefined as 'abusive'. At a lesser level, this includes 'covering' and 'making excuses' for rude or insensitive male behavior in order to preserve the appearance of normal social or domestic relations. At a serious level, women often stay in physically abusive relationships beyond the margins of personal safety. Theoretically, the learned behaviors which produce these different outcomes stem from the same source. When reading women's accounts of offensive male behavior, one might well wonder why most women do not confront those young men who tell derogatory jokes or make insulting comments in their presence. Why do they not make it clear that such behavior is offensive and unacceptable to them? The answer may be that it does not occur to them that they can do this, and that they do not know how. While boys are taught to 'stand up for themselves', girls are encouraged to diffuse or smother situations with a potential for conflict as quickly and quietly as possible. Those few women who did confront their tormentors reported that this had, indeed, settled the matter, and that they had less trouble in the future. However, they seemed mystified by the efficacy of their actions. They seemed not to understand that they had acted as a man would act, and that other men tend to respond positively to this. As we indicated earlier in this chapter, women who had persisted credited their survival partly to the development of assertiveness in dealing with both faculty and peers.

When talking about how they responded to rude peer behavior, female students made comments such as, "It's best to just ignore them," "Reacting just makes it worse," and "They'll grow out of it." Women who felt angry expressed it to each other, rather than directly with the men concerned. In a situation where the power differential is so much to their disadvantage, and there are no guidelines for responding to the situation, women in S.M.E. majors appear to fall back on learned ways of discounting abuse in the exercise of male power. Assuming the traditional female responsibility as 'peace maker' comes at the price of tolerating an abusive situation, and in this case, of offering some rationale for that accommodation to the researcher who questions it.

A second possible explanation, which is not inconsistent with the first, derives from games theory. The outsider who wishes to become a player in a game which is already underway, with a group who knows the rules, are more skilful players, and to which he or she does not belong, has to accept admission tests—even if they seem silly or arbitrary. Although our women informants described the constant implicit demand of their male peers that they 'prove themselves' as foolish and irrelevant—as, indeed, for women, it is—they nevertheless were drawn into proving behavior. They felt constantly forced to demonstrate their 'right' to belong, and part of their motivation to work hard, or harder than the men, was a vain attempt to force this concession. Those women who adjusted their presentation of self to a parody of male style, can be seen as seeking to side-step admission tests by claiming group affinity. Paradoxically, while disputing that unpleasant male behavior bothers them enough to undermine their motivation, the female minority tacitly accepts the rules of the game imposed by the dominant group. Again, the researcher's inquiry threatens to expose the evidence of this compromise.

Our understanding of what looks like denial of the significance of an abusive situation is clearly limited. The issue emerged from our analysis of the transcripts some time after we had left the field, and there was no opportunity to return to our informants for clarification. It is, however, important to tease out the dynamics of this interaction in order to design interventions which help women to understand and cope more effectively with the inner- and outer-dimensions of their problems in S.M.E. majors.

Notes

1. Lipson's study of Harvard-Radcliffe women in science (discussed in Tobias, 1990) illustrates the cross-over into women's college experience of negative self-perceptions developed in childhood/adolescence. Lipson found that women who persisted to graduation tended to evoke external explanations for any difficulties they experienced in science classes. Those who left tended to cite their own inadequacies as the cause.

2. The stronger tendency of women to be drawn into S.M.E. majors through the influence of others was also found by Strenta et al. (1993).

3. This finding runs counter to the theory (proposed by Hall [1985]), and subsequently repeated in a variety of reports and articles, that the loss of women from S.M.E. majors is created or exacerbated by foreign-born male faculty or graduate students who, "may have a great deal of difficulty in perceiving or treating women students as anything but inferior intellectually, and as sexual objects" (ibid., pp. 43-45).

4. Feelings of pressure, isolation, powerlessness, and the constant need to prove themselves, were reported in the Stanford and M.I.T. studies of graduate women in science, and in the Illinois Valedictorian Project. These problems, which are discussed in Widnall (1988), do not diminish beyond graduate school, but are a permanent feature of the working lives of professional women in science.

5. We noted that male science and mathematics seniors planning advanced degrees had begun to take on attitudes which are considered appropriate for their future profession. They were more apt than other S.M.E. seniors to explain switching in terms of incompetence, or unwillingness to work hard, and to express the belief that the weed-out system was a good way to find the best people.

6. Costa (1993) also interprets the ritualistic elements she observes in undergraduate S.M.E. education as being part of a rite of passage. She does not, however, distinguish between the reactions of young men and women to the transitions demanded of them, and may also underestimate the extent to which young men are aware that the "tests" they undergo are part of a process encouraging alignment with dominant traditions of thought, belief and action in the scientific community. We found the testing process and its functions semi-overt to the men, but totally obscure to the women, until, as surviving seniors, some women came to perceive its meaning.

7. The stronger tendency of women to be drawn into S.M.E. majors through the influence of others was also found by Strenta et al. (1993).

8. Manis et al. (1989) also found the "impersonality" of science and mathematics classes to be more problematic for women than for men.

9. This is consistent with Strenta et al.'s (1993) finding that the importance of future family matters correlates positively with persistence for men, and negatively for women.

10. As discussed in our notes on research methods, we regret, given our constraints on the number and location of campuses in our inquiry, that we were unable to talk with students at a wider sample of institutions of different mission, type and location.

11. Dislike, or fear, of being 'wrong' was also noted among female students by Dweck (1986) and Kimball (1989).

12. Among switchers overall, 24.7 percent of men (compared with 9.7 percent of women) described themselves as working in a solitary, unsupported way, and 15.7 percent of men (compared with 7.5 percent of women) ascribed at least some part of their switching decisions to failure to seek out appropriate peer help.

13. Had we chosen a different set of institutions, Women In Engineering Programs (W.I.E.P.) and chapters of the Association for Women in Science (A.W.I.S) were also likely to have been prominent.

6

Issues of Race and Ethnicity

In this chapter, we consider the causes and consequences of S.M.E. attrition from the perspective of those whose loss rates are the highest—students of color. National data for the 1980s (Morrison & Williams, 1993) indicate that only 35.6 percent of students of color entering engineering programs complete degrees in that field, compared with 68.4 percent for white students. Of those who continued into their sophomore year, only 56.7 percent of students of color graduated, compared with 87.4 percent for white sophomores. Thus, the relative graduation rate for students of color in engineering is about half (52%) that of white students. The situation is no better in the sciences. Between freshman and junior years, 65 percent of students of color entering science or mathematics left their major, compared with 37 percent of white students (*Science*, 1992, p. 1209). Switching to non-S.M.E. majors accounts for only part of the loss: half of the students of color who leave engineering drop out of college altogether (Campbell, 1993).

Concern about this situation has generated considerable effort to recruit more people of color into the sciences. Over the past 20 years, the National Science Foundation alone has spent approximately $1.5 billion to increase minority participation in science, and two major programs at the National Institutes of Health have invested $675 million in the same endeavor (*Science*, 1992, p. 1185). In terms of recruitment, these initiatives have been effective in dramatically increasing the enrollment of blacks, Hispanics, and native Americans. Data from the Astins' longitudinal study (1993) indicates that, upon entry, 27.3 percent of white students, 52.6 percent of Asian-American students, and approximately 33 percent of black, Hispanic and native American students choose an S.M.E. major. The increase in engineering enrollment by freshmen of color is particularly striking, with a steady increase from 4.4 percent in 1973 to 12.6 percent in 1993. However, the outcome in terms of retention for students of color other than Asian-Americans is very discouraging: although the number entering increases, the revolving door out of S.M.E. majors merely spins faster. In engineering, for example, the enrollment of freshmen of color has increased five-fold over the last 20 years, while attrition rates remain unchanged (cf., Brown, 1994, 1995; *Science*, 1992; O.T.A., 1988). Across all S.M.E. majors, while white students have an attrition rate of 27.3 percent, and Asian-American students only 17 percent, about half of black and native American students, and two-thirds of Hispanic students leave their S.M.E. majors (Astin & Astin, ibid.). Rates of minority attrition for all majors are also high, and losses are greatest among the most able black and Hispanic students (Ware, Steckler & Leserman, 1985; Lipson & Tobias, 1991; Tinto, 1993), although fewer of the highest-ability black and Hispanic undergraduates choose S.M.E. majors (Baker, 1994)

The question of why students from particular racial or ethnic groups have higher S.M.E. attrition rates than white students has not been satisfactorily answered. Hilton, Hsia, Solorzano, and Benton (1989), and Clewell, Anderson and Thorpe (1992) have suggested that students of color may not realize that academic preparation and planning for careers based on the sciences need to begin as early as junior high school. Students of color are more likely than white students to be under-prepared, especially in mathematics, and this is discernable among Hispanic and black students as early as age nine (Betz, 1990). Lack of preparation in algebra and geometry is a barrier to college entry and persistence, not only in the sciences, but in all majors (Pelavin Associates, 1990 for the College Board). In the case of Hispanic students, achievement in high school mathematics is increased by access to bilingual education (Rios Rodriguez, 1992). Students of color also have less access than white students to information about careers based on science and technology. They are also more likely than white students to develop negative attitudes toward mathematics and science in the junior high school years (Clewell et al., 1992), and not see their relevance to everyday life (Thomas, 1984). Inadequate preparation, and thus, the chance to develop interest in the sciences, are primarily created by a high level of structured inequality nation-wide in pre-college education. This is further reinforced by the common belief that, contrary to the international evidence, mathematical ability is limited to relatively few students who are predominantly male, white, or Asian-American (Beane, 1985; Mullis, Dossey, Owen, & Phillips, 1991).

The small number of students of color to be found in S.M.E. classes in itself creates difficulties for those few who enter them: students of color lack peers, faculty role models and mentors (Brown, 1994; Thomas, Clewell & Pearson, 1992). As Pearson observes (*Science*, 1992), because they are forced to "learn in isolation," students of color do not have the same educational experience as white male peers. Black women, in particular, complain they are often the only minority students (and are often, the only woman) in their S.M.E. classes (Brown, 1994). Their self-confidence is also undermined by the perception that white faculty and students regard students of color (especially black students) as of lower ability. Black students see faculty as unapproachable and report that other students exclude them from study and lab groups (Brown, 1994; McBay, 1986). Because students of color often enter science classes with a narrower career focus than their more broadly educated white peers, they may be more impatient with faculty's failure to apply theoretical class materials to practical problems and are more apt to lose interest (Collea, 1990).

Along with inadequate academic preparation, insufficient financial resources (i.e., to complete an S.M.E. degree) have been consistently identified as among the most serious contributors to the loss of students of color from S.M.E. majors (Bond, Lebodl & Thomas, 1977; Cox, 1982; Mohrman, 1987; Rotberg, 1990; Rodriguez, 1993; Mortenson, 1995). The family responsibilities of many students of color exacerbate their financial problems. These responsibilities, which are more common among students of color than white students, force role conflicts with their academic commitments (Tinto, 1987; Rodriguez, 1993).

Explanations for the failure of students of color to enter or remain in S.M.E. majors in representative numbers are somewhat patchy, and the relative importance of factors—for particular minority groups, or for all students of color—is unclear. There are, however, lay theories for the phenomenon of minority under-representation based on presumptions of racial and ethnic differences in individual motivation, rather than on socio-economic factors, including differential access to educational resources. As with the under-representation of women, the beliefs of high school teachers and counselors and college faculty about the reasons for minority under-representation in the sciences may, in themselves, be regarded as contributing to the problem. For example, Treisman (1992) asked over 1,000 S.M.E. faculty to explain why they thought (non-Asian-American) students of color were at greater risk of leaving their majors than white students. The most frequent of the theories that emerged posited 'a motivation gap' between white and Asian-American students, and students of color—who were assumed to be less well motivated. Students of color were also thought to enter university with less high school science and mathematics, and substantially lower S.A.T. scores, than white and Asian-American entrants. Faculty also believed that minority families provided less moral support, lacked understanding of the higher education system, and that their poorer economic circumstances adversely affected academic performance. As Treisman observes, each of these theories assign responsibility to factors beyond the control of universities or their faculty. Some of our findings with respect to high school preparation and financial difficulties appear to lend support to these faculty explanations for minority attrition rates. However, as we shall discuss, the reasons are complex and require considerable qualification.

One important aim of this study was to learn what distinguishes the experiences of students of color from that of white males which might account for the greater difficulty of minority students in persisting in S.M.E. majors. As the interviews and data analysis progressed, it became increasingly clear that differences among and within different racial and ethnic groups have greater significance for the chances of success than had previously been assumed. As we shall illustrate, failure to take such differences into account may, in and of itself, explain why programs intended to recruit or support "minority students" have not improved their chances of survival in S.M.E. majors.

A total of 88 students of color (i.e., 26 percent of our total sample) were interviewed on seven campuses: 27 were black, 20 were Hispanic, 35 were Asian-American, and six were native American. A breakdown by ethnicity, and status (switcher or non-switcher) in engineering and the sciences (including mathematics) appears in *Appendix A* (Figure A.4). Not every student of color in our sample was born in the United States, but all had attended U.S. high schools. Switchers were almost evenly divided between engineering (24) and science or mathematics (28) majors; persisters in these disciplinary groups were 16 and 20, respectively. The low representation of native American students in our sample is a direct result of their general under-representation in S.M.E. majors: only 0.8 percent of the U.S. higher education student population is native American. At two of the institutions visited, there were no current or former S.M.E. majors who were native American. Nevertheless, the experiences and problems of the six native Americans who were interviewed proved distinctively different from all other students of color. Finally, we decided to include Asian-American students (from several different ethnic groups) in our sample. This decision was based on findings from our preliminary (Hewitt & Seymour, 1991) study which indicated that Asian-American students experience a unique set of problems in S.M.E. majors that have been ignored, both in the literature, and by the institutions they attend.

Comparisons of Students of Color with White Students

It was also a strong finding of our preliminary (1991) study that any statement purporting to summarize the experience and attrition risks of all non-white S.M.E. students tends to distort and mislead. "Minority programs" based on presumption of needs common to all "minorities" tend to founder, quite largely, because they do not address the needs of specific racial and ethnic groups. We have been careful, therefore, to describe the situation of students of color by group, and to avoid global generalizations about "all minorities." This said, there appear to be some risk factors which transcend racial and ethnic differences, and which distinguish students of color from white peers. Table 6.1 compares (by rank and percentage) the 10 reasons for switching most frequently cited by students of color overall with the same 10 factors for white switchers. We found strong differences between the two student groups in seven of these 10 reasons. Students of color were much more likely to cite the following factors as reasons for switching:

TABLE 6.1 Comparison of White and Non-White Switchers in the 10 Most Highly Ranked Factors Contributing to Switching Decisions.

Issue	Non-White Switchers (%)	White Switchers (%)
Non-S.M.E. major offers better education/more interest	37	42
Reasons for choice of S.M.E. major prove inappropriate	35	6
Shift to more appealing non-S.M.E. career option	33	23
Conceptual difficulties with one or more S.M.E. subject(s)	31	5
Lack of/loss of interest in S.M.E.: "turned off science"	29	49
Rejection of S.M.E. careers/ associated lifestyles	27	30
Inadequate high school preparation in basic subjects/study skills	25	11
Discouraged/lost confidence due to low grades in early years	23	23
Poor teaching by S.M.E. faculty	21	42
Curriculum overloaded, fast pace overwhelming	19	41

* inappropriate reasons for their choice of an S.M.E. major (34.6% compared with 6.1%)

* conceptual difficulty with one or more S.M.E. subject(s) (30.8% compared with 5.3%)

* inadequate high school preparation in basic subjects and study skills (25% compared with 10.7%)

A fourth factor—a shift to a more appealing S.M.E. career option—was cited slightly more often by students of color (32.7%) than by white students (22.9%). By contrast, white students more commonly cited the following as factors in their switching decisions:

* lack or loss of interest in their S.M.E. major (48.9% compared with 28.9%)

* poor teaching by S.M.E. faculty (42.0% compared with 21.2%0)

* curriculum overload and fast pace (41.2% compared with 19.2%)

We shall draw upon the text data to explore the reasons for these differences. However, it is important to highlight one dominant theme—the distinctive tendency of students of color to blame themselves rather than departments, faculty or institutions, for all, or most, of their difficulties. As we shall illustrate, the process of switching is especially painful for students of color, and often has long-term consequences which are more serious for them than for their white peers. As with women (with the possible exception of black women), the decision to leave an S.M.E. major is often preceded by loss of confidence in the ability to do science.

Inappropriate Choice
        Choice of an S.M.E. major for reasons which subsequently proved inappropriate was not (at 6.1 percent for both male and female white switchers) a major contributor to switching decisions among white students. Inappropriate choice was, however, mentioned as a problem by 94 percent of all students of color, by 34.6 percent as a reason for switching, and was one of the strongest overall differences between white and non-white S.M.E. students. An important element in inappropriate choice was the active influence of others, which was also mentioned more often by students of color who switched (and by all women switchers) than by those who persisted (13.5 percent for the former and 2.7 percent of the latter). Some misguided choices arose directly from efforts to recruit more students of color into S.M.E. fields. Some students clearly had been encouraged to enter majors for which they had insufficient interest, preparation or understanding:

I was really motivated by the American Indian Science and Engineering Society. They put me through some programs emphasizing science and math. And that increased my motivation to try harder in school because Indians see that, in order to be competitive with the outside world, they have to bring that technology back to the reservation. And that's what I really wanted to do, but now that's changed because of my failing in those classes. (Male native American science switcher)

Some black students had been actively recruited and offered scholarships by schools of engineering. These were powerful inducements, even for students who were unsure about what this choice would require—either in terms of course work or the actual work of engineering:

I was set on being an electrical engineer because several engineering schools recruited me and were ready to pay whatever it took to go or to get me through. That's how my mind was made up. (Male black engineering switcher)

I was associated with Inroads, which is a non-profit organization. It gets corporations to sponsor talented minorities in business and technology. They actively recruited in the high schools. When they first came in 10th grade I was going to be a journalism major. They've been really instrumental as far as deciding my career choices. (Male black engineering switcher)

I was recruited by the minority engineering program. I hadn't picked a specific major at the time. I was in a college prep school and they came out to interview and then they brought me on campus to see the engineering school. (Male black engineering switcher)

Families and communities also played a significant role in encouraging students of color to make choices which reflected social rather than personal career goals:

I feel the need to explain myself to the people back home in practical terms. They see value in the careers that can be practiced on the reservation. Only, you know, doctor, lawyer, teacher, nurse, engineer. It makes it easier to enter these majors, and it would be harder to study humanities and social sciences if that was your inclination. (Male native American science non-switcher)

Although well-intentioned, those who encouraged students of color to choose an S.M.E. major were often mistaken about students' actual interest and abilities, or had limited understanding of what level of ability or preparation was required. Some parents and high school teachers confused students' expressions of interest in mathematics and science with excellence in these subjects.

Many students of color had also been encouraged by their families and schools to select careers that would provide a secure future. Hispanic students reported that, because engineering was seen in their community as synonymous with success, they had been encouraged to pursue engineering to the exclusion of other possibilities:

> In high school the emphasis really was more for minorities to do well in math and science and to go on and become engineers. Looking back, it really didn't reflect all the choices that you have in college. (Male Hispanic engineering switcher)

> The advisors in the Martin Luther King program had their own ideas on majors—no matter what I liked, they wanted me to go into this. One advisor, he'd always ask me when I was going to take my chemistry classes so I could get into engineering. And every time I'd say, 'Well, I don't want to go into engineering.' (Male Hispanic science switcher)

Compliance with family views of appropriate careers was a distinctive aspect of Asian-American students' choices. Indeed, few Asian-American students chose their major without reference to family priorities. Job security, opportunities for advancement and following the same occupational paths as parents were stressed over personal interest in particular academic subjects. Respect for their parents' wishes, and a strong desire to realize them, were major reasons why Asian-American S.M.E. majors were less likely to switch than any other group of students. However, the dominance of family over individual choice among these students was a major contributor to high levels of dissatisfaction among Asian-American non-switchers:

> They were maybe doing it for their parents. Their parents always said, 'My son is going to be a doctor,' 'My son is going to be a scientist.' But when you have to sit here, receive these grades and stay in these difficult classes, *you have to want to do it*. It can't be for anyone else. (Male black science non-switcher)

> I put natural sciences in my application to appease that family drive. There's a family prejudice towards the math and sciences. (Male Asian-American science switcher)

> A lot of Asians got here through being good engineers, which is something America's always needed. Engineers move here because they can have a very good life. A huge part of the reason I chose the major was that my parents are science people. (Male Asian-American engineering switcher)

> A lot of Asians who are starting as pre-meds probably are in it half-heartedly. If their interest is not confirmed, and if they could resolve the problem with their family, they would get out. They can't face their parents and say, 'Well, I don't want to be a doctor. I want to be a writer.' I know a lot of people who are really miserable over this. (Male Asian-American science switcher)

Because the expectation that Asian-American students should major in the sciences is also stressed by teachers and peers, the resultant self-limiting perspective is particularly strong among Asian-American students:

I was a fool. Based on the courses that I took in high school I should have seen which area interested me the most...I mean, you cannot depend on other people to choose your major. (Female Asian-American science switcher)

As with women of all racial and ethnic groups, entering S.M.E. majors largely to please others, or for pragmatic, materialist, or even altruistic reasons, exposes students to the risk of leaving S.M.E. majors once they come to appreciate what it takes to complete them.

Inadequate High School Preparation

One quarter (25%) of the students of color in our sample reported inadequate high school preparation as a reason for switching, compared with only 10.7 percent of white switchers. In addition, nearly one-third (30.8%) of those students of color who switched reported conceptual difficulties in their S.M.E. classes, compared with only 5.3 percent of white students. As Treisman's (1992) survey indicates, many S.M.E. faculty perceived non-Asian students of color as insufficiently prepared for college-level S.M.E. work. This impression was confirmed by those students of color who, soon after entry to their first S.M.E. classes, discovered they were much less well prepared than many white peers. This discovery deeply undermined these students' confidence in their ability to continue:

> The education on a reservation school just doesn't have the resources of an off-reservation school. I knew the quality of education wasn't as good, but I just hoped that whatever I had learned, I could apply here—but obviously not. (Male native American mathematics switcher)

> I went to a big inner-city school, and they couldn't tell me anything about college prep. I remember asking my counselor about some of the courses I thought I needed to prepare for college and he said not to worry about them, so I didn't take them. Unfortunately, one of them was calculus. (Female black engineering switcher)

> Well, I'm from a bad high school—it's considered the worst in the area. But I don't blame the teachers. We had some of the best teachers. I mean, my algebra teacher was amazing. They would start you low where you understood everything and work you up little by little. But they had to take the time to pull everyone along together, so I never really did get the challenge. I was always pulling As, and that felt good, but I always knew it was too easy. There wasn't any A.P. or honors math. (Male black science switcher)

> When I took my introductory math courses I was sitting by people who had already taken the calculus series in high school. When they came here they were just sitting through the courses all over again. So they're maxing out because they've had it before and we're learning it for the first time—and all within 10 weeks. That was the hardest thing. (Male black science non-switcher)

The only thing I was ready for was the calculus. I had a very good calculus teacher. Everything else was new. My first year here I was very upset because my first engineering course was resistors. And these other students knew all of those components 'cause they had a course that taught them that in high school. I was very much upset because I don't think I was prepared for college. I don't think our high school was good at all. (Female Hispanic engineering switcher)

There was just so much that I didn't know. I felt like I wasn't even in the same game as everyone else. (Male black engineering switcher)

Some students of color who knew before they entered college that their high schools had been deficient in science and mathematics preparation did not expect to do well in college. Feelings of inadequacy set in early, and many of these students left before learning whether or not they could actually have surmounted their difficulties:

A lot of people had physics that was beyond what I had in high school, so I was really insecure about whether I belonged here. I dropped a math course and went down to a lower math course right off the bat...I remember the day that I dropped. We had a problem set due that day, and we were all sitting around working last minute, and I remember everyone was really going at it kind of bouncing off each other and I was thinking, 'I'm just not at this level, and I need to sit down by myself and read this slowly.' I wasn't at the level where I knew these things intuitively. And I remember thinking, 'This is horrible.' But it turns out that I was doing pretty good. I had a B when I dropped the class, but I didn't know that. (Female black engineering switcher)

Under-Prepared and Over-Confident. Many of the students of color that we interviewed came from predominantly minority high schools where they had been outstanding students. However, those who had excelled in sub-standard or even average high schools faced an uphill battle in the competitive culture of the university. They were shocked to discover that they had over-estimated their capabilities. Because they had been led to believe that their knowledge and skills were greater than they actually were and had been treated as special by their high school teachers, these students were doubly at risk: they entered S.M.E. classes both under-prepared and over-confident in their ability to undertake them. They were at a loss to comprehend how, in a single semester, they could have gone from the top of their high school class to the bottom of college mathematics or physics classes:

The high school that I went to wasn't one of the best, but I was tops in my class. I graduated student valedictorian of the class and I had what they called 'academically talented' chemistry, math and science courses. (Male black engineering switcher)

I did well in high school and when I came here I didn't do so well, so I figured there must be something wrong with me. I realized later that, talking with other people, 'Hey, my high school is not the strongest academic institution.' I didn't take calculus my senior year. (Male black science switcher)

I went to a small, all-girls' private high school and I graduated in the top 10 of my class. I had taken all the advanced classes in mathematics and science, so by the time I got to this university, I figured I would have an easy time with science. But I found it was a lot harder than I had thought, and I wasn't as prepared as I should have been. But the worst thing—I wasn't used to being average. (Female Asian-American science switcher)

I should have taken the advice from my tutor in high school. He said, 'Go to junior college first.' I just had no idea. I thought I would just go ahead and tough it out. (Male black engineering switcher)

Although many white students also chose their majors inappropriately, suffered from inadequate academic preparation or entered S.M.E. classes with an inflated view of their readiness to undertake the level of work required, these problems were much more common among students of color—among those who switched, they were almost universal. However, inappropriate choice and over-confidence combined with under-preparation were insufficient to explain the higher switching rates among students of color. As with white students, many students of color who began with these difficulties persisted despite this. However, students of color experience a higher incidence of pre-college problems which are then exacerbated by negative experiences unique to minority undergraduates. These campus experiences make it harder to persist even for those who *are* well prepared and choose their field appropriately.

Problems Unique to Students of Color

The text data revealed four broad areas of difficulty which become important beyond college entry and which bear exclusively upon students of color. These difficulties arise from: differences in ethnic cultural values and socialization; internalization of stereotypes; ethnic isolation and perceptions of racism; and inadequate program support. The first set of difficulties reflects distinctive cultural values that conflict with the demands of college science. The internalization of negative stereotypes based on prior experience intensifies in college. Ethnic isolation and perceptions of prejudice reflect structural arrangements within institutions, and vary according to each group's population density on campus. Problems arising from the first three sources mutually reinforce each other; responsibility for inadequate program support for students of color rests squarely on the shoulders of the institution. The following sections describe the burdens arising from these sources which fall exclusively on students of color. Along with white S.M.E. faculty, most white students appeared to be unaware of the extra layer of difficulty which their non-white peers had to contend with.

Patterns of Socialization and Ethnic Cultural Values

The cultural values and socialization patterns of particular racial and ethnic groups can have negative consequences for the success of their members in S.M.E. majors. This is not to impugn such values. However, to succeed in S.M.E. careers, male students of color and all women often find it necessary to alter or over-ride important personal values. Those unable to discard cultural values which hinder individual success are vulnerable either to changing majors or to abandoning the attempt to attain any degree.

All children are socialized through the family and the educational system. That which is modeled for them in family and school forms the foundation not only of beliefs and attitudes, but also of behavior. What are generally referred to as white "middle-class values" (including the "Protestant work ethic"), comprise the dominant pattern of socialization in the United States. Other socio-economic, ethnic and racial communities endorse these values, but vary the emphasis they give to particular elements within this broad framework. Such variations produce a range of behavioral outcomes. For example, two common American values are showing respect for adults and taking responsibility for oneself. Emphasizing one over the other produces different behavioral outcomes. Thus, middle-class white students will question teachers about a grade which they perceive was given in error because their socialization emphasizes personal responsibility over respect for adults. Black students also are likely to pursue the matter since their culture emphasizes looking out for yourself in a social system perceived as oppressive. However, Asian-American, native American and Hispanic students are less likely to question grades, because to do so contradicts the dominant value of respect for elders over personal achievement.

Each culture contains variations in socialization by sub-culture. Thus, the socialization of inner-city blacks, barrio Hispanics, Asian-Americans from immigrant communities, and native American reservation students differs significantly from that of students of color who are less insulated from the middle-class, white population. Values are not tied only to race and ethnicity, but social class also. We discovered, for example, very different attitudes about what it means to be a black S.M.E. major among black students from the inner-city than among those from upwardly-mobile black professional families. Similarly, native Americans raised in urban areas did not adhere to the traditions of those raised on reservations. Social class differences within sub-groups of Hispanic and Asian-American students were less pronounced: most Hispanic students came from working-class families, and most Asian-American students from middle-class families. There were salient contrasts between the socialization of native Americans from reservations and those from urban backgrounds. Native Americans from reservations brought to college a spiritual tradition and first language that are unfamiliar, both to whites, and to other minority groups—including those native Americans who had never experienced reservation life. Their campus experience is more like that of foreign students' than that of other American-born students of color. Like foreign students, native Americans from reservations experience culture shock. However, many foreign students come from middle-class or upper-class families, while native Americans from reservations come from the bottom rung of the socio-economic ladder:

> I come from a part of the country where it's like the Third World. The poverty rate is high; unemployment's high; alcoholism is high; teenage pregnancy is high...Most students on a reservation have never even left it. They have to be aware that it's different out there, and those differences can hinder your goals. (Male native American mathematics switcher)

> Some of us grew up just hating the reservation—hating the way it was, hating the people, found life better outside, and stayed away. Some reject their native American background—their minority identity—for personal improvement. It's really hard if you look and don't act ethnic. You're rejected by your own group because you don't act ethnic, and rejected by white people who see you as ethnic. (Male native American science switcher)

By contrast, native Americans who are raised on reservations and embrace traditional values are torn between two worlds when they move to campus. Because they are apt to perceive their societal problems as the result of policies forced on their people by whites, they experience the unsettling feeling that they are studying with the enemy. Even those who do not distrust white people experience severe difficulties in adjusting to a very unfamiliar setting. Education beyond a basic level is commonly distrusted, resisted or defined as a selfish pursuit by many traditional working-class cultures, including reservation communities:

> There are still those people on the reservation who say, 'Go learn all you can and then bring it back to us. Help us shape it to our needs.' There's a lot of resentment from the elders for people who come back to the reservation as bureaucrats—who don't have respect for or knowledge of the traditional ways. (Male native American science switcher)

By contrast, students who are classified as native American, but who were socialized in white, mainstream society and lack a strong cultural or ethnic identity, do not experience these conflicts:

> I'm one-quarter Indian on my father's side. My parents divorced when I was a baby, so I don't know him or anything about Indian ways—except what I've read and seen in movies. (Female native American science non-switcher)

They did not identify with native American students from reservations or form peer groups with them. Since they did not grow up within the tradition of the reservation, this segment of the native American campus population escapes the problems arising from socialization in a segregated ethnic group. They may, however, experience 'outcast' status and/or lack a sense of direction from their families:

> I don't think it's true that those from the reservations have more problems in college. Those of us who grew up as outcasts in the cities don't have any incentive from home...Blacks and Hispanics and Asians, even the res kids, they have that in their background. Urban Indians don't have any family or community motivation. (Female native American science switcher)

Similarly, black students who had been integrated into white schools and communities resisted identification with those from impoverished backgrounds. They explained, often at some length, how closely they identified with the white mainstream:

> I can relate to whites more than my own because I've never actually lived around my own. I never went to schools that were predominantly of my own, or around people predominantly of my own. The majority of my friends are from other backgrounds. I was always the type of black student that knew what I was talking about—intelligent, competent in the things that I knew. So they've always looked at me as a person, not as a token black. (Male black engineering switcher)

> I can relate more to white people than I can my own black people because I've grown up in a white society. There were only seven blacks in my high school graduating class. (Male black engineering switcher)

> I have had no contact with the minority group here on campus. I've lived in a predominantly white community all my life. I don't think of myself as different from anybody else...I feel like the Minority Student Union is kind of a crutch for people who are having an identity crisis. A lot of black students here came from black schools and they have a completely different idea of life than I do. They might need that group of people, but I don't. I have my own friends. (Female black science non-switcher)

Social class differences among the Hispanic students we interviewed were generally not so pronounced as those evident among black students. However, the classification of several nationalities as 'Hispanic', solely on the basis of a common original language, prompts misleading assumptions. We found evidence of cultural clashes between students from Hispanic groups of different national and regional origins: on campuses in the West, 'Hispanic' referenced people of Mexican ancestry; in the Midwest and on the East Coast, it encompassed students whose roots were Latin American, South American, or Caribbean. The following comments illustrate the lack of a cohesive Hispanic campus identity:

> You see a one-dimensional stereotype of Mexican-American laborers in Texas and southern California. There's more backlash there. Here, there's a distinct difference between Hispanics. My friend is from El Salvador, and our parents are very similar in terms of their immigrant backgrounds, but our experiences are different because we were raised in different environments. I'm Latin American raised in suburban New Jersey. My father is college-educated and travels all over the world. His father owns a restaurant in a Spanish-speaking

neighborhood. Cuban-Americans have been established here for generations and they don't look Hispanic, so to speak. Then, you have Haitians, who mostly are viewed, at first, as blacks. (Male Hispanic engineering non-switcher)

Anglos don't know that Hispanics have different cultures. I had a hard time dealing with the labels. They refer to me as Mexican-American and I was not born in Mexico, I was born here. I'd never been labeled that before I came here. (Male Hispanic engineering switcher)

I know a lot of Hispanic people, you ask 'em, 'Are you Spanish or Mexican?' and they'll say, 'Spanish,' 'Mexican,' or 'Latin American.' I prefer Mexican-American 'cause I was born and raised here in America. I don't have the same cultural upbringing as a Mexican, but my family origin is Mexican. But I would prefer Mexican-American, and not Chicano. My mom says 'We're not Chicano.' I guess the name isn't very nice when it's translated...But here I learned that it's more a political word. (Male Hispanic science switcher)

The Hispanic community here has a very serious identity problem. There used to be a Latin American Student Union here that was dominated by Puerto Rican students. The Puerto Ricans that I'm used to are migrant workers from New Jersey or some of the lower-class areas in New York. And here, you have well-off Cuban-Americans, and people like myself—Latin Americans. My father's an engineer from El Salvador. There are all kinds of people classified as 'Hispanic.' (Male Hispanic engineering senior)

The highest degree of heterogeneity within any ethnic classification is, however, that found among those groups referenced as 'Asian'. Without a common language or dominant religion across all the Asian nationalities represented on their campuses, often the only thing which Asian-American students felt they shared was the perception by non-Asians that they had common physical attributes. Asian-American students reacted strongly to the tendency of non-Asians to see all Asian cultures as one culture, and to ascribe elements particular to one culture to some or all others:

The likelihood that a third-generation Catholic Filipino would have anything in common with an immigrant Hmong student whose family is into animism is so far-fetched, it's ridiculous. (Female Asian-American science non-switcher)

For Koreans, mostly the community revolves around the church. So mainly the support is through religion. And the Vietnamese, I think they have a good system where they help each other out. (Male Asian-American science non-switcher)

I used to attend a lot of Asian functions, but I felt very uncomfortable. I just didn't feel like I belonged. They were all with their own group. Now I don't go to these clubs. I think it actually hurts diversity. (Male Asian-American non-switching engineer)

Since most Asian-Americans we interviewed came from urban middle-class white areas, they were accustomed to seeing few members of their ancestry in school and were usually less self-conscious in the college environment than students of other ethnicities:

> I was always around Caucasians—I was never really around Asians. My mother—she's from Japan, so she's, you know, very Oriental in her outlook. But my father's third-generation, so I feel very comfortable here. (Male Asian-American engineering non-switcher)

Exceptions included a second-generation Chinese-American student, raised in a small town in the Midwest where his family were the only Asians. His father was a dishwasher and his mother, who did not speak English, was a housewife. On campus, he found no peer group with whom he could identify:

> I think I had a pretty tough childhood. It was kind of lonely being Asian. It wasn't the best of times. I don't think my teachers always liked me. I was often made fun of, you know. I, I cried a lot when I was younger. (Long pause.) When I first came here, I experienced a bit of a culture shock. Walking through the student union, you see all these Asian foreign students. I may look like them, but I just don't fit in with that group, and I'm different from Caucasians.

In contrast to Asian-Americans, black and Hispanic students who came from communities and high schools where their race or ethnicity was dominant, were uncomfortable on campuses that lacked a significant representation of their own group. Even where their broad ethnic or racial group representation was greater, intra-group variations in outlook—governed by differences in geography, socio-economic class, or national origin—mitigated against the development of cohesive racial or ethnic communities on campus. Initiatives intended to benefit students of color which do not take into account the variety of cultural forms glossed by the term 'minority students' are unlikely to improve their S.M.E. retention rates.

Cultural Variations in Educational Socialization

One theory offered to explain poor retention by students of color (and women) is that they have different learning styles from those usually encountered in mainstream science and mathematics education. A white senior who left engineering to become a teacher explained the theory thus:

> A lot of research has stated that minority groups learn differently, or learn better by different teaching techniques than the traditional one presented at most schools. This straight lecture style does not work well with African-Americans or Hispanics.

Contrary to the speaker's opinion, it was our constant observation that the "straight lecture style" did not work particularly well for students of *any* ethnicity. However, students who had attended white schools (regardless of ethnicity) had been socialized to *anticipate* it. Furthermore, it was not cultural differences in learning styles, but features in the educational socialization of S.M.E. students which explained their learning difficulties. In every interview with students from 'minority' high schools, the pedagogy of S.M.E. college faculty was poorly rated compared with that of their high school teachers. As with women's descriptions of good teaching, these students stressed individual attention from teachers. In contexts where few students planned to attend college, teachers used their relationships with students to motivate them to continue in mathematics and science. Many students from such high schools had not learned to use peer study groups because they had become highly reliant upon their relationship with particular teachers. Teachers in these settings also motivated students by rewarding effort as well as performance with good grades, and their students carried this expectation into college. Thus, they responded to their first experiences of "objective" grading in S.M.E. classes by defining S.M.E. faculty as unfeeling or discriminatory:

> I went to a predominantly black high school. My math teacher saw that I had a problem and she extended herself. I went to a black junior high, and the same thing. The teachers took hours after school to work with me. The first paper I turned in here, I gave it all I got and he still gave me a C. That can be frustrating. You know, at this school they're quick to tell you, 'Well, you have to work and be responsible for yourself...Hard work pays off.' All of these ethics. But it's like they're playing games with you. You do the work but you're not going to get anything for it. They see a black guy working hard and it's like a game—'I'm going to push you as far as you can go and I'm going to give you the very minimum for what you do.' (Male black engineering switcher)

> I've had very few teachers who gave you the benefit of the doubt. You know, 'I see this student working hard. I see him struggling. If his grade is borderline, I'm going to give him the benefit....' You have a few teachers like that. But the majority are, 'You get what you get,' and that's it. (Male black engineering switcher)

> I feel that minority students are not wanted here. And it boils down to two things. First of all, most minority students come from schools in which teachers were properly trained. They would nourish me. You come to this totally different environment, and it's mostly non-minority instructors who cater to the non-minority students, because their backgrounds are similar. (Male black engineering switcher)

In a non-competitive high school environment emphasizing individual attention and improvement, youngsters who might otherwise drop out are motivated to graduate. While this pedagogical approach is effective for high school retention, it does not prepare students for the competitive culture of S.M.E. courses in a large university where C and D grades are the norm and many students experience discouragement and lowered self-confidence. Indeed, all students from student-centered educational contexts (including, as we argued in the previous chapter, women) were ill-equipped to deal with the impersonality of traditional S.M.E. teaching. They continued to miss the "nurturing" they had received from former teachers:

> My mom graduated from a black college down in Virginia and she said it was totally different. She said teachers were interested in seeing you learn. They wanted you to graduate. You know, you got nurtured. (Male black engineering switcher)

> I learned that the instructors here are very indifferent to the needs of students, especially minority students. This so-called retention is just on paper, but really never exists because they do not go out of their way to try to help you. (Male black science switcher)

Only in one institution (the western, private liberal arts college), where the number of students of color was small, did we hear consistent reports of S.M.E. faculty supporting students of color who expressed the need for a nurturing pedagogical relationship:

> The faculty know who we are because there's so few of us. So I get catered to in a lot of ways. I like them saying, 'Well, if you need help, here's my home phone number.' I picked this school 'cause it was so small, and I was used to individual attention at high school. (Female native American science non-switcher)

> They need to get to know their students. Because what has helped me is the dean of electrical engineering saying, 'Hi, how are you doing? How's your classes?' And you just feel like they really care. He heard I wasn't doing very well in one class and he sent his secretary to find me and make an appointment with me. And he's willing to give me tutoring, and he gives me a little pep talk telling me that he wants to see me graduate. It really helps. (Female Hispanic engineering non-switcher)

This comment was truly singular. No other student reported a dean of engineering or a department head seeking them out to offer counsel or encouragement.

Students from high schools where their own racial or ethnic group was dominant were those most at risk of a learned over-dependence on teachers. Having sought in vain for individual attention from S.M.E. college teachers, they sometimes found emotional support through peer groups. However, they had often not learned how to work in groups. Without a supportive relationship with faculty or peers, these students were at especial risk of switching or of leaving college altogether.

Ethnic Cultural Values

On every campus, we found a set of cultural imperatives, values, role conflicts and patterns of interaction which were specific to particular cultures and sub-cultures, and had specific significance for S.M.E. persistence. The most salient of these are represented in Table 6.2. We would expect to find the same dysfunctional relationship between these factors and the persistence rates of students of color in S.M.E. majors on any other campus.

Obligation to Serve Community. As discussed earlier, many students of color report strong feelings of obligation to serve and 'repay' their communities for the support they have received. This imperative plays a role in the decision to switch majors for those students who see their choice as ill-founded, unless they can use their S.M.E. major in service to their community:

> A big concern of a lot of black students is we feel like we're being prepared to go into white corporate America, and it won't really help our community— we won't have the opportunity through our careers to give back to the community. Anything that we do for the community would be outside of our academic field, and that's a very serious concern. I know it was for me, and it's also something that I hear expressed. People are always trying to find out if there are any corporations owned by black people that really deal with community issues. As there aren't too many opportunities to do that, students are always trying to think of ways to create some. I don't think I'm atypical at all. I think it's a serious concern. (Female black engineering switcher)

Some saw their community obligation as a part of their student role and not as something that could be put off until graduation. They were active in local community initiatives or national organizations and found it difficult to meet these obligations as well as the demands of S.M.E. majors:

> I've always had this obligation. My mother has always stressed how lucky I am, and so I give back to the community. And, you know, I don't think that's work at all. I think that's a good thing to do and I do it all the time. But sometimes I wince through the decisions based on doing that, and neglecting my own needs. I was stretched out for a while, working 15 hours a week as a tutor at the Hispanic Center, being a tour guide, being a panelist, being contributing editor for our newspaper...At some point you've got to stop being the crusader, but you feel kind of guilty, or selfish. (Male Hispanic engineering non-switcher)

Responses to these feelings of obligation follow fairly predictable patterns: some are shared by several groups, and some are specific to particular sub-cultures. For example, black students from inner-city communities, students from many Hispanic groups, and native Americans from reservations broadly share the belief that they should meet their obligations by returning to their community after college and using their education to improve the quality of life of community members. By contrast, many Asian-American students, and native

TABLE 6.2 Comparison by Racial/Ethnic Group of Cultural Values Expressed by Non-White Students.

Value	Blacks		Hispanics	Asian-Americans	Native Americans	
	Inner-city	All others			Reservation	All others
Obligation to serve community	Yes	No	Yes	No	Yes	No
Obligation to be a role model	Yes	Yes	Yes	No	Yes	No
Conflict between student/family roles	Yes	No	Yes	No	Yes	No
Educational goals defined by parents	No	No	No	Yes	No	No
Encouraged to be self-assertive	No	Yes	No	No	No	No
Encouraged to be self-reliant/autonomous	Yes	Yes	No	No	No	Yes
Supportive, effective peer group culture	No	No	Yes	No	Yes	No

Americans from urban areas, share the dominant perspective of white students: although they often expressed altruistic career goals, a service orientation was seen as a matter of individual choice, not as a cultural imperative. The strongest sense of community obligation was expressed by Hispanic students who unanimously stressed the duty to repay their communities. For them, the career dilemma of individual success versus community service never presented itself:

> After I earn my advanced degree in dentistry, I want to go back to my hometown and help those in the community who helped me. That's my pay-back. I want to return the contributions made to me, back to the community. (Male Hispanic science non-switcher)

Being raised in a middle-class environment did not necessarily reduce students' sense of duty to serve their community. There was, however, less agreement among middle-class black students than among other middle-class students of color about how to interpret that responsibility. The children of black professionals raised in the majority community presented their own success as a way to raise the aspirations of younger community members, and as a symbolic achievement for their group. The interpretation dominant among black, urban, working-class students stressed the responsibility of working for political, social and economic change. As a group, middle-class black students expressed more inner-conflict than students of any other group about how best to meet their sense of community obligation:

> Some black people say, 'If I do well then I'm helping the community just because I'm doing well.' Other people see that as a sell-out, saying, 'No, that's not truly helping the community. You need to be involved.' (Female black science switcher)

Within the small group of native Americans interviewed we also found differences of opinion about how the obligation of community service should be addressed. In the following extracts, the first speaker expresses the importance of ensuring the survival of cultural pride and tradition; the second takes a pragmatic approach to the needs of his people and concludes that he cannot meet them:

> After graduating, I plan to study native American Studies and bring our history and a native American curriculum back into the school system on the reservation. Or perhaps I'll apply it to a college where, like here, there's no native American studies at all. (Male native American science switcher)

> Unless you're in psychology or sociology, you can't go back and work with them—work with some of the problems like alcoholism. But not if you're a scientist. I mean, when I came here I pretty much knew I wasn't gonna go back home. I stayed away from having a family when I was home. I didn't want to be tied down. I never did really have friends, so I never got tied down and I can stay away. (Male native American science switcher)

The only students of color who (as individuals) did not express a sense of obligation to serve their community of origin were Asian-American and black middle- and upper-class students.

Obligation to be a Role Model. An important aspect of the sense of community obligation is offering one's self as a role model to younger members of the group. Even middle-class Asian-American and black students, who shared the predominantly individualistic orientation of white students, were aware that other sub-cultures in their group stressed this responsibility:

> If I decided to switch out, I would feel I let people down—let myself down—against people who say, 'I knew she couldn't do it.' And that's, that's a lot of pressure. (Female black science non-switcher)

> There are very few presentations of academic excellence in the black community. So we feel we are supposed to do well, and if we don't, it's kind of devastating. 'Cause it's not just yourself you're representing, it's the whole community. (Female black science non-switcher)

However, persistence in an S.M.E. major was not usually seen as an aspect of role model obligation. Native American students were among those who portrayed community pride as focused primarily on graduation from college, not on any particular major. These students found it easier to switch majors, since they could fulfill their role model obligation in careers outside of the sciences:

> There's a lack of role models on the reservation and also low expectations or horizons. Even though I switched majors, they are counting on me to graduate and be an example for the other kids. (Male native American math switcher)

Students who discussed their obligation to be role models in future-oriented terms saw it as a privilege and a source of pride. Those who perceived this as a current obligation found it an onerous duty which increased the other pressures of their majors:

> Being held up as a role model, it's a big problem. People just want you to succeed so bad...but it's just too much pressure put on you. (Male Hispanic engineering non-switcher)

> If you come from a minority background, everyone is following your every move. I'm used to that, and it sucks sometimes. When things are going great, I mean, you're on top of the world—but when you fall, people have such expectations that everyone's disappointed. No one knows what to say. (Male Hispanic engineering non-switcher)

> Just because you're a minority you're held up as an example for other high school kids to do well—to be on a par with the non-minority engineers. And when you don't.... (Long pause.) Everybody was let down when I couldn't take it in engineering, everybody in the whole valley. I, I let everybody down, not just myself. (Male Hispanic engineering switcher)

Because success in science-based majors is not usually included in definitions of good role-modeling which are common in their sub-culture, the cultural imperative tended to favor switching in order to graduate rather than persistence in an S.M.E. major.

Conflict Between Academic and Family Responsibilities. As already indicated, conflict between responsibility to one's nuclear or extended family and the demands of an S.M.E. major were common themes in interviews with black students from the inner-city, Hispanic students and native Americans from reservations. For the latter two groups, close ties to the extended family created the need to return home for kin celebrations or in response to types of crisis that students from other cultures would see as important only in their nuclear families:

> I come from a rather close-knit family. When both of my grandparents were ill, that took a lot of attention—trying to go home every weekend. My family is not just my immediate family—it also includes my extended family. (Male Hispanic engineering switcher)

> Native Americans stick together back on the reservation. They love going back for all the celebrations and they also feel they have to go back for problems in the family. See, all of this is just from what I hear when I tutor them, 'cause personally, I never experienced it. I grew up here in the city. I just know they like to hold on to their culture, and I can understand that. I think sticking close to home and keeping the ties you grew up with would be better. That's just the way their lifestyle is, and it's harder when you're so far away. (Female native American math switcher)

The family responsibilities of most inner-city blacks and most Hispanics often included making regular financial contributions toward the support of immediate and extended family members. They discussed the conflicts this created, especially making sufficient time for their academic work. Many of these students were also responsible for their own tuition:

> I have my mother and my sister that I've been supporting for the last four and a half years. And in that time period, I've always worked full-time and overtime. So school is like the part-time thing I have to do to get through and finish. (Male Hispanic science non-switcher)

> I work 30 hours. It's a lot. I'm not only working, I have to take care of things at home too—my parents, three younger brothers and two young sisters. That's why my grades are going down. (Female Hispanic science switcher)

Students who shouldered both family economic obligations and paid for much or all of their own college education felt that most faculty were unaware of the heavy burden that they carried and were apt to judge them unfairly:

Sometimes faculty tend to forget that at the same time I was going to school, I was working full-time all the way through to support myself and my aunt and uncle. (Male Hispanic engineering switcher)

I haven't experienced anything negative from any of the departments here. But I do think that faculty are kind of removed from the educational plight of minorities. They feel you should get excited about sciences. But it's kind of hard to do that when you're trying to pay your rent or support your parents...You have a whole bunch of other things that you have to take care of besides science. (Male Hispanic science non-switcher)

They stressed the dominant role played by insufficient educational funding in the difficulties facing all students from lower-income families (both white and nonwhite) on the one hand, and the extra financial load of family responsibilities carried by many of these students on the other. Understanding the economic factors bearing upon all working-class students, especially those in S.M.E. majors where academic demands on students' time are often the greatest, was considered paramount:

Many of the students, like myself, also are putting themselves through school. So on top of that, I'm trying to support my mother and younger brother and sisters—my mother, she's not married and she's too sick to work. So I work two jobs, but it doesn't bring in much. I got need-based tuition, but that's just based on what they think *you* need. There's no recognition of your need to support a family. You're always scraping to get finances, which makes it very difficult at times. (Male black science switcher)

Of the people who do drop out, usually a large chunk of it is financial. I would say 20, 25, maybe even 30 percent is financial. It's hard, and then there's always the burden that to stay at the university I have to work. I'm the first generation of my family to go to college and I'm not coming out of the solid middle-class $80,000 to $100,000 family...White students can go skiing during the weekend. I don't have that luxury. There's definitely a tremendous money gap. (Male black engineering switcher)

I'm on the President's Committee on the Retention of Students. A major issue is financial difficulties. Ethnic groups are the hardest hit. When the tuition goes up, black, Hispanic and native American students suffer most because they have less income coming in...Lack of money for school is a growing problem for all students, but it's compounded because of race. (Male black engineering switcher)

I remember my first couple of years I was actually working my class schedule around my work schedule. You know, I was more worried about, 'Will I have enough time to work?'...As a minority going to school, your work is more important than your academics. (Male Hispanic engineering non-switcher)

Obligation to extended kin was not a problem for any of the Asian-Americans we interviewed. Indeed, the sole family responsibility described by

Asian-American students was that of giving their total attention and very best efforts to their role as full-time students. Being successful in school and in their careers beyond was what the family expected of them. Students across all Asian cultures represented in our sample, reported that their families—even those who were not well-off—sought to provide sufficient financial support to allow their children's total concentration on academic work. To do this, families had set aside funds for college since their children were born. Only three of the Asian-American students in our sample worked while attending school:

> Coming from a lower-class background, it's harder to deal with things I suppose. We haven't always been middle-class. Now we're well-off. I think with a lower-class Hispanic background, it probably would have been harder because of the financial problems. There's no way I could work to pay for rent, food and college tuition, and still get a decent G.P.A. (Female Asian-American science switcher)

The difference made to academic performance—and to their focus and self-confidence—by the experience of being able to take financial help for granted (even briefly) was poignantly described by one black male senior who was offered a place in a Harvard summer program:

> They paid for everything! I had nothing to do but study and that was the first, and only, time as a student where I had nothing to worry about but going to class and studying all day long. It was beautiful. I swear, it was magnificent. Lectures became easy. Class was easy. I was away, you know, not worrying about home. Money was no issue—I even had spending money. It was like being in heaven, and I got As in two very difficult courses in an eight-week program. From that point on I knew that doing well isn't just about intelligence. (Male black science non-switcher)

The impact of economic responsibilities on the retention of many students of color is clear. Many Hispanic, black and native Americans who had left S.M.E. majors expressed the relief they felt in being able to maintain respectable grades in less demanding majors even while fulfilling their economic and other family obligations. Those who were still struggling to resolve this role conflict debated whether it was worth staying in their original major:

> Last year I was working 60 hours a week and I would wait until the day before the exam, then read the five chapters, then wonder, 'Why did I get this C?' I only spent a day studying, so I guess a C was okay. But I wish I had majored in something fuzzy, 'cause I probably could have graduated with all As. (Female black science non-switcher)

Contrary to white students' beliefs, over half (56.9%) of the students of color from poorer families in our sample (i.e. 33 out of 58) had few financial resources other than their own paid employment. This observation underscores the consistent finding that financial difficulties play a major role in minority under-representation in the sciences. It also validates the recent shift in emphasis (for example, by the National Science Foundation) away from "minority programs" in favor of improved financial support for all able students from poorer families.

Educational Goals Defined by Parents. For the most part, switchers who were black, Hispanic or native American reported their families had been supportive when they changed majors. Again, the fact that they did not drop out of college altogether assuaged family or community disappointment that they would graduate without an S.M.E. degree:

> My mom told me—I'm the oldest of three kids—she said, 'You're the trailblazer.' Not doing engineering was really disappointing, but I didn't quit college. So my graduating will be a very important aspect of their lives, because they've seen me do it, so they know that they can do it too. (Male black engineering switcher)

This comment is typical of all students of color who switched, except Asian-Americans. Many Asian-American students depicted their families as goal-oriented, and their parents (especially fathers) as taking an authoritarian approach to child-rearing. The major that they choose, as well as the grades they receive, are important to the family because they are seen as steps on the road to financial success and social prestige. Role-modeling, other than in occupations defined as "successful," is not culturally-supported, and the idea of education for its own sake is de-emphasized and de-valued:

> Many minorities who enter science, do so because their parents, as my father did, recommended they go into the science and math fields. For me it was okay. But for my older brother it was a burden. My father expected him to go into math and science, but in high school he was interested in art and he liked to paint. My parents said, 'Don't go into that. There isn't any future in that.' So my brother listened to my parents and majored in math. But after a while, he decided it wasn't for him and he left school. Now he's married and is working as a cook. (Male Asian-American science non-switcher)

> Asians have pretty tightly-knit families and their parents usually have very high expectations of their children and push them very, very hard to meet those expectations. I really don't see that in other families. They're kind of obsessive about it...They seem to have that final goal in life as simply to hit it big, to be successful. That seems kind of unhealthy, but at the same time that makes you strive very high. (Male Asian-American science non-switcher)

Parental pressure made it very difficult for Asian-American students to declare or switch to a major in a field with no obvious career attached to it. One of the Asian-American engineering students had undertaken a double major rather than completely opt out of his commitment to engineering. He had not told his parents how he felt:

> There's a lot of pressure in my family. That's where I am right now. I mean, if they weren't there, I probably would be doing an English major right now.

For another Asian-American student, the whole university experience was an inadmissible anathema:

> My parents knew I was having some problems, but I never told them I had been kicked out and then readmitted. From then on, I just did not want to go to school. I lost all ambition and I just *hated* school! I still dislike it but I'm doing it because I'm almost done. In an indirect way my parents are putting a lot of pressure on me. They came from Japan and want their kids to have a better life. But I just can't get into studying and going to class. (Female Asian-American science switcher)

For Asian-American students who had never questioned the values of their family and culture, and had not, therefore, explored non-science interests prior to college, the decision to switch was particularly devastating: all they had taken for granted was suddenly called into question. All of the Asian-American students who encountered problems in their original majors reported difficulty in telling their parents. Siblings often had more understanding of their dilemma and could be turned to for support:

> I had already applied to study in Nepal and been accepted, and I didn't tell my parents. I finally called them up and I said, 'Maybe I'll go to Nepal to study philosophy.' They just blew up. So I told my sister and the next day she called up my parents—she's like the diplomat of the family—and she smoothed things out and, like, now it's okay. (Male Asian-American engineering switcher)

The following advice was given to a focus group peer who had not yet told his parents he had switched from 'pre-med' to sociology a year earlier. The strategy advocated was to play off one traditional Asian family value against another, so that changing majors was presented as the lesser of two evils:

> I'll give you a tip that worked when I changed to history. Threaten your parents with bad grades. Tell them, 'Well, if I keep taking these science and math courses I'll get Bs and B-s and a couple C+s.' And then they'll shape up. They want that G.P.A. more than anything else. (Female Asian-American science switcher)

Notwithstanding, the restrictions in their choice of a first or a subsequent major, many Asian-American students expressed a strong sense of certainty about their family's love and concern. Although switching meant challenging strongly-held family values, it was also clear that love and duty were mutually supported in their families. The following response was offered in a focus group of Asian-American non-switchers where we posed the question of how their families would react had they switched to a non-science major. After a thoughtful silence, one young man replied:

My dad would still love me, but he would be very, very disappointed. I wouldn't do that to him.

The subject of parental love arose spontaneously in interviews with both male and female Asian-American students. They chose particular career directions and persevered through periods of academic difficulties because they knew their parents loved them and wanted the best for them. While other students also expressed concern not to disappoint or anger their parents by switching or earning poor grades, no other group of students, including white students, expressed quite this sense of mutual obligation based on the certainty of reciprocal love:

> When I graduated from high school, I didn't know a whole lot, so I followed my father's recommendation and became a physics major. He loves me. He must know what is best for me. (Male Asian-American science non-switcher)

> I'm perfectly happy and it would distress me to feel I was somebody who got scared away from changing their major simply because I made concessions to my parents. I love them. And I'm making these concessions because my parents are totally worth it in the end. (Male Asian-American science switcher)

Cultural Restraints on Self-Assertiveness. Broadly speaking, most students of color were more self-effacing than white students and less prone to take action when they ran into problems on campus. An important exception are those black students from higher socio-economic groups whose culture affirms self-assertiveness, and who are not timid in pursuit of their academic and career interests. By contrast, inner-city blacks have long-standing cultural reasons for believing themselves to be victims of an oppressive system. Their socialization does not encourage assertiveness in the face of individual problems encountered on campus:

> The white guys are very quick to say, 'Well, it was this predicament, or this T.A....' But for minorities it's a lot harder to do that because you're not used to a system behind you. You're used to being on your own, so when you don't do well, then it's your fault. It's just totally your fault. (Female black science non-switcher)

Asian families instill respect for authority in their children, and we found no criticism of teaching methods, or even curriculum overload, from Asian-American students. Thus, when Asian-American students cannot keep their grades at a level approved of by their families, they consistently assume all of the blame:

> I don't want to make them think I was hiding behind excuses. It's been tough. The biggest thing I've been struggling with is this G.P.A. And, and...it's all my fault. I'm just not so smart as everybody thought. (Male Asian-American engineering switcher)

I studied and I tried to get it from the lecture only. I didn't go and talk to them. At the time I felt that school was too big and impersonal. I mean, it could just be an excuse, because I didn't go and talk to the professor when I didn't understand some subject. So I cannot say that they didn't spend enough time with students—because it was me. (Male Asian-American science switcher)

These comments exemplify the self-blaming tendency among students of color who have never considered there may be structural impediments to their progress. They do not see themselves as casualties of a particular educational process because such a representation of their difficulties would be unsupported by their families and cultural values.

The self-effacing, nonassertive behavior of Hispanics and native Americans is similar to that of Asian-Americans in terms of deference to authority, but their response is shaped by fear and awe of authority, rather than simple respect. The socialization experiences of Hispanics and native Americans often include situations where authority is oppressive, rather than admirable. What appears to be respectful behavior by Hispanic and native American students may actually be fear of reprisal. Socialized fear of authority makes it peculiarly difficult for students from these groups to take the initiative with faculty when they need assistance:

My advisor directed me to the Minority Advising Office and the director of that office, he's Latino, he took me around to the chair of the department of earth sciences so I could speak to him about possibly majoring in that department. I wouldn't have gone on my own. (Male Hispanic engineering non-switcher)

Generally, we have a fear of authority, poor assertiveness and low expectations. Competitiveness and self-assertiveness are not culturally-supported, but this is crucial if we are going to survive on campus. You have to ferret out opportunities and take them. The more programs you get into, the more lists you get on, the more people contact you. If you're too timid, you miss opportunities and never catch up. (Male native American science non-switcher)

In our culture, we don't challenge authority. We don't ever question a grade or ask for help. We're used to being told what to do, so it's hard getting used to structuring your own work. Coming here, we don't know how to handle so much freedom. (Male native American science non-switcher)

Native American people drop out of the major and they tend also to drop out of college. They assume the problem is with themselves, not just making the wrong choice. They don't seek help. They take it all on themselves. (Male native American science non-switcher)

Self-Reliance and Autonomy. Many students from Hispanic, native American and Asian cultures described their difficulties in developing self-reliance as young adults. However, the norms that produce what appear to be similar problems are different for each group. Feelings of limited personal control over educational goals and the authoritarian parenting style this reflects, constrain Asian-American students' capacity for autonomy. Across different Asian groups, students portrayed their parents as discouraging independence by making decisions for them long after most other children have begun to make their own choices. Those Asian parents who followed traditional parenting norms had not allowed their children to work while in high school or to attend social functions other than those organized by adults. When they arrived on campus and were free to control their own time and activities, they often felt ill-equipped to do so:

> I think it's just the way that I was raised. I was probably one of the very few high school students that never went out on a Friday or Saturday night. I *never, ever* in my life, until college, went out. I come out here and people are like, 'Come on! Let's go to a bar! Let's go out!' It was a shock. I've never experienced anything like that. (Female Asian-American science switcher)

> My first year here was the first time I was really independent from my parents. I was *free* to do whatever I chose to do. I was doing a lot of other things and then trying to catch up with school work. Even now, I sometimes spend many extra hours with friends when I know I should be studying. (Male Asian-American science non-switcher)

> I think I would have done better if I'd gone to a school near home. But my parents had such a tight grip on me, I don't think I would have become a person on my own. They are so strictly in the Japanese tradition. They told me, 'You're not going to date until you get out of college.' If I had stayed near home, I probably wouldn't have gone out with anyone. I think I'm glad that I came out away from my parents. But, gosh, I miss home *so* much! (Female Asian-American science switcher)

The low level of autonomy and self-reliance observed among both native Americans from reservations and Hispanic students is also culturally-derived. The extended family, which we have described as making demands that conflict with academic work, is also the students' main source of affirmation and security. These supports are difficult to simulate on campus, and both Hispanic and native American students describe feeling homesick for family-centered activities. With few other Hispanic or native American students in their major, they lack an ethnic peer group with whom to share social activities or discuss academic difficulties. They are apt to become lonely and despondent, and meeting groups of their own ethnicity in majors where they are better represented becomes a powerful inducement to switch:

> Most of my friends didn't come as freshmen; they transferred here as sophomores. You feel, 'Well, I could have gone into engineering directly at home.' I had the highest score on the S.A.T.s in my whole town. I often think about, What would have happened if I had stayed home and gone into engineering there? (Male Hispanic engineering switcher)

For reservation Indians, homesickness is a major problem some never surmount. They go home too frequently and that undermines their efforts as students. It is important to build an attachment to others on the campus, but there are so few—and on a large campus like this, we're dispersed. I got married recently and that helps create a sense of community. (Male native American science non-switcher)

Among all the students of color interviewed, the only group that seemed to have been encouraged to be self-reliant were black students. In a culture which values autonomy and independence, they took on responsibilities at a very early age. Many black students had responsibilities that are typical of non-traditional students, because they are often older than the average student and have a pattern of interrupted education. Some were working to support their family of origin, their own children, or both. This group included students who had previously dropped out of college, but who, having discovered how limited their opportunities were without a degree, had returned with a strong motivation to graduate:

I never attended high school. I dropped out of school in the ninth grade. I grew up in an urban environment and I got side-tracked, but I always wanted to be a scientist. I had to go back and get a diploma. I started taking classes, but then I'd stop because I couldn't work and go to school. So then I decided to work two years straight and save up money—which I did from '86 to '88. Then, in 1988, I entered community college, went there for a year, then I transferred here. I'll be 29 next week. So it's been a *long* arduous process for me. (Male black science non-switcher)

I'm not a traditional student. I first joined the military and was in for three years. Then I worked as a nurse for one year. Then I returned to community college and there I realized I had to build up my skills at all the basic levels. Every single one of them. Then I transferred here and I had to drop out once again for two more years to support the family. I came back in '91—working full-time, going to school part-time—and now I'm finally finished. So in reality, it took almost 10 years. (Female black science non-switcher)

Older, non-traditional students who had families to support (whether students of color or white) were less likely to switch than other students—partly because they had clearer goals than their younger peers, but also because their families were a distinctively effective source of support through periods of difficulty. In our recently completed study of S.M.E. graduate and undergraduate majors with disabilities (Seymour & Hunter, 1996) we also found the emotional (and financial) support of the spouses and children of mature students to be a strong factor in their persistence.

Cultural Variations in Peer Group Success Norms. All S.M.E. students, regardless of ethnicity, benefit from effective peer study groups. Some students—most notably, native Americans and Hispanics—also look to a peer group for affective support similar to that provided by their family and community. The demands of the extended family have been discussed in terms of the problems they create for native American and Hispanic students. However, their kin networks also offer affirmation and emotional support. Students from these cultures expressed the need to recreate the functions of the extended family on campus, and when it was possible to do this, were less likely to drop out of the institution:

> There is an Indian university in Kansas that would be better for many of the students from the reservations. The classes are smaller and there's an intimate environment which is like the family support group. The people at home are a great support, but they also pull you back. They feel threatened by your escape. (Male native American science non-switcher)

> We have our own house on campus. There are 20 Latinos who live there and we're all seniors in different majors, but we'll all graduate together in the spring. It's really been great, and it's gonna be hard to leave them. We really are a family. (Female Hispanic engineering non-switcher)

Wherever we found high levels of persistence among Hispanic and native American groups, we also found an institutional effort to simulate the extended family structure of these cultures. An example of this were group living arrangements where all tutorial, academic and financial advising and other support services were offered within these domestic units. These initiatives were effective in retaining S.M.E. students partly because they drew upon both the affective and instrumental strengths of peer groups.

We also found that peer group norms of black and Asian-American S.M.E. students can work against the persistence of their members. There are several aspects to this problem for black students. First, as discussed earlier, cultural emphasis on self-reliance and independence, coupled (for some) with over-dependence on high schools teachers and failure to learn the importance of working with class peers, means that black students often arrive in college without understanding the significance of peer group learning for academic progress and persistence. These black students are at particular risk of struggling on alone in the face of academic difficulty. If they do seek help, it is apt to be from tutors or T.A.s (as surrogate teachers) rather than from peers:

> There was this black guy in engineering with me, but he's gone now. He was just so much of a self-starting person, he didn't want to ask for help. He was used to succeeding on his own. I think that led to his downfall more than anything. You see that often with black students. Nobody can do this totally on their own. (Male Hispanic engineering non-switcher)

> Many groups are much better at working together than others, and if you don't work together, it adds more of a burden on the individual to do well. (Male black science non-switcher)

> Even though I know it's bad and I know that I should study with others, I don't do it. (Male black science non-switcher)

We consistently noted in the accounts of those black students who sought validation from black peers for their academic success, the culture of the peer group made this hard to evoke. This arises, we feel, from the history shared by all black students, regardless of differences in socio-economic background. A tradition of mutual support through years of oppression and the struggle for civil rights defines the character of black campus social groups as both politically active and supportive to members in adversity:

> The Black Student Union is close-knit—pretty tight—for things that are going on, on campus, and larger issues. They're pretty active. They have a political agenda, but they definitely, like, push the social side too. (Female black engineering switcher)

At a personal level, a focus on mutual support through life's adversities permeates the norms of black friendship groups. When a black student has academic problems, the peer group provides a safe and sympathetic context in which to vent frustrations:

> There's not many of us in engineering. Four now: it used to be eight or nine. Nobody is doing very good, just kinda hangin' in there, hoping we can graduate. The other guys, they help, you know. I just got a D on a pop quiz and they said, 'Blow it off, don't let them get you down.' It kinda helps to hear that. (Male black engineering non-switcher)

Unfortunately, this support is conditional. The norm that promotes group encouragement and affirmation when things are not going well is inflexible. There is no support for success. This is not to say that blacks fear or do not value success. Individually, they are highly motivated to succeed. However, the culture of the black peer group offers no affective support for members who are doing well. Black students either isolate or mock those of their group who are earning good grades. The group offers commiseration in adversity, but invokes negative sanctions against celebrating individual (rather than group) success. A black student who is passing courses with minimal difficulty is likely to feel criticized by the group:

> I fear being found out to be successful. You can't admit your success because then they're like, 'Well, get away from me. Just leave us alone.' It's not the right thing to say you've done well. When I do well I keep it to myself. If you do well, then shut up. Let everyone else who didn't do so well speak up. They're happy doing that. If you get above average, that's not cool. But it hurts me if one of my own is undermining my success and making me feel bad about it. (Female black science non-switcher)

They were having a hard time because...well, there's just a lack of peer support for them 'cause they were doing fairly well. (Male black engineering switcher)

So I did what it took to get As and I'd allow them to put me in a few honors classes. But I *hated* being stereotyped that way. There was peer pressure. There was *tremendous* peer pressure from black students for being a know-it-all. When I came to school here almost all the people I associated with initially who were black called me a walking encyclopedia. I was ridiculed through high school and my first couple years here because I knew a lot about a lot of different things. So now all my friends are white. (Female black engineering switcher)

Ostracism of successful black students by their peer group is stronger within S.M.E. majors than in groups formed in the humanities and social sciences because, the more difficult the course work, the more the black peer group focuses on providing support through failure. It does not, therefore, spontaneously develop the function of helping each other to succeed by studying together. This leaves the black students who are doing well in S.M.E. majors with the choice either of being loners throughout college, or of switching to majors where there is less need for peer groups whose sole function is to allow members who are struggling to vent their frustrations.

The norms of Asian-American peer groups in S.M.E. majors were also dysfunctional to persistence for some of their members, but the mechanism worked in the opposite direction from that found in black peer groups in that it placed at risk those in academic difficulties, rather than those who experienced success. Students from Asian backgrounds described themselves (and were described by non-Asian peers) as highly effective in forming peer study groups. However, Asian-American students who experienced difficulties with their course work reported that their peer groups offered no help or sympathy and withdrew from them socially. Only success was supported: 'failure' elicited disapproval and social rejection. This occurs because Asian-American student peer groups replicate family pressures to succeed in the sciences and place as much emphasis on high grades as do their parents; the value placed on high grades that is instilled by parents through active involvement in homework and the monitoring of their children's educational progress is incorporated into the peer group culture. The over-arching peer group norms are that one should be industrious and that one always deserves the grade received. The affective dimension that is so effective in other peer groups in affirming and retaining members who lack self-confidence is missing in Asian-American peer group culture. Support and affirmation is offered to those who are doing well, but not to those seeking emotional support thorough periods of lowered confidence or poor academic performance. The norms are manifested by shunning and blaming those who are not succeeding:

I was telling everybody, 'Hey, I'm doing so terrible, my grades are so bad,' and they're like, 'Well, why don't you study more?' I was like, 'You don't even understand. When I get home I study all night long. I don't even feel like I'm making any progress.' One reason it took me so long to get out of engineering is because they convinced me I just wasn't trying hard enough. (Male Asian-American engineering switcher)

Asian-American students often questioned the purpose of this study. They found it puzzling that we should attempt to determine why students switched majors: they assumed switchers were inferior students who either could not "hack it," or were unwilling to put in the effort to succeed. As a group, they were less inclined than were other students either to complain about the demands of S.M.E. majors or to question the appropriateness of the competitive culture. The following comment is typical:

I think the most effective filter for science is who wants to do it. And people who don't want to do science are selected out. It's better for them, and it's better for me. There should be no attempt to encourage people who wouldn't naturally do it. (Male Asian-American science non-switcher)

Because the Asian-American peer group is largely focused on the instrumental, task-oriented function of study, there is no outlet for its members to vent their frustrations or fears. Because of cultural emphasis on individualism and success, it is taken for granted that to complain or seek support from others is not only unseemly, but is an admission of a flaw in moral character:

Strangely, my Asian friends don't really talk about difficulties they're having. There's some cultural training so that you're not gonna start complaining...I don't hear much complaining from them. (Female white engineering switcher)

Lacking affective support on campus and perceiving themselves to be a disappointment to their families, the solution to the problem of a sinking G.P.A. is often to switch majors. Of all the students we interviewed, Asian-Americans were the least inclined to be either relieved or happy about their decision to switch. They felt they had failed their families, been deserted by their peers and socially isolated in their new major because, outside of S.M.E. majors, Asian-Americans are an under-represented group.

The following comment was offered by an Asian-American senior majoring in physics. He accurately pinpoints some of the problems for students of color in S.M.E. majors. Despite his insight, both he and other Asian-American students did not portray members of their own group experiencing these difficulties:

The way it's set up, people take all of the blame onto themselves when things go wrong—and that's not the whole story. And people go off into another major and spend the rest of their lives thinking they are losers. It's a real problem for everyone, but it's worse for Hispanics and blacks. Blaming yourself, instead of seeing all the ways things are set up for so many people to fail, is really the crucial issue. You feel you have to take responsibility for your own stuff—but that's not all of the problem.

The dysfunctionality of peer groups for black and Asian-American S.M.E. students works on the same principle: students who violate peer group norms defining approved academic performance levels are negatively sanctioned (even ostracized) rather than supported. H' wever, the normative content of the rules for each group is exactly opposite. The following observation by a black woman who had taken several engineering courses with Asian-American students points to the contrast between the success norms of these two groups:

> From my experience here, I think that the Asian community has more of an individualistic attitude to success. I think they very much identify with mainstream success. I know they support each other, but individual success is extremely important to them. And it's not at all the same as the African-American community where a group identity is a lot more important than individual success.

Throughout this section we have stressed the point that particular features of racial and ethnic group cultures have implications for the way in which their members define appropriate behavior and respond to the situations they encounter in S.M.E. majors. We do not, however, mean to imply that people are prisoners of their culture. The values that are instilled as a matter of socialization within any group are guidelines; the longer people are away from the group, the less they feel tied to its values. A native American student stated this quite succinctly, albeit sadly:

> Speaking from my traditional background, you have to sacrifice many things from that tradition in order to come to school, to get an education. That's a big problem for me. It feels the longer I stay here, the more I'm being cut off from those ties. That's why I want to return after I graduate. To go back to get in touch with what I may, or may not, have lost. (Male native American math switcher)

Internalization of Negative Stereotypes and its Consequences

Everyone acquires a social identity that defines who they are in relation to other people. We cannot define or evaluate ourselves without taking into account how we think others see and evaluate us. When this looking-glass self reflects negative stereotypes about who and what we are, there is the danger that people may develop "spoiled identities" (Goffman, 1963). Negative ethnic stereotypes have the power to erode self-esteem because, when negative beliefs that are generalized to an entire racial or ethnic group are absorbed by its individual members, the group hatred generated by others may be converted to self-hatred. At the very least, an internalized negative stereotype can cause those who receive it to have serious doubts about their abilities.

Variations in the ways in which racial and ethnic groups are characterized can be traced to the historical circumstances from which they grew. They can be classified by the ways in which minority groups have interacted with the dominant group. The particular sets of stereotypes applied to blacks, Hispanics and native Americans evolved from the same expressed need of the white majority to dominate these minority groups. By contrast, stereotypes about Asian-Americans focus on undermining or reversing their success in competing with whites. Thus, the stereotypical generalizations of blacks, Hispanics or native Americans as lazy, unintelligent, or lacking in ambition are not applied to Asian-Americans, who are portrayed as overly ambitious, competitive, clannish and intelligent in self-interested ways.

Some stereotypes specifically pertain to racial and ethnic groups on campus—for example, the judgment that black and Hispanic students are less intelligent than white or Asian-American students, as evidenced by the common presumption that entrance requirements are routinely lowered in order to fill quotas. This view, widely expressed by white students, was a source of resentment which reinforced the prejudice that (non-Asian) students of color were less-qualified than white students. Whether affirmative action guidelines on college campuses do or do not lower the admissions criteria for particular students is, in this context, *irrelevant*. It is the stereotype itself that damages inter-racial/ethnic relationships, *not* the particular policy that is in force. More significantly, this stereotype damages the self-concept of black and Hispanic students by undermining their confidence to persist, regardless of their actual level of ability or preparation:

> Some of the Latino students heard remarks like, 'Oh, you're here just to fill quotas,' or, 'You came in with lower standards than other students.' Some minority students begin to feel that the standards were lowered for them, and felt like they were competing with people who were of a higher calibre. That put a lot of stress and anxiety on them. (Female Hispanic engineering non-switcher)

> I'm half Hispanic myself, but I didn't put that down on my card because I felt if I was accepted as a Hispanic student I would forever be wondering if that was why I got in. I didn't want to live with that, so I'm glad I didn't. (Female Hispanic science switcher)

Many students of color who moved to the social sciences were well aware of the distinction between ascribed status (like gender and ethnicity) and achieved status (which is gained through education, occupation or income). Students of color who had attained the grades necessary for college admission were demoralized by the stereotype that discounted their achievement and presented their admission as an ascribed status based on affirmative action:

> Well, a lot of my class-mates thought I got in because of my skin color, and that affected me a lot. You know, they didn't accept me because of my

intelligence. And so I did bad. I've never gotten the grades that I should have, because that was always in the back of my head, and it affected my performance. (Male black science non-switcher)

Because all students of color had experienced the consequences of being stereotyped, their understanding of the nature and implications of the process for students in other minority groups was more profound than that of white students:

All minorities—in some fashion—share common problems...Everybody has the common ground of being minority, but only in your specific group do you understand how you get treated...Because people may see me like a stereotypic thing, 'Well, she's black, she may not know as much.' Or an Asian would be like, 'Oh, they know everything.' So they have different things hitting them, like I have different things hitting me. (Female black science non-switcher)

All non-white students could describe the stereotypes that were used about their own group as well as those in circulation about other groups:

The negative stereotype of a Hispanic is of immigrants and low-paying jobs. Hispanic-hating people have stereotypes of illegal immigrants...Maybe they're used to seeing the maid in their house. (Male Hispanic engineering switcher)

Sensitivity towards minorities is both good and bad. They consider you the epitome of native Americans. And that's really distracting. On this campus you're usually greeted with a little fascination or total ignorance. A lot of people's connotations of native Americans are still connected with old western pictures. (Male native American science switcher)

In the engineering school the stereotype of blacks is: 'Black students always sit in the back of the class,' 'Black students don't ask questions,' 'Black students are all guys,' 'Black students get scholarships because they're black.' God, it's so narrow! (Male Hispanic engineering non-switcher)

However, students in one minority group might also express the dominant (white) stereotype about students in another minority group:

For blacks, the motivation from home isn't that strong to pursue something that could be competitive. (Male Asian-American science non-switcher)

Asian-American students suffered from the consequences of a stereotype with particular significance for S.M.E. enrollment and persistence: that Asian-Americans tend naturally to excel in mathematics and science and have limited interest in other academic fields:

There is this assumption that if you have Oriental parents or grandparents you *must* be good at math and science, which is *so* untrue. I'm really bad at it, to tell you the truth. I mean, I enjoy biology a lot, but chemistry and math just didn't do it for me. (Female Asian-American science switcher)

The Asian-American stereotype, you know, that I'm supposed to be smarter than the average person. There's times when people assume I'm smart and say,

'Oh, you don't have to study as much as I do.' (Female Asian-American science non-switcher)

One switcher described the constraints on his field choices of this well-intentioned ethnic stereotyping by teachers as "being put in a little bamboo cage." Both non-Asian-American students of color and white students expressed facets of dominant stereotypes about Asian-American students, for example, that they have an over-narrow focus on study and, thus, an "unfair competitive advantage":

It's hard to compete with them. Some of them are so dedicated—they bury their heads in the books for days, or weeks. They don't do anything else. If you ask them, 'What did you do over the weekend?' they didn't do anything but study. I'm thinking it's their Asian upbringing, being really dedicated and non-social. (Female Hispanic science non-switcher)

I'm not by *any* means racist. But with the Asian students, it becomes unnerving when you go to the engineering library and it's dark and dingy in the basement...They're all Asian students just buried in there, cramming away. You know, they're technically inclined, smart, and they...they don't have a social life to be perfectly honest. (Male black engineering switcher)

We encountered an even more insidious stereotype of Asian-Americans, mentioned by white students only, and always presented by speakers who were unaware that it was offensive. In asking our informants about race and ethnicity on their campuses, we always clarified that we were inquiring only about those who were American-born. However, we invariably had to redirect the focus of discussion about "Asians" from foreign- to American-born students, and some of our interviewees were unable to make this distinction:

There are 40 people in my chemistry class and I'd say about eight of them are minority students. I think they're Japanese-American—or Japanese. I'm not sure if they're American. (Male white science non-switcher)

Most of our minority students are Asian. A lot of them are coming from overseas, so I'm just not sure if any of them are American-born. (Female white science non-switcher)

Now this sounds like a really, really racist thing to say—I never noticed any American-born minorities in the engineering classes. Maybe I just wasn't paying attention. (Male white engineering switcher)

Americans who are of Oriental descent, who speak with California slang are rapidly being assimilated into the culture. It's almost as though they're deliberately doing it. (Male white engineering non-switcher)

The legal barriers to citizenship for Asians were abolished in 1952, but over 40 years later, Asian-Americans still appear to be stereotyped as foreigners. The negative stereotypes of blacks, Hispanics, and native Americans have functioned to convince them they are inferior to whites. The stereotype of Asian-Americans as foreigners holds the potential of making Asian-Americans feel like aliens in their own country.

In their struggle to be seen as individuals, some students must deal not only with negative racial or ethnic stereotypes, but with the additional stereotypes of gender, or of having an athletic scholarship:

> If I was a man—a Caucasian man with a 2.7—I would have been fine. But there I am with a 2.7 being female and a minority, and I feel like an idiot. I'm not an idiot, but sometimes it's hard to believe that because of what they're always telling you. (Female Hispanic engineering switcher)

> I've felt when I was sitting in class, they were thinking, 'Here's the dumb football player with his hand up,' or, 'Here's a black that doesn't get it.' There's something that goes through *your* mind and sometimes it causes you to be hesitant about asking a question. (Male black engineering switcher)

> Here you are struggling with the course work and athletics and then you have to prove to other people that you're not the dumb jock. A lot of athletes don't need that. And those of us who are black don't need that either. (Male black science switcher)

These students described how the double or triple stereotype is transmitted:

> I went to see the athletic academic advisor and she instantly assumed that I was unintelligent and started signing me up for classes that were insulting to me. I felt that I was being looked at as a black student athlete. I was the only black girl athlete on the campus with a scholarship and I was in completely the 'wrong' sport. Everybody expected me to be track or basketball, not swimming. It just gets to be a hassle when you're having to justify your existence every other day. (Female black engineering switcher)

> One of my teachers would treat this one basketball player differently. Like maybe he was just 'the big guy,' and he'd make jokes—friendly jokes like, 'He'll protect us if someone comes in,' and not talk to him in a real academic way. So I think athletes definitely receive discrimination. (Male white engineering switcher)

As already argued, the greatest danger which stereotypes pose to the members of any group is that they will be internalized:

> I know a black woman who switched to art, she was going to be a physics major. Her physics professor came and told her, 'Why are you in my classroom. What can you possibly want to know about physics?' And it was horrible for her...and, coming from a professor, you know, that is devastating for a student. And black students will internalize it and say, 'Well, this is me. It must be me.' (Female black engineering switcher)

When people apply stereotypical characterizations to themselves, they become unable to act in ways that will change or counter the stereotype, and it is further reinforced:

> Just because you're Chinese you're supposed to just know math. If you don't, then you can't show your face around. If you're black, the stereotype is you shouldn't know math. If you do, then you're just not cool. All you should know is sports and that's where you belong. It's harder for you to open up and try other things because you've been told that you will fail at them. That fear keeps you away from trying it. (Female black science non-switcher)

To overcome the negative feelings toward self and group they have internalized, people are motivated to prove to others and to themselves that they are not "inferior":

> I feel like I have to work twice as hard in order to get the same respect as a non-minority student. (Female black science switcher)

> They say that I will always get a job, and that I don't have to worry because I'm a minority and because I'm a woman. But either way, I know I'm going to catch flak. Even if I get hired, I'm going to have to be twice as good just to prove I am average. (Female Hispanic engineering switcher)

Paradoxically, the students' earliest encounters with particular stereotypes were often in their own communities where the widespread internalization of particular stereotypes had endowed them with a factual, taken-for-granted quality:

> There is this feeling you have no right to be in the university—of not being good enough—which results in feelings of inadequacy and a self-imposed ceiling. It all comes from cultural learning which is constantly reinforced by questioning from home. (Male native American science non-switcher)

> It's like, I can say, 'Well, because I'm Hispanic I wasn't able to do this stuff.' I won't say that, but I've lived that since I was a young kid...Most Hispanic kids aren't even *expected* to go to college. The ones who do, often lack the confidence to do things that they can actually do. (Male Hispanic engineering switcher)

Many students had experienced stereotyping by teachers and counselors, including those of their own race or ethnicity, long before they entered college. In the following focus group excerpts, science seniors of color describe how they had developed a poor self-image early in their education:

> Black woman: All through junior high they put me in easier classes. High school, they started doing it again. Not until I started hearing my peers talking about college and the requirements that you need to take—algebra, geome-try—all that stuff, did I realize, 'Wait a minute, I can't get into college without these classes.' I talked to my counselor and had to beg her to put me into honors and regular classes. If I hadn't done that, I probably wouldn't be here.

Hispanic man: It has a lot to do with counseling in high school. When they see you're a minority, they say, 'Oh, you shouldn't take these classes. I don't think you're going to do good in it.' And they put you in something lower.

Asian-American man: 'Take wood shop.' Yeah, that's what they did with my brother. When we came here, he wanted to take science classes. 'No, no. Your English is not good.' But we didn't listen to them, and he went to science classes and did fine. They shouldn't put you down.

Black man: I made it through high school with good scores because of a teacher that took interest in me. She used to say, 'Take these courses. Don't listen to the counselors. Don't listen to your friends.' I think there were just two of us who made it through high school. So that's also something we should deal with—having our expectations increased.

Black woman: I went to a minority community college...I interacted very closely with all my professors in biology, chemistry, physics and I became friends with them. But every one of them, including minority professors, would give you the message that they didn't expect you to do more than this. *Always! Always!* It was the same problem.

Hispanic woman: Now that I have been here four years I feel at the same level as peers and I know that I belong here. I think we're qualified; we do have the skills. It's the psychological factor that I think we should work with.

Students were shocked and angry to find that some of the same stereotypes they had fought not to internalize during childhood and adolescence were reflected in the structure of minority programs on their campuses. The following are observations on this aspect of minority programs at three different universities:

One thing that I dislike about the minority program is that it tends to look down at you: even the counselors don't expect much of you. I realize that they're trying to keep you from getting into academic problems, but they look at all minority students the same way. I went once to see a counselor and she said, 'You can't take these classes because you're not ready. It's too much for you.' They're just reinforcing what you're already thinking: 'Maybe I'm not strong enough to do that.'...It's a problem if the people who are supposed to be helping you, hold you back. (Female black science non-switcher)

A lot of the minority counselors who are our own people don't expect much. Then it's just a self-fulfilling prophecy if people tell us that we're slightly less-qualified and our own people believe it and say it back to us. Who do we go to, to change this? (Female Hispanic science non-switcher)

Socially, there's Asian groups. I only went once, I didn't like it: I don't need a group to tell me to be proud about who I am, especially if that group subliminally reinforces certain tendencies in my group. There are a lot of pre-meds and a lot of engineering...that's fine. But do I have to hang out with them? I'd rather go where people are interested in the same things I am. (Male Asian-American science switcher)

They have this tutoring thing in engineering. Everybody who is black has to go. It's a workshop for calculus and she gives us extra practice problems. I feel like they put us together so that we know everyone and find someone we can communicate with. But it's separating us and making us different from everyone else—saying that we need extra help because we're black. (Female black engineering non-switcher)

Doubts about one's ability to do the work, coupled with a generalized lack of confidence, were less commonly expressed by white male students, but were common in interviews with both white women and students of color. Feeling incompetent from the outset made it easier for students to become discouraged by grades which were lower than expected. Students of color who experienced academic difficulty often did not ask questions or seek help: they had come to believe that their situation was hopeless:

You're always self-conscious about the *way* that they're looking at you. And you're trying to figure out, 'What are they gonna think about me asking this question?' Not because I don't understand it, but because I'm black and I'm not supposed to understand. (Male black engineering switcher)

There are so many students trying to get attention, trying to get help. And if you're not doing well and the professors have some kind of ready-made idea about your capabilities, it's very hard for you to approach professors. (Female black science switcher)

Well, I always wanted to be in engineering, but it was very intimidating. They didn't seem really encouraging. I just chickened out. I didn't think I could hack it. Actually, the work wasn't too hard. I think I just psyched myself out of that computer class. I just figured it was too hard. You have to believe in yourself to get through the material. And when they cut you down, you just don't think it's possible at all. (Female Hispanic engineering switcher)

The competition makes it difficult when it appears that everyone is prepared for this and you're not. Every time I walked into a classroom or lab I was intimidated just because I felt like I wasn't prepared for the situation. And heaven forbid I should ask a stupid question. (Male black engineering switcher)

It's kind of like a whirlpool effect. You start out on the top and then it just pulls you in and takes you finally to the point where you're becoming depressed because you got a C or a D. You're saying, 'What the hell? No matter what I do now, it's too late to compensate.' (Male black science switcher)

Even students of color who were about to graduate in their original S.M.E. major continued to express feelings of inadequacy. As the wholehearted internalization of a stereotype is more likely under conditions of social isolation, those who had persisted had, in every case, found a student support group which encouraged them to share their feelings and to resist internalizing stereotypes:

> I started off thinking that I was less qualified than some other people here. Even though I did very well on my S.A.T.s and my high school G.P.A. was good, I always had that doubt whether they were putting me here...as sort of a challenge to see if I could make it. I worked very hard and I did very well, but that's always in the back of your mind. You have to have friends here or it will just overpower you. (Female black science non-switcher)

> If you come into a class where you feel like you're not up to par or you don't belong, you begin with that doubt. You set your standards to a lower level than if you come in with confidence...How did I get that confidence? It came from my own group. Definitely! I mean, you don't bring it here with you. (Male Hispanic science non-switcher)

In sum, the values and support of their racial or ethnic group is the floor upon which students of color stand. Unfortunately, an internalized stereotype is the ceiling above which they cannot rise.

Degree of Ethnic Isolation and Perceptions of Prejudice

From our analysis of minority and majority students' views of the state of ethnic relations on their campuses, we constructed a picture of the role played by perception of prejudice in the switching decisions of students of color. Students whose racial or ethnic group formed an insignificant part of the minority population on campus experienced both physical and social isolation. Group isolation has two serious outcomes for students of color in S.M.E. majors: it makes an indirect but very powerful contribution to switching decisions and it heightens their perception of prejudice. We consistently found that racially or ethnically isolated students felt surrounded by white students who were prejudiced toward them. Unpleasant incidents clearly did occur—whether in the classroom or elsewhere on campus. However, they took on even greater significance when there was no one with whom to share the pain and humiliation. This is not to argue that racism does not exist where it is not perceived; nor that it exists on every occasion where it is perceived. On campuses where there were very few native Americans, blacks and Hispanics in S.M.E. majors, these students experienced doubt that they belonged, wondered if others judged them as incompetent, held back from seeking help or asking questions and were miserably lonely without a peer group with whom to share their experiences:

> There are not too many African-American students in *any* of the classes. We have to seek each other out...Common issues bring us together. Students who feel isolated feel like they don't belong, and that somehow their actions and their behaviors may not be up to par. They internalize feelings that may be irrelevant, but they end up *becoming* relevant! (Male black engineering switcher)

> I don't see diversity. In my classes, I'm the only black person and you don't feel as at ease to voice your own opinions in class. You might just want to save it rather than speak up. (Female black engineering switcher)

> Sometimes I ask myself, 'What am I doing here?' I could attend a southwestern university where there's a larger Indian population. I would say, for me, the only interaction with white students is in the classroom. Outside I just have minority connections. It's very important for me to belong to the native American community. If you don't have a support group or cannot find one, then you are lost here. (Male native American science non-switcher)

Gross numbers to the contrary, we discovered Asian-American students in S.M.E. majors also experienced ethnic isolation on all but two of the campuses we studied, and on the other five campuses they were hard pressed to form an ethnic peer group. This problem appears to be greatest for Asian-American women:

> I felt really all alone (pause)...really all alone in physics. The class was huge and it seemed that a lot of people, like, would get together to do problem sets, and I felt like everyone was getting them a lot quicker. (Female Asian-American engineering switcher)

Ethnic isolation creates the sense of being a token representative for one's ethnic group. The pressure to do well is enhanced, and the fear of admitting to inadequacy by asking for help is also greater:

> In engineering, it's not necessarily conscious to administrators or professors, but it's *there*. It makes you feel like they look down on you. And if you are the only one, that makes it difficult to ask a T.A. or professor for help and just confirm that you're stupid like they thought. (Female Hispanic engineering switcher)

The higher the degree of ethnic isolation, the more keenly the isolated individual perceives prejudice. Being the sole target for all the slings and arrows of ethnic stereotypes makes one more vulnerable to their sting. By extension, the more ethnically isolated any S.M.E. student feels, the greater the likelihood of their leaving the major. Feeling self-conscious of being the sole representative of one's group was especially intense for students from ethnically or racially homogeneous communities. Those who had been integrated into the white community throughout their education felt less discomfort in classes where there were few members of their own group:

> It depends on what kind of community they were brought up in. If they were from an all-Asian community, and then come here, where the majority is white, they would feel the tension more. But if they were brought up in an all-white community, then I don't think they have too much difficulty as far as fitting in, making friends. (Female Asian-American science non-switcher)

I was always around Caucasians. I was never really around Asians. I've experienced some racism here, but I mean, it's nothing that's ever bothered me. (Male Asian-American science non-switcher)

White students and faculty sometimes assume that students of color who are isolated will find support by forming social relationships with students from other groups. Students of color do not share this assumption:

I don't see a real mixing of the groups. You notice when you look around the classroom that you're the only Hispanic and there's only one black person. You share a lot of the same feelings, but at the same time, you wouldn't want to go up to them and say, 'It's us against them.' (Male Hispanic engineering switcher)

How could you come to a place this big and still feel isolated? You would think with all the people you'd have people around you at all times. But people pull together within their own group. I find that especially with the Asian students. I've tried to hook up with a few of them because they're smart in math, but it's hard. They help their own and stick together pretty much. (Male black engineering switcher)

Everyone's ethnocentric, so it's not surprising. You always see these clusters of Indian or Chinese students, and, of course, you want to be in your own little cluster of blacks. But you didn't have that opportunity here because there were so few of us. (Male black engineering switcher)

The strong need for same-group affiliation was sometimes met by a shift into the humanities or social science classes where minority groups are represented in larger numbers, open discussion of issues of race and ethnicity is encouraged and students can major in an area of ethnic specialization:

If you're in a class where you're unique, then you have to feel like you don't fit in. And if you're with a whole bunch of people just like you, then you're more likely to stay. It just made sense to me to go to Asian studies. (Male Asian-American engineering switcher)

If you are isolated, especially Koreans, you can become really academically involved because you're not involved much socially. Some people who excel in studying do really well and go into graduate school. But they're always alone and limited to academics. And some people who are isolated just drop out of school. I decided to go to philosophy before that happened to me. (Male Asian-American science switcher)

I was one of only a few blacks, but in sociology we're almost half the majors. You've got peers like yourself and a couple of faculty too. And it's open, you know, race isn't treated like a dirty secret like over in the engineering school. (Male black engineering switcher)

Students are hesitant to come into engineering or stay here because of the hostile, racist environment—just not feeling accepted in classes, or having anybody to have a cup of coffee with, or saying anything to you, ever. (Male Hispanic engineering switcher)

I like it when they offer classes on African and Brazilian literature and black history classes and stuff like that. I sort of understand when people say affirmative action is not fair. But on the other hand, I just remember how I felt in the biology class all by myself. (Female black science switcher)

Analysis of destination majors supports our contention that ethnic isolation makes an important negative contribution to S.M.E. switching by students of color. In their final choice, students often moved to majors where, by the very nature of the discipline, they would be less isolated. These included area studies (such as Asian, African-American and Latin American Studies), a variety of specializations in ethnic history and foreign languages. The social sciences also drew switchers into majors in race relations, cultural anthropology, urban studies and social work.

As to the experience of overt unpleasantness, students of color clearly understood the distinction between prejudice (belief) and discrimination (action), and realized that these operated independently:

There is some discrimination from the faculty, which is subtle. I'm not really sure if it's really racism or just nervousness...But I think that there are also some intentional racist faculty here. (Female black science switcher)

You sit next to them and they'll actually move away. It's rampant in engineering. You know, it is not something subtle. (Male Hispanic engineering switcher)

I would say they're pretty much racist throughout the whole campus, but I would say more so in engineering because that is a very lucrative field. And the more non-white students that they can weed-out the better it is for them. I think it's a systematic way of keeping certain jobs open for certain people. (Male black engineering switcher)

When I asked my last professor what he was looking for in an applicant for a researcher position, he said, 'Somebody like myself.' I was very quiet and I thought, 'I guess I'm in trouble 'cause I don't look very much like you.' I didn't say that to him. I just thought it. (Male black science non-switcher)

You know, the racist attitudes, the discriminatory attitudes have not gone. They've just gone underground. That is the worst. A person will be smiling right in your face and you don't know what they're thinking. (Male black engineering switcher)

It's *real!* When I first came here, I was doing what I thought was good work. I had just taken a course with the professor who gave me a B, and he was teaching a seminar for undergraduates, offered with consent of the professor only. But at that point I didn't know what that meant, so I enrolled. The first day I showed up and he said, 'I didn't talk to you. You need to come and talk to me at my office hours.' When I went to speak to him, he said, 'This class

is by consent of the instructor only.' I said, 'I know, but I'm enrolled in the
class.' Then he began to drill me. Why was I there? He hadn't consented for
me to take the class, and it just wasn't the class for me. It was just blatant
racism in my opinion. Blatant, blatant racism. (Female black science switcher)

White students, however, did not understand the distinction between prejudice
and discrimination and suggested that if no discriminatory acts were committed,
then there was no prejudice. Comments such as, "They're always looking for
racism," "They have a chip on their shoulder," and "They read discrimination
in the simplest thing," reflected their belief that students of color are overly
sensitive, and that the problem, and its resolution, lies largely with students of
color themselves. The pressure to internalize this assessment of the situation was
strong and was difficult to resist:

> Racism is *increasing* in some areas on campus. Again! My husband is white,
> and we went through several *long* conversations about my fears and why they
> really were very realistic. I still get very upset when people suggest it is in my
> imagination or something that can just be overcome. (Female black engineering
> switcher)

> When it comes to multi-culturalism and P.C.-ism, I know a lot of people are
> really turned off by the idea, and don't want to understand what started these
> things. But when you know someone who's personally been affected, that's
> always the changing point. (Female Hispanic engineering switcher)

The belief that faculty or majority students are prejudiced was found to be
as powerful in its effect on the academic performance of students of color as
were more overt acts of discrimination:

> In my biochemistry classes I was the only minority. I would look around to see
> if I could find somebody to study with and like...Usually the people form
> groups within their ethnicity. You feel uncomfortable so you don't push
> yourself to try. (Female black science switcher)

> In most of the classes I've taken, if I've tried to hook up with somebody for
> a study partner, they kind of pull away from you. (Male black engineering
> switcher)

> If the class requires you to have a lab partner, you just keep pulling straws
> until you're the last one. That doesn't help your level of confidence. (Male
> Hispanic science switcher)

Minority Group Enrollment Levels and Perceptions of Racism. All white
students were asked how they felt students of color were treated on their
campus. At the five sites where the white population exceeded 80 percent, the
most common response was that, with so few students of color on their campus,
they did not think that anti-ethnic or racist sentiments existed. They commonly
expressed sympathy for the isolation and greater degree of difficulty which they
believed students of color experienced in S.M.E. classes. Although the tone of

some of the following observations from white students on these campuses may seem somewhat patronizing and informed by stereotypical ideas, they also reflect a generalized goodwill:

We probably have a higher ratio of ethnic professors than we do students. I mean this place is so white and blond it's frightening. I think they could use some more ethnic diversity. Look around. I don't think we have a black person in engineering in the entire department. There aren't even very many brown ones: there's no red ones. There are plenty who are of Oriental descent, you know, who were born here. (Male white engineering non-switcher)

I think it's real important that more minorities should be in engineering. It's probably 90 percent white male and maybe five, six, seven percent Asian, I guess. And that's really terrible. I think a good cultural mix is real important. (White male engineering non-switcher)

On the whole, the minority population is at a much lower economic level than Caucasians. They don't have the opportunity for an education. I don't see anything wrong with trying to help them, because as a group you need to have people that are gonna be role models, that will succeed, for the children to look up to and say, 'Look, I really can do this.' (Female white science non-switcher)

When I see a black student in class it's like, 'Wow, this is so unusual. This is...this is good.' I mean, I think more should come, but I think that starts further back in their upbringing. The high schools they end up going to don't put that much emphasis on it and they don't say, 'Yes, you can do this.' They could succeed with a little more tender loving care. (Female white engineering switcher)

I don't feel that they've let people in who aren't qualified because of their ethnicity. I feel everyone I've met here is very smart, and sometimes more motivated because of their ethnic background—because it's a way out. They grew up not having a lot of money and they felt like their education was gonna get them out, which gave them more drive—which is a good thing. (Female white science switcher)

Lack of contact between dominant and minority groups has often been viewed as a situation in which stereotypes and prejudice are more likely to flourish: where white people see few people of color, negative stereotypes go unchallenged. We, therefore, expected the accounts of white students on predominantly white campuses to confirm the perceptions of students of color that there were high levels of prejudice. By the same logic, on the two campuses where Asian-American representation in S.M.E. majors was high, we also expected to find white students expressing more positive feelings towards them than on campuses where there were few Asian-American students in S.M.E. majors. However, both expectations were contradicted by our findings. This became clear as we analyzed the perspectives of white students towards particular groups who were either the largest racial or ethnic group on campus, or in the case of native Americans, were present in proportions that were larger than the national average.

Table 6.3 shows the percentage of enrollment (in all majors) by ethnicity at each of our seven interview sites. (The percentages for foreign students are given, but these students were not included in our sample.) For comparison, Figure 6.1 provides the national enrollment averages for students of those groups shown in Table 6.3. Within S.M.E. majors, the representation of each racial or ethnic group is generally lower than for the social sciences and humanities. By comparing the dominant perspectives on the inter-racial/ethnic climate which were expressed by S.M.E. students with those expressed by students of color at each of the sites, it became clear the two groups did not share the same view of racial/ethnic relations on their campus. The higher the representation of a racial or ethnic group in S.M.E. majors, the more resentment of that specific group was expressed by white students. Conversely, where representation of a racial or ethnic group was small (or, in the case of native Americans, at a size consonant with white students' expectations), white students expressed less prejudice and more favorable attitudes toward the members of that ethnic group. Thus, those campuses where the students of color believed white S.M.E. students were prejudiced against them were actually campuses where white peers expressed greatest sympathy toward students of color. The strongest prejudice was actually expressed on campuses where S.M.E. students of color said they felt most accepted. For example, at the small, private western college, native Americans were represented at twice the national average, and at the time of the interviews, 20 freshmen had recently been recruited from the same reservation. Although native American students were still less than two percent of the student body, this was the largest representation of native Americans on any campus we visited. Native Americans acknowledged awareness of racism targeted towards other racial and ethnic groups on this campus, but felt they were well-accepted:

> I think it's better here than some places. I mean, I think it's pretty bad for native Americans down South. Sometimes it seems like there's very little racism, and then, all of the sudden, it's big again. I'm sure it's always going to be there. But I think native Americans are well accepted here—as different, but equal. (Female native American science switcher)

This assessment was not, however, echoed in our conversations about attitudes towards native Americans on this campus with current and former white S.M.E. majors:

> At this college there's a large Indian population and there is definitely resentment here. They go to school free. They get paid to go to school, actually. Four hundred dollars a month and they don't have to do a thing. And that makes me upset, that, for them there's a free ride. I never see them

TABLE 6.3 Percentage of Enrollment by Race/Ethnicity at Seven Institutions (1991-1993).

MWPUB1 = Midwest, public, ranking 1; WPUB2 = West, public, ranking 2; WPUB3 = West, public, ranking 3; ECPUB4 = East Coast, public, ranking 4; WCPRI1 = West Coast, private, ranking 1; WPRI2 = West, private, ranking 2; WPRI3 = West, private, ranking 3; with ranking according to a modifed version of the Carnegie Classification of Institutions (cf., *Chronicle of Higher Education*, July 8, 1987).

a = above national average, b = largest minority population on campus

Institution	Native American	Asian-American	Black	Hispanic	White	Foreign-born	Total Enrollment
MWPUB1	0.5	3.9 b	2.1	1.1	87.6 a	4.7 a	56,350
WPUB2	0.7	4.7 a	1.9	5.2 b	83.9 a	3.6 a	28,836
WPUB3	0.9 a	2.2	1.5	4.1 b	88.4 a	2.9	27,080
ECPUB4	0.3	9.5 a	10.0 ab	3.1	69.7	7.4 a	34,621
WCPRI1	0.9 a	14.1 ab	5.4	7.3 a	57.4	14.9 a	15,150
WPRI2	0.6	2.9	3.2	4.1 b	83.3 a	6.0 a	7,878
WPRI3	1.6 a	2.8	2.1	5.7 b	85.5 a	2.3	1,949

FIGURE 6.1 Average Percent Enrollment at 3,100 U.S. Institutions of Higher Education by Race and Ethnicity.

# of Institutions	Native American	Asian-American	Black	Hispanic	White	Foreign-born	Total Enrollment
3,100	0.8	4.4	9.3	6.0	76.5	2.9	14,359,000

Source: U.S. Department of Education, *Chronicle of Higher Education*, March 3, 1993.

study. Hispanics and other minorities seem to work as hard as anyone else.
(Male white science switcher)

If somebody wanted to get governmental funds, they would claim, even if
they're only one-eighth of some tribal group, just because they are rewarded
for being an American Indian. In some, it's not noticeable at all that they're
Indian. The system is being taken advantage of. (White female science
switcher)

A similar situation was found at the East Coast state university with the
largest black student population of any of the seven sites. At 10 percent of the
student body, black students exceeded the national average. In a situation where
black students were strongly represented and had easy academic and social
access to other black students, they described the inter-racial climate on their
campus as comfortable and largely determined by their own attitudes and
behavior:

I have never experienced any prejudice. I've never been called names. I've
never been discriminated against here. And I think a lot of that also has to do
with my attitude. You know, I don't exude a defensive mode. (Female black
science switcher)

We all have experienced some racism somewhere, but I mean, it's nothing
that's ever bothered me. But here I haven't had to deal with it and I feel very
comfortable in engineering. (Male black engineering non-switcher)

Amongst our white S.M.E. discussants on this campus, we found clear evidence
of stereotypical attitudes, resentment and prejudice toward black students, of
which our black informants were apparently unaware:

The university must maintain a 15 percent black population or something. *That*
kinda gets me off. I don't see how you could possibly admit this guy who's 2.1
G.P.A. out of high school, but he's filling that last percent of the quota for
blacks on our campus. So they say, 'Let him in. See how he does.' (White
male engineering non-switcher)

If some rich black decided to take a scholarship he could get it. I've never
applied for a scholarship, but that's where my resentment comes in—I mean,
if someone else gets a scholarship that I could apply for. (Male white
engineering switcher)

I just don't know if they're as qualified, and it's unfair for people who are
qualified and have worked hard and done better than some of these blacks. I
think it should be equal for everybody...I don't think there should be a
program, that says, 'We have to admit this many minority students.' That's
just not fair. We don't talk about that too much because there are so many
black students here. (Female white science switcher)

Blacks could be lacking and be put into the system on the assumption that
they'll adapt or figure a way to learn. Maybe they were screw-offs in high

school; maybe they'll turn serious here in college. I think the university does 'em a *big* favor by letting them in. *Big* favor! (Male white engineering non-switcher)

This pattern repeated itself at the four western campuses where Hispanic students were the dominant minority group (although only at the private West Coast university did Hispanics exceed the national average of 6 percent). At each of these four campuses, we found a well-represented minority group experiencing feelings of acceptance by the white majority population in S.M.E. majors:

I don't think that students or faculty have preconceived notions about the quality of work I do or the kind of person I am based on my last name. (Male Hispanic engineering non-switcher)

I feel very accepted here for who I am. My work, my intelligence, everything about me is taken on an individual basis by non-Latinos. I'm quite comfortable in engineering. (Female Hispanic engineering non-switcher)

Again, these feelings did not square with those of white S.M.E. peers, whose resentment towards Hispanics was based on the belief that they were given unfair advantages, especially waiver of entrance requirements, and that affirmative action programs were abused by students who qualified by race or ethnicity, but not by academic performance or family income level:

I know from my high school this year there are three Hispanic students that got in, and I'm not saying that those people are not bright, 'cause I'm sure they were some of the top students. But I do know that, sometimes, affirmative action does make a difference, and you don't want them to be accepting people just because they feel they ought to. You want the quality of your school to stay high. Three is an awfully big number for a school of 1,500. I could see three from a better quality school, but not from one high school. And the fact that they were all Hispanic. I don't want to sound like I'm discriminating, but.... (Female white science switcher)

I'll tell you something that's really bothered me. At N.I.H. they have a program designed for minority students and my friend who is Hispanic, they gave her this thing. I don't know how much that has to do with her Hispanic background, but since she's been here she's been offered a job for Hispanic or black women. I don't think her background is that different from mine. Her parents both have master's, and she's lived in the United States for the majority of her life. There are going to be cases where people who don't particularly need an advantage are going to get it. (Female white science non-switcher)

Encouraging minorities to come here is fine. There's no reason to withhold a good education from someone on the basis of their ethnic group. However, you should not be financing it for them. There are just as many whites here who are hard up as there are Hispanics. (Male white science non-switcher)

Asian-American students are 4.4 percent of the national undergraduate student population, which is lower than that of both blacks and Hispanics. Although Asian-Americans are more strongly represented in science and engineering majors, in other majors, their presence appears to be larger than it actually is because, as we consistently found, other students tend not to distinguish Asian-American from Asian students from other countries. At two of our sites, Asian-American students were the largest single non-white group. Although they were not a significant proportion of the student body at the midwestern university—which had the highest percentage (88%) of white students of any of our sites—their presence was more noticed because other students of color were so rare. At the private West Coast university, the percentage of white students was below, and the Asian-American campus population nearly three times greater than, the national averages for each group. This university also had the highest percentage of students of color of any of the sites visited; native American and Hispanic enrollment also exceeded the national average with white enrollment slightly over 50 percent. The unusually high degree of diversity at this academically-selective institution has been created as a matter of institutional policy, and the value of diversity is strongly promoted. For example, all freshmen are required to take a course in "ethnic sensitivity." Asian-American students on both of these campuses indicated that they felt comfortable and accepted by their white peers:

> Caucasians that I've talked with or been close with have been very nice. I've never really experienced any racism stuff. (Male Asian-American engineering non-switcher)

> I don't remember any situation where I had a problem. Not really. (Female Asian-American engineering switcher)

> Difficulties? I don't find any—not for myself, or for other Asian students I know who have been raised here. (Male Asian-American engineering non-switcher)

We did not, however, find that official promotion of the idea of a diverse academic community on the West Coast campus had resulted in a greater acceptance of the strong Asian-American presence in S.M.E. majors by white students than that found at the midwestern campus where an official pro-diversity policy existed, but was less overtly stressed. On both campuses, white class-mates repeated the same resentments towards Asian-Americans that we heard expressed towards other strongly-represented groups elsewhere. These included receiving "unfair advantages" in employment opportunities and scholarships, and exploiting programs intended for poorer students:

> I'm paying for my own tuition. I've been saving since I was 13. Basically, I contribute three-quarters of my funding. It's really frustrating to me to see friends who are Asian who are living so well-off. I feel like that they're really

exploiting the system. It's really frustrating because there are all these programs for minority students, but a number of minority students I see getting the funding and getting these programs or scholarships are exactly the ones who don't really need it. (Female white engineering non-switcher)

I applied to work and had all the qualifications for it, but they were taking minorities that semester. So I didn't get into it...They're going to pick Orientals, and...um...other foreigners. That makes me sound a little prejudiced, but I've always been at the wrong place at the wrong time to get jobs. (Male white engineering non-switcher)

Seems to me there are so many more scholarships available for minorities, especially if you're gonna be an engineer. I know a Japanese woman and she's told me they're set! She's got a free ride practically. (Male white engineering non-switcher)

These perceptions are doubly ironic: 'minority programs' tend to exclude Asian-American students because they are not considered to be "under-represented" in the sciences, and middle-class Asian-Americans express resentment about "unfair" competition for funding toward other non-white S.M.E. students:

We have an Office of Minority Student Affairs, but I've always felt that they catered more to African-Americans than to any other minority, which in a way is a bias. People like myself, we don't even have a category. I don't think there is a campus organization that caters to our needs financially, especially if you're from a middle-class background like me. (Female Asian-American science non-switcher)

We also found that Asian-American students actively avoided seeking any special advantage related to ethnicity and often expressed the same disapproving attitude as their white peers toward students who were thought to abuse programs based on affirmative action principles:

I try and stress my academics and my achievements. I think that's more important than saying, 'Look, I'm a minority. You owe me.' I really have a problem with that. As far as scholarships for minorities, if somebody cannot afford to go to school and wants that opportunity, that's fine. But if somebody is trying to take advantage, I have a problem with that. (Female Asian-American science switcher)

I don't advocate race-based scholarships. The African-American community says, 'It's needed because we have historically been cheated of our opportunities.' I don't think your race or your color should give you an edge over someone else. If they do give a scholarship for black people, it should be poor black people or intelligent black people, you know, not just anyone who just wants to go to school. (Male Asian-American science non-switcher)

White students on both campuses expressed an additional set of negatives beliefs and attitudes toward Asian-American students: that they were foreigners; that there were "too many" Asian T.A.s; and that the Asian presence in S.M.E. classes was "overwhelming":

> Asians are going into the science field, and so are a lot of other folks that don't live in the United States. You walk in these classes and the Asian T.A. is in there and somebody goes, 'Oh, god. Look at this guy.' (White male science switcher)

> I don't feel like I'm racist by any means, but there is a very large ethnic population in the engineering program—specifically, Asian. I mean if someone is smart, it doesn't matter what their race is, they'll still make the curve the same way. But a lot of the people that started off in engineering would be Asian, and consequently you have a disproportionate number of them that want to be T.A.s. (Male white engineering switcher)

> I felt especially inadequate in comparison with the Asian students in this engineering class. It seemed to be largely dominated by them. Not that they were discriminatory at all. Just that I felt so overwhelmed that there were *so* many. (Female white engineering switcher)

As the foregoing discussion indicates, the character of ethnic relations on each campus was shaped by variations in the proportions of minority-to-majority students in the S.M.E. population. Indeed, we found an inverse relationship between the level of hostility and resentment expressed by white students and the degree of racism perceived by students of color. When the population ratio of an ethnic group reaches a point that can sustain the perception of acceptance for its own members, it triggers white prejudice and attitudes opposing affirmative action programs. The paradoxical effect of increased ethnic density is expressed in the following hypothesis: as the number of students in an ethnic group increases, expression of white student resentment toward that group also increases, though its members perceive less prejudice. As we have illustrated, students of color in well-represented groups did not notice racism on their campus; others noticed some hostility, but discounted it as being indistinguishable from racism in society at large, or distanced themselves from its consequences. This appears to occur because the group effectively insulates its members from a reality which is harsher than they realize. S.M.E. students of color who belonged to well-represented groups were physically and socially insulated from the white majority on campus. They shared common living arrangements, study groups and social activities, and had little or no contact with white students outside of classes. Enveloped by a close-knit group, they were protected from negative stereotypes, received affective and instrumental support, developed a positive view of the campus ethos and were, thereby, enabled to persist, despite a high level of (unperceived) hostility from white peers.

In considering the sources of white student resentment toward more strongly-represented groups, we need to look more closely at the nature of the negative beliefs and attitudes most commonly expressed by white S.M.E. students. It is often assumed that people with more education are less likely to express racial or ethnic prejudice. This assumption underwrites the expectation that people in lower socio-economic groups are more likely to be prejudiced because they perceive a serious economic threat in competition for unskilled jobs from applicants of color. The findings from this study do not refute this theory, but extend it across class lines to include both income and education. We would argue that it is not the level of education attained, but how likely the chance of achieving economic security is thought to be that governs the extent to which people in the dominant group see those in smaller ethnic or racial groups as a competitive threat. For students, the threat is future-oriented: competition for jobs at a time of shrinking employment opportunities is perceived to be intensified by the admission of more students of color thought to have lower levels of qualifications on entry and preference in hiring on graduation:

> When you talk to people about the job market nowadays, especially with it so bad, comments are said, 'Well, I'll probably get beat out by a black woman anyway, so why should I even try for that?' It's really discouraging, but there is that feeling. (Female white engineering non-switcher)

> I don't like the idea of quotas and allowing people into something just because they're a minority. I think that's an insult to them because, if they're good, everyone should be given an equal chance. I mean, I believe in capitalism and that everyone should work for what they get. I don't believe anyone should ever be given a break for anything. The world's not a perfect place. (Female white engineering switcher)

> I don't think anyone should get a job over someone else because of the color of their skin. And it's upsetting because you feel like you worked so hard to keep your head above water, and then someone who sort of floats along is gonna get the job ahead of me. (Focus group, white women switchers)

> I think they are lowering the entrance requirements for minorities. Definitely! (Male white engineering non-switcher)

> I feel like the system's being exploited. There are a couple of minority students. They're living in these incredibly expensive homes. The only reason they were accepted to this university was not on their scholarly credentials, but because they have an Asian last name. (Female white biology non-switcher)

The racism generated by these fears about the future becomes a strong feature of campus life in the present.

By far the most strongly and most frequently expressed source of white student resentment concerned their own current (and apparently growing) difficulties in securing financial aid and other forms of college funding. Students of color were commonly thought to have unfair access to scholarships or other funds which were seen as difficult for white (or Asian-American) students to get. Anger was greatest where funds presumed to be ear-marked for talented students of color from lower-income families were thought to have been given to students with poorer academic performances or to those who had abused the system—either by making a questionable claim to a particular race or ethnicity or because group membership (rather than actual need) was thought to have determined the award. White students who were uncomfortable about the racism they perceived among their peers saw this as a manifestation of prejudices common in the wider society, but also expressed doubts about the efficacy or equity of the affirmative action approach to educational access:

> I see affirmative action as the wrong approach to the right problem, in that it just creates too much hostility and doesn't address the more deep causes of racial division and inequality. I think being a racist has to come sociologically from somewhere. I think it's ingrained by someone talking to you, especially a parent. (Male white engineering non-switcher)

> Once you're in a classroom it doesn't matter if you're a girl or a boy or a black or from a foreign nation. I mean, it doesn't make a difference and the professors don't care either. Giving minorities an opportunity, if they just can't do it, they're going to fail out sooner or later. It doesn't matter if you help them get in the door to take the class; eventually they won't make it through. (Male white engineering non-switcher)

Neither courses in ethnic sensitivity, nor greater contact with minority groups appear to ameliorate the level of prejudice. Indeed, we found the opposite to occur. The larger the ethnic group, the more its members are perceived as an economic threat to the majority, and the greater the degree of racism and hostility which is expressed against them by all students, including those of other ethnicities. On every campus, it was the largest minority group which was resented the most, and in all cases, this occurred when the group was represented at a higher percentage than the national average. We stress that this was an unexpected finding, and that the nature of both our research design and our data do not allow us to advance a hypothesis about the specific population ratio that would trigger this effect. We see this as an important question for future study.

"Minority Programs"

Over three-quarters (78%) of the students of color who switched reported they received inadequate support either from existing programs or because institutional resources were lacking. Few students of color found a campus-wide program that effectively served the needs of S.M.E. majors or any type of minority assistance program within their S.M.E. departments. Their need for such assistance was, however, strongly evidenced: without exception, every student of color who stayed in their original S.M.E. majors reported that some type of program assistance had been critical to their survival. The types of support most often identified as useful are discussed below.

Academic Assistance

On five of the sites, we found a single, campus-wide "minority" program whose goal was to recruit, retain and assist students of color across all disciplines, rather than by major. Students of color reported three types of problems with academic assistance programs: first, they applied the same approach to all students and did not take the cultural values and experience of different racial or ethnic groups into account; second, they were not field specific; and, third, they emphasized tutoring, short-term skill building and time management—all of which focus on weaknesses in students' preparation—but neglected to encourage interest in their discipline or enhance their intellectual experience.

Programs that define academic support only in remedial terms inadvertently stigmatize those who use them and promote reluctance to seek help among those who may need it most. Students of color at the three largest public universities reported that a free tutoring service was available for them, but not for Asian-American or white students. A student could, therefore, only take advantage of the service by, as one engineering switcher put it, labelling himself as "another black loser." At one of these institutions, all black, Hispanic and native American students (and *only* these students) who enrolled for S.M.E. entry-level classes were informed that registration for a second semester was contingent upon attendance at a twice-weekly mathematics tutorial program. No exceptions were made on the basis of S.A.T. mathematics scores or level of demonstrated competence, and no allowance was made for work schedules. Those who passed the mid-term exam were excused from attendance thereafter. The program, though well-intentioned, had counter-productive effects:

> It was supposed to be a minority math lab, but it was more of a remedial situation. And I really had no need for that. I was doing pretty well on my own. So I quit as soon as I could. (Male Hispanic engineering switcher)

> It was a night lab, you just go there from 6:00 p.m. to 9:00 p.m. and they're supposed to help you. I don't think I really needed it. I didn't try to get out of it. They said we had to go, but it was a waste of time for me. (Male native American science switcher)

> I didn't *want* to go to that program because I felt that it was the most *condescending* situation. I just felt that I don't *need* that kind of assistance. But they made us go. (Female black engineering switcher)

The quality of tutorial services offered to students of color was also called into question, especially when they were centrally rather than departmentally organized. On some campuses, there was no institutional provision for individual or group tutorials:

> From my experience, some of the tutors have a hard time with some of the subjects. (Male black engineering switcher)

> When I came here I started going to those tutorials. Now the group is bigger, so there's no personal help...I don't think discussion alone helps. (Male Hispanic science switcher)

> The black engineering society has some help for you. They have old tests you can use to study from. I guess that's all they had for us. (Male black engineering switcher)

The stereotypic notion that Asian-American students have an innate advantage in science and mathematics is perpetuated where the institution excludes them from access to academic assistance programs. We encountered Asian-American S.M.E. students who struggled with their class work, but who had no recourse to tutorial help:

> You just hang out together which helps some people, but I just didn't feel like that was what I needed when I was so far behind in calculus. I really would have liked to have some kind of tutoring like other minority students have available to them. (Female Asian-American engineering switcher)

> They have an Asian Engineering Society, but they don't offer tutoring. It's more of a social thing. There isn't really any tutoring at all. (Male Asian-American science switcher)

As discussed earlier, Asian-Americans who confessed to academic difficulties were unable to turn to their peers for help. Rather than realizing they were under-prepared or just needed tutorial help, Asian-Americans who experienced academic difficulties were peculiarly at risk of leaving their major in a mood of self-blame:

> All my life I wanted to be a doctor. I never thought of doing anything else.... (Pause.) My dad's a doctor and my grandfather too. But I just couldn't do the math. I tried so hard, I really did. I don't know why I couldn't get it. I'm not inferior in any other subject. Something's lacking in me, I guess. It was just the biggest disappointment I, and my family, ever had to get over. (Female Asian-American science switcher)

Field-specific tutoring was largely an unmet need, except at two sites where we found academic support programs provided by individual departments. The physics department at the East Coast public university had developed a tutorial laboratory staffed by graduate students which was open to all undergraduates. Many white students also took advantage of the individualized assistance they made available. The engineering department at one of the private universities also offered a tutorial program which was open to all students and was well-regarded by them. Students of color did not find it stigmatizing, used its services and found it helpful:

> They've gotten a couple of the best T.A.s in the physics department to have an extra section. They have opened it to everybody in the class now, but they give us preference—as far as getting in. I can see the difference in my grades.

I don't know if I would have gotten this grade in physics had I not had the extra help. (Female black science non-switcher)

I had an extra math class which was really good, because we got a chance to go over things and spend extra time working on stuff like the more challenging problems. That was a really good course. That probably got me through the math. (Female black science non-switcher)

They get a graduate student to work with you in the evenings. There was a big variety of students in those groups, but I think they give preference to minority students. I know it helped me a lot. I did very well in math, considering my background was very bad. In the end, I didn't have any problems at all with my calculus. Just the practicing extra problems is what I liked. I liked it a lot. And they really encourage you to study in groups. (Male Asian-American engineering non-switcher)

Students who lacked the options of field-specific and departmental tutoring suggested the need might be met by recruiting graduates and more senior undergraduates in their field as tutors or study-group leaders, by organizing field-specific clubs and by bringing field-specific program advisors into departments:

Maybe you could set up some kind of system where people who major in physics could help the undergraduates. We don't have such a system. (Female Asian-American science non-switcher)

I don't think there is a minority program that is field-wise. They pretty much just group people together and have native American and Latino programs. I'd like it if it were a group from the same field getting together—like a math or engineering club. (Male Hispanic engineering non-switcher)

After that second year, I was thinking about switching and I met an advisor in the minority advising office. He's helped me the most. He actually sat down and talked to me to help me figure out what directions I could pursue. He's Hispanic and a great guy. A lot of the times when I really need to talk, he's helped me. They should have people like him in engineering. (Male Asian-American engineering switcher)

Discipline-specific workshops for S.M.E. students of color were not offered at any of the sites visited. We are, however, aware of their efficacy. For example, in the first longitudinal study of performance and retention effects of workshops for S.M.E. students of color, Bonsangue and Drew (1992) reported that the achievement and persistence levels of the 133 participants were significantly better than the control group. The researchers tracked 320 black, Hispanic and native American students over a period of five years. They found two lasting benefits: early awareness of academic expectations in these majors and the necessity of remaining connected to student peers, professors and academic advisors throughout college. This work supports Treisman's (1992) conclusion from his calculus workshop for students of color that an academic intervention program stressing excellence rather than remediation is time and cost effective for both students and their institutions. Bonsangue and Drew also argue that the problems of under-prepared but able students of color can be overcome by good academic experiences and high expectations in college. Workshop programs are most effective when collaborative learning and community building are combined, and programs serve all S.M.E. majors, regardless of race or ethnicity. Though we did not find science or mathematics workshops at any of the sites visited, students' evaluations of the support programs which we encountered on two campuses, and the consensus of opinion about the kinds of programs students of color would most like to see, support Bonsangue and Drew's findings.

Finally, two segments of the S.M.E. minority population for whom there was no program support at any interview site were non-traditional students and athletes of color. Non-traditional students of color (who are over-represented compared with white students) and athletes of color both occupy a marginalized status which is exacerbated by the design of minority programs. The demands on their time from their other responsibilities make it impossible to take part in academic support programs designed to fit the schedules of traditional students. Older students, as discussed previously, often found affective support within the nuclear family. However, they do not find academic assistance there. Because students with athletic scholarships are assumed to be served by the advisors and tutors employed by the athletic department, S.M.E. departments do not make any effort to accommodate their need for academic help. On every campus we found athletes of color who were former S.M.E. majors, but none who had been able to persist in these majors.

Advising and Counseling Programs

A central office for the advising and counseling of students of color (including foreign students) was available on all seven campuses. Where a separate office provided student services for foreign students, Asian-Americans were served along with them. This, again, reinforced the belief of other students that all Asian-Americans share the same culture and are in this country on a temporary basis. On campuses with a single program serving all students of color, attempts to integrate different groups through social events were sometimes made. This is not usually successful because students who have suffered from negative stereotyping are just as likely to be prejudiced toward students of other racial and ethnic groups as white students who have never experienced it. Attempts to promote social mixing across racial and ethnic lines tend not to work. The assumption that not being white offers sufficient common ground to make students of different racial and ethnic groups wish to bond together is spurious and may cause offense. Students get together when they feel something in common, not on the basis of their cultural differentness from white students or from each other:

You can see that not only in engineering, but everywhere on campus. If you have lunch in the union, you'll see groups of blacks in one corner, Japanese in one corner, Koreans in one corner, Indians in one corner, and Hispanics in another corner. They're not able to relate to other groups because they have nothing in common. (Male black engineering switcher)

However, provision of offices serving individual different racial and ethnic groups on a campus-wide basis does not guarantee students will use them. We found campus-wide minority counseling and advising offices on every campus, but they were neither well-used, nor highly regarded by students of color. Under-use occurs when: students do not know about the service or the nature of service offered; they are seeking field-specific advice; they have experienced cultural insensitivity; they have been given inaccurate information; or they fear that the price of using the service is stigma:

There was a minority advisor but I was unaware of who she was and she didn't know about me. Towards the end when I talked to her, she said, 'You should have come and seen me sooner.' Well, I would have if I had known she existed, but it was too late then to stay in biology. (Female native American science switcher)

My student advisor on the floor said, 'Well, there isn't really much we can do.' I couldn't get to sleep at night—everything was just terrible! I didn't know about the minority help center or any of those things. I had no clue as to what help was around. No one helped me in going to them. It was terrible. I can't believe it. Then, after I dropped out, then, I found there was an Asian Student Counseling Services. (Female Asian-American science switcher)

When I was on probation, I got letters from the Office for Services for Asian-American Students saying they've got tutors and could help me. But then I was embarrassed so I didn't want to go to them for help. I felt stupid for getting letters like that and my reaction was, 'What business do they have looking at my grades? It's *my* business and *mine* alone!' I felt violated. It made me feel really dumb. So it kind of backfired. I should have gone in and said, 'I really need help. I don't know how to organize my time so I can study right.' It was too late when I realized. I learned on my own how to do all those things. I did it the hard way. (Female Asian-American science switcher)

I think, for some blacks, it's a stigma. It's like, 'Why go there when there's a lot of other advisors?' I've been there only *once*, just to get information. It's just so culted by skin color going to that type of advisor. (Male black engineering switcher)

The Office for Minorities were all telling me, 'Don't take any more than 12 credits.' The book is saying I should at least take 15. If I take 12 credits I'm gonna be here for six years. And they're like, 'Don't worry about that. You can take summer classes. Take 12 credits.' So I took 15 and that was fine; my grades were good. But I should have gone to the regular engineering advisor because I didn't do the right core requirement courses and the minority office doesn't tell you about that. I got way behind and I, I had to drop out of the program. (Male black engineering switcher)

Departments which had their own advising and counseling programs for each ethnic group received the most favorable comments. Students found it was especially helpful to have peer counselors who were either graduate students or upper-classmen of their own discipline and ethnicity:

> It's helpful in that it gives minorities a chance to help each other out. If for some reason they don't want to ask the question in class, they can put it off and ask their friend, a senior who's been there before. (Male Hispanic engineering non-switcher)

> I'll be able to do it. It's just gonna take me a little longer. But I was kinda getting anxious for a while 'cause I could see my friends moving on through the course work and I've had to backtrack a few times. The Latino adviser got me connected to a graduate student, a Latino guy in M.C.D.B., and he keeps me encouraged. (Male Hispanic science non-switcher)

> I've worked for the Services for Asian-American Students office and I was a peer counselor this past year. We were assigned students who were in the same major and I think that helped the students a lot. They would get feedback from somebody whose been through it as far as how to prepare for exams, and what kind of courses to take. (Female Asian-American science non-switcher)

> I wish I had, not a tutor, but more of a peer counselor. There weren't any in engineering. I could have gone over to Black Student Services, but there weren't any engineering or math students. If I'd had a peer mentor in engineering, it would have made a big difference. (Female black engineering switcher)

On campuses with no peer counseling by discipline, attending minority professional society meetings (e.g., for black and for Hispanic engineers) was a way to get advice from upper-classmen or graduate students. Students also found these organizations helpful in arranging contacts with professionals, either as mentors or as potential employers.

Orientation Programs

Many institutions offer special programs to students of color between their acceptance into an undergraduate program and the start of their first semester: these range from one-day orientations to intensive academic programs lasting several weeks. Regardless of program type, student evaluations contained an important warning: where they encourage students of color who do not yet realize they are under-prepared to believe that all they need to succeed is a high level of confidence, they are set up not only for failure, but also for self-blame:

> They invite prospective minority students—about 800 or so. And they tour you, feed you, put on the whole show. I went and it was great. And they kept saying, 'You can do anything you want.' But you know, you can't really if you

don't have the proper background. I think it's fine for those who can, but it's misleading for those who can't, and it really isn't good to give them false hope and make them feel like they didn't do so good, because they didn't have enough confidence in themselves. (Male Hispanic engineering non-switcher)

I was in the bridge program and there were students there who I didn't think could handle it—because they weren't well-prepared. It wasn't their character or their intelligence or anything. It was who they were competing against. They were just too far behind. (Male Hispanic science non-switcher)

The summer program before freshman year gives you help in time management, learning to use the library, how to study. They also give you hands-on experience in the working worlds you might wish to enter. However, they push people toward certain disciplines which lead to work roles needed on reservations. That's okay if you are temperamentally and intellectually suited to these, but there is a danger that you may drop out if you discover you are unsuited, rather than just changing majors. (Male native American science non-switcher)

The college does offer a minority program in the summer. Since the students from my high school have been coming here, half have left. So I think they need to work more on retention. (Male native American science switcher)

Students stressed that orientation programs could not address a number of problems they saw as fundamental and widespread—deficiency in the quality and depth of high school science and mathematics, and in the provision of appropriate counseling in those high schools where students of color are numerically dominant:

My understanding of the big problem is that you don't get prepared enough. Therefore, you should deal with the problem at the lower levels—K through 12. Because once we get here, attrition rates are horrible. I think trying to fix the problem at a later stage...I mean, a month in the summer to make up for 12 years! That's unrealistic. They should be dealing with the problem back there. You're going to have to spend billions of dollars, like you would in the defense budget to solve the problem. But you know that's not going to be likely. (Male black science non-switcher)

Students also pointed out the difficulties of attending a summer bridge program where no financial provision was offered: in the summer prior to college entry, many students need to work in order to save money for tuition and living expenses.

Retention Programs

When students of color who have been actively recruited by particular S.M.E. departments arrive on campus and find there are no retention efforts within those departments, they feel angry and abandoned. Institutions often measure the success of their retention efforts by the number of students of color who remain enrolled regardless of major and offer only campus-wide retention programs. Not only do these programs fail to support students in their original majors, their staff tend to redirect students experiencing difficulty into majors where they are more likely to graduate:

> The reason I came to this university was because I was contacted by them. I had heard of the minority engineering program, but I don't think it exists...I found there's just a minority retention office over on the main campus. (Female black engineering switcher)

> I got a letter from, I believe the provost, saying that they're starting a program to recruit minorities. But since the letter, I have not had any follow-up. (Male Hispanic science switcher)

> After I failed that math course, the advisor in the Martin Luther King program said, 'Just pick out classes that sound interesting. And do that for a couple quarters. It doesn't matter if they count for anything or not. Just see what you like to do.' That's why I took communications. (Male Hispanic science switcher)

From the students' perspective, their chances of persistence are most effectively increased by what is offered by their departments rather than their institutions. Departments that were described as making a serious effort to help them persist were those which: provided peer counseling; encouraged or organized mentoring by faculty or graduate students; set up study groups; offered tutorial sessions with T.A.s or other students; and hired male and female faculty of color. Although they also welcomed offers of practical help or encouragement from all faculty, students of color described faculty of color as performing additional functions that were relevant to their persistence: they act as role models in bonding them to the major; act as reminders that people of all races and ethnicities can succeed; preserve cultural connections and understand cultural constraints; and by demanding high standards from students, demonstrate the fallacies of stereotypes:

> The Arabs and even the Japanese think a lot less of blacks. But you put a black instructor with a Ph.D. in front of them and they have to learn from that instructor. It gives them a different perspective. (Male black engineering switcher)

> There are role models on the faculty for black students here—in every department, nearly. It's pretty good *now*, actually. It's good to see. It gives you a lot to look forward to. You see diverse backgrounds there, and it makes you feel good walking down to class. Maybe one day.... (Male black engineering switcher)

All students, regardless of race or ethnicity, appreciated those departments and faculty who had given them a discipline-specific work-study opportunity or the chance to be involved with a research project. We found that research opportunities for *any* undergraduates were rare on all seven campuses. However, students who had been involved in departmental research were very enthusiastic about their experience and felt it greatly enhanced their interest in the field. For students of color especially, working alongside senior students and faculty creates a sense of belonging, and dispels their sense of isolation. Research experience and work-study programs were also a source of financial assistance, which, in some cases, had been critical in allowing students of color to continue in their major:

> I just started doing research because I thought I would gain a better working knowledge of the material. And I found that being involved in research, I didn't feel like one of a 1,000 minnows trying to swim upstream. It gave me a place that was almost like home. I feel a *part* of something. So that gives me more stability here. (Male black science non-switcher)

> The Student Research Opportunities Program is for people of color within the university. It's in the Big 10 schools, and you did a research project one-on-one with a professor in your area. You picked whatever you wanted to do and it took all summer. At the end of the summer you did a presentation. I know it got more of us interested in grad school. (Male native American science non-switcher)

> I think that if they set up a program where your tuition and living expenses are paid for and then got you a research position in something relevant, you would cut out a lot of the middle cost of running a minority program and you're dealing more directly with the problems that students have, especially financial. And since we're isolated from the faculty, you get some individual contact. (Male black science non-switcher)

Unfortunately, most programs intended to benefit students of color were *not* connected to departments, were *not* staffed by S.M.E. faculty, staff, or students, were *not* open to all students, and were *not* connected to departmental research activities. Some existing departmental programs (for both students of color and women) were seen as of limited value because of their marginal status. Where programs are understaffed, run in a makeshift fashion, or where faculty discount or undermine the efforts made on their behalf by program staff, it is hard for students of color to believe that the department considers them important to its mission. A token minority program stigmatizes and demoralizes students of color and reinforces their suspicion that they are unwanted and unwelcome.

Conclusions

Some of the problems faced by students of color in S.M.E. majors parallel those experienced by white students. Other problems are experienced exclusively by students of color, and their character and impact varies both between and within racial and ethnic groups. The problems which white and non-white students share are not a random array, but arise from similarities in their socio-economic circumstances and educational experiences. For example, we found choosing a major for inappropriate reasons to be a strong pattern among women (of all ethnicities) and also among those men of color who have been socialized to accommodate the career aspirations of families, teachers and community role models. For these students, choosing to please others (unless this coincides with personal interests and goals) often leads to unhappiness in the major and places them at high risk of leaving it. Conceptual difficulties linked with inadequate pre-college preparation in mathematics and science are also problems that are shared by many white and non-white students who attended schools which were deficient in facilities, funding and qualified teachers. Thus, the under-preparation of many students of color reflects not only the structured inequalities of race and ethnicity, but also those of social class (particularly gross regional and local disparities in standards and provision for public schools). Recent recruitment drives intended to encourage S.M.E. enrollment among high school students of color have foundered in no small part because they have sought to foster individual motivation, self-confidence and aspiration to science-based careers, while the uneven quality of pre-college education remains under-addressed.

Institutions of higher education have the knowledge, resources and power to promote change in both campus and societal attitudes that perpetuate problems of stereotyping and prejudice for students of color. In recent years, some institutions have made strong commitments to diversity, equity and civility on their campuses. Colleges can also shape the quality and supply of teachers throughout the educational system. Some college science departments (as well as the National Laboratories) have been active in efforts to improve the quality of pre-college mathematics and science teaching through out-reach and enrichment programs for elementary, junior and high school teachers. At the same time, the number of pre-college teachers with a baccalaureate degree in the sciences continues to fall. As we described in Chapter 4, even in science departments involved in teacher enrichment programs, S.M.E. faculty continue to discourage their own graduate and undergraduate students from choosing a career in science or mathematics teaching.

The problems faced by students whose level of confidence exceeds their level of preparation is one unhappy result of the uneven attention given to science promotion and recruitment among minority school children on the one hand, and the uneven quality of their pre-college education on the other. The contribution of colleges and S.M.E. departments to the national effort to increase enrollment by students from traditionally under-represented groups is, as we have illustrated, often counter-productive. Schools who covertly reduce their entrance requirements for students from particular racial or ethnic groups—especially where departments make insufficient effort to support the students thus admitted—expose undergraduates to stigma and high risk of failure. Summer orientation programs which focus on confidence-building, but pay insufficient attention to gaps in entry-level knowledge and skills, and to the provision of a coherent departmental support system, also increase their participants' risk of early disenchantment and failure.

Lack of structural coherence also undermines institutional minority recruitment efforts. Where the advisory, tutorial, financial and mentoring functions of departments and central administration are ill-coordinated, ill-publicized or missing, and the attitudes of faculty or advisors toward students of color do not live up to the public statements of college administrators, students express doubt about the sincerity of institutional commitment to increased diversity:

> The fact of the matter is 90 percent of most blacks are under-prepared for a university curriculum. If the university gives them the opportunity and they don't make it, they're off the hook. They can say the chance was afforded to them. (Female black engineering non-switcher)

> The government helps fund this institution if they recruit so many minority students. This is the reason that they've let minority students into engineering. The school gets credit for the head-count coming in, but they don't count how many are chopped down. (Male black engineering non-switcher)

> They open the flood gates and then they wonder why these people suffer. But they can say, 'We've given them the opportunity.' The administration's attitude is, 'You've only got such and such on your S.A.T., but we'll let you in anyway because we *believe* in you.' Belief is *not* going to get you through. It's preparation and support. (Male Hispanic science switcher)

The social class basis of some serious problems that are shared by white and non-white students is particularly evident in the growing financial burden directly shouldered by undergraduates. All students from families of modest means feel under-served by the present level of financial aid. They also work longer hours than the predominantly white, male middle- and upper-class students of previous generations to pay for their education and living expenses, and worry they may not be able to find work appropriate to their degree and which can sustain their college debt burden. The effect of these concerns upon the current and future student profile of graduate and professional schools cannot be underestimated. Whether or not they are a reality for most students of color, the existence of funds ear-marked for under-represented groups, and the suspicions of white and Asian-American students that some questionable claims to minority status are made in order to gain access to them, are major contributors to the increases in campus racism noted by ourselves and other observers. In addition to the growing financial problems of all working-class, and many middle-class, students, black and Hispanic students with economic responsibilities for their family-of-origin, as well as all single parents, carry an additional financial burden which mitigates against their persistence in those undergraduate or graduate majors which make the heaviest demands on students' time.

One important difference with white students is that students of color overall assign more blame for failure to complete an S.M.E. major to their own perceived shortcomings than to inadequacies in their education. For students of color, the decision to leave an S.M.E. major is not taken lightly. Switching provokes a more profound sense of personal inadequacy, shame and failure than is experienced by most white switchers. How these are expressed varies according to the expectations of particular sub-cultures and the degree to which students feel they have failed to meet them. However the tendency to self-blame is common across minority groups. It is responsible for the greater risk of leaving college altogether (rather than simply switching majors) observed among students of color. Loneliness, feelings of rejection by the dominant group and the perceived importance of college graduation, *per se*, contribute more to minority switching decisions than informed preference for alternative fields of study or careers.

Other problems bearing upon the loss of students of color both from S.M.E. majors and from college which are not shared by white males, are those deriving from conflicts between cultural values, family roles, educational socialization, community obligations and career expectations on the one hand, and the values and demands of college science and engineering on the other. Helping students to confront and resolve these conflicts requires an understanding which is sub-culturally specific. Broad programs of "minority" support (including advising or mentoring), which lack understanding of the needs and perspectives of particular student groups will not improve retention. As we discussed with reference to women, many of the personal difficulties faced by students of color follow predictable patterns. When their origin and nature are understood by program directors, counselors or advisors, they can be anticipated, planned for and pre-empted. Even where the traditional teaching, advising, and mentoring practices of faculty and S.M.E. departments are slow to respond to the broadening of their client base, students can survive when they are encouraged to share their concerns, helped to understand the sources of their problems (especially lapses in confidence) and offered practical strategies to surmount them.

The well-publicized failure of minority recruitment and retention initiatives has prompted a search for more effective alternatives. One danger in this second round of initiatives (already discernable in our participants' accounts), is to grasp at over-simple versions of strategies which can be useful when their strengths and limitations for particular purposes and groups are understood. Such is the case with efforts to formalize relationships which, on an informal basis, have traditionally promoted persistence among white male students—most commonly, the organization of collaborative learning, tutorial and workshop programs, and faculty-student mentoring. As we have illustrated, these initiatives tend to mis-fire unless they are based on a culturally-specific understanding, including how peer groups actually work, how to serve students in need of tutorial support without stigmatizing them, and what kinds of mentoring relationships students of color actually need. As Pearson (1995) has pointed out, the academic experiences of many students and young faculty of color often give them little understanding of how progress in professional (including academic) careers is accomplished. Meeting this need requires active recruitment of senior faculty mentors who are professionally-active, well-connected and who insist on high standards of work and presentation from their protégés. Pearson observes that those faculty most apt to volunteer as mentors are often the least productive or professionally active members of departments. In a situation where male faculty of color and both white and non-white female faculty are still limited in number, non-minority and opposite gender faculty can be effective mentors for students of color. However, to be a good mentor requires an understanding of the specific constraints and needs of students from particular sub-cultures.

Ill-conceived or poorly run academic programs can contribute to the difficulties of the people they are intended to serve. This is not to argue that students of color would be better off without them. As non-switchers especially made clear, relevant and timely support had been essential to their persistence. However, they were also clear about which kinds of academic support services work best. They are: well-advertised, departmentally-based, field-specific, open to all students and accessible. They may include interactive computer programs, but must include live discussion with faculty, T.A.s or student tutors—whether as individuals or in small groups. They must also be offered at times which allow access to employed students and athletic scholars. Academic enrichment and support can be effectively organized for students sharing the same dormitories (or other domestic units), or offered through minority professional societies. Students strongly advocated the use of same-discipline (where possible, same minority group) student tutors who are paid for their work. They also welcomed any opportunity to work with faculty in teaching, research or organizational tasks. This seemed also to be the most effective, natural way for students to acquire mentors, bond to the discipline and learn how science is done. While our understanding of and experience with what works best is still limited, asking students to assess how well student support experiments are working, and adjusting them in the light of what they say, is more productive than blind adherence to any particular set of strategies.

As to the broad, national strategy to increase enrollment and persistence among students of color in the sciences, it is clear that the achievement of greater numbers alone does not resolve the unique problems of students of color that we have described. Though a larger racial or ethnic cohort can clearly insulate students of color from personal damage caused by expressions of peer hostility, it does not address other persistence factors, and, as we have discussed, can increase the level of racism on campuses: programs intended to increase the participation of students of color have also increased white peer hostility by widening and highlighting inequities in access to college education for the children of all families with modest incomes.

The first round of minority recruitment and retention programs, which began in the 1980's, attempted to address the predicted national shortfall in scientific "man"-power without questioning the traditional practices of science education, or the assumptions on which they were based. Important among these was the belief that the existing system of college science teaching effectively recruited from the white, male 'talent pool' most of those thought able to do science. Casting a wider net among women, students of color and students with disabilities so as to draw in talent hitherto missed made good sense in these terms. It also seemed the right thing to do at a time when the idea of diversity was gaining wider acceptance. As concern about a shortage of scientifically-trained workers shifted to concerns about the shortage of jobs for such people, new inequities and racial tensions began to emerge. It also became clear that the pool of ability to do science was not, as traditionally supposed, small and fixed, but grew as our understanding of how to teach mathematics and science broadened. We discovered that all students benefit from improvements in pedagogy, but that the benefits to under-represented groups are even greater. As the rationale for intervention shifts more clearly in the direction of equity in educational access, both the goals and methods of "minority programs" and our dependence on community and junior colleges to bridge gaps in the college preparation of many high school seniors, have to be viewed as interim strategies. Sooner or later, we need to decide how to address the structural inequalities in public pre-college education and in the national system of student financial support.

7

Some Conclusions
and Their Implications

We began this inquiry as part of the national effort to clarify the factors contributing to high attrition rates from S.M.E. majors—whether for white men, or for women and students of color. In discussing our findings at a variety of institutions, it has become clear that, although most faculty accept that it has proved harder to retain than to recruit students from under-represented groups, they do not necessarily accept there is 'a problem' of wastage for the white male majority. It is for this reason that we sought the help of the Higher Education Research Institute, U.C.L.A., in establishing the rates of loss for S.M.E. majors compared with other groups of majors.

The desire to marginalize the issue of wastage is understandable, given the size of the problem, and the consequences of taking it seriously. The loss of 40 to 60 percent of a group of students with higher than average abilities within two years of taking their first college science or mathematics class would be a serious matter notwithstanding the evidence of higher loss rates among those minority students (by gender, race or ethnicity) on whose recruitment and retention much money and effort has been expended. Our observations support the conclusions from successive C.I.R.P. studies that the problem of wastage is not marginal, but affects the white male majority in most or all S.M.E. departments on most or all campuses. We, or others, may point to institutions of particular type, mission, or history which are exceptions to this generalization, but this does not change its validity for most S.M.E. undergraduates.

The difficulty for faculty would appear to be that of redefining something as 'a problem' which has long been taken for granted as an appropriate and normal consequence of a pedagogy that serves established, and largely unchallenged, student selection objectives. Switching is not defined as a problem when it is believed to be caused, on the one hand, by wrong choices, under-preparation, lack of sufficient interest, ability or hard work, or on the other, by the discovery of a passion for another discipline. Either way, there is little that faculty feel they can, or should, do about people who leave for such reasons. The difficulty about our data is that they support neither type of explanation for switching. We find no support for the hypothesis that switchers and non-switchers can be sufficiently distinguished in terms of high school preparation, performance scores or effort expended, in order to explain why one group leaves and the other group stays. Nor do switchers neatly divide into those who are pushed out (by inappropriate choice of major choice, lower ability, poorer preparation, lower levels of interest, or unwillingness to work), and those who are pulled out (because they discover a vocation elsewhere). Rather, our data suggest a new hypothesis—that the most common reasons for switching arise in response to a set of problems experienced by switchers and non-switchers alike. There was a high level of agreement across the whole student sample about the issues that lead to defection by switchers and to dissatisfaction among non-switchers, and to strong similarities in the importance members of each group ascribed to each set of concerns. On the basis of their relative perceived significance, we posit that problems which arise from the structure of the educational experience and the culture of the discipline (as reflected in the attitudes and practices of S.M.E. faculty) make a much greater contribution to S.M.E. attrition than the individual inadequacies of students or the appeal of other majors.

The assumption that most switching is 'appropriate' obscures the loss of two groups of students whom S.M.E. faculty might prefer to retain. They might be described as the 'more pulled than pushed', and the 'more pushed than pulled'. The first group includes very able, often multi-talented, students who have a strong interest in science and mathematics and would have stayed had the teaching been more stimulating and the curricula more imaginative. Although they are drawn to majors which promise a fuller educational experience, they retain their scientific interest and modes of thought and seek ways to combine these interests with their new majors and/or career plans. These students expressed ambivalence about switching and harbored thoughts of resuming their scientific studies at some future date. They attributed their decision to leave almost exclusively to the poverty of the educational experience created by the weed-out system. Notwithstanding the future contributions of graduates whose abilities span the arts, sciences and humanities, they represent an important loss to science, mathematics and engineering.

The second group of students (who are more pushed than pulled), are those who feel they have the ability to complete an S.M.E. degree, were adequately prepared, and entered their S.M.E. major largely on the basis of interest. They become discouraged by poor teaching and aspects of the weed-out process and, although they would prefer to stay in the sciences, they move into majors which they regard as a poor compromise. These were among the most angry, regretful and frustrated of all the students whom we interviewed. They felt their choice of an S.M.E. major had been appropriate, and that they could have completed it, given some faculty support and a less cut-throat atmosphere. The accounts of many women and students of color who switched could be described in this manner. Though we, of course, encountered students whose switching was 'appropriate', in that they had chosen unwisely, were under-prepared, or did not (by their own admission) work hard enough, our data lead us to hypothesize that, on every campus, there are substantial numbers of able students who could be retained in S.M.E. majors were appropriate changes made in departmental practices.

Another common assumption encountered among faculty and challenged by our data is that switching involves the discovery of errors in student choices, judgments or self-perceptions, and represents logical action to correct these. By this interpretation, the weed-out system is defined as 'cruel to be kind'. As indicated above, the Cartesian view of students as either 'scientists' or 'not scientists' obscures the loss of many students with the ability to do science— including some who could have done it very well. The nature of the switching process revealed in students' accounts is very different from that imagined by S.M.E. faculty. We found the decision to leave an S.M.E. major was always the culmination of a dialogue with self and others over time, in which students were drawn back and forth between the options that seemed open to them. Typically, the process began with poor experiences in S.M.E. classes in their first year and, for some, the discovery of under-preparation. It was deepened by a series of academic crises and disappointments that provoked anger towards particular faculty, advisors or teaching assistants. Students began to experience self-doubt and lowered confidence in their ability to do science. They became disillusioned with science and the science-based careers to which they had aspired, and questioned whether getting the degree would be worth the effort and distress involved. Only then did they begin to consider a switch to those non-S.M.E. classes where they had experienced better teaching and/or more satisfaction with their academic work. Potential switchers discussed these experiences with others, and, even at a late stage, some who came very close to switching decided to stay. The process of moving back and forth between thoughts of leaving and staying lasted from a few months to over two years. However, the final decision was typically triggered by a 'last straw' incident or an institutional deadline. This explains why the reasons for switching given by students in exit interviews (in the rare instances where these are offered) are often so puzzling to the dean or advisor who hears them.

With respect to the choice of S.M.E. majors, our data offer clear evidence that a combination of interest in the discipline and the career(s) to which it leads, realism about career goals and some measure of altruism, are conducive to persistence. However, many non-switchers who enter S.M.E. majors for what they subsequently report as the 'wrong' reasons, nevertheless survive. The survival of some students, but not others, despite very similar problems, depends partly on their acquisition of particular attitudes and strategies. Whether they find sufficient academic and personal support (from institutional, faculty, peer and other sources) to sustain their motivation and morale is also critical. Their interest in the discipline must also be strong enough to survive a pedagogical style dictated by weed-out objectives. Students must develop a perspective which effectively insulates them from loss of self-confidence. This includes viewing faculty behavior toward under-classmen as "a game," and not taking their displays of indifference personally; seeking help with academic difficulties as they arise from any available source; and developing criteria for academic progress that are independent of grades. We were rather dismayed also to discover the role in survival played by luck (in locating the resources needed) and by cheating.

We found no evidence to support contentions that significant contributions to S.M.E. attrition are made by the size of classes, *per se*, the (alleged) poor tutorial abilities of teaching assistants, the inadequacy of laboratory or computer facilities, or flaws in the linguistic, pedagogical or social skills of foreign faculty or (foreign) teaching assistants. Focus on these non-problems rather than on the central issues of pedagogy, student assessment, curriculum design and advising, is another way to marginalize the problem of attrition.

It is also clear from our data that the most effective way to improve retention among women and students of color, and to build their numbers over the longer-term, is to improve the quality of the learning experience for all students—including those non-science majors who wish to study science and mathematics as part of their overall education. Though faculty sometimes like to begin a program of reform with discussions of curriculum content and structure, this is unlikely to improve retention unless it is part of a parallel discussion of how to secure maximum student comprehension, application and knowledge transfer, and give students meaningful feedback on their academic performance. We have no illusion that faculty will find this easy. Even to begin so fundamental a debate requires a willingness to explore the body of knowledge about how people learn that has largely been developed by faculty who are not members of S.M.E. departments.

To effectively address student concerns about lack of faculty engagement in their learning in the first two years of S.M.E. classes, involves a shift of objectives from selection to education. This too is difficult, partly because it involves change in deeply socialized attitudes, and partly because it has implications for the criteria by which students are (or are not) admitted into particular S.M.E. colleges, departments or classes. Abandonment of student selection as an important objective of introductory science and mathematics classes in favor of intellectual stimulation, conceptual grasp and student support, also has profound implications for high school science and mathematics. Reducing or eliminating the need for a selection process in the first two years of college (which is currently accomplished by the weed-out process), requires that the process of student admission become more selective, the selection process more reliable and that a better fit is created between enrollment numbers and disciplinary resources. This, in turn, implies the adoption of common learning standards for science and mathematics by which both colleges and high school seniors, can, with greater confidence, compare levels of knowledge and skill. However, national or regional teaching and student performance standards by discipline are not yet part of the United States' educational tradition. Without such standards, large numbers of able students will continue to be wasted because they enter college unaware that they are insufficiently prepared to tackle their first college science and mathematics classes. The negative consequences of the present state of affairs fall most heavily on precisely those under-represented minority groups whose higher level of enrollment is the target of many current initiatives. Especially for students of color, encouragement to reach beyond their level of readiness (though not ability) is especially disastrous. The increasing financial burden of college education on students themselves, combined with the variable quality of their science and mathematics preparation, makes the high level of S.M.E. attrition also an indicator of incoherence and inequity in pre-college and college educational provision, standards and funding.

In many ways, our most distressing finding comes as an aside to our main research concerns. This was the consistent discovery, campus by campus, that science and mathematics teaching is devalued as a career for S.M.E. baccalaureates, and that students with a strong interest in teaching science and mathematics are effectively discouraged from pursuing this career path. As described earlier, we have visited a number of campuses and Department of Energy laboratories which offer 'teacher enrichment programs' to existing elementary and high school science and mathematics teachers who are, for the most part, not science or mathematics baccalaureates. However, among large state universities, research institutions and liberal arts colleges, we have encountered only one initiative[1] which encourages S.M.E. majors to consider a career in science and mathematics teaching by offering an integrated (five-year) program of teacher education concurrent with a science degree. We think there may be others, but that they are not to be found in the mainstream institutions which most S.M.E. undergraduates attend. We have also found the level of contact between S.M.E. faculty and the science and mathematics specialists in Colleges of Education on the same campuses to be low or non-existent. The lack of such a dialogue inhibits discussion of ways to promote science and mathematics teaching as a career, or to ease the path to professional certification for S.M.E. majors who would like to teach. It also represents the loss of an opportunity to draw upon the pedagogical and program evaluation knowledge and skills of education faculty that are available to S.M.E. departments on most campuses. In a forthcoming study, we intend to further explore the extent of interest in teaching careers in the sciences among both S.M.E. undergraduate and graduate populations, the nature and relative importance of barriers to teaching careers for S.M.E. graduates and alternative ways to surmount them.

Finally, we offer some observations on the nature of the evidence described in this report. In discussing our data with S.M.E. faculty, we sometimes encounter the objection that the state of affairs collectively portrayed in students' accounts is based on 'anecdotal' evidence. Strictly speaking (from its Greek root), an 'anecdote' is an unpublished account. In more general usage, it is a story which is casually heard and has no coherent, patterned connection to other stories on the same theme. By either usage, the accounts which form the text data for this study are not anecdotes. Accounts which are gathered and analyzed in a systematic manner allow the investigator to discover things that cannot easily be discovered by any other means. In complex human affairs, noticing the patterns in the independent accounts of expert witnesses plays the same role as laboratory observations in the formation of hypotheses. As the reader will perhaps concede, there is much to be learned by treating such accounts with respect.

All of the themes and patterns we have identified in these data are offered as hypotheses, propositions, indications or caveats. However, since the conclusion of this study we have conducted a shorter, companion study (Seymour & Hunter, 1996) of graduate and undergraduate students with disabilities in S.M.E. majors. An entirely unexpected, but very strong, finding from this second study was the degree to which the experiences of students with disabilities reflect and confirm those of the switchers and persisters described in this account. By their accommodation requests, students with disabilities inadvertently challenge rules which S.M.E. faculty see as necessary for the protection of high academic standards and are thereby forced into conflict with the formal and informal rules which govern progress in S.M.E. majors. Thus, students with disabilities "stress-test" the tacit rules by which S.M.E. faculty operate, and in doing so, bring the essentially moral character of these rules into even sharper focus than do the accounts of switchers and persisters in this study.

We continue to discuss our findings with students in a growing variety of institutional contexts, and feel we can offer the hypotheses presented here with some confidence. We hope that some readers will test our hypotheses among other student populations that are available to them. We have received a number of communications from colleagues who have done so, and who confirm particular aspects of our experience. Given the modest nature of our research design, it is important that such work be continued. There is much we do not understand about the processes which constrain the academic and career achievement patterns of students from particular racial and ethnic groups, especially those of women of color. Other facets of growing diversity in the student population—returning older learners, single parents, students with disabilities and employed students—will have consequences for the structure, norms and pedagogy of college science, mathematics and engineering of which we are, as yet, only dimly aware.

As educational reform in the sciences progresses, we will continue to need feedback from our students to be sure that we have correctly diagnosed the nature of their problems and are addressing the right issues. We also need to learn the skills of evaluation the better to understand how our educational experiments are working. We have colleagues on our own campuses who can, and will, help us with these unfamiliar tasks. For our students, research and evaluation hold more than a scholarly interest: they explore matters of great personal consequence. The course of their future lives is shaped by our attitudes and skills, and they have every good reason to keep us honest.

Notes

1. The P.R.I.S.M. initiative—developed jointly by the Los Alamos Laboratory Education Program, the University of New Mexico and the State of New Mexico Education Office.

Appendix A

FIGURE A.1 Disciplines Included in Each Group of Majors in the C.I.R.P. Data.

Biological Sciences   Biology (general); Biochemistry/Biophysics; Botany; Marine (life) Science; Microbiology/Bacteriology; Zoology.

Physical Sciences   Astronomy; Atmospheric Science; Chemistry; Earth Science; Marine Science; Physics; Other physical science.

Engineering   Aeronautical or Astronautical; Civil; Chemical; Electrical or Electronic; Industrial; Mechanical; Other.

Mathematics/Statistics   Mathematics; Statistics.

Agriculture   Agriculture; Forestry.

History/Political Science   History; Political Science.

Social Sciences   Anthropology; Economics; Ethnic Studies; Geography; Psychology; Social Work; Sociology; Women's Studies; Other social sciences.

Fine Arts   Art, Fine and Applied; Music; Speech; Architecture/Urban Planning.

English   English (language or literature).

Other Humanities   Languages (except English); Philosophy; Theater or drama; Theology or Religion; Other.

Health Professions   Nursing; Pharmacy; Pre-medicine; Pre-dentistry; Pre-veterinary; Clinical Therapies (Physical, Occupational, Speech).

Computer Science/ Technical   Computer Science; Data Processing or Computer Programming; Communications; Drafting or Design; Mechanics; Electronics; Other technical.

Business   Accounting; Business Administration; Finance; Marketing; Management; Secretarial Studies; Other business.

Education   Business; Elementary; Music or Art; Physical Education or Recreation; Secondary; Special.

Other Non-Technical   Journalism; Home Economics; Library/Archival Science; Law Enforcement; Military Science; Other.

FIGURE A.2 Profile of Switchers and Non-Switchers by Discipline.

Discipline	Switchers		Non-Switchers		Total	
	N	%	N	%	N	%
Science & Mathematics	92	27.5	86	25.7	178	53
Engineering	91	27.2	66	19.7	157	47
Total	183	54.6	152	45.4	335	100

FIGURE A.3 Profile of Switchers and Non-Switchers by Discipline, Sex and Race/Ethnicity.

Informants	Number of Participants at Each Study Site							Total	%
	MW PUB 1	W PUB 2	W PUB 3	EC PUB 4	WC PRI 1	W PRI 2	W PRI 3		
Science Switchers	23	6	12	14	21	2	14	92	27
Science Non-Switchers	6	12	15	12	12	12	17	86	26
Engineering Switchers	21	15	12	20	22	1	0	91	27
Engineering Non-Switchers	11	14	17	13	11	0	0	66	20
White Men	23	19	20	21	22	3	11	119	48
White Women	21	17	25	20	23	9	13	128	52
All Races/ Ethnicities: (Men/Women)	17	11	11	18	21	3	7	88	26
Totals & Percents for all Institutions	61	47	56	59	66	15	31	335	100
	18%	14%	17%	18%	20%	5%	9%	100%	

FIGURE A.4   Profile of Non-White Switchers and Non-Switchers by Discipline and Race/Ethnicity.

Non-White Participants	Switchers			Non-Switchers			Totals	
	Eng.	Sci.	All	Eng.	Sci.	All	N	% of Non-White Sample
Black	12	7	19	5	3	8	27	30.7
Hispanic	4	7	11	7	2	9	20	22.7
Asian-American	8	10	18	4	13	17	35	39.8
Native American	-	4	4	-	2	2	6	6.8
Totals	24	28	52	16	20	36	88	100

Appendix B

Topics Explored with S.M.E. Switchers and Non-Switchers
in Semi-Structured Interviews and Focus Groups

Topics were not necessarily explored in the order in which they are listed below.

Throughout the interviews with women and minority interviewees, we solicited comments on perceived differences between their experiences and those of their white male counterparts.

The same topics were covered with both switchers and non-switchers, with adjustments according to the nature of their experiences.

Topics

* Major: current and former. When switched.

* Why chose S.M.E. Who and what influenced decision. Family occupations, interest in science or engineering. Teachers and other mentors: how interest was fostered. Nature of motivation.

* High School: type and location, quality and level of preparation for college math and science, study skills learned, mentors, teacher expectations, grades, level of interest in science/motivation for science-based career, comparison of high school and college science and mathematics.

* Experience of college S.M.E. work:

    G.P.A. (incoming, & pattern before/after switch)

    Class size, course load/overload, curriculum structure, syllabus content, degree-completion time

    Financial issues: parental/other support (grants, scholarships, loans, internships), paid work, time constraints, stresses, length of degree

    Quality/styles/effectiveness of/commitment to teaching by faculty and T.A.s

    Labs: facilities, instruction, assessment

    Grades & assessment, weed-out experiences and theories, how weed-out system was learned and transmitted

    Assessment of own work habits, motivation, study techniques

    Strategies for survival

* Academic program evaluation: structure, length, advising and information distribution system.

    Assessment of S.M.E. faculty as advisors, counselors, mentors, resources for research experience & careers.

    Assessment of academic support and advising for women and students of color.

* Foreign faculty and T.A.s: experiences, nature of difficulties, rate in switching decisions.

* Support systems: the importance of informal (peers, room-mates) and formal (clubs, societies) support.

* Special programs (e.g. students of color, women, R.O.T.C., science and engineering dorms).

* Variations in the educational experiences (including problems) in S.M.E. majors of women and different minority groups.

    White male students' views of the perceived difficulties or advantages of women and students of color in their majors solicited.

* Culture of S.M.E. disciplines: prestige and ranking of majors/careers; faculty attitudes and objectives; the ethos of science and engineering; competition and cooperation; education vs. training.

* Experiences in non-S.M.E. courses. Comparisons of teaching and learning experiences, perceived differences in the nature of the social sciences and humanities, level/type of difficulty, assessment and grading practices.

* Experience of switching (self and peers).

    Factors which contribute to change of major: their relative importance, the process of decision-making. Feelings about switching: self, friends, parents, career plans, costs and benefits.

    Theories about switching—why others switch.

    Upper-classmen: Difficulties of remaining in S.M.E. schools/departments: costs and benefits.

* Career plans: influences (prestige, money, intrinsic interest, parental expectations).

    Plans for graduate study. Why/why not.

    Changes in career plans related to switching. Consequences of, and feelings, about career shift.

    Attitudes toward teaching as a career.

* Interviewee's advice on improving enrollment and persistence in S.M.E. majors addressed: to high schools, S.M.E. schools and departments, faculty, special program heads, education policy makers.

Bibliography

Alliance for Undergraduate Education. 1990. *The Freshman Year in Science and Engineering: Old Problems, New Perspectives for Research Universities.* Report of a Conference held April 6-7, 1990, at the University of Michigan. Washington, D.C.: A.U.E.

American Association for the Advancement of Science. 1989. *Project 2061: Science for all Americans.* Washington, D.C.: A.A.A.S.

American Association of University Women. 1992. *How Schools Short-change Girls: The A.A.U.W. Report.* Washington D.C.: A.A.U.W. Educational Foundation: National Education Association.

American Council on Education. 1992. *College Freshmen with Disabilities: A Statistical Profile.* Washington, D.C.: H.E.A.T.H. Resource Center.

Arnold, K.D. 1987. "Values and vocations: The career aspirations of academically-gifted females in the first five years after high school." Paper presented at the Annual Meeting of the American Educational Research Association, Washington, D.C.

Astin, A.W. 1985. *Achieving Educational Excellence: A Critical Assessment of Priorities in Higher Education.* San Francisco, CA: Jossey-Bass.

Astin, A.W. 1993. *What Matters in College? Four Critical Years Revisited.* San Francisco, CA: Jossey-Bass.

Astin A.W., & H.S. Astin. 1993. *Undergraduate Science Education: The Impact of Different College Environments on the Educational Pipeline in the Sciences.* Los Angeles, CA: Higher Education Research Institute, U.C.L.A.

Astin, A.W., Green, K.C., Korn, W.S., & M. Schalit. 1985. *The American Freshman: National Norms for Fall 1985.* Los Angeles, CA: Higher Education Research Institute, U.C.L.A.

Astin, A.W., Green, K.C., & W. S. Korn. 1987. *The American Freshman: Twenty-Year Trends, 1966-1985.* Los Angeles, CA: Higher Education Research Institute, U.C.L.A.

Astin, A.W., Green, K.C., Korn, W.S., & E.R. Riggs. 1991. *The American Freshman: National Norms for Fall 1991.* Los Angeles, CA: Higher Education Research Institute, U.C.L.A.

Atkinson, Richard C. 1990. "Supply and Demand for Scientists and Engineers: A National Crisis in the Making." Presidential Address, A.A.A.S. National Meeting, New Orleans, LA, February 18.

Baker, D. 1990. "Gender differences in science: Where they start and where they go." Paper presented at the meeting of the National Association for Research in Science Teaching, Atlanta, GA.

Baker, J.G. 1994. *Gender, race and progression to the natural science and engineering doctorate*. Report to the National Science Foundation, Directorate for Education and Human Resources, Washington, D.C.

Banzinger, George. 1992. Women-in-the-sciences program at Marietta College: Focusing on how to keep women in science. *Journal of College Science Teaching, March/ April*: 279-283.

Barber, Elinor G., et al. 1989. To pursue or not to pursue a graduate engineering degree. *Engineering Education, July/August*: 550-556.

Baruch, R., & J. Nagy. 1977. *Females and Males in the Potential Scientist Pool: A Study of the Early College Years*. Final Report to the National Science Foundation.

Baum, Eleanor. 1989. Why so few women in engineering? *Engineering Education, July/August*: 556-557.

Bazler, Judith A., & Doris A. Siminis. 1990. Are women out of the picture? Sex discrimination in science texts. *Science Teacher, 57*(9): 24-26.

Beane, D.B. 1985. *Mathematics and science: Critical filters for the future of minority students*. Washington, D.C.: Mid-Atlantic Center for Race Equity, American University.

Belenky, M.F., Clinchy, B.M., Goldberger, N.R., & J.M. Tarule. 1986. *Women's Ways of Knowing: The Development of Self, Voice and Mind*. New York, NY: Basic Books.

Berg, H.M., & M.A. Ferber. 1983. Men and women graduate students: Who succeeds and why? *Journal of Higher Education, 54*(6): 629-648.

Berryman, S.E. 1983. *Who Will Do Science? Trends and Their Causes, in Minority and Female Representation Among Holders of Advanced Degrees in Mathematics*. New York: The Rockefeller Foundation.

Betz, N.E. 1990. *What stops women and minorities from choosing and completing majors in science and engineering*. Washington, D.C.: Federation of Behavioral, Psychological and Cognitive Sciences.

Bleier, R. 1984. *Science and Gender*. New York, NY: Pergamon Press.

Bleier, R. 1986. *Feminist Approaches to Science*. New York, NY: Pergamon Press.

Blum, L., & S. Givant. 1982. "Increasing the Participation of College Women in Mathematics-Related Fields." In S.M. Humphreys, ed., *Women and Minorities in Science: Strategies for Increasing Participation*. Boulder, CO: Westview Press.

Boli, J., Allen, M.L., & A. Payne. 1985. High ability women and men in undergraduate mathematics and chemistry courses. *American Educational Research Journal, 22*: 605-626.

Bond, A.J., Lebodl, W.K., & M. Thomas. 1977. *Factors associated with attracting and retaining black Americans in engineering*. Washington, D.C.: American Society for Engineering Education.

Bonsangue, M.V., & D.E. Drew. 1992. *Long-term effectiveness of the calculus workshop model.* Report to the National Science Foundation, Washington, D.C.

Bowen, C.W. 1992. Myths and metaphors: Their influence on chemistry instruction. *Journal of Chemical Education, 6:* 479-482.

Bowen, W.G., & A. Sosa. 1989. *Prospects for Faculty in the Arts and Sciences.* Princeton, NJ: Princeton University Press.

Boyer, Ernest L. 1989. *The Condition of the Professorate: Attitudes and Trends, 1889.* The Carnegie Foundation for the Advancement of Teaching. Princeton, NJ: Princeton University Press.

Boyer, Ernest L. 1990. *Campus Life: In Search of Community.* The Carnegie Foundation for the Advancement of Teaching. Princeton, NJ: Princeton University Press.

Brainard, Suzanne G. 1992. *First annual report of the freshman intervention program at the women in engineering initiative, the University of Washington.* Report to the Alfred P. Sloan Foundation.

Brophy, S.G. 1985. "Interactions of Male and Female Students with Male and Female Teachers." In L.C. Wilkinson, and C.B. Marrett, eds., *Gender Influences in Classroom Interaction,* New York, NY: Academic Press.

Brown, S.V. 1994. *Under-represented Minority Women in Science and Engineering Education.* Princeton, NJ: Educational Testing Service.

Brown, S.V. 1995. *Profiles and Persistence of Minority Doctorate Recipients.* Final report to the Graduate Records Examination Board. Princeton, NJ: Educational Testing Service.

Browne, Malcolm W. 1992. "Amid 'shortage,' young physicists see few jobs." *The New York Times, March 10:* C1, C7.

Bruer, J.T. 1984. Women in science: Toward equitable participation. *Science, Technology and Human Values, Summer,* 1984: 230-245.

Brush, L.R. 1985. "Cognitive and Affective Determinants of Course Preferences and Plans." In S.F. Chipman, L.R. Brush, and D.M. Wilson, eds., *Women and Mathematics: Balancing the Equation,* Hillsdale, NJ: Lawrence Erlbaum Associates.

Brush, S.G. 1991. Women in science and engineering. *American Scientist, 79:* 404-419.

Campbell, George Jr. 1993. Visions of Engineering Education in Century II. The Porth Distinguished Lecture, University of Missouri at Rolla, Rolla, MO, March 31.

Carnegie Foundation. 1987. Carnegie foundation's classification of more then 3,300 institutions of higher education. *Chronicle of Higher Education, 33:* 22.

Carnegie Foundation. 1989. *The Condition of the Professoriate: Attitudes and Trends, 1989.* The Carnegie Foundation for the Advancement of Teaching. Princeton, NJ: Princeton University Press.

Carrier, Sam C., & David Davis-Van Atta. 1987. *Maintaining america's scientific productivity: The necessity of the liberal arts colleges.* Final report for the second conference on "The Future of Science at Liberal Arts Colleges." Oberlin, OH, June, 1985.

Carter, Carolyn S., & Nancy W. Brickhouse. 1989. What makes chemistry difficult? Alternative perceptions. *Journal of Chemical Education, 66:* 223-225.

Casserly, P., & R. Rock. 1979. "Factors Related to Young Women's Persistence and Achievement in Mathematics." In S.F. Chipman, L.R. Brush, and D.M. Wilson, eds., *Women and Mathematics: Balancing the Equation.* Hillsdale, NJ: Lawrence Erlbaum Associates.

Chipman, S.F., Brush, R.L., & D.M. Wilson, eds., 1985. *Women and Mathematics: Balancing the Equation.* Hillsdale, NJ: Lawrence Erlbaum Associates.

Chipman, S.F., & V.G. Thomas. 1987. The participation of women and minorities in mathematical, scientific and technical fields. *Review of Research in Higher Education, 14:* 387-430.

Clayton, Julie. 1992. Can They do Science? *New Scientist, 135(1837):* 31-34.

Clewell, B., Anderson, B., & M. Thorpe. 1992. *Breaking the Barriers: Helping Female and Minority Students Succeed in Mathematics Science.* San Francisco, CA: Jossey-Bass.

Collea, F.P. 1990. Increasing minorities in science and engineering. *Journal of College Science Teaching, 20:* 1.

College Board. 1988. *College-Bound Seniors: 1988.* New York, NY: College Entrance Examination Board.

Committee on Science, Space, and Technology, the U.S. Congress. 1992. *The Quality of Undergraduate Science Education: Hearing Before the Subcommittee on Science.* Washington, D.C.: G.P.O.

Committee on the Status of Women in Ontario Universities. 1988. *Attracting and Retaining Students for Science and Engineering.* Toronto, Ontario: Ontario Council of Universities.

Constantinople, A., Cornelius, R., & J. Gray. 1988. The chilly climate: Fact or artifact? *Journal of Higher Education, 59(5):* 527-550.

Costa, V.B. 1993. School science as a rite of passage: A new frame for familiar problems. *Journal of Research in Science Teaching, 30(7):* 649-668.

Cox, E.L. 1982. *Some indicators for a program of industry aid to colleges for retention of black students in engineering.* Dissertation Information Service, University of Michigan, Ann Arbor, MI.

Daniels, J., Landis, R., McGee, M., & P. Parker. 1990. *Realizing the Potential of Women and Minorities in Engineering: Four Perspectives from the Field.* Washington, D.C.: National Governors' Association.

Davis, Barbara G., & Sheila Humphreys. 1985. *Evaluating Intervention Programs: Applications from Women's Programs in Math and Science.* New York, NY: Teachers College Press.

Davis-Van Atta, David, Carrier, Sam C., & Frank Frankfort. 1985. "Educating American Scientists: The Role of the Research Colleges." A Report for the Conference on "The Future of Science at Liberal Arts Colleges." Oberlin, OH, June 9-10.

Department of Education. 1989. *Profile of Handicapped Students in Post-Secondary Education, 1987.* Washington, D.C.: National Center for Education Statistics, Data Series SP- NPSAS-86/87-10.

Dey, E.L., Astin, A.W., & W.S. Korn. 1991. *The American Freshman: Twenty-five Year Trends.* Los Angeles, CA: Higher Education Research Institute, U.C.L.A.

Dweck, C.S. 1986. Motivational processes affecting learning. *American Psychologist, 10:* 1040-1048.

Eccles, J. 1989. "Bringing Young Women into Math and Science." In M. Crawford and M. Gentry, eds., *Gender and Thought: Psychological Perspectives.* New York, NY: Springer-Verlag.

Eccles, J. 1994. Understanding women's educational and occupational choices. *Psychology of Women Quarterly, 18:* 585-609.

Eccles, J., Kaczala, C.M., & J.L. Meece. 1982. Socialization of achievement attitudes and beliefs: Classroom influences. *Child Development, 53:* 322-339.

Eckley, Robert S. 1987. Liberal arts colleges: Can they compete? *The Brookings Review, 5:* 32-37.

Educational Testing Service. 1988. *The Science Report Card: Elements of Risk and Discovery Research Report No. 17-S-01.* Princeton, NJ: Educational Testing Service.

Ellis, R.A. 1992. Access to engineering: Measuring participation of persons with disabilities. *Engineering Manpower Bulletin, 121.* Washington, D.C.: E.M.C. & A.A.E.S.

Emmett, Arielle, & David F. Noble. 1992. A world without women. *Technology Review, 95*(4): 44-52.

Engineering Deans' Council. 1988. Findings and recommendations from the "Report of the Task Force on the Engineering Student Pipeline." *Engineering Education, May:* 778-781.

Erickson, L.J. 1981. "Intervention Techniques: Assessment and Recommendations." In, Science Council of Canada, *Who Turns the Wheel?: Proceedings of a Workshop on the Science Education of Women in Canada.* Ottawa, Ontario: Minister of Supply and Services.

Etzkowitz, Henry. 1994. "Barriers to Women in Academic Science and Engineering" In Willie Pearson, Jr., and Alan Fechter, eds., *Human Resources in Science*. Baltimore, MD: Johns Hopkins University Press.

Etzkowitz, Henry, Kemelgor, Carol, Neuschatz, Michael, & Brian Uzzi. 1992. Athena unbound: Barriers to women in academic science and engineering. *Science and Public Policy, 19*(3): 157-179.

Etzkowitz, Henry, Kemelgor, Carol, Neuschatz, Michael, Uzzi, Brian, & Joseph Alonzo. 1995. "Gender Implosion: The Paradox of 'Critical Mass' for Women in Science." Paper to the N.A.C.M.E. Research and Policy Conference: Minorities in Mathematics, Science, and Engineering, Wake Forest University, Wake Forest, NC.

Fennema, E. 1990. "Justice, Equity, and Mathematics Education." In E. Fennema and G.C. Leder, eds., *Mathematics and Gender*. New York, NY: Teachers College Press.

Fausto-Sterling, Anne. 1985. *Myths of Gender: Biological Theories about Women and Men*. New York, NY: Basic Books.

Fausto-Sterling, Anne. 1991. Race, gender and science. *Transformations, 2* (2): 32-39.

Frazier, K.S., et al. 1992. *Women in Mathematics and Physics: Inhibitors and Enhancers*. Ann Arbor, MI: The University of Michigan.

Gardner, April L., Mason, Cheryl L., & Marsha Matyas. 1989. Equity, excellence, and 'just plain good teaching'. *American Biology Teacher, 51*(2): 72-77.

Gardner, Philip D., & Angela Broadus. 1990. Pursuing an Engineering Degree: An Examination of Issues Pertaining to Persistence in Engineering. East Lansing, MI: Collegiate Employment Research Institute, Michigan State University.

Gerson, Kathleen. 1985. *Hard Choices: How Women Decide about Work, Career, and Motherhood*. Berkeley, CA: University of California Press.

Gilligan, C. 1979. Women's place in man's life cycle. *Harvard Educational Review, 49*(4): 431-444.

Gilligan, C. 1982. *In a Different Voice: Psychological Theory and Women's Development*. Cambridge, MA: C.U.P.

Ginorio, A.B., Brown, M.D., Henderson, R.S., & N. Cook. 1993. "Patterns of Persistence and Attrition Among Science and Engineering Majors at the University of Washington, 1985-1991." Report to the Alfred P. Sloan Foundation.

Goffman, E. 1963. *Stigma: Notes on the Management of Spoiled Identity*. Englewood Cliffs, NJ: Prentice-Hall.

Gomery, Ralph, & Hirsh Cohen. 1993. Science: How much is enough? *Scientific American, July*: 120.

Grandy, J.L. 1995. *Persistence in Science of High-Ability Minority Students, Phase V: Comprehension Data Analysis*. Princeton, NJ: Educational Testing Services.

Green, Kenneth C. 1989a. A profile of undergraduates in the sciences. *The American Scientist, 78*: 475-480.

Green, Kenneth C. 1989b. "Keynote Address: A Profile of Undergraduates in the Sciences." In *An Exploration of the Nature and Quality of Undergraduate Education in Science, Mathematics and Engineering, National Advisory Group, Sigma Xi, the Scientific Research Society.* Racine, WI: Report of the Wingspread Conference.

Greene, Bernard, & Linda Zimbler. 1989. *Profile of Handicapped Students in Post-Secondary Education, 1987.* Washington, D.C.: National Center for Education Statistics.

Hacker, R.G. 1990. *Doing it the Hard Way: Investigations of Gender and Technology.* Boston, MA: Unwin Hyman.

Hacker, R.G. 1991. Gender differences in science-lesson behaviors. *International Journal of Science Education, 13*(4): 439-445.

Hall, R.M. 1985. "Foreign Faculty and Graduate Students: How do they Affect the Learning Climate for Women?" In *The International Flow of Scientific and Technological Talent: Data, Policies, and Issues.* Proceedings of the 1985 Joint Meeting of the Scientific Manpower Commission and Engineering Manpower Commission, Washington, D.C., May 7, 1985. Prepared by S.V. Barthel & J.A. Early: 43-45. Washington, D.C.: Scientific Manpower Commission.

Hall, R. M., & B. Sandler. 1982. *The Classroom Climate: A Chilly One for Women?* Project on the Status and Education of Women. Washington, D.C.: Association of American Colleges.

Hall, R.M., & B. Sandler. 1984. *Out of the Classroom: A Chilly Campus Climate for Women?* Project on the Status of Women. Washington, D.C.: Association of American Colleges.

Hall, R.M., & B. Sandler. 1986. *The Campus Climate Revisited: Chilly for Women Faculty, Administrators, and Graduate Students.* Project on the Status and Education of Women. Washington, D.C.: Association of American Colleges.

Harding, J. 1986. *Perspectives on Gender and Science.* London: The Falmer Press.

Heller, J.F., Puff, C.R., & C.J. Mills. 1985. Assessment of the chilly college climate for women. *Journal of Higher Education, 56*(4): 446-461.

Henderson, Cathy. 1993. *College Students with Disabilities: Interest in Engineering and Other Technical Fields.* Unpublished report to the A.A.A.S.

Hewitt, Nancy M., & Elaine Seymour. 1991. Factors Contributing to High Attrition Rates Among Science, Mathematics, and Engineering Undergraduate Majors: Preliminary Report to the Alfred P. Sloan Foundation. University of Colorado: Bureau of Sociological Research.

Hewitt, Nancy M., & Elaine Seymour. 1992. A long, discouraging climb. *Prism: Journal of the American Society for Engineering Education, February*: 24-28.

Heylin, Michael. 1987. Editorital. *Chemical News and Engineering, 65(3)*.

Higher Education Research Institute. 1992. *The American College Student, 1991: National Norms for the 1987 and 1989 Freshmen Classes*, Los Angeles, CA, U.C.L.A.

Hill, Oliver W., Pettus, Clinton W., & Barbara A. Hedin. 1990. Three studies of factors affecting the attitudes of blacks and females toward the pursuit of science and science-related careers. *Journal of Research in Science Teaching, 27*: 289-314.

Hilton, Thomas L., & Valerie E. Lee. 1988. Student interest and persistence in science: Changes in the educational pipeline in the last decade. *Journal of Higher Education, 59*: 510-526.

Hilton, Thomas L., Hsia, J., Solorzano, D.G., & N.L. Benton. 1989. *Persistence in Science of High-Ability Minorty Students*. Princeton, NJ: Educational Testing Service.

Holland, Dorothy C., & Margaret A. Eisenhart. 1990. *Educated in Romance: Women, Achievement, and College Culture*. Chicago, IL: University of Chicago Press.

Hollingshead, A.C. 1991. Taste, talent and tenacity: Secrets of success for undergraduate and graduate women in science. *Journal of College Science Teaching, September/ October*: 235-243.

Hollingshead, A.C., et al. 1992. "Academic Climate, Intervention and Institutional Change: Women in Science, Mathematics and Engineering." In C.M. Demo, ed., *Proceedings of the 1992 WEPAN National Conference*, West Lafayette, IN: Purdue University, May-June.

Hornig, L.S. 1979. "Scientific Sexism." In A. Briscoe & S. Phafflin, eds., *Expanding the Role of Women in the Sciences. Annals of the New York Academy of Sciences*, 323, New York, NY: New York Academy of Science.

Hudson, H.T. 1986. A comparison of cognitive skills between completes and dropouts in a college physics course. *Journal of Research in Science Teaching, 23*: 41-50.

Humphreys, Sheila M. 1982. *Women and Minorities in Science: Strategies for Increasing Participation*. Boulder, CO: Westview Press.

Humphreys, Sheila M., & Robert Freeland. 1992. Retention in Engineering: A Study of Freshman Cohorts. Berkeley, CA: University of California at Berkeley, College of Engineering.

Independent Colleges Office. 1991. *Volume I: What Works: Building Natural Science Communities*. Washington, D.C.: Project Kaleidoscope.

Independent Colleges Office. 1992. *Volume II: What Works: Resources for Reform*. Washington, D.C.: Project Kaleidoscope.

Independent Colleges Office. 1995. *Structures for Science: A Handbook for Planning Facilities for Undergraduate Natural Science Communities*. Washington, D.C.: Project Kaleidoscope.

Industry, Science and Technology, Canada. 1991. *Women in Science and Engineering, Volume I: Universities.* Ottawa, Ontario: I.S.T.C., University and Colleges Affairs Branch, Science Sector.

International Association for the Evaluation of Educational Achievement. 1988. *Science Achievement in Seventeen Countries: A Preliminary Report.* Oxford: Pergamon Press.

Jackson, Philip W. 1983. The reform of science education: A cautionary tale. *Daedelus: Scientific Literacy, 112*(2): 143-166.

Jacobi, Maryann. 1991. Choosing and Changing Majors: Results of Five Student Focus Groups. Project Report to Offices of Academic Planning, and Student Affairs Information and Research Office, Los Angeles, CA: U.C.L.A.

Jacobs, Lucy C., & Charles B. Freidman. 1988. Student achievement under foreign teaching associates compared with native teaching associates. *Journal of Higher Education, 59*: 551-563.

Jagacinski, C.M. 1987a. Androgyny in a male-dominated field: The relationship of sex-typed traits to performance and satisfaction in engineering. *Sex Roles, 17*: 529-547.

Jagacinski, C.M. 1987b. Engineering career: women in a male-dominated field. *Psychology of Women Quarterly, 11*: 97-110.

James, R.L., & S. Smith. 1985. Alienation of students from science in grades 4-12. *Science Education, 69*(1): 39-45.

Johnson, R.T., & D.W. Johnson. 1987. "Cooperative Learning and the Achievement and Socialization Crisis in Science and Math Classroom." In A.B. Champagne, and L.E. Hornig, eds., *Students and Science Learning.* Washington, D.C: A.A.A.S.

Jones, M.G., & J. Wheatley. 1990. Gender differences in teacher-student interactions in science classrooms. *Journal of Research in Science Teaching, 27*: 861-874.

Kahle, J.B., ed. 1985. *Women in Science: A Report from the Field.* Philadelphia, PA: Falmer Press.

Kahle, J.B. 1990. "Real Students Take Chemistry and Physics." In K. Tobin, J.B. Kahle, and B.J. Fraser, eds., *Windows into Science Classrooms: Problems Associated with Higher-Level Cognitive Learning,* New York, NY: Falmer Press.

Kahle, J.B., & L.J. Rennie. 1993. Ameliorating gender differences in attitudes about science: A cross-national study. *Journal of Science Education and Technology, 23 (1): 321-333.*

Katz, Joseph, & Rodney T. Harnett. 1976. *Scholars in the Making: the Development of Graduate and Professional Students.* Cambridge, MA: Ballinger Pub. Co.

Keller, Evelyn Fox. 1988. Feminist perspectives on science studies. *Science, Technology, and Human Values, 13*(3,4): 34-47.

Kemelgor, Carol. 1989. *Research groups in molecular biology: A study of normative change in academic science.* B.A. thesis, S.U.N.Y, Purchase.

Kimball, M.M. 1989. A new perspective of women's math achievement. *Psychological Bulletin, 105*(2): 198-214.

Kistiakowski, V. 1980. Women in physics: Unnecessary, injurious, and out-of-place? *Physics Today, 33(2)*: 32-40.

Koehler, M.S. 1990. "Classroom, Teachers and Gender Differences in Mathematics." In E. Fennema, and G.C. Leder, eds., *Mathematics and Gender*. New York, NY: Teachers College Press.

Komarovsky, M. 1985. *Women in College: Shaping New Feminine Identities*. New York, NY: Basic Books.

Krupnick, C.G. 1984. *Sex Differences In College Teachers' Classroom Talk*. Ph.D. diss., Harvard University: Cambridge, MA.

Lee, Valerie E. 1988. "Identifying Potential Scientists and Engineers: An Analysis of the High School-College Transition." In *Elementary and Secondary Education for Science and Engineering, Grade School to Grad School*, Office of Technology Assessment, Washington, D.C.

Levin, James, & John Wyckoff. 1988. Effective advising: Identifying students most likely to persist and succeed in engineering. *Engineering Education, 78*: 178-182.

Levy, Sidney J. 1979. "Focus Group Interviewing." In James B. Higginbotham and Keith Cox, eds., *Focus Group Interviews: A Reader*, Chicago, IL: American Marketing Association.

Lin, H. 1982. Learning physics vs. passing courses. *The Physics Teacher, March*: 151-157.

Linn, M.D., & J.S. Hyde. 1989. Gender, mathematics and science. *Educational Researcher, 31*: 27-35.

Lipson, Abigail. 1990. "Why College Students Drop Science." Report for Sheila Tobias and The Research Corporation, Tucson, AZ. Based on data from Susan Bailey, Barbara Burrell, and Norma Ware, *Concentration Choice Study, 1978-1983*. Archived at the Henry A. Murray Research Center, Radcliffe College, Cambridge, MA.

Lipson, Abigail. 1992. The confused student in introductory science. *College Teaching, 40* (3): 91-95.

Lipson, Abigail, & Sheila Tobias. 1991. Why do some of our best college students leave science? *Journal of College Science Teaching, 21*: 2.

Lofland John L., & Lyn H. Lofland. 1984. *Analyzing Social Settings: A Guide to Qualitative Observation and Analysis, 2nd Edition*. Belmont, CA: Wadsworth.

Lollar, Cynthia. 1991. Access to engineering: New project for students and faculty with disabilities. *Science, Vol. 251 (4996)*: 952.

Lubinski, D., & C.P. Benbow. 1992. Gender differences in abilities and preferences among the gifted: Implications for the math-science pipeline. *Current Directions in Psychological Science, 1* (2): 61-66.

Lucky, Luretha F. 1989. Boosting science careers for the physically handicapped student. *Florida Scientist, 52 (3)*: 145-153.

Malcolm, Shirley. 1989. Increasing the participation of black women in science and technology. *Sage, 6*(2): 67-75.

Manis, J., Frazier-Kouassi, S., Hollenshead, C., & D. Burkham. 1993. *A Survey of the Graduate Experience: Sources of Satisfaction and Dissatisfaction Among Graduate Students at the University of Michigan.* Ann Arbor, MI: The University of Michigan Center for the Education of Women.

Manis, Jean M., Sloat, Barbara F., Thomas, Nancy G., & Cinda-Sue Davis. 1989. *An Analysis of Factors Affecting Choices of Majors in Science, Mathematics and Engineering at the University of Michigan.* University of Michigan, MI: Center for Continuing Education of Women.

Mappen, E.F. 1990. "The Douglass Project for Rutgers Women in Math, Science, and Engineering: A Comprehensive Program to Encourage Women's Persistence in these Fields." In J.Z. Daniels, ed., Women in Engineering Conference: A National Initiative, conference proceedings, West Lafayette, IN: Purdue University.

Massey, Walter. 1989. Science education in the United States: What the scientific community can do. *Science, 245*: 915-921.

Matyas, Marsha L. 1985. "Factors Affecting Female Achievement and Interest in Science and in Scientific Careers." In J.B. Kahle, ed., *Women in Science,* Philadelphia, PA: Palmer Press.

Matyas, Marsha L., & Linda Skidmore Dix, eds. 1992. *Science and Engineering Programs: On Target for Women?* Committee on Women in Science and Engineering, O.S.E.P., the National Research Council. Washington, D.C.: National Academy Press.

Matyas, Marsha L., & Shirley M. Malcolm, eds . 1991. *Investing in Human Potential: Science and Engineering at the Crossroads.* Washington, D.C.: A.A.A.S.

Mayer, M., & M.S. Koehler. 1990. "Internal Iinfluences on Gender Differences in Mathematics." In E. Fennema, and G.C. Leder, eds., *Mathematics and Gender.* New York, NY: Teachers College Press.

Mayo, Elton. 1966. *Human Problems of an Industrial Civilization.* New York, NY: Viking.

McBay, S.M. 1986. *The Racial Climate on the M.I.T. Campus.* Massachussetts Institutie of Technology, Office of the Dean for Student Affairs.

McClelland, L. 1993. Students Entering Science, Mathematics, and Engineering Majors as Fall Freshmen, 1980-1988. Unpublished data provided by L. McClelland, University of Colorado, Boulder, Office of Research and Information.

McDonald, J., Clark, M., & E. Dobson. 1990. *Increasing the Supply of Minority and Women Engineers: An Agenda for State Action.* Washington, D.C.: National Governors' Association.

McNeal, Ann P. 1989. Real science in the introductory course. *New Directions for Teaching and Learning, 38*: 17-24.

Merton, Robert K. 1942. Science and technology in a democratic order. *Journal of Legal and Political Science, 1*: 115-126.

Merton, Robert K. 1970. Originally published 1938. *Science, Technology, and Society in Seventeenth Century England.* New York, NY: Howard Fertig.

Merton, Robert K. 1973. *Sociology of Science: Theoretical and Empirical Investigations.* Norman W. Storer, ed., Chicago, IL: University of Chicago Press.

Merton, Robert K. 1987. The focused interview and focus groups: Continuities and discontinuities. *Public Opinion Quarterly, 51*: 550-556.

Mestre, J. 1986. "The Latino Science and Engineering Student: Recent Research findings. In M.A. Olivas, ed., *Latino College Students.* New York, NY: Teachers College Press.

Miller, J.B. 1991. "The Development of Women's Sense of Self." In J.V. Jordan, A.G. Kaplan, J.B. Miller, I.P. Stiver, and J.L. Surrey, eds., *Women's Growth in Cconnection: Writings from the Stone Center.* New York, NY: The Guildford Press.

Mohrman, Kathryn. 1987. Unintended consequences of federal student aid policies. *The Brookings Review, Fall*: 24-30.

Morgan, David L. 1988. *Focus Groups as Qualitative Research, Qualitative Research Methods Series, Volume 16.* Beverly Hills, CA: Sage.

Morrison, C., & L.E. Williams. 1993. "Minority Engineering Programs: A Case for Institutional Support." *N.A.C.M.E. Research Letter, Vol. 4,* No. 1.

Morse, L.W., & H.M. Handley. 1985. "Listening to Adolescents: Gender Differences in Science Classrooms. In L.C. Wilkinson and C.B. Marrett, eds., *Gender Influences in Classroom Interactions,* Madison, WI: Academic Press.

Mortenson, Thomas G. 1995. "Financing opportunity for postsecondary education." Paper presented at the N.A.C.M.E. Research and Policy Conference: Monorites in Mathematics, Science and Engineering, Wake Forrest University. Wake Forest, NC, Jan. 26-29.

Mullis, I.V.S., & Lynne B. Jenkins. 1988. *The Science Report Card: Elements of Risk and Recovery. Trends and Achievements based on the 1986 National Assessment.* Princeton, NJ: Educational Testing Service.

Mullis, I.V.S., Dossey, J.A., Owen, E.H., & G.W. Phillips. 1991. *The state of mathematics achievement.* Educational Testing Service for National Center for Education Statistics, report no. 21-ST-03. Washington, D.C.: G.P.O.

National Academy of Sciences. 1987. *Nurturing Science and Engineering Talent: A Discussion Paper*. The Government-Industry Research Roundtable. Washington, D.C.: N.A.S.

National Advisory Board on Science and Technology. 1988a. *Committee on the Participation of Women in Science and Technology*. Report to the Prime Minister of Canada. Ottawa, Ontario: N.A.B.S.T.

National Advisory Board on Science and Technology. 1988b. *University Committee*. Report to the Prime Minister of Canada. Ottawa, Ontario: N.A.B.S.T.

National Advisory Group, Sigma Xi, the Scientific Research Society. 1989. *An Exploration of the Nature and Quality of Undergraduate Education in Science, Mathematics and Engineering*. Racine, WI: Report of the Wingspread Conference.

National Association of State Universities and Land-Grant Colleges. 1989. *Quality of Engineering Education 111. Committee on the Quality of Engineering Education, Commission on Education for the Engineering Professions*. Washington, D.C.: N.A.S.U.L.G.C.

National Center for Education Statistics. 1989. *Profile of Handicapped Students in Post-Secondary Education, 1987: National Post-secondary Student Aid Study*. Washington, D.C.: U.S. Department of Education, Office of Educational Research and Improvement.

National Governors' Association. *Increasing the Supply of Women and Minority Engineers: An Agenda for State Action*. Washington, D.C.: N.G.A.

National Research Council, Committee on Women in Science and Engineering. 1991. *Women in Science and Engineering: Increasing their Numbers in the 1990s*. Washington, D.C.: National Academy Press.

National Research Council, National Committee on Science Education Standards and Assessments. 1993. *National Science Education Standards Working Papers: An Enhanced Sampler, February 1993 & July 1993 Progress Report*. Washington D.C.: National Research Council.

National Science Foundation. 1986. *Undergraduate Science, Mathematics and Engineering Education. N.S.B. Task Committee on Undergraduate Science and Engineering Education*. Washington, D.C.: N.S.F.

National Science Foundation. 1987. *Report of the N.S.B. Committee on Foreign Involvement in U.S. Universities*. Washington, D.C.: N.S.F.

National Science Foundation. 1988, 1989a. *Changing America: The New Face of Science and Engineering. Interim and Final Reports, The Task Force on Women, Minorities, and the Handicapped in Science and Technology*. Washington, D.C.: N.S.F.

National Science Foundation. 1989b. *Report on the N.S.F. Disciplinary Workshops on Undergraduate Education*. Washington, D.C.: N.S.F.

National Science Foundation. 1989c. *Report on the National Science Foundation Workshop on Science, Engineering and Mathematics Education in Two-Year*

Colleges. Directorate for Science and Engineering Education, Division of Undergraduate Science, Engineering and Mathematics Education. Washington, D.C.: N.S.F.

National Science Foundation. 1989d. *Meeting the National Need for Scientists to the Year 2000. Commission on Professionals in Science and Technology.* Washington, D.C.: N.S.F.

National Science Foundation. 1989e. *Foreign Students Account for Most Growth in Graduate Science and Engineering Enrollment. Science Resources Studies.* Washington, D.C.: N.S.F.

National Science Foundation. 1989f. *Report on the N.S.F. Disciplinary Workshops on Undergraduate Education.* Washington, D.C.: N.S.F.

National Science Foundation. 1990a. *The State of Academic Science and Engineering.* Directorate for Science, Technology and International Affairs, Division of Policy Research and Analysis. Washington, D.C.: N.S.F.

National Science Foundation. 1990b. *Women and Minorities in Science and Engineering.* Washington, D.C.: N.S.F.

National Science Foundation. 1990c. *Report on the N.S.F. Task Force on Persons with Disabilities.* Washington, D.C.: N.S.F.

National Science Foundation. 1990d. *Women and Minorities in Science and Engineering.* Washington, D.C.: N.S.F.

National Science Foundation. 1990e. *Future Scarcities of Scientists and Engineers: Problems and Solutions.* Washington, D.C.: N.S.F.

National Science Foundation. 1991a. *Enhancing Women in Science and Engineering.* Washington, D.C.: N.S.F.

National Science Foundation. 1991b. *Survey on Retention at Higher Education Institutions.* Washington, D.C.: N.S.F., with The National Endowment for the Humanities, & the U.S. Department of Education.

National Science Foundation. 1993a. *Indicators of Science and Mathematics Education, 1992.* Division of Research, Evaluation and Dissemination, Directorate for Education and Human Resources. Washington, D.C.: National science Foundation.

National Science Foundation. 1993b. *Beyond National Goals and Standards: Excellence in Mathematics and Science Education K-16.* Proceedings of an N.S.F. Invitational Conference, February 9-11, 1993. Washington, D.C.: N.S.F.

National Science Foundation. 1994. Women, minorities and persons with disabilties in science and engineering: 1994. Arlington, VA, N.S.F.: 94-333.

Neale, Abraham, Gerhart, James B., Hobbie, Russell K., McDermott, Lillian C., Romer, Robert, & Bruce R. Thomas. 1991. The undergraduate physics major. *American Journal of Physics, 59*: 106-111.

Nevitte, N., Gibbons, R., & P.W. Codding. 1988. The career goals of female science students in canada. *The Canadian Journal of Higher Education, 18*: 31-48.

Oakes, Jeannie. 1990a. *Lost Talent: The Under-participation of Women, Minorities, and Disabled Persons in Science.* Washington, D.C.: N.S.F. with the Rand Corporation.

Oakes, Jeannie. 1990b. "Opportunities, Aachievement and Choice: Women and Minority Students in Science and Mathematics." In C.B. Casden, ed., *Review of Educational Research, 16*: 153-222.

Office of Scientific and Engineering Personnel. 1986. *Leaving the Pipeline: Documenting Losses in the Science Talent Pool.* Washington, D.C.: National Research Council.

Office of Scientific and Engineering Personnel. 1987a. *Minorities: Their Under-representation and Career Differentials in Science and Engineering.* Washington, D.C.: National Academy Press.

Office of Scientific and Engineering Personnel. 1987b. *Women: Their Under-representation and Career Differentials in Science and Engineering.* Washington, D.C.: National Academy Press.

Office of Technology Assessment. 1985. *Demographic Trends and the Scientific and Engineering Work-force.* Washington, D.C.: G.P.O.

Office of Technology Assessment. 1988. *Educating Scientists and Engineers: Grade School to Grad School.* Washington, D.C.: G.P.O.

Office of Technology Assessment. 1989. *Higher Education for Science and Engineering: A Background Paper.* Washington, D.C.: G.P.O.

Pascarella, E.T., & P.T. Terenzini. 1991. *How College Affects Students.* San Francisco, CA: Jossey-Bass.

Pearson, W., Jr. 1995. "The Sociological Effects of the Mentoring Process for Minority Students," Paper presented at the American Educational Research Association, San Francisco, CA, April 20.

Pelavin and Associates. 1990. *Changing the odds: Factors increasing access to college.* Publ. No. 003969. New York, NY: The College Board.

Peterson, P.L., & E. Fennema. 1985. Effective teaching: Student engagement in classroom activities and sex-related differences in learning mathematics. American Education Research Journal, 22: 309-335.

Phelan, W. 1979. Undergraduate orientations toward scientific and scholarly careers. *American Educational Research Journal, 16:* 411-422.

Pool, Robert. 1990. Who will do science in the 1990s? *News and Comment, 27*: 433-435.

Porter, Oscar. 1990. *Undergraduate Completion and Persistence at Four-Year Colleges and Universities: Completers, Persisters, Stop-outs, and Drop-outs.* Washington, D.C.: National Institute of Independent Colleges and Universities.

Rayman, P. 1992. "Opportunities for Women in Science: The Undergraduate Experience." National Research Council Office of Scientific and Engineering Personnel, Conference: *Science and Engineering Programs: On Target for Women?* Washington, D.C., Published Proceedings, 1992.

Rigden, John S., & Sheila Tobias. 1992. Tune in, turn off, drop out: Why so many college students abandon science after the introductory courses. *The Sciences, January, 31*(1): 16-20.

Rios Rodriguez, C. 1992. *Hispanic student achievement program of study and gender differences in attitutdes toward mathematics at the high school level: An explanatory study.* Ph.D. diss., University of Massachusetts, Amherst.

Robinson, J. Gregg, & Judith S. McIlwee. 1989. Women in engineering: A promise unfulfilled. *Social Problems, 36*: 455-472.

Rodriguez, Carlos Mario. 1993. *Minnorities in science and engineering: Patterns for success.* Ph.D. diss., University of Arizona, Department of Educational Administration and Higher Education.

Rosser, Sue V. 1989. Teaching techniques to attract women to science: Applications of feminist theories and methodologies. *Women's Studies International Forum, 12*(3): 363-377.

Rosser, Sue V. 1990. *Female-Friendly Science: Applying Women's Study Methods and Theories to Attract Students.* New York, NY: Pergamon.

Rossiter, M. 1982. *Women Scientists in America.* Baltimore, MD: Johns Hopkins University Press.

Rotberg, Iris C. 1990. Sources and reality: The participation of minorities in science and engineering education. *Phi Delta Kappan, 71*: 672-679.

Roychoudhury, A., Tippins, D., & S. Nichols. 1993. An exploratory attempt towards a feminist pedagogy for science education. *Action in Teacher Education, 15*(4): 36-46.

Sadker, D., & M. Sadker. 1985. Is the ok classroom ok? *Phi Delta Kappan, 55*, 358-361.

Sadker, M., & D. Sadker. 1992. Ensuring equitable participation in college classes. *New Directions for Teaching and Learning, 49*: 49-56.

Science editorial. 1992. Minorities in science: The pipeline problem. *Science, 258* (5085), November 13, 1992.

Schwartz, Howard, & Jerry Jacobs. 1979. *Qualitative Sociology: A Method to the Madness.* New York, NY: MacMillan.

Seidel, John V., Kjolseth, J. Rolf, & Elaine Seymour. 1988. *The Ethnograph: A User's Guide.* Littleton, CO: Qualis Research Associates.

Seymour, Elaine. 1992a. The student's experience of teaching and advising in science mathematics and engineering majors: Gender differences in a study of undergraduate attrition. *Journal of College Science Teaching, 21*(5): 284-292.

Seymour, Elaine. 1992b. 'The problem iceberg' in science, mathematics and engineering education: Student explanations for high attrition rates. *Journal of College Science Teaching, 21*(4): 230-238.

Seymour, Elaine. 1995a. Revisiting the 'problem iceberg': Science, mathematics, & engineering students still chilled out. *Journal of College Science Teaching, 24*(6): 392-400.

Seymour, Elaine. 1995b. Guest comment: Why undergraduates leave the sciences. *American Journal of Physics,63*(3): 199-201.

Seymour, Elaine, & Nancy M. Hewitt. 1994. *Talking about leaving: Factors contributing to high attrition rates among Science, mathematics, and engineering undergraduate majors.* Final Report to the Alfred P. Sloan Foundation on an ethnographic inquiry at seven institutions.

Seymour, Elaine, & Anne-Barrie Hunter. 1996. *Talking about disability: The education and work experiences of graduates and undergraduates with disabilities in science, mathematics, and engineering majors.* Washington, D.C.: A.A.A.S.

Silberman, R.G. 1981. Problems with chemistry problems: Student perception and suggestions. *Journal of Chemistry Education, 58* (1036).

Smail, B. 1985. An attempt to move mountains: the 'girls into science and technology' G.I.S.T. project. *Journal of Curriculum Studies, 17*: 351-354.

Spertus, E. 1991. *Why are there so few Female Computer Scientists?* M.I.T. Artificial Intelligence Laboratory Technical Report.

Spradley, J.P. 1979. *The Ethnographic Interview.* New York, NY: Holt, Rinehart & Winston.

Stage, F.K., & S. Maple. 1993. *Dropping out of the mathematics/science pipeline: Narratives of women doctoral candidates.* Paper presented at the Annual Meeting of the Association for the Study of Higher Education, Pittsburg, PA.

Staver, John R., & Larry Small. 1990. Toward a clearer representation of the crisis in science education. *Journal of Research in Science Teaching, 27*: 79-89.

Steen, L., ed. 1987. *Calculus for a New Century: A Pump not a Filter.* Washington, D.C.: Mathematics Association of America.

Sternglanz, S.H., & S. Lyberger-Ficek. 1977. Sex differences in student-teacher interaction in the college classroom. *Sex Roles, 3*: 345-351.

Stevenson, Robert J. 1994. Where do all the sociologists come from? *Footnotes, 21*(9): 11-12. Washington, D.C.: American Sociological Association.

Strenta, C., Elliott, R., Matier, M., Scott, J., & R. Adair. 1993. *Choosing and leaving science in highly selective institutions: General factors and the question of gender.* Report to the Alfred P. Sloan Foundation.

Surrey, J.L. 1991. "The 'self-in-relation': A theory of Women's Development." In J.V. Jordan, A.G. Kaplan, J.B. Miller, I.P. Stiver, and J.L. Surrey, eds., *Women's growth in connection: Writings from the Stone Center.* New York: The Guildford Press.

Tetreault, Mary Kay Thomson. 1986. The journey from male-defined to gender-balanced education. *Theory into Practice, 25*(3): 89-96.

Thomas, G. 1984. *College students and factors influencing their major field choice.* Atlanta, GA: Southern Education Foundation.

Thomas, G., Clewell, B., & W. Pearson, Jr. 1992 . *The role and activities of American graduate schools in recruiting, enrolling, and retaining United States' Black and Hipanic students.* GRE Report 87-08, Princeton, NJ: Educational Testing Service, Graduate Record Examinations Board.

Thomas, W.I. 1928. *The Child in America.* New York, NY: Knopf.

Tidball, E.M. 1988. "Women's Colleges: Exceptional Conditions, not Exceptional Talent, Produce High Achievers." In C.S. Pearson, D.L. Shavlik, and J.G. Touchton, eds., *Educating the Majority.* New York, NY: American Council on Education.

Tinto, V. 1987, 1993. *Leaving College: Rethinking the Causes and Cures of Student Attrition.* Chicago, IL: University of Chicago Press.

Tobias, Sheila. 1978, 1993a. *Overcoming Math Anxiety.* New York, NY: W.W. Norton.

Tobias, Sheila. 1990. *They're not Dumb, They're Different: Stalking the Second Tier.* Tucson, AZ: Research Corporation.

Tobias, Sheila. 1992a. *Revitalizing Undergraduate Science: Why Some Things Work and Most Don't.* Tucson, AZ: Research Corporation.

Tobias, Sheila. 1992b. Women *in* science – women *and* science. *Journal of College Science Teaching, April/May*: 276-278.

Tobias, Sheila. 1993b. Science education reforms: What's wrong with the process? *Change, 24*(3): 13-19, May/June, 1993.

Tobias, Sheila. 1993c. *Overcoming Math Anxiety: Revised and expanded.* New York, NY: W.W. Norton.

Tobin, K., & P. Garnett. 1987. Gender-related differences in science activities. *Science Education, 71:* 91-103.

Treisman, U. 1992. Studying students studying calculus: A look at the lives of minority mathematics students in college. *The College Mathematics Journal, 23*(5): 362-372.

Tucker, A. 1964. *Factors Related to Attrition among Doctoral Students.* Cooperative research project No. 1146, U.S. Office of Education with Michigan State University.

Unger, R., & M. Crawford. 1992. *Women and gender: A feminist perspective.* Philadelphia, PA: Temple University Press.

U.S. Bureau of the Census. 1991. *Statistical Abstract of the United States, 11th Edition.* Washington, D.C.: U.S. Department of Commerce.

U.S. Government. 1989. *Changing America: The New Face of Science and Engineering. Final Report, the Task Force on Women, Minorities, and the Handicapped in Science and Technology.* Washington, D.C.: G.P.O.

Vetter, Betty M. 1980. Working women scientists and engineers. *Science, 207:* 28-34.

Vetter, Betty M. 1987. Women's progress in science. *Sigma Delta Epsilon Report,* Summer; also in *Mosaic, 18*(1): N.S.F.,1987.

Vetter, Betty M. 1988. Demographics of the engineering student pipeline. *Engineering Education, 78:* 735-740.

Vetter, Betty M., & Eleanor L. Babco. 1989a. *Measuring National Needs for Scientists to the Year 2000: Report of a Workshop.* Washington, D.C.: Commission on Professionals in Science and Technology.

Vetter, Betty M., & Eleanor L. Babco. 1989b. *Professional Women and Minorities: A Manpower Data Resource Service, Eighth Edition.* Washington, D.C.: Commission on Professionals in Science and Technology.

Ware, N.C., Steckler, N.A., & J. Leserman. 1985. Undergraduate women: Who chooses a science major? *Journal of Higher Education, 56:* 73-84.

Ware, N.C., & D. Dill. 1986. *Persistence in science among mathematically able male and female college students with pre-college plans for a scientific major.* San Francisco, CA: Paper presented at the Annual Meeting of the American Educational Research Association.

Ware, N.C., & V.E. Lee. 1988. Sex differences in choice of college science majors. *American Educational Research Journal, 25*(4): 593-614.

Whatley, Marianne H. 1989. A feeling for science: Female students and biology texts. *Women's Studies International Forum, 12*(3): 355-361.

White, P.E. 1992. *Women and Minorities in Science and Engineering: An Update.* Washington, D.C.: N.S.F.

Whyte, J. 1986. *Girls into Science and Technology: The Story of a Project.* Boston, MA: Routledge and Kegan Paul.

Widnall, S. 1988. "A.A.A.S. Presidential Lecture: Voices from the Pipeline," *Science, 24:* 1740-1745.

Wilson, Robin. 1990. Only fifteen percent of students graduate, a new study finds. *Chronicle of Higher Education, February 21, 1990*: A1, A42.

Zuckerman, H., & J. Cole. 1987. Marriage, motherhood and research performance in science. *Scientific American, 256*(2): 24-35.

Zuckerman, H., et al., eds. 1991. *The Outer Circle: Women in the Scientific Community*. New York, NY: W.W. Norton.

Name Index

Subject Index

About the Book and Authors

This intriguing book explores the reasons that lead undergraduates of above-average ability to switch from science, mathematics, and engineering majors into nonscience majors. Based on a three-year, seven-campus study, the volume takes up the ongoing national debate about the quality of undergraduate education in these fields, offering explanations for net losses of students to non-science majors.

Data show that approximately 40 percent of undergraduate students leave engineering programs, 50 percent leave the physical and biological sciences, and 60 percent leave mathematics. Concern about this waste of talent is heightened because these losses occur among the most highly qualified college entrants and are disproportionately greater among women and students of color, despite a serious national effort to improve their recruitment and retention.

The authors' findings, culled from over 600 hours of ethnographic interviews and focus group discussions with undergraduates, explain the intended and unintended consequences of some traditional teaching practices and attitudes. *Talking about Leaving* is richly illustrated with students' accounts of their own experiences in the sciences.

This is a landmark study—an essential source book for all those concerned with changing the ways that we teach science, mathematics, and engineering education, and with opening these fields to a more diverse student body.

Elaine Seymour and **Nancy M. Hewitt** are sociologists at the Bureau of Sociological Research, the University of Colorado at Boulder.